REGULATING (FROM) THE INSIDE

This book examines a key aspect of the post-financial crisis reform package in the EU and UK—the ratcheting up of internal control in banks and financial institutions. The legal framework for internal controls is an important part of prudential regulation, and internal control also constitutes a form of internal gatekeeping for financial firms so that compliance with laws and regulations can be secured. This book argues that the legal framework for internal control, which is a form of meta-regulation, is susceptible to weaknesses, and such weaknesses are critically examined by adopting an interdisciplinary approach. The book discusses whether post-crisis reforms adequately address the weaknesses in regulating internal control and proposes an alternative strategy to enhance the 'governance' effectiveness of internal control.

Regulating (From) the Inside

The Legal Framework for Internal Control in Banks and Financial Institutions

Iris H-Y Chiu

•HART•
PUBLISHING
OXFORD AND PORTLAND, OREGON
2018

Hart Publishing
An imprint of Bloomsbury Publishing Plc

Hart Publishing Ltd
Kemp House
Chawley Park
Cumnor Hill
Oxford OX2 9PH
UK

Bloomsbury Publishing Plc
50 Bedford Square
London
WC1B 3DP
UK

www.hartpub.co.uk
www.bloomsbury.com

Published in North America (US and Canada) by
Hart Publishing
c/o International Specialized Book Services
920 NE 58th Avenue, Suite 300
Portland, OR 97213-3786
USA

www.isbs.com

First published in hardback, 2015
Paperback edition, 2018

British Library Cataloguing-in-Publication Data
A catalogue record for this book is available from the British Library.

ISBN: PB: 978-1-50992-009-9
HB: 978-1-84946-525-0

Typeset by Compuscript Ltd, Shannon

Acknowledgements

I would like to thank Richard Moorhead, Director, UCL Centre for Ethics and the Law, for reading earlier drafts and providing comments on the book, and for involving me in the 'Legal Risk' project from which some empirical insights regarding compliance officers were drawn for the writing of this book. I am also grateful to all members of the Centre for providing me with feedback formally or informally in the process of developing this book—special thanks to Anna Donovan and Marc Moore. I would also like to thank the editorial team at Hart Publishing for supporting this work and for their meticulous efforts in bringing this to publication. This work is dedicated to my family.

Table of Contents

Part II: Making Internal Control Effective in Banks and Financial Institutions

Table of Cases

Table of Legislation

European Union

International

United Kingdom

Part I

The Elements of Internal Control in Banks and Financial Institutions

1

The Role of Internal Control in the Meta-Regulation of Financial Institutions

THIS BOOK EXAMINES the role of internal control in banks and financial institutions. Although internal control functions form part of the back office of banks and financial institutions, and do not hog prominent headlines in popular discussions relating to financial regulation, they have become increasingly important as part of (a) the prudential regulation framework that governs risk-taking at financial firms; (b) the conduct of business regulation framework that governs behaviour of firms vis a vis markets, regulators and stakeholders; and (c) the wider question of financial sector culture that has fallen into notoriety since the onset of the global financial crisis of 2008–09. Regulatory obligations for financial sector firms have increased dramatically post-crisis and regulators look to a range of methodologies to secure firm compliance with regulatory objectives. The role of internal control is an important piece in the mosaic of methodologies towards securing regulatory objectives. Internal control, located within a firm, can provide support to secure the firm's meeting of regulatory objectives, and thus also meet regulatory expectations. The role of internal control in financial sector firms can now be regarded as supporting regulators' meta-regulation of firms where prescriptive and command-and-control type regulations are inappropriate. As regulators now see the role of internal control in securing the compliance of firms as becoming much more pronounced with the advent of greatly increased demands on firms to meet new regulatory obligations, internal control functions are also subject to new regulatory frameworks and expectations.

Internal control functions in financial sector firms are first and foremost self-monitoring mechanisms and therefore act as lines of defence before firm irregularities may become externalised. Firms have an essential self-interest in instituting effective internal control, but firm-centric notions of the effectiveness of internal control may not be socially optimal in the view of regulators. Regulators have increasingly come to regard firm internal control as a plank of governance that secures regulatory objectives. This is because internal control functions are well placed to monitor the firm from the inside, and reaches where regulatory supervision and enforcement may not. The role of internal control at firms is therefore regarded as having the potential to support the attainment of regulatory objectives. In the post-crisis environment, the role of internal control at financial sector firms is subject to enhanced regulatory expectations. This is manifested in regulatory reforms that have established more prescriptive regulatory frameworks for internal control functions.

The book will discuss the pre-crisis and post-crisis regulatory frameworks for internal control and critically discuss to what extent internal control functions in banks and financial institutions can meet enhanced regulatory expectations and serve a governance function in the overall financial regulation agenda. Regulatory expectations would introduce upheaval in terms of how the role of internal control is perceived by the organisations and the individuals concerned. This book will critically analyse how and to what extent the efficacy of internal control functions in meeting enhanced regulatory expectations is affected by (a) the regulatory framework for internal control; (b) conceptions of professionalism; and (c) regulatory enforcement. The book will conclude with some suggestions towards enhancing the efficacy of internal control functions in light of such heightened regulatory expectations.

A. INTRODUCTION TO INTERNAL CONTROL

Internal control in the financial sector has had a long history of development. It is generally regarded both as a principal means to manage business risks in order to further the success of a business,[1] as well as a means to assure regulators of compliance with securities reporting obligations.[2] The institution of effective internal control is regarded as a best practice, the responsibility for which is reposed at the highest level of management—the Board of Directors.[3] In the UK, the Turnbull Guidance[4] which

[1] KPMG, *Internal Control: A Practical Guide* (1999) at www.ecgi.org/codes/documents/kpmg_internal_control_practical_guide.pdf.

[2] Peter Ferola, 'Internal Controls in the Aftermath of Sarbanes-Oxley: One Size Doesn't Fit All' (2006) 48 *South Texas Law Review* 87 and Lawrence A Cunningham, 'The Appeal and Limits of Internal Controls to Fight Fraud, Terrorism, Other Ills' (2003) at ssrn.com/abstract=444600 (2003) 29 *Journal of Corporation Law* 267 both contain a succinct account of the historical development of internal control, albeit from the American point of view.

[3] See UK Corporate Governance Code 2012 at www.frc.org.uk/Our-Work/Publications/Corporate-Governance/UK-Corporate-Governance-Code-September-2012.aspx, para C.2.

[4] Financial Reporting Council (FRC), *Internal Control: Revised Guidance for Directors on the Combined Code* (October 2005) at www.frc.org.uk/FRC/media/Documents/Revised-Turnbull-guidance-October-2005.pdf. The Council is consulting on whether the Revised Guidance needs to be further updated at the end of 2012.

supports the implementation of the Corporate Governance Code defines internal control as a system that

> encompasses the policies, processes, tasks, behaviours and other aspects of a company that, taken together:
>
> Facilitate its effective and efficient operation by enabling it to respond appropriately to significant business, operational, financial, compliance and other risks to achieving the company's objectives. This includes the safeguarding of assets from inappropriate use or from loss and fraud and ensuring that liabilities are identified and managed.
>
> Help ensure the quality of internal and external reporting. This requires the maintenance of proper records and processes that generate a flow of timely, relevant and reliable information from within and outside the organisation.
>
> Help ensure compliance with applicable laws and regulations, and also with internal policies with respect to the conduct of business.

The US Committee of Sponsoring Organizations of the Treadway Commission (COSO) also defines internal control similarly, referring to it as a process 'designed to provide reasonable assurance regarding the achievement of objectives … in relation to operations, reporting and compliance'[5] With regard to financial institutions, the Basel Committee on Banking Supervision[6] defines the role of internal control at banks to be for three purposes: to assist in achieving profitability and performance, to ensure the reliability and integrity of financial information relating to the bank and to assist in external compliance with regulations. In sum, internal control may be regarded as an internal form of gatekeeping[7] to prevent businesses from succumbing to wrongdoing, and to ensure that business objectives and accountability requirements are met.

In the case of financial institutions, internal control has also evolved to meet changing regulatory requirements such as in relation to internal

[5] See COSO, *Internal Control: Integrated Framework* (2013) at www.coso.org/documents/990025P_Executive_Summary_final_may20_e.pdf, 3.

[6] 'A system of strong internal control can help to ensure that the goals and objectives of a banking organisation will be met, that the bank will achieve long-term profitability targets, and maintain reliable financial and managerial reporting. Such a system can also help to ensure that the bank will comply with laws and regulations as well as policies, plans, internal rules and procedures, and decrease the risk of unexpected losses or damage to the bank's reputation.' See Basel Committee on Banking Supervision, *Framework for Internal Control in Banking Organisations* (1998).

[7] The role of monitoring and providing reasonable assurance to management that business objectives are being met could be described as a form of gatekeeping. The role of gatekeeping is, however, not only the premise of a particular department in the firm, but is increasingly a part of all employees' job descriptions as a front line of defence, so that specific internal control departments act as second and third lines of defence; see COSO, *Internal Control: Integrated Framework* (December 2011) at www.coso.org/documents/coso_framework_body_v6.pdf, paras 11, 21.

fraud, financial crime, prudential regulation and compliance with capital markets reporting and client-facing regulation.[8] With the advent of intensive European legislative harmonisation in financial services regulation from 2000, internal control in banks, investment firms, collective investment schemes and now alternative investment fund managers has become a subject of regulation in itself. However, the regulatory framework for internal control, as will be discussed in detail in chapters two to four, has been skeletal in nature in the years prior to the global financial crisis of 2008–09. Post-crisis, the regulatory framework for the organisation and efficacy of internal control in financial institutions has been significantly ramped up.

Regulatory interest in the institution of internal control at banks and financial institutions lies in its organisational position and role. Internal control has proximity to inside knowledge and issues, and acts as an internal gatekeeper for banks and financial institutions. It may be argued that such an organisational position and role could also serve the regulator's objective of securing the financial institution's compliance with regulatory requirements. In other words, internal control is increasingly being fashioned as an internal gatekeeper which also serves gatekeeping purposes for the regulator.

The move towards reframing the role of internal control post-crisis has its roots in the diagnosis of what went wrong in the crisis. In the wake of the global financial crisis of 2008–09, poor risk management has been highlighted as a key factor in the failure of a number of financial institutions,[9] and the role of internal control is thus questioned as to its efficacy in overseeing risk-taking in financial institutions. Further, a number of long-running retail mis-selling scandals that have reignited public attention due to regulatory enforcement in the UK,[10] and the scandals

[8] Ray Kinsella (ed), *Internal Controls in Banking* (Chichester: John Wiley & Sons, 1995); Steven Maijoor, 'The Internal Control Explosion' (2000) 4 *International Journal of Auditing* 101.

[9] M Brunnermeier, A Crockett, C Goodhart, AD Persaud and Hyun Shin, *The Fundamental Principles of Financial Regulation* (London: Centre for Economic Policy Research, Geneva Reports on the World Economy, 2009); Gabriele Sabato, 'Financial Crisis: Where Did Risk Management Fail?' (2009) at papers.ssrn.com/sol3/papers.cfm?abstract_id=1460762; Anette Mikes, 'Risk Management at Crunch Time: Are Chief Risk Officers Compliance Champions or Business Partners?' (2008) at papers.ssrn.com/sol3/papers.cfm?abstract_id=1138615; Hans J Blommestein, Lex Hoogduin and JJW Peeters, 'Uncertainty and Risk Management after the Great Moderation: The Role of Risk (Mis)Management by Financial Institutions' (28th SUERF Colloquium, Utrecht, September 2009) at papers.ssrn.com/sol3/papers.cfm?abstract_id=1489826; Michel Crouhy, 'Risk Management Failures During the Financial Crisis' in Robert W Kolb (ed), *Lessons from the Financial Crisis* (New Jersey: John Wiley & Sons, 2010) 283; Elizabeth Sheedy, 'The Future of Risk Modelling' in Robert W Kolb (ed), *Lessons from the Financial Crisis* (New Jersey: John Wiley & Sons, 2010) 301; Frank Partnoy, 'On Rogues, Risk-taking and Restoring Trust in Banks' *Financial Times* (23 September 2011).

[10] The mis-selling of Payment Protection Insurance (PPI) to retail customers, see Gfk NOP (for the FSA), 'The Sale of Payment Protection Insurance—Mystery Shopping Results'

relating to the manipulation of the London-Interbank Offered Rate[11] and foreign exchange rates[12] implicating a number of large well-known banks all point to failures in financial institutions relating to compliance and internal control. In the post-crisis era, regulatory expectations have ratcheted up in relation to the role of internal control in serving the regulator's objective by securing the compliance of financial institutions. The post-crisis regulation of the role of internal control therefore serves as one of the planks in the regulatory toolkit towards fundamentally changing cultures in financial institutions that are indifferent to, or indeed relaxed about sharp and miscreant behaviour.[13]

Langevoort and Thompson argue that subjecting internal control to a form of regulation manifests a melding of market and social interests in private sector risk-taking.[14] Internal control is regarded as positioned like a gatekeeper, not only to monitor the use of corporate wealth in accountability to capital providers. They are also increasingly being relied on to monitor the impact of corporate decisions or behaviour upon wider society. Regulatory reform in the financial sector now arguably frames internal control as a gatekeeper for serving wider interests beyond the financial institution in which it is positioned. This book examines the extent to which such regulatory reforms have reframed the role of internal control functions and whether internal control functions can assume such a role effectively.

(November 2005) CR45 at www.fsa.gov.uk/pubs/consumer-research/crpr45.pdf; FSA, 'The Sale of Payment Protection Insurance: Thematic Update' (September 2007) at www.fsa.gov.uk/pubs/other/ppi_thematic_update.pdf; FSA, 'The Assessment and Redress of Payment Protection Insurance Complaints: Feedback on CP 09/23 and Further Consultation' (March 2010) CP10/6 at www.fsa.gov.uk/pubs/cp/cp10_06.pdf; FSA, 'The Assessment and Redress of Payment Protection Insurance Complaints: Feedback on the Further Consultation in CP10/6 and Final Handbook Text' (August 2010) PS10/12 at www.fsa.gov.uk/pubs/policy/ps10_12.pdf; FSA Handbook DISP 3; Eilis Ferran, 'Regulatory Lessons from the Payment Protection Insurance Mis-Selling Scandal in the UK' (2012) *European Business Organisation Law Review* 248. On the mis-selling of interest rate swaps to small businesses, see FSA, 'FSA Confirms Full Review of Interest Rate Swap Misselling' (31 January 2013) at www.fsa.gov.uk/library/other_publications/interest-rate-swaps.

[11] See 'LIBOR Manipulation: Done for you, Big Boy' *Financial Times* (27 June 2012). A parliamentary Commission has been instituted as of 2 June 2012 in the UK to look at wider implications for reform of the banking sector in light of this scandal. 'Barclays Fined for Attempts to Manipulate LIBOR' *BBC News* (27 June 2012); 'UBS Fined £1.5bn for LIBOR Rigging' *BBC News* (19 December 2012); 'LIBOR Scandal: RBS Fined £390m' *BBC News* (6 February 2013).

[12] 'Foreign Exchange: The Big Fix' *Financial Times* (12 November 2013) discussing 15 banks including JP Morgan in potential enforcement action against foreign exchange fixing; 'Big Banks Slapped With £2.6bn FX "Rate Rigging" Fines But Will They Ever Learn?' *Forbes.com* (15 November 2014); Martin DD Evans, 'Forex Trading and the WMR Fix' (2014) at papers.ssrn.com/sol3/papers.cfm?abstract_id=2487991.

[13] 'Banks need a generation to change culture, report says' *Financial Times* (26 November 2014).

[14] Donald C Langevoort and Robert B Thompson, '"Publicness" in Contemporary Securities Regulation after the Jobs Act' (2013) 101 *Georgetown Law Journal* 337.

It may be argued that given the complexity and difficulties in regulating financial activities effectively, regulators' reliance on the enhanced role of internal control is merely a form of 'latching on' to 'management speak'. Regulatory reforms that boost the role of internal control merely create perceptions of credible governance in financial institutions and regulators are still far from engaging with effectively changing organisational cultures and behaviours in the financial sector.[15] This book will examine in detail the nature of the post-crisis legislative reforms to the roles of internal control functions, tease out the regulatory expectations that seem to underlie the reforms, consider the impact of such reforms upon the governance of financial institutions and the internal control professions, and critically evaluate the extent to which such reforms will indeed address real behaviour change in the financial sector.

Evolution of the Role of Internal Control Broadly Understood

In the years prior to the global financial crisis of 2008–09, the role of internal control at financial institutions has been shaped by a 'positive' strand and a 'negative' strand. This framework is derived from Cunningham's analysis which views internal control functions as having a 'positive strand' when they are positioned as part of the means to achieve the business objectives of the firm, and as having a 'negative strand' when their main purpose is to prevent wrongdoing by the firm.[16]

The positive strand in internal control at financial institutions relates largely to prudential risk management and compliance with prudential regulation and the negative strand relates to prevention of financial crime and securities mis-reporting. The explosion of customer-facing regulation in the EU since 2004[17] has also introduced further obligations for internal control in terms of compliance, ie, falling within the 'negative strand'. Pre-crisis, the role of internal control is arguably facilitative in nature where risk-taking is concerned. In many firms, the treatment of prudential risk management and compliance is framed towards achieving business objectives for the financial institution, rather than towards self-restraint and

[15] Herbert Smith Freehills and London School of Economics, 'What Appetite for Conduct Risk' (Roundtable, London, 2 July 2014).

[16] Cunningham, 'The Appeal and Limits' (n 2).

[17] European Parliament and Council Directive 2004/39/EC of 21 April 2004 on markets in financial instruments amending Council Directives 85/611/EEC and 93/6/EEC and Directive 2000/12/EC of the European Parliament and of the Council and repealing Council Directive 93/22/EEC [2004] OJ L145/1 (Markets in Financial Instruments Directive (MiFID 2004).

achieving regulatory objectives in safety and soundness.[18] Where the negative strand is concerned, efforts are focused on avoiding wrongdoing in specific areas that are intensely watched by regulators, such as in securities reporting and avoiding financial crime. Such gatekeeping is targeted towards necessary compliance almost like a necessary evil, and not carried out in the spirit of holistic promotion of a healthy business culture. Hence, conduct irregularities such as mis-selling and benchmark manipulation, which were not highlighted by regulators in the pre-crisis era, were by and large thinly managed by many financial institutions.

As prudential regulation for banks and financial institutions moved from a prescriptive approach in the late 1980s to a flexible approach incorporating firm internal governance in the late 1990s/early 2000s, the role of internal control functions in prudential risk management became increasingly facilitative of business objectives. This movement will be discussed in section B below as part of the rise in new governance approaches in regulation. The upshot of this development is that, as regulators allow firms' internal governance, systems and procedures to form part of the implementation of prudential risk regulation, firms are allowed to treat prudential risk management systems and procedures as serving both the purposes of regulatory compliance and business objectives.[19] This treatment is not illegitimate as there is an essential trade-off between risk-taking and safety which is not a judgement that should be made exclusively from the regulatory or business points of view. In practice, firms have practically been devolved with primary responsibility to make appropriate judgements regarding the trade-off, as regulatory supervision was inadequate in this area. Firms have become incentivised to under-provision for risk so that more growth and profits can be pursued in risk-taking activities.[20] Firms have tended to compromise prudential regulatory objectives in favour of business objectives and this has hardly been checked by the role of internal control functions.

As to the 'negative strand' relating to the role of internal control functions in preventing wrongdoing or non-compliance, internal control functions have focused on two areas: securities reporting and financial crime prevention. This has largely been shaped by the need to respond to

[18] Robert W Kolb (ed), *Lessons from the Financial Crisis* (New Jersey: John Wiley & Sons, 2010) generally.

[19] Robert F Weber, 'New Governance, Financial Regulation, and Challenges to Legitimacy: The Example of the Internal Models Approach to Capital Adequacy Regulation' (2010) 62 *Administrative Law Review* 783.

[20] A Sinan Cebenoyan and Philip Strahan, 'Risk Management, Capital Structure and Lending at Banks' (2001) at ssrn.com/abstract=293378; Jukka Vaukhonen, 'Bank Safety and Basel II' (2009) Bank of Finland Research Paper at papers.ssrn.com/sol3/papers.cfm?abstract_id=1513239.

regulatory emphases, but has resulted in a rather piecemeal approach to scoping the monitoring functions of internal control.

On securities reporting, a number of high-profile collapses such as the fall of Polly Peck and BCCI in the 1990s in the UK, the dot.com bubble and collapses of World.com and Enron in the US in the 2000s and Parmalat's collapse in Italy, pushed the integrity of corporate reporting and corporate governance into the spotlight. Against this backdrop, the role of internal control is framed around the firm's needs to meet the requirements of capital markets accountability, although it has been acknowledged much earlier that internal control deals with a wider range of monitoring and verification.[21] Moore[22] points out that UK corporate governance has developed based on the need for audit and accounting integrity in response to the failure at BCCI in 1990.[23] Subsequently, the Turnbull Review[24] further emphasised the need to have reliable internal and external reporting systems as part of 'internal control' and 'risk management'. The language of 'internal control' used in the Cadbury and Turnbull reports deals with systems that process financial information and reporting and how to ensure that such systems would bring about integrity in financial reporting. Although the Turnbull Guidance views internal control as a form of risk management that 'enable[s] [companies] to respond appropriately to significant business, operational, financial, compliance and other risks to achieving the company's objectives',[25] the more precise language surrounding risk management and internal control boils down to the prevention of accounting fraud and ensuring the integrity of financial reporting. The previous Codes preceding the current UK Corporate Governance Code 2010 have always placed the issue of 'internal control' as key to safeguarding shareholders' interests and corporate assets, and tasks the audit committee of the Board to have supervisory oversight. The development of internal control in corporate governance reforms is thus very much led by the securities regulation objective of supporting transparency to facilitate market discipline. Van der Elst argues that the evolution of 'internal control' as being a corporate governance issue in the EU has been led by the need for reliable securities disclosure.[26] Further, developments

[21] James B Bower and Robert E Schlosser, 'Internal Control—Its True Nature' (1965) 40 *The Accounting Review* 338; DR Carmichael, 'Hypotheses of Internal Control' (1970) 45 *The Accounting Review* 235.

[22] Marc T Moore, 'The Evolving Contours of the Board's Risk Management Function in UK Corporate Governance' (2010) 10 *Journal of Corporate Law Studies* 279.

[23] Culminating in Sir Adrian Cadbury's review of corporate governance in general and the promulgation of the Cadbury Code of Corporate Governance 1992. Adrian Cadbury, *Report of the Committee on the Financial Aspects of Corporate Governance* (London, Gee, 1992).

[24] See Turnbull Guidance (2005) at www.frc.org.uk/documents/pagemanager/frc/Revised%20Turnbull%20Guidance%20October%202005.pdf.

[25] ibid, para 19.

[26] Christoph Van der Elst and Marijn van Daelen, 'Risk Management in European and American Corporate Law' (2009) ECGI Law Working Paper 122/2009 at ssrn.com/abstract=1399647.

in the US after Enron's collapse also focused on the role of internal control as safeguarding the integrity of financial reporting and auditing.[27] The emphasis placed on accounting and reporting integrity is found in the Sarbanes–Oxley Act which prescribes for certain forms of internal control such as controls over auditor appointment[28] and mandatory certifications by Chief Financial Officers.[29]

The emphasis on improving the integrity of corporate reporting to capital markets and the robustness of corporate governance to support strong securities regulation[30] is based on the importance of market discipline to control corporate behaviour.[31] The importance of market discipline has to be understood within the wider context of regulatory retreat in the pre-crisis years coupled with the rise in trust in the role of market-based governance.[32] Hence, the role of internal control to safeguard the integrity of financial reporting primarily frames the role of internal control within the private paradigm of corporate governance. This conception of internal control is arguably firm-centric in nature and positions the accountability of internal control towards shareholders and creditors.[33] The perspective of internal control as serving the objectives of the regulator is relatively absent in the pre-crisis years. Such a perspective is being changed in the present post-crisis era of regulatory resurgence[34] as chapters two to four will flesh out.

[27] Donald C Langevoort, 'Internal Controls after Sarbanes–Oxley: Revisiting Corporate Law's "Duty of Care as Responsibility for Systems"' (2006) 31 *Journal of Corporation Law* 949; Ferola, 'Internal Controls' (n 2).

[28] ss 502, 503, Sarbanes–Oxley Act 2002.

[29] ibid, s 302.

[30] See, eg, the corporate governance and securities regulation topics discussed in John Armour and Joseph A McCahery (eds), *After Enron: Improving Corporate Law and Modernising Securities Regulation in Europe and in the US* (Oxford: Hart Publishing, 2006) generally.

[31] The empirical research on the relationship between market discipline and perceptions of the strength of internal control in firms is mixed. Some findings indicate that market discipline is not influenced by or related to internal control: see Thomas J Lopez, Scott J Vandervelde and Yi-Jing Wu, 'The Auditor's Internal Control Opinions: An Experimental Investigation of Relevance' (2006) at ssrn.com/abstract= 905796; J Altamuro and A Beatty, 'How does Internal Control Regulation Affect Financial Reporting?' (2010) 49 *Journal of Accounting and Economics* 584. Some findings indicate the contrary, or at least a much less pronounced relationship: see Maria Ogneva, KR Subramanyam and K Raghunandan, 'Internal Control Weakness and Cost of Equity: Evidence from SOX: Section 404 Disclosures' (2006) at papers.ssrn.com/sol3/papers.cfm?abstract_id=766104; H Ashbaugh-Skaife, D Collins and W Kinney, 'The Discovery and Consequences of Internal Control Deficiencies Prior to SOX-Mandated Audits' (2006) Working Paper, University of Wisconsin-Madison at https://tippie.uiowa.edu/accounting/phd/publications/collins_discovery.pdf.

[32] Discussed in FSA, 'The Turner Review: A Regulatory Response to the Global Banking Crisis' (March 2009) at www.fsa.gov.uk/pubs/other/turner_review.pdf, 39–42.

[33] Langevoort, 'Internal Controls after Sarbanes–Oxley' (n 27), although he argues that wider public accountability may also be envisaged as the cost of instituting expensive internal control mechanisms may not be fully supported by shareholders.

[34] Mads Andenas and Iris H-Y Chiu, *The Foundations and Future of Financial Regulation: Governance for Responsibility* (Oxford: Routledge, 2014).

As for the prevention of financial crime, international consensus on money laundering, financial crime and terrorist financing was being forged in the 1990s[35] and then accelerated after the tragedy of the September 11 destruction of the Twin Towers in New York in 2001.[36] Banks and financial institutions have been enrolled into the front lines of fighting financial crime,[37] but in a negatively-framed manner, as severe penalties loom over banks and financial institutions if money laundering indeed occurs in the chain of money transmission handled by them. The law compels banks and financial institutions to make suspicious activity reports and provide intelligence to regulators in order not to be regarded as being liable for money laundering themselves.[38] The development of anti-money laundering control in banks and financial institutions has become a specialised activity, often departmentally separate from general legal and compliance departments. Banks and financial institutions often institute specific systems to deal with customer due diligence, thresholds for alerts and money laundering reporting.[39] The separation of anti-money laundering control from internal control generally may hint of how banks and financial institutions view this particular negative strand of internal control—as specialist and not necessarily integrated into the bigger picture of firm culture.

In sum, the concept of 'internal control' at banks and financial institutions is multifaceted and possibly fragmented in order to meet particular regulatory requirements. Business-centric purposes permeate prudential risk management, while market-based accountability frames the purposes of internal control for financial reporting. Liability-avoidance concerns dominate the institution of anti-money laundering control. Post-crisis, 'internal control' is to be reframed into a more integrated and comprehensive gatekeeping function that has an overall view of risks assumed by the bank or financial institution concerned, and would be positioned to assist in securing regulatory compliance. Such changes to the role of internal control at banks and financial institutions would be kick-started by new regulation that would have to be implemented by firms.

[35] Financial Action Task Force 40 Recommendations, 1989, revised incorporating below in 2012.

[36] Financial Action Task Force 9 Special Recommendations on Terrorist Financing 2004, incorporated into revised version of the FATF Recommendations 2012.

[37] R Barry Johnston and John Abbott, 'Placing Bankers in the Front Line' (2005) 8 *Journal of Money Laundering Control* 215.

[38] See ss 327, 328, 330, 333 and 338 of the UK Proceeds of Crime Act 2002; *K v National Westminster Bank* [2006] EWCA 1039; *Shah v HSBC* [2012] EWHC 1283 (QB) acknowledging that banks are subject to draconian anti-money laundering obligations but attempts to provide some accountability safeguards for clients.

[39] Tim Bennett, *Money Laundering Compliance*, 2nd edn (W Sussex: Tottel Publishing, 2007) ch 14. Procedures and systems have been developed based on the Joint Money-Laundering Steering Group guidance at www.jmlsg.org.uk/jmlsg-guidance and the Wolfsberg Group of Anti-Money Laundering Principles and Compliance.

Post-crisis reforms in the financial sector in the UK and EU are premised largely on a public interest concept of 'financial stability'[40] which would justify greater regulatory monitoring over risk-taking by financial firms.[41] Thus, risk-taking by firms is no longer an issue that resides merely in the private or business realm. The role of internal control relates to the new need for instilling appropriate 'self-control' on the part of financial firms,[42] having regard to their wider impact upon financial stability as monitored by regulators. Regulatory monitoring or control over levels of risk assumed by financial firms is however a delicate issue as entrepreneurial risk-taking should not be unduly stifled and cannot be centrally prescribed.[43] However, regulators are in a better position to monitor system-wide trends and risks.[44] In order to maintain socially tolerable states of financial stability, regulators are increasingly involved in the mediation of the interface between firm-centric decision-making and wider systemic impact.[45] The internal control functions at banks and financial institutions are now situated at this point of mediation, being involved in risk control for firm-centric purposes as well as for the purposes of accountability to regulators.

Internal control in financial institutions is defined as comprising of a compliance function, a risk control function and an internal audit function.[46] These specialist functions are nested within broader internal

[40] See generally, Andenas and Chiu, *The Foundations and Future of Financial Regulation* (n 34).

[41] Klaus Hopt, 'Better Governance of Financial Institutions' (2012) at ssrn.com/abstract=2212198; KJ Hopt, 'Corporate Governance of Banks after the Financial Crisis' in E Wymeersch, KJ Hopt and G Ferrarini (eds), *Financial Regulation and Supervision: A Post-Crisis Analysis* (Oxford: Oxford University Press, 2012); and Part B in (2013) 13 *Journal of Corporate Law Studies* 219; Roman Tomasic and Folarin Akinbami, 'Towards a New Corporate Governance after the Global Financial Crisis' (2011) *International Company and Commercial Law Review* 237.

[42] Moore, 'The Evolving Contours' (n 22).

[43] Peter O Mülbert and Ryan D Citlau, 'The Uncertain Role of Banks' Corporate Governance in Systemic Risk Regulation' (2011) ECGI Working Paper at ssrn.com/abstract=1885866; Karl S Okamoto and Douglas O Edwards, 'Risk-Taking' (2010) 32 *Cardozo Law Review* 159.

[44] Known as 'macro-prudential regulation', see G30 Working Group on Macroprudential Policy, *Enhancing Financial Stability and Resilience: Macroprudential Policy, Tools and Systems for the Future* (Washington DC: Group of Thirty, 2010); Committee on the Global Financial System (Bank of International Settlements), 'Macroprudential Instruments and Frameworks: A Stocktaking of Issues and Experiences' (May 2010) CGFS Paper 38 at www.bis.org/publ/cgfs38.pdf; Priya Nandita Pooran, 'Macro-prudential Supervision—A Panacea for the Global Financial Crisis?' (2009) 3 *Law and Financial Markets Review* 534; Bart PM Joosen, 'The Limitations of Regulating Macro-Prudential Supervision in Europe' (2010) 25 *Journal of International Banking Law and Regulation* 493.

[45] In both micro- and macro-prudential supervision. For an overview of macro-prudential supervision, see Andenas and Chiu, *The Foundations and Future of Financial Regulation* (n 34) Part 4.

[46] European Banking Authority, *EBA Guidelines on Internal Governance* (September 2011) 37, para 24.4. The EBA was established by European Parliament and Council Regulation (EU) 1093/2010 of 24 November 2010 establishing a European Supervisory Authority (European Banking Authority), amending Decision No 716/2009/EC and repealing Commission

governance frameworks which include senior management responsibility and the overall risk management culture.[47] As will be discussed later in the book, each of these elements of internal control is now subject to regulatory reframing so that their roles are more explicitly of a monitoring or governance nature intended to ensure that financial institutions meet the public interest objectives underlying financial regulation. The regulatory framework for internal control also extends to wider aspects of corporate governance in order to support effective and robust internal control.

B. THE META-REGULATION OF INTERNAL CONTROL AND THE RISE IN META-REGULATION IN FINANCIAL REGULATION GENERALLY

This section now provides a general overview of the nature of the regulatory framework for internal control functions and how this fits with the broader financial regulation agenda. The regulatory framework for internal control may be regarded as a form of 'meta-regulation'.[48] 'Meta-regulation' broadly means that regulators provide a broad outline of a

Decision 2009/78/EC [2010] OJ L331/12 (EBA Regulation 2010). This approach is not only limited to banks, see: European Securities and Markets Authority (ESMA), *Guidelines on Certain Aspects of the MiFID Compliance Function Requirements* (6 July 2012); ESMA, *Consultation Paper: MiFID II and MiFIR* (22 May 2014). The concept of internal control in the EU is arguably converging; see also application to the regulatory frameworks dealing with retail collective investment schemes and alternative investment fund managers. European Parliament and Council Directive 2009/65/EC of 13 July 2009 on the coordination of laws, regulations and administrative provisions relating to undertakings for collective investment in transferable securities [2009] OJ L302/32 (UCITS recast Directive) Arts 17–19, supplemented by Commission Directive 2010/43/EU of 1 July 2010 implementing Directive 2009/65/EC of the European Parliament and of the Council as regards organisational requirements, conflicts of interest, conduct of business, risk management and content of the agreement between a depositary and a management company, Arts 10–12; for alternative investment fund managers, see European Parliament and Council Directive 2011/61/EU of 8 June 2011 on Alternative Investment Fund Managers and amending Directives 2003/41/EC and 2009/65/EC and Regulations (EC) No 1060/2009 and (EU) No 1095/2010 [2011] OJ L174/1 (AIFM Directive), Arts 15, 18, and supplemented by the European Commission, see Commission Delegated Regulation (EU) No 694/2014 supplementing Directive 2011/61/EU of the European Parliament and of the Council with regard to exemptions, general operating conditions, depositaries, leverage, transparency and supervision, Arts 61 and 62.

[47] EBA, *EBA Guidelines on Internal Governance* (September 2011), 7–8, paras 1.18–1.21.

[48] Cary Coglianese and Evan Mendelson, 'Meta-Regulation and Self-Regulation' in R Baldwin, M Cave and M Lodge (eds), *The Oxford Handbook of Regulation* (Oxford: Oxford University Press, 2010); John SF Wright, Paul G Dempster, Justin Keen, Pauline Allen and Andrew Hutchings, 'The New Governance Arrangements for NHS Foundation Trust Hospitals: Reframing Governors as Meta-Regulators' (2012) 90 *Public Administration* 351; Christine Parker, *The Open Corporation* (Cambridge: Cambridge University Press, 2002); Christine Parker, 'Meta-Regulation: Legal Accountability for Corporate Social Responsibility' (2006) at papers.ssrn.com/sol3/papers.cfm?abstract_id=942157; Colin Scott, 'Regulating Everything: From Mega- To Meta-Regulation' (2012) 60 *Administration* 61.

framework which is not excessively prescriptive and sets out certain regulatory objectives to be attained. The regulated firm has the discretion to implement systems and processes to achieve the regulatory objectives. This is a form of delegated governance by regulators to firms, and firms can have considerable discretion in designing the implementation systems and processes. As such, the firm's own governance is the primary means by which regulatory objectives may be attained, while the regulator's role is at a meta-level, providing a broad blueprint and supervising the implementation by the firm.

In the EU, pre-crisis legislation has provided for the meta-regulation of internal control at banks and financial institutions in a very skeletal manner. For example, the (now superseded) Markets in Financial Instruments Directive 2004 (MiFID) and supplementing legislation provided for broad principles of organisational soundness and the establishment of internal controls such as a compliance function, risk management systems, an internal audit function, and the responsibility of senior management for internal control generally.[49] The legislation did not prescribe further as to what the roles and functions of internal control entailed, leaving regulated firms to flesh out and implement their own systems and procedures within the contours of the framework. Organisational structures and arrangements cannot be excessively prescribed as regulators are not in a position to micro-manage firms. Further, firms have an incentive to institute self-monitoring mechanisms in their own interests in order to protect assets and safeguard against various business and financial risks. Hence, over-prescription as to how internal control functions should be constituted and what they should do seems unnecessary. However, firms are relied on to design a proportionate and appropriate form of compliance that meets regulatory objectives. Can it be assumed that firm-centric organisational and governance structures would necessarily fall in line with the attainment of regulatory goals? Would firm implementation of internal control meet its private objectives but nevertheless fall short of socially optimal outcomes?

Meta-regulation has been described as a regulatory approach that empowers and enhances the capacity of corporations to self-regulate, but connects 'the private justice of the internal management system' to the 'public justice of accountability'.[50] Parker proposes that such capacity to self-regulate may be enhanced by value orientation, management

[49] Commission Directive 2006/73/EC of 10 August 2006 implementing Directive 2004/39/EC of the European Parliament and of the Council as regards organisational requirements and operating conditions for investment firms and defined terms for the purposes of that Directive [2006] OJ L241/26 (MiFID Commission Directive 2006) Arts 5–9.

[50] Parker, *The Open Corporation* (n 48) 246.

commitment, the acquisition of skills and knowledge, and the design of internal processes and systems. The 'self-regulation' of each firm should then be accountable to regulators and stakeholders in order to achieve not just 'compliance' but responsibility towards the democratic polity. Parker envisages that 'meta-regulation' would improve the permeability of the corporation to public accountability.[51]

In the pre-crisis context, there was arguably a belief in the alignment between a firm's implementation of internal control (in its self-interest) and the attainment of regulatory objectives in relation to prudential management and general regulatory compliance by firms. The skeletal nature of the meta-regulation of internal control arguably manifests such belief. It may also be argued that meta-regulation in general is extensively used in the financial sector based on social trust for the integrity and legitimacy of the financial sector, and hence the nature of meta-regulation in financial regulation has been highly facilitative and non-prescriptive.

This section will discuss the nature of meta-regulation generally and its importance in financial regulation. It will then discuss the meta-regulatory framework for internal control and highlight the weaknesses inherent in the meta-regulatory framework that may affect the efficacy of internal control functions in meeting regulatory expectations. In particular, post-crisis reforms in reframing the role of internal control have continued in a meta-regulatory framework although more prescriptions have been introduced to enhance the framework. Meta-regulation remains an important overall approach in financial regulation and in the regulatory framework for internal control at financial sector firms.

We first turn to the need for meta-regulatory frameworks in financial regulation generally and the limitations of meta-regulation. This section will highlight the achievements and inherent weaknesses and limitations in meta-regulation, but will also discuss how certain post-crisis reforms attempt to address the fallibilities.

The Rise of Flexible and Alternative Models of Regulation

The rise of flexible and alternative regulatory models such as meta-regulation in contemporary regulation theory is supported by a few factors. The decreasing perceived efficacy of traditional command-and-control methods in regulation has resulted in the rise of contemporary flexible strategies in regulation where regulators recognise that they do not have a monopoly over the regulatory space and that other actors in

[51] ibid.

the financial sector are able to exercise governance in many aspects.[52] Regulators have thus embraced new dynamics in regulatory relationships with their regulated, delegating aspects of governance and co-opting the regulated to play a role in governance generally.[53] Such an approach allows regulators to engage with alternative and experimental strategies in regulation and governance, within the resource constraints of the regulatory budget.[54] Further, the financial sector has become a powerful epistemic community capable of generating governance and has been in a position to assume self-regulatory governance and co-governance with regulators.[55] Meyer and Drori argue that contemporary areas of governance are dominated by knowledge-based individuals and communities whose collective role provides a form of governance that is perceived as legitimate and credible because of their expertise, professionalism and purported rationality in operation and action.[56] Hence, 'knowledge-based' actors are

[52] Contemporary literature is generally acknowledging the rise of governance, which is a pluralistic concept that explains how spaces for problem solving and dialogue are populated by many actors, and not monopolised by regulators or governments. See James N Rosenau and Ernst-Otto Czempiel, *Governance without Government: Order and Change in World Politics* (Cambridge: Cambridge University Press, 1992) as an earlier classic treatise on this issue; Stephen P Osborne (ed), *The New Public Governance?: Emerging Perspectives on the Theory and Practice of Public Governance* (Oxford: Routledge, 2009) Part I. On financial regulation specifically, see Isabelle Huault and Chrystelle Richard (eds), *Finance: The Discreet Regulator* (Abingdon: Palgrave Macmillan, 2012) on how non-regulatory actors provide leadership in governing finance.

[53] Julia Black, 'Enrolling Actors in Regulatory Systems: Examples from UK Financial Services Regulation' [2003] *Public Law* 63; Julia Black, 'Mapping the Contours of Contemporary Financial Services Regulation' (2002) 2 *Journal of Corporate Law Studies* 253. See also a concurring account from the sociological point of view: Laureen Snider, 'The Conundrum of Financial Regulation: Origins, Controversies, and Prospects' (2011) 7 *Annual Review of Law and Social Science* 121.

[54] Often referred to as risk-based regulation, see Julia Black, 'The Emergence of Risk-Based Regulation and the New Public Risk Management in the United Kingdom' [2005] *Public Law* 512; Joanna Gray and Jenny Hamilton, *Implementing Financial Regulation: Theory and Practice* (Chichester: John Wiley & Sons, 2006). Risk-based regulation is a modern compromise between the acknowledgement of the realities of the de-centred regulatory space and the limitations of the regulators in providing public goods. Risk-based regulation seeks to define the regulator's responsibility within the parameters of economic resources, efficiency and cost–benefit analyses.

[55] Sol Picciotto and Jason Haines, 'Regulating Global Financial Markets' (1999) 26 *Journal of Law and Society* 351; Stephen L Harris, 'Regulating Finance: Who Rules, Whose Rules?' (2004) 21 *Review of Policy Research* 743; Geoffrey RD Underhill, 'Markets beyond Politics? The State and the Internationalisation of Financial Markets' (1991) 19 *European Journal of Political Research* 197; Geoffrey Underhill and Xiaoke Zhang, 'Norms, Legitimacy, and Global Financial Governance' (2006) WEF Working Paper 13 at papers.ssrn.com/sol3/papers.cfm?abstract_id=941389 accessed 4 January 2013.

[56] Gili S Drori and John W Meyer, 'Global Scientization: An Expanded Environment for Organization' in Gili S Drori, John W Meyer and Hokyu Hwang (eds), *Globalization and Organization* (Oxford: Oxford University Press, 2009) 50; Gili S Drori, 'Governed by Governance' in Gili S Drori, John W Meyer and Hokyu Hwang (eds), *Globalization and Organization* (Oxford: Oxford University Press, 2009) 91.

likely to have the authority to lead or participate in governance. The financial sector, leading in innovation and standardisation has maintained, and is likely to maintain, this position of 'authority' in governance even in the post-crisis landscape.

Flexible and alternative strategies in regulation abound in financial regulation.[57] Such regulation could take the form of principles-based regulation, process-oriented regulation, outcomes or performance-based regulation, or meta-regulation.[58] The following will discuss how the various alternative regulatory techniques have been used in different aspects of financial regulation.

Flexible and Alternative Regulatory Strategies in Financial Regulation

First, financial regulators in the UK[59] have always embraced principles-based regulation.[60] Principles-based regulation according to Black features the following key elements: a purposive approach to interpretation of regulatory norms; a reliance on the internal management of firms; a focus on ensuring that regulatees attain the purposes or outcomes of the regulation rather than technical compliance with detailed rules; a targeted approach to enforcement; and a redistribution of responsibilities within the regulatory regime for ensuring and demonstrating compliance.[61] Principles-based regulation may be regarded as a form of outcomes-based regulation[62] which means that certain known outcomes are prescribed in regulation while leaving a significant amount of discretion and responsibility to firms to take actions to ensure the attainment of those outcomes. The UK's principles-based approach to regulation takes the form of a set of 11 high-level principles that form the basis on which detailed rules are further enacted.[63] These principles are themselves capable of giving rise

[57] Cristie Ford, 'Macro- and Micro-Level Effects on Responsive Financial Regulation' (2011) 44 *University of British Columbia Law Review* 589.

[58] Folarin Akinbami, 'Is Meta-Regulation All it is Cracked Up to Be? The Case of UK Financial Regulation' (2013) 14 *Journal of Banking Regulation* 16.

[59] The Financial Services Authority until April 2013, and now the Prudential Regulation Authority that oversees systemically important banks, insurers and investment firms and the Financial Conduct Authority.

[60] FSA, 'Principles-based Regulation: Focusing on the Outcomes that Matter' (April 2007) at www.fsa.gov.uk/pubs/other/principles.pdf; Julia Black, Martyn Hopper and Christa Band, 'Making a Success of Principles-based Regulation' (2007) 6 *Law and Financial Markets Review* 191.

[61] Julia Black, 'Paradoxes and Failures: "New Governance" Techniques and the Financial Crisis' (2012) 75 *Modern Law Review* 1037.

[62] Mary Condon, 'Canadian Securities Regulation and the Global Financial Crisis' (Walter S Owen Lecture, University of British Columbia, 26 March 2009).

[63] FSA Handbook, PRIN module.

to regulatory obligations on the part of regulated firms and can be used as a basis for enforcement.[64]

The 11 principles require regulated firms to:

1. Conduct business with integrity.
2. Conduct business with due skill, care and diligence.
3. Organise effective organisation and controls, in particular risk management systems.
4. Maintain adequate financial resources.
5. Observe proper standards of market conduct.
6. Treat customers fairly and pay due regard to their interests.
7. Provide effective and fair communication to clients.
8. Manage conflicts of interests.
9. Take reasonable care in ensuring suitability of investment advice and other discretionary decisions.
10. Provide adequate protection for clients' assets.
11. Maintain open and cooperative relationships with regulators, including appropriate disclosure.

These 11 principles are not indicia for compliance but outcomes that should be achieved in the regulation of investment firms. Firms may be free to employ different risk-mitigating measures to achieve the outcomes and the regulator's supervisory function will concentrate on ascertaining how firms' systems and procedures meet the outcomes. The principles also reflect the key areas of risk in investment firms' conduct of business.

The common concerns with principles-based regulation are that such regulation is too open-ended and could either result in sub-optimal implementation[65] which is undetected by regulators or forms of over-implementation for fear of enforcement.[66] However, commentators have argued that principles-based regulation is often supported by an interpretive community[67] where the relational engagement between regulator and regulated produces interpretations and understandings and give the principles more certainty. Commentators have also argued that in financial regulation where complex innovations abound, traditional prescriptive techniques are likely to fare worse and principles-based regulation provides the necessary flexibility to make regulation more relevant and

[64] FSA Enforcement Notice against Kensington Mortgage Co Ltd (12 April 2010); *BBA v FSA and FOS* [2011] EWHC 999 (Admin), [2011] ACD 71.

[65] Black, 'Paradoxes and Failures' (n 61).

[66] Steven L Schwarcz, 'The "Principles" Paradox' (2009) *European Business Organization Law Review* 175.

[67] See Julia Black, *Rules and Regulators* (Oxford: Clarendon, 1998); Andromachi Georgosuli, 'Regulatory Interpretation: Conversational or Constructive?' (2010) 30 *Oxford Journal of Legal Studies* 361.

durable.[68] It is generally agreed[69] that the implementation of one of the principles—'Treating Customers Fairly'—has been successful as the regulator and regulated have consistently engaged in the interpretation of this requirement. Regulatory clarifications—including through regulator enforcement—of what 'fairness' means have allowed the regulated firms to conduct business with more certainty.

Principles-based regulation should be distinguished from the UK's embrace of risk-based regulation. The risk-based approach is technically a regulatory strategy that seeks to maximise efficiency. Risk-based regulation seeks to define the regulator's responsibility within the parameters of economic resources, efficiency and cost–benefit analyses.[70] The UK regulator has been committed to risk-based regulation since its establishment in 2000.[71] The intention of risk-based regulation is to ensure that regulatory attention and resources are prioritised in an efficient manner to address the riskiest issues that may affect the delivery of regulatory goals. This approach has been accepted in many other countries, such as Australia and parts of Canada.[72] A risk-based approach in regulation allows regulators to carry out variable levels of supervision depending on the risk profiles of firms and hence allocate resources according to those priorities. In this way, Black critically comments that risk-based regulation could be used to redefine blame and the parameters of accountability.[73] Risk-based

[68] See Dan Awrey, 'Regulating Financial Innovation: A More Principles-Based Alternative?' (2010) at ssrn.com/abstract= 1702457; Dan Awrey, William Blair and David Kershaw, 'Between Law and Markets: Is there a Role for Culture and Ethics in Financial Regulation?' (2013) 38 *Delaware Journal of Corporate Law* 191, and at papers.ssrn.com/sol3/papers.cfm?abstract_id=2157588.

[69] Awrey, Blair and Kershaw, 'Between Law and Markets' (n 69); Andromachi Georgosuli, 'The FSA's Treating Customers Fairly (TCF) Initiative: What is so Good About it and Why it May not Work' (2011) 38 *Journal of Law and Society* 405.

[70] Black, 'The Emergence of Risk-Based Regulation' (n 54); Gray and Hamilton, *Implementing Financial Regulation* (n 54).

[71] See Michael Foot, 'Our new approach to risk based regulation risk and what will be different for firms' (speech at the FSA, London, 12 December 2000) at www.fsa.gov.uk/Pages/Library/Communication/Speeches/2000/sp69.shtml. The historical context of strong self-regulation in the financial sector prior to the establishment of the FSA may be important to the adoption of risk-based regulation, which promises proportionality and a relational paradigm in the FSA's approach. For some history, see Black, *Rules and Regulators* (n 67) chs 2 and 3. This is also the general thrust of public regulation in the new millennium, see Stephen Bundred, 'The Future of Regulation in the Public Sector' (2006) 26 *Public Money and Management* 181.

[72] Julia Black, 'The Development of Risk-based Regulation in Financial Services: Canada, the UK and Australia—A Research Report' (ECRC Centre for the Analysis of Risk and Regulation, LSE, 2004) at www.lse.ac.uk/collections/law/staff%20publications%20full%20text/black/risk%20based%20regulation%20in%20financial%20services.pdf.

[73] Black, 'The Emergence of Risk-Based Regulation (n 54). The limitations and subjective tendencies of risk-based regulation are also discussed in relation to the medical profession in Sally Lloyd-Bostock and Bridget M Hutter, 'Reforming Regulation of the Medical Profession: The Risks of Risk-Based Approaches' (2008) 10 *Health, Risk and Society* 69; Allen L Camp, 'Treatment of Uncertainties in Risk-Based Regulation' (December 1994) at www.osti.gov/bridge/servlets/purl/46555-dl5dVd/webviewable/46555.pdf.

regulation has become 'light-touch' regulation in the pre-crisis years partly because regulators were over-relying on firm-based governance.[74] As the regulator was hardly performing meta-level scrutiny and trusting in firms to implement the right procedures and systems, flexible strategies of regulation such as principles-based regulation could descend into sub-optimality. In 2006, the then Chairman of the UK Financial Services Authority (FSA) Callum McCarthy identified about 1500 firms that were subject to medium-to-high risk-based supervision, which entailed regular visits and continuous monitoring by the FSA. The remaining 28,349 firms were subject to low-risk supervision, which meant compliance only with reporting requirements established under the then FSA rules. Pre-crisis, much of the financial sector was arguably subject to a form of self-certifying discipline.[75] It is arguable that the global financial crisis that hit two of the UK's largest high street banks, namely Halifax Bank of Scotland and the Royal Bank of Scotland in late 2008 and early 2009,[76] could be due to the misperception of each bank's health under the risk-based regulatory framework,[77] resulting in a light-touch supervisory approach and over-reliance on the firms' own assessments of risks. Although flexible and alternative regulatory strategies do not necessarily import of light-touch and deficient regulatory supervision, the tendency to over-rely on firm governance did play out prior to the crisis and the UK FSA acknowledged its failings.[78]

[74] This danger was highlighted in Gray and Hamilton, *Implementing Financial Regulation* (n 54) way prior to the onset of the global financial crisis in 2008–09.

[75] Bazley and Haynes argue that risk-based regulation relies heavily on enhancing the internal compliance and risk management processes within firms, see Stuart Bazley and Andrew Haynes, *Financial Services Authority Regulation and Risk-based Compliance* (London: Tottel Publishing, 2006) 4.46ff.

[76] In relation to the Royal Bank of Scotland, the FSA's self-critical report attributes its inadequate supervision to inadequate data, due to which a more intelligent risk profile of the bank could not be put together for regulators, and the lack of liquidity supervision, which was not subject to regulatory oversight or international convergence anyway. See FSA, 'The Failure of the Royal Bank of Scotland: Financial Services Authority Board Report' (December 2011) at www.fsa.gov.uk/static/pubs/other/rbs.pdf.

[77] Most representations to the Regulatory Reform Select Committee of Parliament after the onset of the financial crisis seemed to agree that the application of risk-based regulation by the FSA had been faulty but the approach itself remained valid. See Regulatory Reform Select Committee, *Themes and Trends in Regulatory Reform* (HC 2008–09, 329-I) paras 5–42. Kern Alexander also commented that the risk-based approach to regulation had been faulty for its failure to consider systemic risk in its risk profiling, see Kern Alexander, 'Principles v Rules in Financial Regulation: Re-assessing the Balance in the Credit Crisis' (2009) 10 *European Business Organization Law Review* 169. The FSA's self-critical report reviewing the failure of Northern Rock points out that assessments made by the FSA about Northern Rock's sound risk profile have become sticky and unchanged in spite of new information and signals for concern. See, eg, FSA, 'The Supervision of Northern Rock: A lessons learned review' (March 2008) at www.fsa.gov.uk/pubs/other/nr_report.pdf, 49, 51.

[78] FSA, 'The Turner Review' (n 32) 88, which acknowledged that the FSA's approach in relational outworking with firms was not aggressive enough and a more intrusive and systemic approach was needed.

Outcomes-based regulation may be inappropriate where the certainty of outcomes cannot be defined, and in such a case, a process-oriented or meta-regulatory approach may be warranted.[79] Process-oriented or meta-regulation focuses more on systems and internal procedures which approximate towards soundness of control and governance, even if the outcomes are not entirely known.[80] The regulator may provide a broad framework such as requiring 'organisational soundness' or the institution of an 'independent' compliance function, providing for certain desirable attributes that firms need to ensure in their processes and systems. But the regulated are delegated the discretion to design the exact technologies and implementation of the systems and procedures. In regulation theory, different variants of process-oriented or meta-regulation has been discussed such as 'management-based regulation'[81] as a form of process-oriented regulation that emphasises organisational innovation and procedures to meet public regulatory goals; and 'new governance'[82] which is another form of process-oriented regulation that refers to the regulated being empowered to design compliance strategies and procedures accountable to an engaged regulator who constantly scrutinises at a meta-level.

The Importance of Meta-Regulation in Financial Regulation

Process-oriented or meta-regulation has been used widely in financial regulation. Prudential regulation and aspects of conduct of business regulation such as in conflicts of interest management, and the duty of best execution owed to clients, are process-oriented in nature. Process-oriented or meta-regulation strikes a balance between creating a template for regulatory scrutiny while avoiding micro-managing firms where regulators are not in the best position to do so. However, if regulatory scrutiny is inadequate or incompetent, firms may be incentivised to design and implement procedures and systems that deviate from regulatory objectives.[83]

The micro-prudential regulation framework developed for the most sophisticated banks and financial institutions in 2006 is a form of process-oriented or meta-regulation.[84] The Basel II Capital Accord which was

[79] Sharon Gilad, 'It Runs in the Family: Meta-regulation and its Siblings' (2010) 4 *Regulation & Governance* 485. Gilad however conceptualises process-oriented regulation more broadly as encompassing meta-regulation; this has been queried by other commentators such as Cristie Ford, see Ford, 'Macro- and Micro-Level Effects' (n 57).

[80] Ford, 'Macro- and Micro-Level Effects' (n 57).

[81] Cary Coglianese and David Lazer, 'Management-Based Regulation: Prescribing Private Management to Achieve Public Goals' (2003) 37 *Law & Society Review* 691.

[82] Cristie Ford, 'New Governance, Compliance, and Principles-Based Securities Regulation' (2008) 45 *American Business Law Journal* 1.

[83] Black, 'Paradoxes and Failures' (n 61).

[84] Also discussed in Weber, 'New Governance' (n 19).

implemented in the EU Capital Requirements Directive 2006 made provision for differential treatment between banks in implementing compliance with the capital adequacy requirements.[85] Essentially, the Accord allowed banks with more sophisticated internal risk management systems to exercise more discretion in implementing systems and procedures to comply with capital adequacy requirements. This was a move away from the formerly prescriptive regime under the Basel I Capital Accord which was regarded as outdated and insensitive to modern risk management developments.

Under the Basel I Capital Accord of 1988, a prescriptive, simple and one-size-fits-all approach was taken to determine the extent of capital to be set aside for credit risk. Categories of risk weights were established that determined how much capital was to be set aside against different types of loans. The categories of risk weights were few (five main categories), not very refined and applied across the board. The Basel II Capital Accord introduced three tiers of increasingly sophisticated approaches to determine how capital charges for credit risk were to be worked out. The first tier was the Basel I Capital Accord's approach with standardised risk weights. An innovation was however introduced to allow banks to apply more precise risk weights according to the published and recognised credit ratings of borrowers.[86] The second tier was a 'foundation internal ratings based' approach (or foundation IRB) allowing banks to use their internal methodologies to assess the risk of their loans and therefore their capital needs. Such banks however needed to demonstrate that they had already put in place adequate risk management and evaluation systems to determine the probability of default, but they were required to use standard measures for estimating loss and exposure at default.[87] The third tier of the Basel II Capital Accord's approach to credit risk allowed some of the most sophisticated banks to use the 'advanced internal ratings based' approach (or advanced IRB). The advanced IRB approach let banks with sophisticated and established risk management and evaluation systems determine the probability of default, loss and exposure at default of the loans in their books, in order to determine the precise capital charge required. Hence, the foundation and advanced IRB approaches gave banks significant discretion in determining capital charges against their assets. The IRB approaches were supposed to be supplemented by Pillars 2 and 3 of the Basel II Capital Accord, referring to regulatory and

[85] European Parliament and Council Directive 2006/48/EC of 14 June 2006 relating to the taking up and pursuit of the business of credit institutions (recast) [2006] OJ L77/1 (Capital Requirements Directive 2006).

[86] ibid, Arts 80–83 European Parliament and Council Directive 2006/48/EC of 14 June 2006 relating to the taking up and pursuit of the business of credit institutions (recast) [2006] OJ L77/1 (Capital Requirements Directive 2006) and Annex VI.

[87] ibid, Arts 84–89 and Annex VII.

supervisory oversight, and transparency to shareholders and stakeholders in order to facilitate market discipline.

The IRB approaches clearly treated the more sophisticated banks, mostly financial conglomerates, as being in the best position to deliver sound outcomes. The IRB approaches were meta-regulatory in nature. A broad framework for determining credit risk was first put in place, ie, that credit risk is evaluated by putting together the elements of probability of default, exposure at default and loss given default. Under the IRB approaches, banks have the discretion to implement systems and procedures to work out how each element of credit risk should be calculated in order to determine the capital adequacy required to be set aside. Although it has been intended that regulatory scrutiny should be exercised over firm implementation, so that regulators are operating at a meta-level of supervision, regulators have found it hard to make judgements on the technical robustness of banks' systems and procedures. Hence, the meta-regulatory approach in micro-prudential regulation has actually become a form of self-regulation in banks, and that is a chief weakness of meta-regulation frameworks.[88] In reality, as commentators have pointed out, banks that were in a position to determine their own capital charges have tended to set aside less capital and take on more risk,[89] and put their profit objectives above the regulatory objective of soundness and prudence.

It is to be noted that post-crisis, the meta-regulatory aspects of prudential regulation have been cut back significantly as regulators in the EU and internationally have decided to introduce prescriptive capital charges that apply across the board that are not balance-sheet based. For example, the Basel III Accord[90] has introduced the capital conservation and counter-cyclical buffers that were incorporated in new EU legislation.[91] The Financial Stability Board has prescribed absolute capital charges for internationally systemically important financial institutions.[92] National regulators such

[88] Larisa Dragomir, *European Prudential Banking Regulation and Supervision* (Oxford: Routledge, 2010) 124ff.

[89] See Michael McAleer, Juan-Angel Jiménez-Martin and Teodosio Pérez-Amaral, 'What Happened to Risk Management During the 2008–2009 Financial Crisis?' in Robert W Kolb (ed), *Lessons from the Financial Crisis* (New Jersey: John Wiley & Sons, 2010) 307; Paul H Kupiec, 'Financial Stability and Basel II' (2006) FDIC Research Paper 10/2006 at papers.ssrn.com/sol3/papers.cfm?abstract_id=942297; Michael Jacobs, 'An Empirical Study of the Returns on Defaulted Debt and the Discount Rate for Loss-Given-Default' (2009) at papers.ssrn.com/sol3/papers.cfm?abstract_id=1425146; Vaukhonen, 'Bank Safety and Basel II' (n 20).

[90] At www.bis.org/publ/bcbs189.pdf.

[91] Directive 2013/36/EU of the European Parliament and of the Council of 26 June 2013 on access to the activity of credit institutions and the prudential supervision of credit institutions and investment firms, amending Directive 2002/87/EC and repealing Directives 2006/48/EC and 2006/49/EC (CRD IV Directive) Arts 123, 125.

[92] See, eg, Financial Stability Board, *2014 Update of List of Global Systemically Important Banks (G-SIBs)* at www.financialstabilityboard.org/2014/11/2014-update-of-list-of-global-systemically-important-banks.

as the UK Prudential Regulation Authority may also impose absolute capital charges on domestically significant financial institutions.[93] Further, the discretionary aspects in the IRB approaches to credit risk and other discretionary approaches to provisioning for market and operational risks in the Basel II framework have also been adjusted towards tighter parameters for discretion and enhanced supervisory scrutiny.[94] Although the balance-sheet based framework for working out capital adequacy, and the use of firm models in risk profiling their trading books are not completely superseded and remain a form of meta-regulation, it is to be noted that the post-crisis technique of addressing the weaknesses of pre-crisis meta-regulation is to introduce more prescription and reduce the room for firms to exercise discretion. The book is of the view that such adjustments are inevitable for the development of meta-regulation as a viable regulatory technique, but the healthy development of meta-regulation should be more broadly considered. Increasing prescription and cutting back on meta-regulation may achieve immediate short-term impact, but it remains important to consider how the technique of meta-regulation could be positively refined for the future as it remains a relevant technique in the context of de-centred and complex financial regulation. This book, in its examination of the meta-regulation of internal control, hopes to offer some broader insight in strengthening and refining meta-regulation.

As for conduct of business regulation, process-oriented or meta-regulation also featured in the regulatory framework for investment firms in the management of conflicts of interest and the duty to carry out best execution for customers. I will highlight how meta-regulation works in these two areas before returning to the subject of internal control.

The now superseded EU Markets in Financial Instruments Directive (MiFID 2004)[95] provided a meta-regulatory framework for how investment firms should deal with conflicts of interest. Regulated investment firms were not prohibited from engaging in transactions that feature conflicts of interest. Rather, they were required to identify, manage and

[93] Capital Requirements (Capital Buffers and Macro-prudential Measures) Regs 2014; Pillars 2A and 2B charges discussed in PRA Consultation Paper on implementing CRD IV at www.bankofengland.co.uk/pra/Documents/publications/policy/2013/implementing-crdivcp513.pdf.

[94] EBA, *Consultation Paper: Draft Regulatory Technical Standards On the specification of the assessment methodology for competent authorities regarding compliance of an institution with the requirements to use the IRB Approach in accordance with Articles 144(2), 173(3) and 180(3)(b) of Regulation (EU) No 575/2013* (12 November 2014); Financial Stability Board, *Adequacy of Loss-Absorbing Capacity of Global Systemically Important Banks in Resolution* (10 November 2014); Basel Committee, *Consultative Document Operational Risk–Revisions to the Simpler Approaches* (October 2014).

[95] Art 18.

disclose conflicts of interests.[96] Disclosure was not regarded as a panacea for replacing management of conflicts of interest. The aspects of identification and management of conflicts of interest were very much delegated to the regulated firms although there were forms of non-exhaustive regulatory guidance. There was also a list of non-exhaustive criteria[97] to assist in identifying conflicts of interest, as well as suggestions for how they ought to be managed (using Chinese walls, the removal of cross-subsidising remunerative incentives and avoidance of personnel sharing across different departments, for example).[98] It has been largely up to firms to draw up their own conflicts of interest policy to identify the conflicts of interests they faced and the strategies for managing such conflicts.[99] Such is characteristic of a meta-regulatory approach where firms are primarily responsible for tailor-making strategies for governing certain issues, over which they have control, in order to deliver outcomes according to broader regulatory principles.[100] Where inducements are concerned, there were more precise rules demanding that firms only engage in giving or receiving inducements if benefits could be demonstrated for clients and duties owed to clients were not compromised.[101] Firms were still in control of how such justifications would be made and so the regulatory approach was arguably one of meta-regulation. The controls over investment research production and labelling were arguably more prescriptive.[102] In general, there were few prescriptive bright lines imposed on financial institutions in the area of management of conflicts of interest.

Enriques has argued that leaving primary responsibility to firms to write up their own conflicts of interest policy is likely to be an ineffective regulatory approach.[103] Policies may be written in a general boilerplate so that no real wisdom can be garnered as to what conflicts of interest may actually arise and how they will be dealt with in practice. Firms may also

[96] See the discussion of the regulatory framework for financial services in the European Union by Mads Andenas and Frank Wooldridge, *European Comparative Company Law* (Cambridge: Cambridge University Press, 2009) ch 11 (Investor Protection); Jakob de Haan, Sander Oosterloo and Dirk Schoenmaker, *European Financial Markets and Institutions* (Cambridge: Cambridge University Press, 2009).

[97] MiFID Commission Directive 2006, Art 21.

[98] ibid, Art 22; FCA Handbook SYSC 10.1, 10.2.

[99] MiFID Commission Directive 2006, Art 22.

[100] Gilad, 'It Runs in the Family' (n 79); Sharon Gilad, 'Process-Oriented Regulation: Conceptualisation and Assessment' in David Levi-Faur (ed), *Handbook on the Politics of Regulation* (Cheltenham: Edward Elgar, 2011) 423; Parker, *The Open Corporation* (n 48).

[101] MiFID Commission Directive 2006, Art 26; FSA Handbook COBS 2.3, 11.6.

[102] Such as prohibiting investment analysts from undertaking personal transactions, promising issuers favourable coverage or showing issuers drafts of research reports, see MiFID Commission Directive 2006, Art 25; FCA Handbook COBS 12.2, 12.3.

[103] Luca Enriques, 'Conflicts of Interest in Investment Services' in Guido Ferrarini and Eddy Wymeersch (eds), *Investor Protection in Europe: Corporate Law Making, the MiFID and Beyond* (Oxford: Oxford University Press, 2006).

not be motivated to monitor and evaluate their policies regularly. Kumpan and Leyens point out that firms do not often see refraining from acting for a client as being part of the suite of strategies they will employ in the management of conflicts of interest.[104] Although the regulatory framework is targeted towards investor protection, firms could implement policies in such a way as to tick the boxes of the procedures required in the meta-regulatory approach and in fact place their business interests above those of their clients. Supervisors may find it difficult to check how firms have dealt with conflicts of interest and whether there has been any adverse impact.[105] Civil litigation is likely to be an ineffective instrument as contractual limitations to fiduciary duties could be upheld by the court and causation of loss may sometimes be hard to prove.[106]

As for the duty of best execution,[107] this duty has been imposed in order to protect investors in executing securities transactions, as firms are bound by law to achieve a best possible transaction for them. This duty prevents investment firms from favouring their own interests if a conflict of interest should arise, and combats the potential for fraudulent transactions.[108] Under the superseded MiFID 2004, the implementation of the duty of best execution was in the hands of the firms, and the regulators' role would be at the meta-level of regulatory scrutiny and enforcement. The regulated firms have been primarily responsible for determining how they would secure best execution within a broad framework. MIFID 2004 defined best execution with respect to a range of factors, ie 'price, costs, speed, likelihood of execution and settlement, size, nature or any other consideration relevant to the execution of the order'.[109] However, in relation to the retail customer, the MIFID Commission Regulation 2006 was more prescriptive: best execution with regard to a retail investor is measured according to the total consideration for the securities less cost, and that in order to determine best execution comparison has to be made between terms offered by trading venues.[110]

[104] Christoph Kumpan and Patrick C Leyens, 'Conflicts of Interest of Financial Intermediaries' (2008) 5 *European Company and Financial Law Review* 72.

[105] Ingo Walter, 'Reputational Risk and Conflicts of Interest in Banking and Finance: The Evidence So Far' in J Richard Aronson, Harriet L Parmet and Robert J Thornton (eds), *Variations in Economic Analysis* (New York: Springer, 2010).

[106] In *Seymour v Ockwell* [2005] EWHC 1137 (QB), [2005] All ER (D) 297 for example, although the financial adviser did not disclose a commission obtained after the sale of an investment product, and hence was in breach of fiduciary duty, the losses suffered by the investors in this case were attributed to unsuitable and negligent advice rather than the breach of fiduciary duty.

[107] MiFID 2004, Art 21; FCA Handbook, COBS 11.

[108] Francis J Facciolo, 'A Broker's Duty of Best Execution in the Nineteenth and Early Twentieth Centuries' (2005) 26 *Pace Law Review* 155 discusses the historical origins of the best execution rule and its regulatory rationale.

[109] MiFID 2004, Art 21(1).

[110] MiFID Commission Regulation 2006, Art 44.

Investment firms were given the discretion to design and implement best execution policies according to the broad framework of six and other factors mentioned in MiFID 2004. Such policies had to show what execution venues are selected by the firms and the factors affecting choice of venues. The firms also had to communicate their policies to clients. Firms were responsible for drafting the details of the policies and their implementation. Like the situation with regulating the management of conflicts of interest, regulators could find it difficult to impeach a reasonably drafted execution policy, and substantive judgement on 'best execution' is itself difficult to make,[111] as 'best execution' is not necessarily compromised even if the policy is deviated from. Further, civil enforcement is also highly difficult and unlikely.

It is to be noted that conduct of business regulation under the recast Markets in Financial Instruments Directive 2014 (MiFID II)[112] have embarked on more prescriptive aspects in order to mitigate the weaknesses of meta-regulation. Where conflicts of interest management and the duty for best execution are concerned, the broad framework is still one of meta-regulation,[113] but specific provisions have been introduced to combat identified problems. For example, firms engaged in portfolio management would be subject to a more stringent inducements regime and would be expected to account for all separate aspects of the package of service.[114] Independent financial advisers are mandated to survey the market for diverse options to meet clients' needs and are not permitted to retain commissions or inducements provided by third parties.[115] Further, firms are prohibited from designing remuneration incentives related to sales targets in order to prevent mis-selling.[116] Firms are also not allowed to receive payment for order flow or execution venue kickbacks as these may affect choice of execution venue.[117] The UK Financial Conduct Authority (FCA) has also beefed up its enforcement front[118] and issued specific guidance to constrain misconduct in the mis-selling of financial products.[119]

[111] Jonathan R Macey and Maureen O'Hara, 'The Law and Economics of Best Execution' (1997) 6 *Journal of Financial Intermediation* 188.

[112] Directive 2014/65/EU of the European Parliament and of the Council of 15 May 2014 on markets in financial instruments and amending Directive 2002/92/EC and Directive 2011/61/EU (MiFID II Directive).

[113] Arts 23, 27, MiFID II Directive.

[114] ibid, Art 24(11).

[115] ibid, Art 24(7).

[116] ibid, Art 24(10).

[117] ibid, Art 27(2).

[118] Such as the mis-selling of payment protection insurance, dealt with under FSA Handbook DISP App 3 and the mis-selling of endowment mortgages, dealt with under FSA Handbook DISP App 1.

[119] This area is reformed by the Retail Distribution Review, which came into force in 2013. The UK regulator has published a guidance, see FSA, *Final Guidance: Risks to Customers from Financial Incentives* (January 2013) at www.fca.org.uk/static/fca/documents/finalised-guidance/fsa-fg13-01.pdf.

The approach in the MiFID II shows that there are limits to prescriptive regulation as regulation cannot micro-manage for particular outcomes in myriad investor trades or purchases of investment products. Hence, the meta-regulatory frameworks centred upon the requirement for firms to draw up and implement effective conflicts of interest management and best execution policies remain. Although specific prescriptions attempt to deal with particular problems, they can also result in unintended consequences. The need to make inducements proportionate and transparent may serve investors' needs for accountability, but may then reduce the scope for subsidising non-revenue generating forms of services such as investment research that can genuinely be useful for investors. Specific prescriptions are not a panacea for the weaknesses in meta-regulation, and this book advocates exploration into developing and adjusting meta-regulation with learning,[120] and will in chapter eight provide some suggestions to support the viability of meta-regulation.

Meta-regulation produces in Krawiec's words, 'incomplete contracts'[121] between the regulator and regulated and gives rise to the basic agency problem. The following will discuss the key weaknesses in meta-regulation that could result in firm deviation from regulatory goals. First, meta-regulation could produce 'excessive proceduralisation'[122] in firms, giving an appearance of compliance and making it difficult for regulators to tell if the compliance is genuine or cosmetic, shielding underlying problems. Second, meta-regulation can also result in legal endogenity,[123] which is a form of legitimation of firm procedures and systems as achieving procedural justice. This means that firms treat the implementation of processes and systems as an end in themselves and fail to engage with whether the systems and processes genuinely meet regulatory objectives, missing the wood for the trees. However, this book suggests that the manifestation of concrete problems such as product mis-selling does not mean that meta-regulation has failed as a regulatory technique. The book will address the need for improvements to meta-regulatory designs through the study of the meta-regulation of internal control.

[120] 'London banks and brokers face research business shake-up' *Financial Times* (24 July 2014).

[121] Kimberly D Krawiec, 'Cosmetic Compliance and the Failure of Negotiated Governance' (2003) 81 *Washington University Law Quarterly* 487, 522.

[122] Michael Power, *The Audit Society* (Oxford: Oxford University Press, 1997) and Michael Power, *Organized Uncertainty: Designing a World of Risk Management* (Oxford: Oxford University Press, 2008).

[123] Lauren B Edelman, Christopher Uggen and Howard S Erlanger, 'The Endogeneity of Legal Regulation: Grievance Procedures as Rational Myth' (1999) 105 *American Journal of Sociology* 406; Lauren B Edelman, Linda H Krieger, Scott R Eliason, Catherine R Albiston and Virginia Mellema, 'When Organizations Rule: Judicial Deference to Institutionalized Employment Structures' (2011) 117 *American Journal of Sociology* 888.

Meta-Regulation and its Limitations

Excessive Proceduralisation

Power discusses the phenomenon of proceduralisation in his treatises on audit and risk management,[124] and observes that the legitimacy of corporate management is very much bound up with the development and standardisation of 'control procedures'. The existence of 'control procedures' entails the perception that the firm is 'in control' or has achieved a state of 'manageability' or a 'control environment.' Firms engage in proceduralisation as they perceive support from the wider context for such an approach. First, the wider context of corporate governance emphasising the monitoring Board in firms has shaped firm preferences towards instituting various forms of proceduralisation to show that the Board is able to and indeed 'monitors'. Proceduralisation provides the necessary appearance of systems and information relay and thus assures the Board that it is discharging its monitoring functions. Second, the wider context of corporate social responsibility puts pressure on corporations to institute procedures and systems to appear more engaged with stakeholder concerns. Third, proceduralisation is supported by professionals such as auditors who could provide services in designing procedures and systems; and legal professionals who view proceduralisation as steps taken to eliminate risk in order to manage the scope of any future liability. Hence, firms respond to these contexts and welcome proceduralisation as the firm may itself be reassured and is able to attain a sense of 'comfort' that external legitimacy may also be achieved.[125] The meta-regulation of financial institutions provides opportunities for firms to engage in proceduralisation, such as in the design, implementation and review of various policies such as the best execution policy.[126]

Proceduralisation tends towards an approach that is comfortably nested within the organisation, being rational and professional but not tending towards disruption and antagonism.[127] As Scott-Simmons puts it:

> Procedures and structures often serve as a default heuristic for quality. Corporate constituencies find it easier to coalesce around procedures that, in part, resemble familiar democratic values such as independence, disclosure, and voting. Transplanting these democratic principles to a corporate setting … resonates with the public and some shareholders. But the overall effectiveness of such mechanisms remains a question.[128]

[124] Power, *Organized Uncertainty* (n 122) especially chs 2, 3 and 6; *The Audit Society* (n 122) ch 6.

[125] Power, *The Audit Society* (n 122) ch 6.

[126] Cunningham, 'The Appeal and Limits' (n 2).

[127] Power, *Organized Uncertainty* (n 122).

[128] Omari Scott-Simmons, 'The Corporate Immune System: Governance from the Inside Out' (2013) *University of Illinois Law Review* 1131.

Proceduralisation may also be a reductionist way of working, and this accords with firms' natural tendencies to compartmentalise tasks and roles.[129] Hence, firm implementation may be characterised by 'box-ticking'[130] and encouraging myopia. Such qualities may become contrary to the qualities needed for critical monitoring and scrutiny of front line operations and activities. At worst, proceduralisation could foster merely cosmetic forms of compliance.[131] Proceduralisation could also be excessively biased towards predictability and entail a form of stickiness against change.[132] It could be susceptible to ossification[133] and renders the firm unable to dynamically respond to changing situations. This may especially be so if the proceduralisation has been adopted based on the working of certain technological systems, and becomes welded to the relevant technological limitations. Technologically limited forms of proceduralisation may fail to capture new information needs in the dynamic and complex businesses banks and financial institutions engage in.[134] Firms may continue to derive false comfort from such systems even if the systems become outdated. It has also been commented that firm procedures and systems are chiefly for the purposes of achieving firm efficiency and objectives, so regulatory goals would likely be reinterpreted within the firm's frames.[135] Firm procedures may actually become disengaged from securing substantive regulatory objectives even if such procedures and systems appear to be in compliance and legitimate. In sum, proceduralisation can create an appearance of panacea while masking the underachievement of substantive outcomes.

Further, firm procedures, especially if presented as complex systems and technologies, provide an impression of endeavour, credibility and legitimacy and thus justify themselves, creating a form of legal endogeneity. Legal endogeneity occurs when the systems and procedures implemented by firms are taken as capable of defining what the needs of substantive justice or regulation are, ie, that organisational governance and structures are taken as filling in for the meaning of substantive outcomes and therefore

[129] ibid.

[130] Power, *Organized Uncertainty* (n 122) 164.

[131] Krawiec, 'Cosmetic Compliance' (n 121) 487.

[132] eg, see Lloyd-Bostock and Hutter, 'Reforming Regulation of the Medical Profession' (n 73).

[133] Kenneth A Bamberger, 'Technologies of Compliance: Risk and Regulation in a Digital Age' (2009/10) 88 *Texas Law Review* 669; JW Williams, 'Envisioning Financial Disorder: Financial Surveillance and the Securities Industry' (2009) 38 *Economy and Society* 460.

[134] Gillian Tett, 'The Banks that are too Complex to Exist' *Financial Times* (8 June 2012) citing Henry TC Hu, 'Too Complex to Depict? Innovation, "Pure Information" and the SEC Disclosure Paradigm' (2012) 90 *Texas Law Review* 1601. Complexity in information has been empirically researched as one of the key reasons for internal control failure, see Jan Pfister, *Managing Organizational Culture for Effective Internal Control* (Berlin: Physica-Verlag, 2009) ch 4.

[135] Kenneth A Bamberger, 'Regulation as Delegation: Private Firms, Decisionmaking, and Accountability in the Administrative State' (2006) 56 *Duke Law Journal* 377.

satisfying the requirements of legal compliance as such.[136] Edelman et al have studied internal firm procedures for redressing employment grievances in great detail and observe that courts tend to hold that a firm's compliance with its internal grievance policies is evidence of its compliance with employment law.[137] Hence, organisational or managerial governance could become institutionalised, standardised and widely accepted as legal compliance, resulting in legal endogeneity. In terms of applying to financial regulation, it could also be argued that the lack of regulatory scrutiny of banks in the pre-crisis era applying the meta-regulatory IRB approaches in determining capital adequacy has encouraged a form of legal endogeneity. In the absence of thematic reviews,[138] regulators would unlikely be able to evaluate firms' conflicts of interest management systems and best execution procedures in terms of their substantive outcomes. The existence of the systems and procedures has the potential to create a form of legal endogeneity in the eyes of clients and regulators.

Meta-regulation offers an alternative way of reaching into firms without over-prescription or micro-management, but it is not without its limitations. The inappropriateness of traditional command-and-control regulation, resource constraints for regulators and the acknowledgment for the governance capacity of the regulated are reasons that continue to support such regulatory approaches. Of course, one could also suspect that the continued prevalence of meta-regulation in post-crisis financial regulation is due to the lack of political will to re-regulate where necessary, and that meta-regulatory methods strike an acceptable compromise with the powerful financial sector.[139] In the post-crisis landscape, it is observed that meta-regulation continues to be used in new reform measures, despite the weaknesses pointed out above. However, meta-regulatory techniques are now supported by increased prescription to address known problems, such as in the regulation of internal control functions as this book will study in detail. One example of the continued use of meta-regulation in new reforms relates to the regulatory requirement that financial institutions have to draw up 'recovery and resolution plans'[140] in order to set out *ex ante* how they would deal with a potential crisis.

[136] Russell J Funk and Daniel G Hirschman, 'Endogenous Legal Change: How Organizations Re-Shaped Glass-Steagall' (2012) University of Michigan Working Paper.

[137] Edelman et al, 'The Endogeneity of Legal Regulation' and 'When Organizations Rule' (n 123).

[138] FCA, *Commercial Insurance Intermediaries —Conflicts of Interest and Intermediary Remuneration: Report on the Thematic Project* (27 May 2014); FCA, *Thematic Review: Best Execution and Payment for Order Flow* (31 July 2014).

[139] Scott-Simmons, 'The Corporate Immune System' (n 128).

[140] s 139B Financial Services Act 2010 amending the Financial Services Markets Act 2000; also EU Bank Recovery and Resolution Directive, Directive 2014/59/EU of the European Parliament and of the Council of 15 May 2014 establishing a framework for the recovery and resolution of credit institutions and investment firms and amending Council Directive

Recovery plans, more popularly known as the 'living will', are internationally endorsed measures in order to facilitate orderly resolution of a troubled financial institution at minimum social cost.[141] It is also meta-regulatory in nature. The recovery plan requires a financial institution to provide: (a) information regarding its structures, business and vulnerabilities;[142] (b) suggested triggers for recovery based on stressful scenarios that firms propose;[143] and (c) a range of diverse options for recovery that can be credibly executed within a reasonable time.[144] The recovery plan has to be submitted for regulatory approval, and regulators may require amendments to be made to the plans or business structures to be changed to make firms more resolvable.[145] However, it is envisaged that firms would be responsible for triggering and implementing the recovery plan should the identified stresses occur, and play a responsible part in ensuring their own safety, soundness and survivability.

The persistence of the importance of meta-regulation in financial regulation is not in doubt. Black advocates that regulators need to learn from the weaknesses in meta-regulation exposed in the global financial crisis in order to fine-tune the meta-regulatory approach.[146] Meta-regulation is experimental in nature and there is a need to learn from the implementation and review of meta-regulatory frameworks.[147] From now on, the book will focus on the pre-crisis and post-crisis regulation of internal control in order to flesh out how the meta-regulation of internal control has become an important facet in financial regulation to secure the attainment of regulatory objectives, and how such meta-regulation can be further enhanced, providing broader insights for the viability of meta-regulation as a regulatory technique generally.

82/891/EEC, and Directives 2001/24/EC, 2002/47/EC, 2004/25/EC, 2005/56/EC, 2007/36/EC, 2011/35/EU, 2012/30/EU and 2013/36/EU, and Regulations (EU) No 1093/2010 and (EU) No 648/2012, of the European Parliament and of the Council.

141 Financial Stability Forum, 'FSF Principles for Cross-border Cooperation on Crisis Management' (2 April 2009) at www.financialstabilityboard.org/publications/r_0904c.pdf, Principle 8.

142 Arts 4–7, Directive 2014/59/EU of the European Parliament and of the Council of 15 May 2014 establishing a framework for the recovery and resolution of credit institutions and investment firms and amending Council Directive 82/891/EEC, and Directives 2001/24/EC, 2002/47/EC, 2004/25/EC, 2005/56/EC, 2007/36/EC, 2011/35/EU, 2012/30/EU and 2013/36/EU, and Regulations (EU) No 1093/2010 and (EU) No 648/2012, of the European Parliament and of the Council (BRRD); EBA Final RTS for Recovery Plans (July 2014).

143 EBA Final RTS for Recovery Plans (July 2014).

144 Art 9, BRRD, para 183; Basel Committee on Banking Supervision, *Resolution Policies and Frameworks—Progress So Far* (6 July 2011) at www.bis.org/publ/bcbs200.pdf. See further, Financial Services Authority draft FINMAR rules on recovery plans (May 2012) and EBA Final RTS for Recovery Plans (July 2014).

145 Arts 15–18, BRRD.

146 Black, 'Paradoxes and Failures' (n 61).

147 Gilad, 'It Runs in the Family' (n 79); Gilad, 'Process-Oriented Regulation' (n 100) 423.

C. THREE PARADIGMS IN THE REGULATORY FRAMEWORK FOR INTERNAL CONTROL IN BANKS AND FINANCIAL INSTITUTIONS

Although internal control can be defined as a form of general organisational governance,[148] the specific functions of internal control departments in banks and financial institutions, ie, the compliance, risk management and internal audit functions assume particular roles and responsibilities. These internal control departments are regarded as 'second' or 'third' lines of defence (applicable to Internal Audit only) in an organisation.[149] The regulatory framework for internal control discussed in the book relates to the regulation of the compliance, risk management and internal audit functions as well as the overall organisational governance framework that supports these functions. The regulatory frameworks for internal control functions and the internal control governance of firms remain meta-regulatory in nature although increased prescriptions have been made in post-crisis reforms. It will be argued that the role and functions of internal control should be understood in three paradigms: the organisational, professional and regulatory paradigms. This book will argue that understanding the three paradigms is crucial to appreciating what can be achieved by the meta-regulatory framework for internal control.

The pre-crisis regulatory framework for internal control functions at banks and financial institutions was meta-regulatory but skeletal in nature. European legislation on banks or credit institutions did not require the institution of any particular internal control functions, leaving it to the regulated firms to define what 'adequate internal control' may be proportionate to the 'nature, scale and complexity' of the firm's activities.[150] However, the MiFID 2004 which applied to investment firms mandated the establishment of separate and permanent compliance and internal audit functions in investment firms,[151] leaving firms the discretion to decide if a separate risk management function[152] would be necessary and proportionate to the nature, scale and complexity of the firm's business. In the UK, the regulator applied the MiFID 2004 requirements across the board to authorised financial institutions that are not insurers, reinsurance underwriting agents or building societies.[153]

The pre-crisis framework of internal control only outlined the mandatory institution of permanent and independent compliance and internal

148 COSO, *Internal Control: Integrated Framework* (December 2011) (n 7) paras 15, 415, 441.

149 ibid, paras 154, 417.

150 Capital Requirements Directive 2006, Art 22.

151 MiFID Commission Directive 2006, Arts 6 and 8.

152 ibid, Art 7. Even if firms consider that a separate risk management function is not necessary, Art 7 does require firms to put in place effective and adequate risk management policies and procedures.

153 FSA Handbook, SYSC 1A.

audit functions. Risk management policies and procedures may or may not be undertaken by a specialist risk management function. No further regulatory detail was provided on the roles, tasks and objectives of these functions. Such a skeletal approach could have been taken because of several possible reasons. One is that regulators see internal control functions as organisational phenomena, ie, a form of organisational governance that firms would be willing to establish anyway and hence there was no need to provide any further regulatory detail on these functions. This perspective would also mean that regulators perhaps did not have governance expectations of what internal control functions could do in terms of securing regulatory objectives. The meeting of regulatory objectives is the primary responsibility of the firm, and internal control being part of the firm would not be subject to any special scrutiny. However, if regulators saw internal control as a purely firm-level phenomenon, then why even prescribe the skeletal framework for internal control? The mandatory institution of these functions seems to suggest that some regulatory expectations may exist in relation to how these functions work at the firm level in securing firms' adherence to regulatory objectives.[154]

Further, it could be argued that the skeletal nature of the pre-crisis regulatory framework was due to there being certain regulatory assumptions of what internal control functions did and there was thus no need for regulation to spell such out. Such assumptions may be based on well-accepted organisational understandings of internal control, although as chapters two to four will show subsequently, the organisational understanding of all three internal control functions is far from uniform. In other words, it could be argued that regulators' assumptions were based on the perception of professionalism surrounding internal control functions and hence there was no need for regulation to spell out what professionals ought to do. This book will show that although the three internal control functions are arguably at different stages of professional development,[155] the professional understanding of the scope of responsibilities is yet to be uniformly

[154] The expectations point is also raised in Cunningham, 'The Appeal and Limits' (n 2); Langevoort, 'Internal Controls after Sarbanes–Oxley' (n 27).

[155] Discussed in chapters 2–4. For the compliance profession, see Andrew Newton, *The Handbook Of Compliance Making Ethics Work in Financial Service* (London: Financial Times Management, 1998) ch 4; Annie Mills, *Essential Strategies for Financial Services Compliance* (Chichester: John Wiley & Sons, 2008) 38ff. For the Internal Audit function, see The Institute of Internal Auditors, *International Standards for the Professional Practice of Internal Auditing (Standards)* at www.theiia.org; Dominic SB Soh and Nonna Martinov-Bennie, 'The Internal Audit Function: Perceptions of Internal Audit Roles, Effectiveness, and Evaluation' (2011) 26 *Managerial Auditing Journal* 605. For the Risk Management function, see Laura Spira and Michael Page, 'Risk Management: The Reinvention of Internal Control and the Changing Role of Internal Audit' (2003) 16 *Accounting, Auditing and Accountability Journal* 640; Douglas Hubbard, *The Failure of Risk Management: Why It's Broken and How Do we Fix It?* (Chichester: John Wiley & Sons, 2009) ch 4; Power, *Organized Uncertainty* (n 122) especially chs 1–3.

established. Hence, the regulatory framework for internal control, even in the pre-crisis era, already suffers from disjunctions between regulatory expectations and the organisational and professional practices relating to internal control. These disjunctions will augment the weaknesses inherent in the meta-regulatory framework for internal control and such weaknesses have played out in the global financial crisis, highlighting 'weak internal control' in a number of stricken banks in the crisis.[156]

The taciturn characteristic of the meta-regulatory framework for internal control is changing. In the wake of the global financial crisis and the post-crisis revelations of misdemeanour and mis-selling in financial institutions, internal control functions at banks and financial institutions have been perceived to be weak or deficient,[157] and in need of reform. Further, the UK regulator has also increased regulatory enforcement against internal control personnel[158] although such liability is arguably secondary to the firm's primary liability. The crisis has exposed a gap between regulatory expectations of the role of internal control functions and the actual practice of those functions. This book argues that the weaknesses of pre-crisis internal control functions expose disjunctions, some of which are being addressed by post-crisis reforms. These are:

a. The regulatory–organisational disjunction[159] in the framing of internal control functions.
b. The regulatory–professional disjunction in the framing of internal control functions.
c. The professional–organisational disjunction in the framing of internal control functions.

The regulatory–organisational disjunction refers to the disjunction between regulatory expectations of the role of internal control and the outworking of these roles within the constraints of the organisational fabric. For example, internal control functions could perceive themselves or be

[156] Eg, the Halifax Bank of Scotland whose internal control weaknesses were highlighted in the House of Commons and House of Lords, Parliamentary Commission on Banking Standards, *An Accident Waiting to Happen: The Failure of HBOS* (2012–13, HL 144, HC 705) (4 April 2013).

[157] Weaknesses are discussed with reference to different characteristics, such as methodology, lack of review and weak organisational influence over adverse front line decision-making, see Jézabel Couppey-Soubeyran, 'Financial Regulation in the Crisis: Regulation, Market Discipline, Internal Control: The Big Three in Turmoil' (2010) 123 *International Economics* 13; Hubbard, *The Failure of Risk Management* (n 155) chs 1 and 2; Eric Pichet, 'What Governance Lessons Should Be Learnt from the Societe Générale's Kerviel Affair?' (2008) 3 *La Revue Française de Gouvernance d'Entreprise* 117 exploring the weakness of internal control from the organisational power point of view.

[158] See chapter 7.

[159] Organisational deficiencies resulting in compliance shortfalls is generally discussed in Timothy F Malloy, 'Regulation, Compliance and the Firm' (2003) 76 *Temple Law Review* 451.

perceived as serving mainly firm-centric purposes as they are defined within organisational governance frameworks and capacities, and not be conscious of a wider role in assisting regulators to secure firms' compliance. Or, regulators may have expectations of a certain level of efficacy on the part of internal control functions but they may in reality fall short of achieving those expectations due to constraints in power or resources within the organisational context.

The regulatory–professional disjunction refers to the disjunction between regulatory expectations of what internal control functions do and what internal control functions actually carry out as a matter of professional understanding of their functions. This means that internal control functions may be carrying out functions according to their professional consciousness and these may or may not be in sync with regulatory expectations of their roles. Finally, the professional–organisational disjunction refers to the disjunction between the perception on the part of internal control functions as to what their roles and responsibilities encompass and the perception on the part of the organisation as to the scope and nature of their roles and responsibilities. Organisational framing can distort and limit the professional exercise of internal control functions.

The three disjunctions highlighted above augment the weaknesses of the meta-regulatory framework for internal control. Post-crisis reforms have increased prescription in the regulatory framework for internal control, but this book will argue that the reforms are mainly targeted towards mitigating only one of the disjunctions identified: the regulatory–organisational disjunction. This book will flesh out these reforms in chapters two to six. This book argues that mitigating the regulatory–organisational disjunction improves the governance capacity of internal control functions but does not do enough to define such governance roles and responsibilities. Reforms are needed to address the regulatory–professional disjunction in order to better articulate the scope and nature of internal control roles and responsibilities. The book therefore proposes an approach in chapter eight that will address the regulatory–professional disjunction in order to clarify the professional role of internal control functions in the governance landscape and place regulatory expectations on a firmer footing. Addressing the regulatory–professional disjunction will also lead to enhanced professionalism on the part of the internal control professions and help in mitigating the–professional- organisational disjunction.

It may be argued that regulatory reach into reframing the roles and powers of internal control functions at banks and financial institutions would not necessarily have a direct impact upon changing questionable financial sector behaviour, as firms would only focus on the minimal adjustments needed in order to carry on business as usual. However, it may be counter-argued that such reforms are structural in nature and work on bottom-up processes in firms that could have a gradual but more enduring impact upon long-term changes to firm culture and behaviour. Changes to firm behaviour is a gradual process,[160] and the regulation of internal control functions and governance in firms goes towards changing the incentives and values underlying financial business, an essential support to direct forms of prudential and conduct of business regulation. This book will examine to what extent the post-crisis reforms overcome the three disjunctions outlined above and what remains to be done to enhance the efficacy of the meta-regulation of internal control.

It should be noted that the organisational perspectives of internal control functions that will be presented in this book are based on a literature review of management and organisation literature which includes empirical studies and findings. The book will present an overview perspective as it would not be practicable to identify detailed differences in the way different financial institutions frame and institutionalise their internal control functions. The book will also draw from an empirical research focusing on compliance officers which the UCL Centre for Ethics and the Law has carried out, and in which the author has been involved.[161] This book is intended to be an interdisciplinary study towards the achievement of an appropriate, proportionate and effective framework for regulating internal control functions in banks and financial institutions that contributes towards the wider regulatory governance of financial institutions.

D. STRUCTURE OF THE BOOK

This book will comprise two parts. Part I focuses on the three internal control functions, namely compliance, risk management and internal audit and the wider organisational governance framework in which the three functions are situated. This part consists of five chapters. Chapters two to four will discuss the pre-crisis regulatory framework for the three functions of internal control and the post-crisis reforms that deal largely with the regulatory–organisational disjunction. These chapters will critically discuss the strengths and weaknesses of the pre- and post-crisis meta-regulatory frameworks for internal control. These chapters will also point out where the regulatory–professional and professional–organisational disjunctions lie, how these affect the governance role of internal control

[160] 'Banks need a generation to change culture, report says' *Financial Times* (26 November 2014).

[161] Richard Moorhead and Steven Vaughan, 'Legal Risk: Definition, Management and Ethics' (UCL Centre for Ethics and the Law, April 2015) at www.ucl.ac.uk/laws/law-ethics/research/papers/erc-executive-report-legal-risk-definition-management-ethics.pdf.

functions, as well as to what extent these have been addressed or otherwise in post-crisis reforms.

Chapter five discusses the post-crisis realisation that the efficacy of internal control is affected by broader organisational contexts and structures such as corporate governance and organisational culture. This chapter discusses the specific findings from empirical research identifying weaknesses in internal control as being shaped and affected by governance and culture factors, highlighting how such regulatory–organisational disjunctions have affected the efficacy of internal control functions.

Part II the book comprises three chapters and focuses on evaluating the regulatory strategies that have been employed to make internal control more effective in securing firms' adherence to regulatory objectives. Chapter six deals first with the regulatory framework for aspects of corporate governance and organisational culture as a form of reinforcement for the meta-regulatory framework for internal control functions. This is an important strategy in reframing and enhancing the role of internal control, by addressing the regulatory–organisational disjunctions at the higher level of corporate governance. It is however to be noted that this strategy is also meta-regulatory in nature and its achievements and limitations will be discussed. Chapter seven then discusses recent regulatory enforcement decisions against internal control personnel and senior management as a novel strategy in boosting the governance and gatekeeping roles of internal control. However, the chapter highlights the problems with this strategy in light of the regulatory–professional and professional–organisational disjunctions. Enhanced enforcement may not achieve much in making the governance and gatekeeping roles of internal control more effective if the abovementioned disjunctions are not addressed. Enhanced enforcement may only give rise to increased uncertainty in the professionalism of internal control and raise questions of fairness surrounding regulatory enforcement.

Chapter eight will argue that the post-crisis reforms have overwhelmingly focused on the regulatory–organisational disjunction in order to address the essential weaknesses of the meta-regulatory framework for internal control, but that such are inadequate for boosting the governance capacity of internal control if lack of attention is paid to the regulatory–professional and–professional- organisational disjunctions. These disjunctions are arguably due to the weaknesses surrounding the professional dimension of internal control functions. Chapter eight suggests that a new approach is needed to bridge the regulatory–professional disjunction in order to complement the organisation-based regulatory reforms that have taken place. The new approach is based on enhancing the professionalism of internal control with regulatory input, and securing a clearer and wider sense of responsibility and accountability in the professional discharge of internal control functions. Addressing the regulatory–professional disjunction this way would also mitigate the professional–organisational disjunction so that organisational emasculation or manipulation of internal control functions may be constrained. Finally, chapter eight suggests that the study in this book that addresses the challenges posed by the meta-regulatory framework for internal control functions would also provide insights to constructively add to the theoretical understandings and accounts of meta-regulation generally.

2

The Role of Compliance

A. THE COMPLIANCE FUNCTION: A PROFILE SKETCH

COMPLIANCE IS DESCRIBED as a burgeoning profession,[1] but the role of compliance in financial institutions is mapped out by the interaction of regulatory requirements, organisational implementation and the 'professional consciousness' of compliance officers. Drawing on regulatory requirements in the EU, UK and internationally, as well as empirical studies and practice-oriented literature on the implementation of the compliance function in firms, this section will first sketch a profile of the compliance role in relation to its job scope, organisational positioning, reporting and accountability channels and qualifications of compliance officers in financial institutions. This section lays down the necessary descriptive groundwork for understanding the role of compliance. There are many differences in the observed organisational implementation of the compliance function and hence this chapter will point out the key or common features as gleaned from literature review. Sections B and C then provide a critical discussion that highlights the discrepancies between the descriptive profile of the compliance function and regulatory expectations of the compliance function, referring to the three disjunctions discussed in chapter one. Section D provides a brief conclusion to the chapter.

EU legislation has since 2004 required the institution of a compliance function in all financial institutions that conduct investment business.[2] This requirement is applicable to banks too where they conduct investment

[1] Annie Mills, *Essential Strategies for Financial Services Compliance* (Chichester: John Wiley & Sons, 2008) 39.

[2] European Parliament and Council Directive 2004/39/EC of 21 April 2004 on markets in financial instruments amending Council Directives 85/611/EEC and 93/6/EEC and Directive 2000/12/EC of the European Parliament and of the Council and repealing Council Directive 93/22/EEC [2004] OJ L145/1 (Markets in Financial Instruments Directive) Art 13. (MiFID); Commission Directive 2006/73/EC of 10 August 2006 implementing Directive 2004/39/EC of the European Parliament and of the Council as regards organisational requirements and operating conditions for investment firms and defined terms for the purposes of that Directive [2006] OJ L241/26 (MiFID Commission Directive 2006) Art 6. Although the 2004 Directive is now superseded by the MiFID II Directive 2014, ESMA has mentioned that the compliance function would be included in technical standards to be promulgated, incorporating the guidelines it issued in 2012. See ESMA, *Consultation Paper: MiFID II and MiFIR* (22 May 2014) 18–21.

business. EU legislation sets out certain attributes that need to be instituted in firms' organisation,[3] one of which is the establishment of a permanent and effective compliance function.[4] This requirement was however not fleshed out further in terms of what objectives the compliance function served or what functions in particular compliance had to carry out. Hence, the role of compliance in financial institutions was sketched in a minimal manner in the years before the onset of the global financial crisis of 2008–09. The UK regulator (then the Financial Services Authority (FSA) 1997–2013) applied the requirement to all regulated firms including banking and credit institutions.[5] The UK regulator also added a couple of key details in the regulatory framework for the compliance function that were drawn from earlier recommendations at the international level made by the Basel Committee on Banking Supervision. On the whole, however, the regulatory framework for the compliance function was minimal and skeletal.

The Basel Committee in 2005 defined the compliance function as having a role that assists senior management to monitor and manage compliance risk. Compliance risk was defined as 'the risk of legal or regulatory sanctions, material financial loss, or loss to reputation a bank may suffer as a result of its failure to comply with laws, regulations, rules, related self-regulatory organisation standards, and codes of conduct applicable to its banking activities'.[6] The objectives of securing compliance therefore revolve around the avoidance of financial loss and the management of reputational risk. The responsibility for compliance with laws and regulations by the financial institution lies with senior management, and the compliance function should perhaps be viewed more as dedicated to assisting senior management in discharging its responsibility for compliance. The 2011 *Guidelines on Internal Governance* established by the European Banking Authority (EBA) define 'compliance risk' in a similar way, viz, 'the current or prospective risk to earnings and capital arising from violations or non-compliance with laws, rules, regulations, agreements, prescribed practices or ethical standards can lead to fines, damages and/or the voiding of contracts and can diminish an institution's

[3] Art 13, MiFID, now Art 16, MiFID II Directive 2014.

[4] MiFID Commission Directive 2006, Art 6, which is likely to be carried into the new subsidiary legislation made by the Commission pursuant to the MiFID II Directive 2014. EU-level 'subsidiary' legislation, or 'level-2' legislation, refers to the framework for legislative enactments established in the Alexandre Lamfalussy et al, 'Final Report of the Committee of Wise Men on the Regulation of European Securities Markets' (Brussels, 15 February 2001) at ec.europa.eu/internal_market/securities/docs/lamfalussy/wisemen/final-report-wise-men_en.pdf.

[5] FSA Handbook, SYSC 3.2.7 and 6.1.3.

[6] Basel Committee on Banking Supervision, *Compliance and the Compliance Function in Banks* (April 2005) 7, para 3.

reputation'.[7] The inclusion of 'ethical standards' for compliance may now suggest that compliance objectives also include supporting a culture of ethics in financial institutions (to be shortly discussed in section B). Although the management of compliance risk is a firm-centric concern, regulators have a clear interest in securing firm compliance in order to meet regulatory objectives. Hence, the role of compliance may not only be to safeguard the firm, but to gate-keep the firm from failure to meet regulatory objectives.[8]

The Basel Committee's recommendations in 2005 provided considerable detail as to *how* the compliance function would carry out its responsibilities.[9] The Basel Committee envisaged that the compliance function would develop firm-wide written guidance and policies on how compliance risk is to be managed, and undertake advisory and educational responsibilities to senior management and all staff. The compliance function should also develop frameworks to identify compliance risk and develop measures to assess compliance risk in the firm, and assess the appropriateness of firm procedures and systems by monitoring and testing such procedures and systems. The compliance function should develop a compliance programme for its work plan and report to senior management as to its assessment of how the firm is managing its compliance risk. The Basel Committee recommendations further provided recommendations in terms of the organisational position of compliance (independence and formal establishment),[10] the organisational structure for compliance (avoidance of conflicts of interest and to be headed by a Head of Compliance),[11] resources[12] and power (in terms of access to information).[13] The UK regulator has fleshed out some details in the regulatory framework for the compliance function based on the Basel Committee's approach—the compliance function is responsible for regularly assessing the adequacy of measures and procedures established to manage the firm's compliance risk and assisting senior management in achieving actual compliance with the relevant regulatory framework.

[7] European Banking Authority, *EBA Guidelines on Internal Governance* (27 September 2011) 43, para 28.2.

[8] Marc Lenglet, 'Ambivalence and Ambiguity: The Interpretive Role of Compliance Officers' in Isabelle Huault and Chrystelle Richard (eds), *Finance: The Discreet Regulator* (Abingdon: Palgrave Macmillan, 2012) 59 sees the compliance function as a bridge between the regulator and regulated and the role of compliance as 'ambivalent' in that it is an institution mandated by regulation and serves regulatory purposes but is primarily situated in the firm and therefore serves the firm's interests too.

[9] Basel Committee, *Compliance and the Compliance Function* (n 6) 13–14, Principle 7, paras 34–41.

[10] ibid, 10–11, Principle 5, paras 20–23.

[11] ibid, 11–12, paras 24–29, Principle 5.

[12] ibid, 13, para 33, Principle 6.

[13] ibid, 12, paras 30–32, Principle 5.

The Basel Committee's framework is meta-regulatory in nature as it provides a high-level framework for the objectives and responsibility of the compliance function, and a skeletal profile of the procedural nature of tasks that the compliance function should undertake. The high-level framework leaves to firms to determine the compliance work programmes, the drafting of policies and guidance by the compliance function, the development of indicators of compliance risk and the measures designed to assess firm procedures and systems. It could be impracticable for the high-level framework to prescribe further detail, or such detail would become a form of micro-management of firms without having appropriate regard for firms' organisational structures. Regulatory requirements provide a meta-level framework for the compliance function and outline its profile, but the details relating to *what compliance does* and *how compliance carries out its tasks* are determined in two dimensions: first, in the organisational dimension in which the compliance function is situated; and second, in the professional dimension in terms of what the compliance profession conceives as its role and responsibilities.

This chapter builds up a descriptive understanding of the compliance function by exploring the following aspects: the job scope of the compliance function; the professional backgrounds of compliance officers, which the chapter categorises as the professional dimension; and the organisational positioning of the compliance function and its accountability channels, which this chapter categorises as the organisational dimension. The descriptive understanding of the compliance function is important as it provides a basis for analysing the effectiveness of the compliance function in securing the firm's compliance with regulatory objectives, to be discussed in sections B and C.

The compliance function has not been in the limelight in the initial stages of the global financial crisis of 2008–09. As the crisis has been attributed to failures of risk management functions in banks and financial institutions to prevent excessive risk-taking,[14] regulatory reforms focused on enhancing the risk control function.[15] The recognition of prudential failures in the crisis has paved the way for re-examination of financial regulation in general, but from 2011 onwards, a wave of 'conduct crisis'[16] has hit the UK and EU in relation to the discovery of long-running misconduct in

[14] M Brunnermeier, A Crockett, C Goodhart, AD Persaud and Hyun Shin, *The Fundamental Principles of Financial Regulation* (London: Centre for Economic Policy Research, Geneva Reports on the World Economy, 2009); Michael McAleer, Juan-Angel Jiménez-Martin and Teodosio Pérez-Amaral, 'What Happened to Risk Management During the 2008–2009 Financial Crisis?' in Robert W Kolb (ed), *Lessons from the Financial Crisis* (New Jersey: John Wiley & Sons, 2010) 307.

[15] *EBA Guidelines* (n 7) generally.

[16] Remarks made by Andrew Bailey (seminar at the UCL Centre for Ethics and the Law, 20 February 2013).

manipulating the London Interbank Offered Rate (LIBOR) submissions made by banks,[17]misconduct in the manipulation of foreign exchange markets,[18] the culmination of mis-selling scandals,[19] empirical fact-finding on adverse client-facing conduct[20] carried out by the UK regulator, and violations of anti-money laundering regulations,[21] sanctions regulations[22] and tax regulations[23] by two of the largest banks headquartered in the UK. The conduct crisis, which is essentially a spate of high-profile non-compliances by banks, hints of shortfalls in the compliance functions in those banks.

Post-crisis reforms have now provided more guidance on specific aspects of the compliance function across a range of financial institutions.[24] The European Securities and Markets Authority (ESMA) [25] has since issued guidelines to recommend greater prescriptions for the roles, responsibilities and organisational aspects regarding the compliance function in investment firms. As mentioned earlier, these requirements would apply to banking institutions too as long as investment business is carried out. These measures focus on enhancing the organisational dimension of the

[17] 'LIBOR Manipulation: Done for you, Big Boy' *Financial Times* (27 June 2012); 'Barclays hit with £290m Fine over LIBOR Fixing' *Telegraph* (27 June 2012); 'UBS Latest Bank to be Hit with Multimillion LIBOR Fine' *Guardian* (13 December 2012); 'RBS Fined £390m for Rigging LIBOR Interest Rate' *Guardian* (6 February 2013). Martin Wheatley, *The Wheatley Review of LIBOR* (September 2012).

[18] 'Citigroup forex trader fired amid global probe' *Financial Times* (10 January 2014); 'Deutsche Bank braced for fines in forex probes: sources' *Reuters* (28 May 2014); 'Barclays suspends six foreign exchange traders' *Financial Times* (1 November 2013); 'UBS First to Report FX Rigging Shows EU Immunity Flaws' *Bloomberg* (2 April 2014); 'Foreign exchange trading faces SFO criminal investigation' *Guardian* (21 July 2014).

[19] eg, in payment protection insurance, see FSA, 'The Assessment and Redress of Payment Protection Insurance Complaints: Feedback on the Further Consultation in CP10/6 and Final Handbook Text' (August 2010) PS10/12 at www.fsa.gov.uk/pubs/policy/ps10_12.pdf. See Eilis Ferran, 'Regulatory Lessons from the Payment Protection Insurance Mis-Selling Scandal in the UK' (2012) *European Business Organisation Law Review* 248. For the Arch Cru funds, see FSA, *Consumer Redress Scheme in Respect of Unsuitable Advice to Invest in Arch Cru Funds* (December 2012).

[20] FSA, *Final Guidance: Risks to Customers from Financial Incentives* (January 2013); FSA, *Conflicts of Interests between Asset Managers and their Customers: Identifying and Mitigating the Risks* (November 2012).

[21] 'HSBC to Pay £1.2bn over Mexico Scandal' *Guardian* (11 December 2012).

[22] 'Standard Chartered Hit by $3m in Iran Fines' *BBCNews* (10 December 2012).

[23] 'Bank of England Signal Possible HSBC Tax Probe' *Financial Times* (13 February 2015); 'UK Watchdog to Tackle HSBC on Standards' *Financial Times* (16 February 2015).

[24] ESMA, *Guidelines on Certain Aspects of the MiFID Compliance Function Requirements* (6 July 2012); ESMA, *Final Report: ESMA's technical advice to the European Commission on possible implementing measures of the Alternative Investment Fund Managers Directive* (16 November 2011) ESMA/2011/379 at www.esma.europa.eu/system/files/2011_379.pdf 2012, 101–02. This is now adopted by the European Commission, see Commission Delegated Regulation (EU) No 694/2014 supplementing Directive 2011/61/EU of the European Parliament and of the Council with regard to exemptions, general operating conditions, depositaries, leverage, transparency and supervision, Art 61.

[25] ESMA, *Consultation Paper: Guidelines on Certain Aspects of the MiFID Compliance Function Requirements* (December 2011); ESMA, *Guidelines* (n 24).

compliance function and will be critically discussed in sections B and C. But it remains to be seen if such increased prescription in regulating compliance as a matter of internal control would secure greater efficacy in its gatekeeper role for both the firm and regulators.[26]

The Job Scope of the Compliance Function

Practice-oriented literature as well as empirical studies provide insight into the descriptive understanding of the role of compliance in financial institutions as well as in the general corporate sector. As mentioned above, European regulation and the Basel Committee recommendations in 2005 provide some guidance on *what* compliance should do. However, there is still a lack of convergence in the job scope of the compliance function in practice. For example, the Basel Committee surveyed the implementation of its 2005 framework by international banks and recognised differences in implementation by firms in the types of compliance risks focused on, the different levels of senior management engagement in managing compliance risk, and the different systems implemented to detect and monitor compliance risk, such as having internal reporting and whistleblower channels.[27] Different aspects of organisational implementation therefore shape the scope of the compliance function's role. Birindelli and Ferretti surveyed a sample of Italian banks and found that although the role of compliance converges around the main Basel Committee framework, ie, drafting internal policies and guidance, internal codes of conduct and rolling out training and educational programmes in compliance risk for staff, there were also significant differences in the tasks that the compliance function undertakes in different banks.[28] There was less convergence in tasks of proactive monitoring[29] and prevention of non-compliance, in advising senior management on compliance risk, in supporting the development of new products or markets, in updating and informing of new regulatory developments, in exercising powers in corrective actions and in managing relations with external bodies such as regulators.

The annual Thomson Reuters survey of financial sector compliance professionals across the world shows that there is some commonality in what compliance professionals regard as basic compliance tasks, ie,

[26] There is still a balance between what may be prescribed at a high level to be implemented by firms and what may be specifically prescribed. See Parveen P Gupta, *COSO 1992 Control Framework and Management Reporting on Internal Control: Survey and Analysis of Implementation Practices* (2006) at ssrn.com/abstract=1417604.

[27] Basel Committee, *Implementation of the Compliance Principles: A Survey* (August 2008).

[28] Giuliana Birindelli and Paola Ferretti, 'Compliance Risk in Italian Banks: The Results of a Survey' (2008) *Journal of Financial Regulation and Compliance* 335.

[29] This was also borne out in ESMA's survey, see ESMA, *Guidelines* (n 24) para 20.

updating policies and guidance based on regulatory changes, reporting to senior management, coordinating with other internal control functions, regulatory filings and reporting.[30] Exceptional tasks include liaison with regulators, advising on business queries and undertaking investigations or past business reviews.[31] It is to be noted that the procedural aspects of the compliance function seem to be more pronounced generally. There are a number of treatises that help foster a more convergent or aggregate perspective of what compliance does, and such literature could be both a reflection of practice as well as a manifestation of the growing 'professional consciousness' of compliance supporting greater coherence in the content of compliance's responsibilities. Several compliance professionals[32] in financial institutions have produced treatises that could have the effect of consolidating the professional profile of compliance.[33] On the other hand, it could be argued that a convergent sense of what the compliance function entails is not necessary as the function deals with a wide range of legal and reputational risks unique to the institution concerned.

There are emerging professional bodies for compliance officers, but these remain rather modest in scale and have yet to attain influence in contributing towards convergent understandings of the compliance job scope. These bodies focus on bringing compliance professionals together for the sharing of knowledge and networking.[34] Legally qualified compliance officers who are also general counsel could be part of the General Counsel Forum.[35] Legal qualifications are not a prerequisite for the compliance function[36] although many compliance officers are

[30] Stacey English and Susannah Hammond, *Costs of Compliance Survey 2012* and Susannah Hammond and Jane Walshe, *Costs of Compliance Survey 2013* (Thomson Reuters, 2012, 2013 respectively) at accelus.thomsonreuters.com/sites/default/files/Cost%20of%20Compliance%20Survey%202012.pdf and accelus.thomsonreuters.com/sites/default/files/GRC00186.pdf.

[31] English and Hammond, *Costs of Compliance Survey 2012*, ibid, 2; but liaison with regulators seems to have become a more regular task in the 2013 Survey, ibid.

[32] Andrew Newton, *The Handbook of Compliance: Making Ethics Work in Financial Services* (London: Financial Times Management, 1998; rep Mind Into Matter, 2002); Mills, *Essential Strategies* (n 1).

[33] Broadly similar, see Newton, *The Handbook of Compliance* (n 32) 76–79, profiling the tasks of compliance as relating to training, advising on regulatory matters, monitoring the implementation of compliance risk management procedures and systems, testing and sampling, communicating upwards and downwards, handling reporting and promoting an ethical culture. Mills, *Essential Strategies* (n 1) refers to training, documenting policies and manuals, reviewing implementation of policies, advising senior management and staff, keeping on top of new regulations, managing relations with regulators and filing regulatory reports.

[34] eg, the International Compliance Association based in the UK, see www.int-comp.org/; the Ethics and Compliance Officers' Association based in the US, see www.theecoa.org.

[35] At www.tgcf.org.

[36] Mills, *Essential Strategies* (n 1) 39.

legally trained.[37] The qualifications of compliance officers will shortly be discussed. In the corporate sector generally, a Corporate Compliance Committee has been established under the auspices of the American Bar Association since 2005 providing yearly consolidated reviews of compliance work and the main compliance risks faced.[38]

Supported by the University College London Centre for Ethics and the Law, the author was involved in a qualitative empirical study regarding legal and compliance officers in the corporate sector in general.[39] The study focused on legal and compliance officers' understanding of and responsibility for managing legal risk. The study involved substantial semi-structured interviews with in-house legal counsel and compliance officers in banking institutions and in the general corporate sector. The author will draw from some findings in the study as well as other empirical and practice-oriented literature in order to construct a descriptive profile of the compliance function in terms of its job scope, organisational positioning, accountability and professionalism. The descriptive profile is then critically analysed in sections B and C in terms of how the effectiveness of the compliance function in securing compliance with regulatory objectives is shaped.

One of the findings from the UCL empirical study relates to how compliance officers perceive their job scope. We find that compliance officers generally see their roles in designing procedures for the organisation to secure compliance, but there are also advisory and adjudicative aspects in the role. Different emphases may be placed on different aspects in different organisations.[40] As regulatory requirements have been sketchy on exactly *what* compliance does, the gaps are filled by organisational implementation of the role of compliance. This gives rise to divergences in some respects of the job scope of compliance officers in different financial institutions. As sections B and C will further explore, the lack of a convergent understanding of the compliance function's job scope is important in facilitating organisational shaping and articulation of the compliance function's role. The importance of organisational framing has a marked impact upon the effectiveness of the compliance function in securing the firm's compliance with regulatory objectives. The dominance of organisational shaping of the compliance role may also impact negatively upon the coalescing of distinct professionalism in the compliance professional's

[37] John B McNeese, 'The Ethical Conflicts of the Hybrid General Counsel and Chief Compliance Officer' (2012) 25 *Georgetown Journal of Legal Ethics* 677.

[38] eg, The Corporate Compliance Committee, ABA Section of Business Law, 'Corporate Compliance Survey' (2005) 60 *Business Lawyer* 1759; post-crisis reviews in (2008) 64 *Business Lawyer* 253; (2009) 65 *Business Lawyer* 193; (2010) 66 *Business Lawyer* 125.

[39] See Richard Moorhead and Steven Vaughan, 'Legal Risk: Definition, Management and Ethics' (UCL Centre for Ethics and the Law, April 2015)at www.ucl.ac.uk/laws/law-ethics/research/papers/erc-executive-report-legal-risk-definition-management-ethics.pdf. at.

[40] ibid.

perception of their roles and responsibilities. Further, such dominance may also be used towards the manipulation of the compliance function's role away from meeting regulatory expectations of the role.

The Qualifications of Compliance Officers

Compliance officers in financial institutions may be drawn from fields of expertise including legal, audit and risk management.[41] Even in the general corporate sector, Ford and Hess report that compliance personnel may come from different backgrounds.[42] ESMA recommends that compliance officers should be sufficiently knowledgeable and have adequate professional experience.[43] It is queried if the use of the word 'professional' may limit the fields of expertise compliance can draw from such as legal or accounting backgrounds.[44] However, insights from the industry suggest that compliance is largely drawn from experienced business unit personnel and less emphasis may have been placed on the professional qualifications of such personnel compared to experience in the organisation.[45]

Nevertheless, the rise of regulatory burdens means that legally trained personnel are generally seen as appropriate to undertake the compliance function, and there may be a rise in the preference for legally trained professionals to be appointed to compliance.[46] In financial institutions, however, professionals who employ predominantly quantitative methods may be preferred as a range of business risks in banking need to be

[41] Mills, *Essential Strategies* (n 1) 39.

[42] Cristie Ford and David Hess, 'Can Corporate Monitorships Improve Corporate Compliance?' (2009) 34 *Journal of Corporation Law* 679.

[43] ESMA, *Consultation Paper* (2011) (n 25).

[44] See, eg, the Institute of Risk Management as a symbol of the burgeoning professionalism of risk management at www.theirm.org. Further, the profession of risk management is also increasingly converging around quantitative expertise and application, see Joël Bessis, *Risk Management in Banking* (Chichester: John Wiley & Sons, 2011); Philippe Carrel, *The Handbook of Risk Management: Implementing a Post-Crisis Corporate Culture* (Chichester: John Wiley & Sons, 2010) emphasising both a quantitative and managerial approach to risk management.

[45] Anecdotal insights from discussions with the programme directors Professor Jonathan Westrup and James B McCarthy of the MSc in Management of Compliance offered by University College Cork and the Irish Management Institute.

[46] Martin J Weinstein, 'The World of International Compliance: What Transactional Lawyers Need to Know to Perform Ethically and Responsibly' (2007) 29 *Houston Journal of International Law* 311; Deborah A DeMott, 'The Discrete Roles of General Counsel' (2005) 74 *Fordham Law Review* 955; Sung Hui Kim, 'Gatekeepers Inside Out' (2008) 21 *Georgetown Journal of Legal Ethics* 411; Tanina Rostain, 'General Counsel in the Age of Compliance: Preliminary Findings and New Research Questions' (2008) 21 *Georgetown Journal of Legal Ethics* 465; Christine E Parker, Robert Eli Rosen and Vibeke Lehmann Nielsen, 'The Two Faces of Lawyers: Professional Ethics and Business Compliance With Regulation' (2009) 22 *Georgetown Journal of Legal Ethics* 201; Lenglet, 'Ambivalence and Ambiguity' (n 8) 59.

measured and managed using quantitative methods. Hence, professionals in auditing who employ more quantitative methods could be hired as part of the compliance function in financial institutions.[47] Empirical research carried out in European banks shows that compliance personnel generally have a diverse range of business knowledge and skills in order to deal with the wide range of legal and reputational risks faced by banks.[48] The UCL Centre for Ethics and Law empirical study confirms this and shows that compliance manages a range of regulatory risks and compliance personnel are thus not necessarily drawn exclusively from legal backgrounds. However, in some organisations, the Head of Compliance could simultaneously be Head of Legal. The diversity of background and training in the compliance profession may be advantageous for organisations as organisations have a range of hiring options to meet different needs. This diversity may however have an impact upon reinforcing the lack of convergence in the job scope of the compliance function, some consequences of which have been outlined earlier.

The Organisational Positioning of the Compliance Function

It has been mentioned earlier that legislation requires the compliance function to be 'permanent' and independent.[49] In terms of 'permanence', the understanding of this drawn from the Basel Committee recommendations of 2005 is that there should be a dedicated function with appropriate standing and authority. The Basel Committee also recommends appointing a Head of Compliance with sufficient seniority to support the organisational 'permanence' of the compliance function. Empirical research on European banks show that the compliance function is generally well implemented, as the Head of Compliance is of sufficiently seniority.[50] The provision of adequate resources for the compliance function also supports the 'permanence' of the compliance function.[51] However, the Basel Committee's survey carried out in 2008 shows that the effectiveness of the compliance function can be undermined by the inadequacy of resources.[52] The question of adequacy of resources remains a live one for compliance

[47] Marc Lenglet, 'From Internal Control to the Compliance of Financial Practices. The Crossed Influences of Two Normative Bodies' (2010) EBS Working Paper at ssrn.com/abstract=1646256.

[48] See Paola Musile Tanzi, Giampaolo Gambi and Daniele Previati, 'Managing Compliance Risk after MiFID' (2013) *Journal of Financial Regulation and Compliance* 51.

[49] MiFID Commission Directive 2006, Art 6.

[50] See Musile Tanzi, Gambi and Previati, 'Managing Compliance Risk' (n 48).

[51] FSA Handbook, SYSC 6.1.4; Basel Committee, *Compliance and the Compliance Function* (n 6) 13, Principle 6, para 33.

[52] Basel Committee, *Implementation of the Compliance Principles* (n 27) 13, para 72.

functions in the financial sector in light of the uncertainty of demands placed on them, as will be discussed in section B.

The 'independence' of the compliance function is understood as not being affected by conflicts of interest[53] and perverse incentives such as tying the remuneration of compliance officers to certain business profits.[54] Such a quality is akin to a form of 'objectivity',[55] and it appears that the independence of the compliance function may not be an end in itself but is seen as crucial for achieving 'objectivity' in the discharge of compliance functions. Hence, 'independence' does not mean that the compliance function has to be a distinct department in organisational terms. Depending on the scale, size and complexity of the financial institution's business, the compliance function can be exercised by a separate department[56] or as part of risk management or legal,[57] although fusion with internal audit is frowned upon by the Basel Committee.[58]

Empirical studies from the US especially point to the fusion of legal and compliance in financial institutions and the corporate sector generally.[59] However, an international survey of large banking institutions around the world[60] and an empirical study[61] focusing on European banks show that the compliance function in banks and financial institutions is by and large implemented as a distinct function,[62] although fusion with legal and risk management is observed in some cases. ESMA in particular has expressed a preference for the separation of legal and compliance functions in order to protect the independence of the compliance function.[63] Further, the empirical study conducted by the UCL Centre for Ethics and the Law also provides some findings in relation to the aspects of organisational implementation of the compliance function. The study finds that the compliance function in financial institutions in the UK is generally distinct from other departments such as legal or risk management, but compliance interacts intensively with these other departments.[64]

53 Basel Committee, *Compliance and the Compliance Function* (n 6) 12, paras 28–29.

54 FSA Handbook, SYSC 6.1.4(4).

55 Richard Moorhead, 'Precarious Professionalism: Some Empirical and Behavioural Perspectives on Lawyers' (2014) *Current Legal Problems* 1.

56 FSA Handbook, SYSC 6.1.3A.

57 *EBA Guidelines* (n 7) 42, para 28.4. But ESMA does prefer the separation of compliance and legal, see ESMA, *Guidelines* (n 24) para 62ff.

58 Basel Committee, *Compliance and the Compliance Function* (n 6) 15, paras 44–45.

59 See Deborah A DeMott, 'The Stages of Scandal and the Roles of General Counsel' (2012) *Wisconsin Law Review* 463; Rostain, 'General Counsel in the Age of Compliance' (n 46); McNeese, 'The Ethical Conflicts' (n 37); Omari Scott Simmons and John D Dinnage, 'Innkeepers: A Unifying Theory of the In-House Counsel Role' (2011) 41 *Seton Hall Law Review* 77.

60 See English and Hammond, *Costs of Compliance Survey 2012* (n 30).

61 See Musile Tanzi, Gambi and Previati, 'Managing Compliance Risk' (n 48).

62 The UCL empirical study confirms this for financial institutions involved in the study.

63 ESMA, *Guidelines* (n 24) para 62ff; Annex II.

64 Moorhead and Vaughan, 'Legal Risk' (n 39) 60.

The meta-regulatory framework for the institution of a 'permanent' and 'independent' compliance function has not gone very far in securing the organisational positioning and profile of the function. Thus, firm implementation plays the key part in determining the organisational attributes of the compliance function. The significant scope for organisational shaping of the compliance function is arguably key to the ultimate effectiveness of the function.

Accountability Channels of the Compliance Function

The accountability channels of the compliance function are important for determining its organisational positioning and power. The norm is that compliance is accountable to senior management.[65] This is based on the Basel Committee recommendations in 2005 that provide that compliance officers should report to a Head of Compliance who may be part of the senior management team, or otherwise having accountability and reporting obligations to senior management anyway.[66] Senior management generally bears ultimate responsibility for effective internal control and is therefore positioned to receive reports from compliance, risk management and internal audit and assess and evaluate their effectiveness. Empirical research[67] carried out on European banks bears this out as the compliance function surveyed in these banks state that they report to a member of the senior management team such as the Chief Risk Officer or the Chief Financial Officer, who report to the Chief Executive Officer, and rarely report to or have access to the Board directly or to any executive or non-executive Board members.

The American regulation of mutual funds requires all mutual fund Boards to ensure that a Chief Compliance Officer is appointed to each fund in order to be responsible for the administration of a compliance programme for the fund.[68] Although responsibility is reposed in the Board to ensure the appointment of the Chief Compliance Officer, there are no requirements that direct the accountability of the Chief Compliance Officer back to the Board. The usual practice is for Chief Compliance Officers to report to senior management. Some commentators are of the view that the independence of the compliance function may be compromised by accountability to senior management, and

[65] MiFID Commission Directive 2006, Art 9.

[66] Basel Committee, *Compliance and the Compliance Function* (n 6) paras 25, 26, 32 and 41.

[67] See Musile Tanzi, Gambi and Previati, 'Managing Compliance Risk' (n 48).

[68] Securities and Exchange Commission (SEC) Rule 38a-1.

advocate that the Chief Compliance Officer should report directly to the Board.[69]

Accountability to senior management provides opportunities for senior management to shape the role and job scope of the compliance function to be supportive of business objectives. It may be argued that senior management may also be able to learn from the interaction with compliance in order to shape business strategies and objectives in a way that manages compliance and reputational risk. However, it may be useful to consider if the independence and integrity of compliance work may be safeguarded by an additional channel of accountability to the Board. Perhaps this issue may also be resolved by the institution of appropriate whistle-blowing or internal reporting channels that will be discussed in chapter seven.

The survey of practice-oriented and empirical literature discussed above provide some descriptive findings relating to the job scope, professional backgrounds, the organisational positioning and accountability channels of the compliance function. These descriptive findings provide a basis for the analyses that will be carried out in the next two sections.

Section B analyses the aspects of organisational positioning and accountability of compliance officers and argues that there is a persistent regulatory–organisational disjunction in the pre-crisis firm implementation of the compliance function within the meta-regulatory framework. As the meta-regulatory framework for the compliance function is skeletal in nature, firms have tended to implement the function in a business-centric manner without necessary concern for meeting regulatory expectations. The regulatory–organisational disjunction, which entails the relative organisational weakness of the compliance function, has been extensively picked up in academic literature and policy documents and is addressed to a large extent in post-crisis reforms. This section discusses the achievements of the reforms and what issues may remain. Section C then discusses a key unaddressed issue of emerging professionalism in the compliance function. This section analyses the aspects of job scope and professional backgrounds of compliance officers and argues that relative weaknesses in the professionalism of the compliance function will continue to affect the efficacy of the compliance function in spite of organisational reforms discussed in section B. Such gives rise to a regulatory–professional disjunction that augments the weaknesses in the meta-regulation of the compliance function. This section will also discuss how post-crisis reforms have attempted to address the abovementioned weaknesses.

[69] See W Michael Hoffman et al, 'An Investigation of Ethics Officer Independence' (2008) 78 *Journal of Business Ethics* 87; W Michael Hoffman, John D Neill and O Scott Stovall, 'Mutual Fund Compliance Officer Independence and Corporate Governance' (2008) 16 *Corporate Governance: An International Review* 52.

B. DISJUNCTIONS BETWEEN THE PERFORMANCE OF THE COMPLIANCE FUNCTION AND REGULATORY EXPECTATIONS IN SECURING FIRMS' COMPLIANCE: ANALYSING THE ORGANISATIONAL DIMENSION

In this section, the aspects of firm implementation of the organisational positioning, powers and accountability of the compliance function will be examined, in order to explore as to how the organisational dimension of the compliance function may be shaped or manipulated to affect its efficacy in meeting regulatory expectations.

Distinct Department or Fused with General Counsel?

Empirical literature from the US shows that in the general corporate sector, there may be a fusion of the roles of compliance and legal.[70] The legal department is a natural candidate for assisting senior management in understanding laws and regulations and hence compliance may become part of legal work in general, and the General Counsels of many corporations are also Chief Compliance Officers. However the Thomson Reuters surveys in 2012 and 2013 pertaining to the financial sector in jurisdictions across the globe seems to show that the compliance function is largely distinct from the legal department although it works in close coordination with legal, risk management and internal audit.[71]

Pre-crisis, there has been no prescription as to how the compliance function may be organised vis a vis the legal function in firms. A number of commentators have however pointed out the hazards of fusing the legal and compliance roles. Commentators have in general observed that the role of the in-house counsel has over the years been shaped by business perspectives, and in-house counsel are increasingly playing the part of consultant to management.[72] Such a development may be a natural outworking of the emphasis on loyalty to clients in legal professional ethics. This could be viewed as a positive development as lawyers gain a fusion between business and professional perspectives that could

[70] See DeMott, 'The Stages of Scandal' (n 59); Rostain, 'General Counsel in the Age of Compliance' (n 46); McNeese, 'The Ethical Conflicts' (n 37); Simmons and Dinnage, 'Innkeepers' (n 59).

[71] English and Hammond, *Costs of Compliance Survey 2012* (n 30) 2; Hammond and Walshe, *Costs of Compliance Survey 2013* (n 30) 7.

[72] See Simmons and Dinnage, 'Innkeepers' (n 59); Jonathan C Lipson, Beth Engel and Jami Crespo, 'Foreword: Who's in the House? The Changing Nature and Role of In-house and General Counsel' (2012) *Wisconsin Law Review* 237; Robert Eli Rosen, '"We're All Consultants Now": How Change in Client Organizational Strategies Influences Change in the Organization of Corporate Legal Services' (2002) 44 *Arizona Law Review* 637.

contribute to the corporation.[73] Others however are more concerned about lawyers compromising their professional integrity or ethics in becoming too aligned with business perspectives and getting 'too comfortable' with business practices.[74] These commentators advocate a clear separation between legal and compliance functions.[75] The financial services industry's aggressive profit-chasing business interests have also arguably affected the perspectives of in-house counsel, making them compromised gatekeepers against inappropriate and unethical conduct.[76] In light of the concerns above, the fusion of the compliance and in-house legal functions is arguably not appropriate.

As the Thomson Reuters survey indicates that the compliance function is generally distinct from legal, the concerns raised by commentators regarding the fusion of legal and compliance functions may be negligible in the international banking sector. However, the separation of legal from compliance may be more prevalent in the large banking groups surveyed than in medium to smaller sized financial institutions that seek economies of scale in the compliance–legal amalgamation.[77] Regulators have been careful not to mandate a separate compliance function as they bear in mind the different scopes, scales and complexities of different financial institutions. However, post-crisis, an express preference for the distinctness of the compliance function has been made at the European level, so that fusion may only be allowed subject to express exemptions.[78] Regulators would thus be given the opportunity to consider the suitability of the organisational structure of the compliance function.

Centralisation or Decentralisation?

The compliance function may be structured as a centralised or a decentralised model. A centralised model means that all compliance officers are placed in one department and carry out exchanges and interaction with the rest of the organisation from that position. In the alternative, the compliance function may be organised in a decentralised manner, where compliance

[73] Simmons and Dinnage, 'Innkeepers' (n 59); Lipson, Engel and Crespo, 'Foreword' (n 72).

[74] See Donald C Langevoort, 'Getting (Too) Comfortable: In-house Lawyers, Enterprise Risk and the Financial Crisis' (2011) at ssrn.com/abstract=1932398; Parker, Rosen and Nielsen, 'The Two Faces of Lawyers' (n 46); Donald C Langevoort, 'Chasing the Greased Pig Down Wall Street: A Gatekeeper's Guide to the Psychology, Culture and Ethics of Financial Risk-taking' (2011) 96 *Cornell Law Review* 1209.

[75] Langevoort, 'Getting (Too) Comfortable' (n 74); McNeese, 'The Ethical Conflicts' (n 37).

[76] Langevoort, 'Chasing the Greased Pig' (n 74).

[77] See *EBA Guidelines* (n 7) 43, para 28.3. This position seems to be accepted by ESMA, *Guidelines* (n 24) 13, para 61; 20, para 13.

[78] ESMA, *Guidelines* (n 24) 20, para 13; Annex II, para 64.

officers may be embedded in different business units to provide front line support and monitoring, but report back to the Head of Compliance. Empirical research carried out in European banks shows a preference for the decentralised model so that the compliance function is informationally empowered by proximity and interaction with business units.[79]

Mills succinctly compares the two structures and suggests that the centralised function may be in receipt of more high level information from senior management generally and the Head of Compliance may be more in control of managing the compliance agenda.[80] Some commentators regard the centralised approach as being able to construct multiple linkages within the firm in order to promote a compliance culture.[81] Others are more sceptical, painting a picture of the compliance function being elevated to a level of corporate consultant,[82] having a bird's eye view only and also liable to be entangled with management perspectives[83] which may compromise the objectivity of the compliance function. Moreover, relations with other business units may be more formalised, resulting in the generation of more administrative procedures, and so it may be queried whether day to day compliance risks may be detected sufficiently quickly for preventive interventions to take place. The compliance function and business units may rely on procedural indicators and fail to engage with the spirit of attaining compliance with regulatory objectives. Further, relationships with business units may also be more confrontational in nature if business units perceive the compliance function to be in a policing or adjudicating position.[84] Confrontational relationships are generally disadvantageous to the efficacy of the compliance function as distrust could result in information conveyance that is less open and honest.

A decentralised structure allows compliance officers to be embedded in the front line offices and this allows them to overcome local information asymmetry. A decentralised structure also provides an opportunity for compliance officers to spread the compliance culture to front line units, embedding the compliance objective within business culture more effectively. However, a decentralised structure may mean that the Head of Compliance is in less control over the compliance agenda and may not be aware if compliance officers have become too aligned with business objectives and compromised their objectivity. The Head of Compliance may then be burdened with procedural tasks in relation to monitoring the

[79] See Musile Tanzi, Gambi and Previati, 'Managing Compliance Risk' (n 48).

[80] Mills, *Essential Strategies* (n 1) 21ff.

[81] See Simmons and Dinnage, 'Innkeepers' (n 59); Lipson, Engel and Crespo, 'Foreword' (n 72).

[82] See Rosen, '"We're All Consultants Now"' (n 72).

[83] McNeese, 'The Ethical Conflicts' (n 37).

[84] Miriam Hechler Baer, 'Governing Corporate Compliance' (2009) 50 *Boston College Law Review* 949.

decentralised compliance officers. However, it may be argued that this is not an extra burden for the Head of Compliance as she or he should be evaluating the performance of compliance officers anyway.

The KPMG survey also opines that there is no clear winner between the centralised and decentralised approaches: a decentralised approach achieves the chief advantage of placing the compliance function at the front lines to detect and deter potential violations while the centralised approach achieves a more high-level perspective and may be more effective for holistic organisational monitoring.[85] A centralised structure may need to be supported by more resources, powers of access to information and powers of monitoring and review. This is extensively provided in the European framework.[86] For a decentralised structure, there may perhaps be a need for frequent rotation so that embedded compliance officers do not get 'too comfortable'[87] nor have their perspectives compromised by prolonged proximity with, and perhaps sympathy for, the front line business perspectives.

Although this issue is not dealt with in the European regulatory frameworks, firms are mandated to institute an overall compliance culture, and the compliance function should regularly assess the effectiveness of systems and procedures that constitute such a compliance culture.[88] A centralised or decentralised structure may present different organisational weaknesses and the compliance function may be expected to be able to review its own efficacy in the compliance culture of the organisation. The essentially meta-regulatory nature of the regulatory framework for the organisation of the compliance function remains, although it is supported by more overt references to responsibilities and powers.

Risk-Based Approach to Compliance

European measures advocate that firms adopt a risk-based approach to implementing the compliance function.[89] This means that the compliance function should design a work plan whose scope is commensurate with the optimal allocation of resources to compliance. Newton's guide for compliance professionals also advocates that a risk-based approach to implementing the compliance function be taken.[90]

[85] KPMG, 'The Future of Compliance' (2012) at www.kpmg.com/UK/en/IssuesAndInsights/ArticlesPublications/Documents/PDF/Advisory/future-of-compliance_web_Acc4.pdf.

[86] ESMA, *Guidelines* (n 24) Annex II, paras 46–48.

[87] Langevoort, 'Getting (Too) Comfortable' (n 74).

[88] ESMA, *Final Report: ESMA's Technical Advice to the Commission on MiFID II and MiFIR* (December 2014) 18.

[89] ESMA, *Guidelines* (n 24) Annex II, para 14.

[90] Newton, *The Handbook of Compliance* (n 32) 81.

The risk-based approach is one that emphasises cost-effectiveness, so that resources can be deployed in areas susceptible to the highest risk and therefore used efficiently. Where this applies to the implementation of the compliance function, it likely refers to setting priorities for the compliance function. Newton is of the view that adopting a risk-based approach to compliance also helps compliance to speak the 'same language' as the rest of the organisation as cost-efficiency is a major driving factor that shapes all business units. However, expressly mandating a risk-based approach may detract from monitoring compliance risks comprehensively.[91] It is questioned whether the adoption of a risk-based approach or otherwise ought to be standardised in the regulatory framework as it is for the firm to demonstrate adequate implementation of the meta-regulatory framework for the compliance function.

Moreover, why should the regulator introduce a prescriptive guideline in relation to the internal efficiency concerns of firms?[92] Does a risk-based approach bear any relationship with the output of securing compliance? Black is of the view that the risk-based approach has the effect of delineating the parameters of blame, as it allows priorities and scope of work to be set out upfront, and defines the parameters of responsibility.[93] Would this encourage firms to under-resource their compliance functions or narrowly define the scope for compliance in order to under-implement the regulatory requirements relating to the compliance function? Black and Baldwin further warn that adopting a risk-based approach could induce legitimate ignoring of low-level risks that may nevertheless have high impact as they develop over time.[94] A risk-based approach may then excuse a firm for ignoring risks of an improbable nature which could become a 'black swan'.

Reporting Channels and Accountability

The accountability channels of internal control affect its organisational position and power. Where accountability lies with senior management, the objectivity of the compliance function may be affected if it feels inhibited

[91] Acknowledged by ESMA, *Guidelines* (n 24) 6–7, para 17.

[92] Julia Black, 'The Emergence of Risk-Based Regulation and the New Public Risk Management in the United Kingdom' [2005] *Public Law* 512. The limitations and subjective tendencies of risk-based regulation are also discussed in relation to the medical profession in Sally Lloyd-Bostock and Bridget M Hutter, 'Reforming Regulation of the Medical Profession: The Risks of Risk-Based Approaches' (2008) 10 *Health, Risk and Society* 69; Allen L Camp, 'Treatment of Uncertainties in Risk-Based Regulation' (December 1994) at www.osti.gov/bridge/servlets/purl/46555-dl5dVd/webviewable/46555.pdf.

[93] Black, 'The Emergence of Risk-Based Regulation' (n 92).

[94] Julia Black and Robert Baldwin, 'When Risk-based Regulation Aims Low: A Strategic Framework' (2012) 6 *Regulation & Governance* 131.

from pointing out critical matters in relation to the approach taken by senior management, or if the careers and remuneration of compliance officers may be directly affected by their relations with senior management. Commentators (in relation to the role of compliance in mutual funds in the US) are of the view that where accountability lies with the Board directly, the compliance function could advise the Board in relation to monitoring senior management and empower the Board in terms of information.[95] These observations may apply generally in other financial institution contexts. Accountability to the Board may also insulate the compliance function from adverse influences from senior management or perverse incentives that may result from senior management influence.

European measures now support ultimate accountability to the Board, although this section will show that ESMA has initial preference for the accountability of the compliance function to lie with senior management.[96] The EBA also supports accountability directly to the Board.[97]

The ESMA Consultation paper earlier suggested that the compliance function should report to senior management, in relation to non-compliance matters warranting attention as well as periodic reports on the implementation and performance of the compliance function.[98] This has been resisted by industry, opining that regular reporting of desk-based reviews may be ineffective and costly, and that the relationship between compliance and senior management should more broadly be framed as one of instituting a good compliance culture.[99] A compromise position was reached such that compliance reporting to senior management should be a summary of key findings. However, ESMA's final advice to the Commission recommended that the Compliance function should be appointed by the Board, and should report annually to the Board and on an ad hoc basis should the need arises.[100] The EBA envisages that internal control should be accountable to the 'management body',[101] a generic term that refers to Boards and accommodates the different Board structures found across European jurisdictions. The earlier Basel Committee recommendations for compliance in banks refer to accountability to senior management,[102] but recommend a yearly meeting between the Board and the compliance function in order for the Board to be apprised of senior management

[95] See Hoffman, Neill and Stovall, 'Mutual Fund Compliance Officer Independence' (n 69); Thomas M Majewski, 'Conflicts of Interest Chief Compliance Officers Face in Implementing Compliance Programs for Investment Funds and Investment Advisers' (2006) 7 *Journal of Investment Compliance* 23.

[96] ESMA, *Guidelines* (n 24) Annex II, para 27.

[97] *EBA Guidelines* (n 7) 43, para 28.4.

[98] ESMA, *Consultation Paper* (2011) (n 25) para III.III.

[99] ESMA, *Guidelines* (n 24) paras 35–38.

[100] ESMA, *Final Report* (2014) (n 88) 18–19.

[101] *EBA Guidelines* (n 7) 43, para 28.4.

[102] Basel Committee, *Compliance and the Compliance Function* (n 6) 14, para 41.

effectiveness in managing compliance risk as a whole.[103] Although the practice of compliance reporting to the Board is rare in the industry, this may be set to change under the new European measures.

Power

The main organisational weakness in internal control identified in the wake of the global financial crisis is the relative disempowerment of such functions especially in relation to risk management.[104] Hence, post-crisis reforms have addressed to a large extent the need to enhance the power of all internal control functions including the compliance function. The exercise of power in an organisation is a phenomenon that organisational behaviour academics study as 'organisational power'. Kanter proposed that an individual's power in an organisation is the 'power to get things done' and is related to effectiveness in the job.[105] Such power is a structural phenomenon based on an individual's formal position and informal supporting aspects, rather than on the personal attributes and characteristics of the individual. In that sense, the formal structure of power could be important and regulatory conferment of rights could be key to empowering the compliance function. Formal attributes that affect power include organisational positioning, reporting and accountability channels, remuneration and career prospects. Sung argues that formal attributes affect compliance officers' willingness to interdict and monitor, and their capacity to do so.[106]

For example, in terms of the established attributes of 'permanence' and 'independence', European measures now provide more supporting guidance as to how these are to be safeguarded. Permanence is explained in relation to instituting a dedicated compliance function and having arrangements in place to ensure that such permanence is ongoing.[107] 'Independence' is explained in terms of the non-interference by senior management and business units and the safeguarding of tenure for compliance officers.[108] Further, there are specific prescriptions for the

[103] ibid, 12, para 32.

[104] Hans J Blommestein, Lex Hoogduin and JJW Peeters, 'Uncertainty and Risk Management after the Great Moderation: The Role of Risk (Mis)Management by Financial Institutions' (28th SUERF Colloquium, Utrecht, September 2009) at papers.ssrn.com/sol3/papers.cfm?abstract_id=1489826; Michel Crouhy, 'Risk Management Failures During the Financial Crisis' in Robert W Kolb (ed), *Lessons from the Financial Crisis* (New Jersey: John Wiley & Sons, 2010) 283; Elizabeth Sheedy, 'The Future of Risk Modelling' in Robert W Kolb (ed), *Lessons from the Financial Crisis* (New Jersey: John Wiley & Sons, 2010) 301; Frank Partnoy, 'On Rogues, Risk-taking and Restoring Trust in Banks' *Financial Times* (23 September 2011).

[105] Rosabeth Moss Kanter, *Men and Women of the Corporation* (New York: Basic Books, 1977, rep 1983) 166ff.

[106] Sung Hui Kim, 'Gatekeepers Inside Out' (n 46).

[107] ESMA, *Guidelines* (n 24) paras 53–54.

[108] ibid, Annex II, para 60.

compliance function to enjoy certain powers such as access to information on a firm-wide basis,[109] and access to staff for the purposes of interviewing and monitoring. The compliance function is to have access to all relevant databases. Further, in order to have a permanent overview of the areas of the investment firm where sensitive or relevant information might arise, the compliance function will have access to all relevant information systems within the investment firm as well as any internal or external audit reports or other reporting to senior management or the supervisory function. Where relevant, compliance officers should also be able to attend meetings of senior management or the supervisory function. Where this right is not granted, the compliance function should document this in writing. The compliance function should also be empowered to have in-depth knowledge of the firm's organisation, corporate culture and decision-making processes in order to be able to identify which meetings are important to attend. Further, the enhanced powers of the compliance function would be supported by increased resources.[110]

However, studies have also found that formal attributes of power have to be supported by organisational commitment and culture,[111] so that the exercise of formal powers such as in internal investigations is meaningfully supported at the highest level, and is reinforced by feedback, encouragement and review.[112] Even if regulatory rules or guidelines prescribe formal attributes of power for the compliance function, a supportive firm culture may still be necessary to realise the efficacy of the compliance function. Financial sector culture is pro-risk-taking and regulatory avoidance, so aggressive and critical compliance voices may be regarded as unpopular and could be unsupported.[113] Further, compliance officers could be swept up in the general perspectives and values to which the organisation subscribes. The perspective from organisational culture will be fleshed out in chapter five. Further, the compliance function may refrain from asserting 'critical' power so that it would not run the risk of being targeted for subsequent blame, such as if profits are affected. Hence, there may be perverse incentives encouraging the compliance function to slim down its responsibility despite the formal expansion of powers.[114]

[109] ibid, para 48.

[110] ibid, paras 45–47.

[111] James Rathz, 'Compliance as the Competitive Differentiator' (2009) 12 *Duquesne Business Law Journal* 13, arguing that senior management commitment can be improved if the quality of compliance can be seen as a competitive advantage.

[112] eg, Kathryn McDermott, Heather K Spence Laschinger and Judith Shamian, 'Work Empowerment and Organizational Commitment' (1996) 27 *Nursing Management* 44.

[113] Langevoort, 'Getting (Too) Comfortable' (n 74); Rostain, 'General Counsel in the Age of Compliance' (n 46); Parker, Rosen and Nielsen, 'The Two Faces of Lawyers' (n 46).

[114] Lawrence A Cunningham, 'The Appeal and Limits of Internal Controls to Fight Fraud, Terrorism, Other Ills' (2003) at ssrn.com/abstract= 444600, (2003) 29 *Journal of Corporation Law* 267.

Commentators have also observed that the exercise of power by the compliance function is a process of navigating many challenges in the organisational dimension. For example, as compliance officers are dedicated to a specific role of compliance, they may be perceived as having 'expert power',[115] ie, the power to exert influence within the organisation by virtue of expertise, especially professional expertise. 'Expert power' tends however to be exercised in narrow confines and business units may attempt to define narrowly the relevant scope of the power of the compliance function.[116]

Where the compliance function may be working against a resistant tide, Gilad observes that in order to augment the importance of securing compliance with regulatory objectives and to mitigate resistance in the organisation, compliance officers may overstate the threat of enforcement.[117] Adopting such a form of persuasion could achieve the conveyance of the message relating to the importance of managing compliance risk. However, such a stance could also result in a fear environment[118] and cause annoyance and lack of cooperation if pushed too far. Cunningham also argues that persuasion based on the threat of enforcement may only work if the risk of non-compliance is perceived to be manageable internally and not driven by external factors beyond the firm's control.[119] Hence, the challenges for the compliance function may be especially acute if the firm's organisational culture is not warm to the compliance function or a compliance culture.[120] ESMA therefore places emphasis on the institution of a compliance culture in firms.[121] It is however queried whether culture can be susceptible to regulatory manipulation and how regulation can exert a measured influence upon culture.[122]

Informal attributes such as networks of information, informal groupings and alliances of interest are also important in affecting the exercise

[115] Eugene McKenna, *Business Psychology and Organizational Behaviour*, 4th edn (New York: Taylor & Francis Psychology Press, 2006) 423.

[116] ibid.

[117] Sharon Gilad, 'Institutionalizing Fairness in Financial Markets: Mission Impossible?' (2011) 5 *Regulation & Governance* 309.

[118] Fear of enforcement is however not an unhealthy phenomenon and to a certain extent helps secure compliance, see Robert A Kagan, Neil Gunningham and Dorothy Thornton, 'Fear, Duty and Regulatory Compliance: Lessons from Three Research Projects' in Christine Parker and Vibeke Lehmann Nielsen (eds), *Explaining Compliance: Business Responses to Regulation* (Cheltenham: Edward Elgar, 2011) 37.

[119] Cunningham, 'The Appeal and Limits' (n 114).

[120] More in chapter 5.

[121] ESMA, *Guidelines* (n 24) Annex II, para 34.

[122] Hector Sants, 'Can Culture be Regulated?' (Mansion House Conference on Values and Trust, London, 4 October 2010) at www.fsa.gov.uk/pages/Library/Communication/Speeches/2010/1004_hs.shtml; Dan Awrey, William Blair and David Kershaw, 'Between Law and Markets: Is there a Role for Culture and Ethics in Financial Regulation?' (2013) 38 *Delaware Journal of Corporate Law* 191, and at papers.ssrn.com/sol3/papers.cfm?abstract_id=2157588.

of power.[123] How persuasive the compliance function is in relation to encouraging more firm-wide ownership of managing compliance risk depends on many informal factors such as whether the compliance function 'speaks the same language',[124] and its relations with business units and with senior management. Perhaps the Head of Compliance or Chief Compliance Officer should be part of the senior management team[125] so that peer relations with senior management can support the exercise of power by the compliance function. However Pfeffer observes that personal attributes can affect the exercise of power too.[126] Parker and Gilad observe empirically[127] that compliance officers in banks tend to take on a 'harmonising' stance. This refers to compliance officers being eager to speak the language of business perspectives and emphasising that the compliance function pursues the same objectives. However, it remains uncertain if such a stance is a product of being shaped by organisational culture, professional conviction or personal attributes. Such a stance risks not being sufficiently critical where business practices may border on being aggressively close to incurring regulatory risks, and further empirical research may be needed to shed light on the personal attributes of compliance officers and the compliance record of firms. In sum, the interaction between formal attributes, informal aspects and personal characteristics will ultimately determine how organisational power is exercised.

Finally, firms may experience changes that will cause them to reorganise internally in order to regroup. A scandal that causes reputational damage to a firm may cause a firm to step up its formal empowerment of the compliance function and take steps to change firm culture.[128] As regulatory prescriptions for empowering the compliance function have to work in a dynamic landscape of changing organisational configurations, soft organisational culture and interpersonal relations, it remains open as to how far formal enhancement of the compliance function's power may change its organisational profile and voice. The post-crisis reforms have enhanced the meta-regulation of the compliance function by increasing prescriptions to boost its organisational positioning and power. This section has critically questioned the extent of its achievements, but will argue that such reforms neglect an important aspect that affects the efficacy of

[123] Kanter, *Men and Women* (n 105).

[124] Newton, *The Handbook of Compliance* (n 32) 81.

[125] This is not mandatory under the Basel Committee, *Compliance* (n 6) 12, para 26.

[126] Jeffrey Pfeffer, *Managing with Power: Politics and Influence in Organizations* (Boston, MA: Harvard Business School Press, 1992) 71, 165.

[127] Christine Parker and Sharon Gilad, 'Internal Corporate Compliance Management Systems: Structure, Culture and Agency' in Christine Parker and Vibeke Lehmann Nielsen (eds), *Explaining Compliance: Business Responses to Regulation* (Cheltenham: Edward Elgar, 2011) 170.

[128] DeMott, 'The Stages of Scandal' (n 59).

the compliance function. Section C will now discuss the neglected issue of emerging professionalism.

C. DISJUNCTIONS BETWEEN REGULATORY EXPECTATIONS AND THE ROLE OF THE COMPLIANCE FUNCTION: ANALYSING THE PROFESSIONAL DIMENSION

This section argues that the meta-regulatory framework for the compliance function in banks and financial institutions fails to take into account the emerging nature of the professional dimension of the compliance function, resulting in a regulatory-professional disjunction. This section examines to what extent there exists a distance between the profession dimension of the compliance function and the meeting of regulatory expectations, especially enhanced expectations in the wake of the global financial crisis. First, compliance professionals may have certain perspectives as to what their professional roles and responsibilities are, and these may not be on all fours with regulatory expectations. Second, there may be weaknesses in the professional dimension which allow the dominance of organisational shaping of the role of the compliance function, and such organisational manipulation may not drive towards consistency with meeting regulatory expectations, resulting in a regulatory–organisational disjunction.

The discussion in this section does not mean to indicate that issues affecting the efficacy of the compliance function are necessarily causative of a financial institution's regulatory breach. The exercise here is intended to be investigative and constructive, with an aim towards making observations as to the characteristics of an effective compliance function that secures firm compliance with regulation and meets regulatory expectations.

Lack of Convergence in the Job Scope of the Compliance Function

As discussed above, a convergent or uniformly accepted understanding is yet to be achieved with regard to the job scope of the compliance function. This section does not advocate prescriptive rigidity in defining the job scope for compliance, but a lack of convergence in professional understanding of the job scope provides room for the job scope to be shaped by organisational needs. Firms naturally have incentives to frame the job scope of compliance to be consonant with firm needs, which may or may not be completely aligned with regulatory objectives. According to empirical research, the Mission Statement or Charter for the compliance function which sets out the broad parameters of its job description and powers is usually a document agreed with senior management,[129] or the Board.[130] In practice, there is extensive firm discretion in the implementation of the role and responsibilities of the compliance function[131] and this may completely dominate how the job scope of the compliance function is shaped.

Convergence in the job scope of the compliance function has been more substantially achieved in relation to the aspects susceptible to proceduralisation, such as drafting policies and guidance, training and advising staff and management, developing indicators and procedures to measure, test and monitor compliance risk, and reporting to senior management.[132] Much less convergence seems to be observed where responsibilities such as handling irregularities, internal complaints and whistle-blowing, and contributing to the institution of a firm-wide compliance culture are concerned.[133] Hence, it may be the norm in practice that the compliance function executes largely procedural tasks that secure the appearance or rituals of managing compliance risk, but more controversial responsibilities such as handling irregularities, escalation and whistle-blowing are not readily observed in empirical research.[134] The UCL empirical study also shows that a significant number of compliance officers see themselves as 'coordinators' and not 'doers'.[135] This is not only an issue of the parameters of job scope but also of efficacy. The compliance function could become predominantly concerned with maintaining rituals to sustain the firm's appearance of regulatory compliance while being substantively non-critical. Although it may be argued that the responsibility for handling irregularities and escalation of internal enforcement may be better reposed in either senior management or independent committees of the Board such as the Audit Committee (where irregularities regarding financial misrepresentations may be concerned), the compliance function which is positioned to detect irregularities could have a more defined role and be empowered in accordance with that role in relation to initial handling of irregularities. This could enhance the critical oversight faculties of the compliance function and bring it closer to achieving a form of efficacy nearer to regulatory expectations.

[129] See Mills, *Essential Strategies* (n 1) 41.

[130] See PriceWaterhouseCoopers, 'Realising the Full Value of Compliance' (2009) at download.pwc.com/ie/pubs/realising_the_full_value_of_compliance.pdf, 11.

[131] Parker and Gilad, 'Internal Corporate Compliance' (n 127) 170.

[132] Basel Committee, *Implementation of the Compliance Principles* (n 27). Also see Birindelli and Ferretti, 'Compliance Risk in Italian Banks' (n 28) based on an empirical survey of Italian banks; and Newton, *The Handbook of Compliance* (n 32) and Mills, *Essential Strategies* (n 1) writing in the UK context.

[133] Basel Committee, *Implementation of the Compliance Principles* (n 27).

[134] See, eg, ESMA requires that compliance should have a greater role in dealing with and ensuring the protection of whistle-blowers, see ESMA, *Guidelines* (n 24) Annex II, para 55.

[135] Moorhead and Vaughan, 'Legal Risk' (n 39) 59.

Further, the engagement in excessively procedural work may of itself engender a form of insularity and monotony that discourages proactive perspectives from being developed in compliance work. Birindelli and Ferretti in their survey of Italian banks' implementation of the compliance function show that there is a mixed picture as to whether the compliance function engages in proactive functions to prevent irregularities.[136] Proactive intervention could involve engaging with business units, challenging certain business decisions and resolving conflict. However, greater involvement of the compliance function in proactive detections or preventive interventions could assist in securing compliance with regulatory objectives by the firm. Gabbi et al, in surveying Italian investment firms, also conclude that the compliance function is relatively weak in proactive roles.[137]

In general, it may be said that compliance professionals are less in agreement or perhaps less supportive of undertaking potentially 'lone' and disruptive tasks such as proactive interventions. Firms can reinforce such a stance by emphasising the procedural and facilitative nature of the compliance function and hence curtail the monitoring power of the compliance function. In the wake of the Barclays LIBOR scandal, former Financial Services Authority chief Hector Sants was appointed to be Chief Compliance Officer at Barclays. Sants resigned from the position after 10 months, citing exhaustion and stress. It remains speculative whether the stress and exhaustion resulted from the extreme challenges in fixing a 'broken compliance culture' at the bank,[138] which would have required proactive and substantive changes. Organisational determination to limit the compliance role to a more procedural nature could be effective if not countervailed by a strong professionalism on the part of the compliance function.

Further, the Thomson Reuters 2012 survey points out that many compliance professionals see part of their job as assisting in the firm's lobbying efforts regarding prospective regulation.[139] The role of assisting the firm in regulatory lobbying may reinforce the identification between the compliance function and business objectives and could have an effect upon compromising the objectivity of the compliance function in securing regulatory objectives. This book is of the view that taking on a lobbying-assistance role may be undesirable from the point of view that the objectivity

[136] Birindelli and Ferretti, 'Compliance Risk in Italian Banks' (n 28).

[137] Giampaolo Gabbi, Paola Musile Tanzi and Loris Nadotti, 'Firm Size and Compliance Costs Asymmetries in the Investment Services' (2011) *Journal of Financial Regulation and Compliance* 58.

[138] 'Sants' Resignation from Barclays Shows Pitfalls of Poaching' *Financial Times* (18 November 2013).

[139] English and Hammond, *Costs of Compliance Survey 2012* (n 30) 3. This point does not seem to be picked up again in the 2013 survey.

and therefore the 'independence' of the compliance function may be compromised.[140] Existing regulatory frameworks do not deal with this issue. However, it may be appropriate for regulatory guidance or international standards to not only provide certain core tasks as part of the remit of the compliance function, but to expressly discourage the compliance function from taking up particular tasks.

In the post-crisis reforms, regulators have increasingly articulated particular responsibilities for the compliance function. One example of this is European regulation in relation to involving the compliance function in new product development. The Basel Committee survey in 2008 showed that a number of international banks involved the compliance function in the development of new products or new business practices although that is not yet a converging practice. As the global financial crisis has cast a long shadow upon financial sector innovation especially in structured finance products,[141] ESMA[142] and the EBA[143] both highlight the necessity to involve the compliance function in groups or committees engaged in developing new products so as to highlight conduct and selling risks early on in the developmental stages of product innovation. Further, ESMA also explicitly requires that the compliance function monitors the operations of the firm's complaints-handling process and use information gathered in those processes to monitor the firm in its compliance culture.[144] European initiatives also provide that compliance should be consulted on material non-routine decisions and changes in business.[145] Such strategic involvement could enhance the profile of the compliance function and contribute towards developing stronger professionalism.

In sum, it is suggested here that the lack of convergence in the job scope of the compliance function reflects an emerging form of professionalism which can be taken advantage of by the organisation. Organisations could take the opportunity to frame the role of compliance, affecting its effectiveness and in meeting regulatory expectations. In other words, the regulatory–professional disjunction that arises out of the emerging nature of professionalism reinforces the regulatory–organisational disjunction, and affects the efficacy of the compliance function meeting regulatory expectations. Practitioner opinion also suggests that greater standardisation

[140] The qualities of objectivity and independence have been discussed earlier in section A as qualities that regulators try to protect through meta-regulation of organisational structures.

[141] Richard E Mendales, 'Collateralized Explosive Devices: Why Securities Regulation Failed to Prevent the CDO Meltdown, and How to Fix it' [2009] *University of Illinois Law Review* 1359.

[142] ESMA, *Consultation Paper* (2011) (n 25) Part III; ESMA, *Guidelines* (n 24) Annex II, para 41; ESMA, *Final Report* (2014) (n 88) 56 and 60.

[143] *EBA Guidelines* (n 7) 43, para 28.6.

[144] ESMA, *Final Report* (2014) (n 88) 19.

[145] ESMA, *Guidelines* (n 24) Annex II, paras 40–42.

in the role of the compliance function would assist in mitigating firms' compliance risk.[146] This section recognises however that the flexibility in the job scope of the compliance function meets the organic needs of many financial institutions. While not arguing for prescriptive standardisation or rigidity in formulating the job scope for compliance professionals, a useful and constructive amount of guidance on key functions and particular tasks may assist in consolidating the job scope of the compliance professional and forge a stronger sense of professionalism that can countervail organisational dominance. The convergence issue will be taken up again in chapter eight as enhanced professionalism for internal control is discussed.

Excessive Proceduralisation in the Job Scope of the Compliance Function

As discussed earlier, excessive proceduralisation in the job scope of the compliance function may result in an insular and non-critical mindset that impedes proactive behaviour and effective monitoring of firm obligations to meet regulatory expectations. As discussed in chapter one, excessive proceduralisation may also compromise the effectiveness of internal control functions if they become excessively comfortable with the procedures and systems[147] and fail to apply a broader and more inquiring mind generally towards compliance risk. Krawiec warns that many compliance procedures and programs in the general corporate sector are merely 'window-dressing' to boost the legitimacy of business operators and stave off further regulatory intervention.[148] Cunningham is also sceptical that procedural approaches such as supported by automated and information technology systems would be able to effectively engage with the overall spirit of managing compliance risk, as reliance on procedures and systems is a 'leaky' approach.[149] The Thomson Reuters international surveys of compliance professionals in 2012[150] and 2013[151] both indicate that about a quarter of a compliance officer's time is spent on the procedural matters of drafting and updating guidance. It is queried whether compliance officers could get routinised and become less alert to detecting problems.

[146] Gregory Husisian, 'US Regulation of International Financial Institutions: It's Time for an Integrated Approach to Compliance' (2010) 127 *Banking Law Journal* 195.

[147] Michael Power, *The Audit Society* (Oxford: Oxford University Press, 1997).

[148] Kimberly D Krawiec, 'Cosmetic Compliance and the Failure of Negotiated Governance' (2003) 81 *Washington University Law Quarterly* 487.

[149] Cunningham, 'The Appeal and Limits' (n 114).

[150] English and Hammond, *Costs of Compliance Survey 2012* (n 30) 2.

[151] Hammond and Walshe, *Costs of Compliance Survey 2013* (n 30) 3.

The procedural emphasis of the compliance function's job may be attributed to the Basel Committee's standards. The Basel Committee's recommendations in 2005 provide for a procedural approach to implement the management of compliance risk: ie, the compliance function should be engaged in drafting policies and guidance, training and advising staff and management, developing indicators and procedures to measure, test and monitor compliance risk and reporting to senior management.[152] Although such guidance provides clarity for the job scope of the compliance function, excessive emphasis on these may have unintended negative effects as discussed above. However, Parker and Nielsen's empirical survey found that the institution of procedures and systems signal senior management commitment to manage compliance risk, and can result in the practical effect of constraining and monitoring behaviour.[153] The existence of systems and procedures facilitate information collection, and more systematic preparation of reports for the Board can be carried out. Board reporting is a key aspect of the compliance officer's job as pointed out by the Thomson Reuters 2013 survey.[154] The UCL empirical study also shows that procedures in organisations help to 'move their understanding and responsiveness forward by generating knowledge and learning about risk'.[155] Parker and Nielsen also found that staff training systems and systems for handling consumer complaints are examples of procedures and systems established to manage compliance risk that have a positive impact upon changes in behaviour in the organisation. Hence, proceduralisation is not in itself a negative phenomenon.[156] The contextual framework for the operation of procedures in terms of organisational structures, governance and culture would determine whether proceduralisation empowers the compliance function through systematisation or results in emasculation.

Post-crisis, the European approach has embraced more prescription that details the procedural aspects of the compliance function.[157] The compliance function is tasked to develop policies and procedures to detect compliance risk[158] and to develop a monitoring programme for all of the firm's lines of business in a comprehensive and holistic manner.[159] The compliance function is also responsible for written reports to

[152] Basel Committee, *Implementation of the Compliance Principles* (n 27). Also see Birindelli and Ferretti, 'Compliance Risk in Italian Banks' (n 28) based on an empirical survey of Italian banks, and Newton, *The Handbook of Compliance* (n 32) and Mills, *Essential Strategies* (n 1) writing in the UK context.

[153] Christine Parker and Vibeke Lehmann Nielsen, 'Corporate Compliance Systems: Could They Make Any Difference?' (2009) 41 *Administration & Society* 3.

[154] Hammond and Walshe, *Costs of Compliance Survey 2013* (n 30) 3.

[155] Moorhead and Vaughan, 'Legal Risk' (n 39) 55.

[156] Parker and Nielsen, 'Corporate Compliance Systems' (n 153).

[157] ESMA, *Consultation Paper* (2011) (n 25) paras III.II, III.IV.

[158] ESMA, *Guidelines* (n 24) Annex II, para 15.

[159] ibid, para 18.

senior management[160] and for drafting staff training policies and day to day advisory policies.[161] The advisory function seems a little more proactive, and the compliance function is regarded as key to the establishment of a healthy compliance culture in firms.[162] These post-crisis initiatives seem to have introduced a balance of measures that define clarity for the compliance function while at the same time enhancing the importance of the role in specific business decisions. It will be suggested that regulatory leadership is crucial for boosting the professionalism of internal control functions, and chapter eight will discuss this further.

Expanding Remit and Work Overload

The explosion of regulatory requirements imposed on business in general has been acknowledged as a form of regulatory capitalism.[163] General regulations in employment, health and safety, environmental protection, anti-bribery and corruption and trade have emerged in the modern regulatory state. Financial sector specific regulation has in particular exploded under the legal harmonisation programme[164] carried out pursuant to the Financial Services Action Plan of 1998 endorsed by European policymakers, and after the global financial crisis of 2008–09 pursuant to the recommendations in the de Larosière report.[165] The post-crisis regulatory reforms in the US and EU have added on to an already heavy workload that has developed for the compliance function over the years, and now borders on overload.[166]

The overload of the compliance function may cause compliance officers to be excessively engaged with 'firefighting' and less capacity may be devoted to developing enhanced critical functions that are closer to meeting regulatory expectations. The Thomson Reuters survey of compliance professionals in 2012 reports that compliance officers find that basic compliance tasks have expanded due to increased regulatory burdens and

[160] ibid, para 28.

[161] ibid, paras 32–33.

[162] ibid, para 33.

[163] David Levi-Faur, 'The Global Diffusion of Regulatory Capitalism' (2005) 598 *The Annals of the American Academy of Political and Social Science* 12; John Braithwaite, *Regulatory Capitalism* (Cheltenham: Edward Elgar, 2008) 4–29.

[164] See, eg, Iris H-Y Chiu, *Regulatory Convergence in EU Securities Regulation* (The Hague: Kluwer Law International, 2008) generally.

[165] Jacques de Larosière, *High Level Group on Financial Supervision in the EU* (2009) at ec.europa.eu/internal_market/finances/docs/de_larosiere_report_en.pdf.

[166] Expressed in relation to the compliance function's role in mutual funds, as prescribed by SEC Rule 38a-1, see Rob Sobol, 'Conversations at the Top: The Tone of the Independent Chief Compliance Officer' (2009) 10 *Journal of Investment Compliance* 10. Also see 'Shop Talk: Dodd-Frank and Data Overload' *Compliance Week* (17 April 2012); English and Hammond, *Costs of Compliance Survey 2012* (n 30) 2.

reporting, and less time is available for exceptional tasks such as advising business units, undertaking investigations or past business reviews, and managing relationships with regulators.[167] The 2013 survey continues to report that tracking regulatory changes occupies a significant fraction of compliance officers' time.[168]

Practice-oriented literature and empirical studies have pointed out that increased compliance workload has resulted in compliance professionals being unable to take part closely in day to day operational decisions.[169] Hence, excessive workload could increasingly hollow out the important critical and monitoring scrutiny compliance is expected to apply across the firm's business. The KPMG survey has pointed out the risk of minimising the role of compliance in early intervention.[170] The survey observes that compliance officers have adopted more distanced monitoring of day to day compliance issues, encouraging front line offices to be aware of and take ownership of these issues so that the responsibility for securing firm compliance is more diffuse. If such a structure is adopted strategically towards implementing a firm-wide compliance culture, there could be advantages in the form of distance monitoring undertaken by compliance. However, it is queried whether the approach is taken due to the inability of the compliance function to cope with the workload and hence overall reduces the efficacy of the function. High workload augments the problems associated with emerging professionalism, as compliance officers may not be able to define clearly their priorities under such stressful conditions. Further, the priorities that need attention may be defined by organisational framing, compelling the compliance function to respond to needs, rather than to clearly chart its professional role and responsibilities.

Background Qualifications and Training of Compliance Officers

As mentioned earlier, compliance officers could be drawn from legal, accounting and risk management, as well as other backgrounds.[171] The European initiatives do not specify any particular professional background

[167] English and Hammond, *Costs of Compliance Survey 2012* (n 30).

[168] Hammond and Walshe, *Costs of Compliance Survey 2013* (n 30) 3.

[169] See Gilad, 'Institutionalizing Fairness in Financial Markets' (n 117); Mills, *Essential Strategies* (n 1) 18–19. In the US context for mutual funds, see Michael R Rosella and Domenick Pugliese, 'The Investment Company Chief Compliance Officer: Three Years Later: An Assessment of the Evolution of the Role of the CCO' (2006) 7 *Journal of Investment Compliance* 16.

[170] KPMG, 'The Future of Compliance' (2012) at www.kpmg.com/UK/en/IssuesAndInsights/ArticlesPublications/Documents/PDF/Advisory/future-of-compliance_web_Acc4.pdf, 13.

[171] Section A.

for the compliance function but emphasises sufficiently broad knowledge, experience and high level of expertise.[172] Firms must hire appropriate persons to the compliance function and so there is arguably a certain level of eligible competence to support the efficacy of the function. However, this chapter queries whether the open-endedness in qualifications for the compliance function may disadvantage the forging of stronger professionalism for the function, and allow firms to hire based on business needs rather than for the purposes of securing effective internal control to meet regulatory objectives. However, there is a legitimate need for compliance officers to be drawn from a variety of backgrounds such as risk management and other fields in order to enhance the general commercial and business awareness of compliance.[173] This may be particularly important for financial services businesses which can evolve very quickly with new innovations.

Nevertheless, it is observed that legally trained professionals may dominate the compliance landscape especially if the departments of compliance and legal are fused, as discussed in section C. Even if the departments of compliance and legal are not fused, legally trained persons bring to the compliance function certain skills and mindsets. Lenglet in particular suggests that legally trained personnel dominate the compliance landscape and points out that the key role of the compliance function is to supply the law in practice, and act as regulatory interpreters of the relevant laws including their gaps.[174] Further, increased liaison with regulators may require compliance officers not only to be legally trained, but perhaps skilled in communication and external dialogue as well.[175]

The legal domination of the compliance function can however give rise to two different attitudes towards securing firm compliance with regulatory objectives. Parker, Rosen and Nielsen's empirical study of lawyers in the general corporate sector show that an equal number of in-house legally trained persons could take on diametrically opposite roles.[176] One group of legally trained in-house personnel genuinely acts as compliance champions and gate-keeps potential misconduct and non-compliance in and by the firm. The other group acts as 'gamesters',[177] exploiting the gaps

172 *EBA Guidelines* (n 7) 44. ESMA, *Guidelines* (n 24) Annex II, para 44.

173 PriceWaterhouseCoopers, 'Realising the Full Value of Compliance' (n 130) 12.

174 Lenglet, 'Ambivalence and Ambiguity' (n 8) 59.

175 ibid.

176 Parker, Rosen and Nielsen, 'The Two Faces of Lawyers' (n 46); Ashoke S Talukdar, 'The Voice of Reason: The Corporate Compliance Officer and the Regulated Corporate Environment' (2005) 6 *UC Davis Business Law Journal* 2; Soren Winter and Peter J May, 'Information, Interests, and Environmental Regulation' (2002) 4 *Journal of Comparative Policy Analyses: Research and Practice* 115, 135.

177 Parker, Rosen and Nielsen, 'The Two Faces of Lawyers' (n 46); Jill Fisch and Kenneth M Rosen, 'Is there a Role for Lawyers in Preventing Future Enrons?' (2003) 48 *Villanova Law Review* 1097.

and loopholes in the law and encouraging or reinforcing management desires to comply minimally while aggressively pushing the boundaries to further business interests. The latter predisposition could even be due to the general emphasis on loyalty to clients[178] as part of legal professional ethics. Hence, appointing legally trained compliance officers need not be aligned with the securing of regulatory objectives, even if they may have a greater understanding and awareness of how regulations are interpreted and applied.

Further, there is a need to consider whether the compliance function also acts as the ethical champion in the firm. A survey of empirical and practice-oriented literature shows that the role of the compliance function may be fused with ethical gatekeeping.[179] The UCL empirical study shows that compliance officers are uncertain and ambivalent about their ethical roles, some regarding ethics as underlying the job while others are less sure.[180]

The Role of Ethics in Enhancing the Professionalism of the Compliance Function

This book is however of the view that an ethical dimension[181] could provide a unifying framework for the job scope and professional competencies of the compliance function, therefore strengthening the professionalism of compliance officers. Even if compliance officers may be drawn from diverse backgrounds, an ethical framework could steer the discharge of skills towards the broader objective of encouraging ethical conduct in and by the firm and protecting the reputational capital of the firm.[182] Such a framework may provide the necessary coalescing drive for forging a stronger professionalism on the part of the compliance function. Such a framework is able to embrace a diversity of skill sets in the compliance function without diluting professionalism, and accommodate the changing needs of the job scope of compliance while resisting organisational manipulation of the role of compliance. This framework also complements the more detailed prescriptive reforms that regulatory measures have introduced. Klebe et al

[178] DeMott, 'The Discrete Roles of General Counsel' (n 46).

[179] See Weinstein, 'The World of International Compliance (n 46); W Michael Hoffman and Mark Rowe, 'The Ethics Officer as Agent of the Board: Leveraging Ethical Governance Capability in the Post-Enron Corporation' (2007) 112 *Business & Society Review* 553.

[180] Moorhead and Vaughan, 'Legal Risk' (n 39) 57.

[181] Newton, *The Handbook of Compliance* (n 32) 97.

[182] This perspective seems quite well accepted, at least in the US, see Ford and Hess, 'Can Corporate Monitorships Improve Corporate Compliance?' (n 42); Scott A Roney et al, 'Leading Corporate Integrity: Defining the Role of the Chief Ethics and Compliance Officer (CECO)' (2007) at www.ethics.org/ceco.

is in fact of the view that legally trained compliance officers tend to take a narrower approach to compliance and do not frame compliance risk as part of a wider landscape of ethical conduct in business,[183] hence there are advantages in drawing compliance personnel from diverse backgrounds.

Lenglet observes that overt reference to 'ethics' has been dropped from EU regulation concerning the compliance function and this could be due to concerns that a reference to 'ethics' would foster differences in regulatory interpretation.[184] The reference to 'ethics' could be interpreted to give national regulators the open-ended discretion to implement different ethical considerations in regulatory interpretation, detracting from supervisory convergence. Although this book appreciates the view that instituting ethics in the regulatory framework for the compliance function may bring about certain challenges in regulatory interpretation, regulatory initiatives can help to forge the otherwise slow and incremental process of developing professionalism.

Emerging Representative Professional Bodies

There appear to be loose forms of professional groupings for compliance officers, but such groupings or bodies have yet to attain a stature comparable to other professions such as for solicitors or accountants where professional bodies are engaged in a wide range of services such as admissions, standard-setting, discipline and representation. In the UK, the International Compliance Association[185] has been established only since 2001 although it boasts of international membership and is increasingly engaged in certification of compliance expertise. In the US, a membership body called the Ethics and Compliance Officers' Association[186] has been established since 1991 under the auspices of the American Bar Association, to share knowledge and updates and facilitate networking. This body does not however appear to be internationally oriented. There also exist national membership bodies for compliance officers in a number of jurisdictions such as Ireland, Switzerland, Jersey and the British Virgin Islands. The lack of a strong and perhaps internationally representative body for compliance officers may to a certain extent affect the professionalism of the compliance function, as chapter eight will argue that professionalism is often manifested and supported by the existence of a strong professional body. Arguably, the lack of a strong professional body for

[183] Linda Klebe Trevino, Gary R Weaver, David G Gibson and Barbara Ley Toffler, 'Managing Ethics and Legal Compliance: What Works and What Hurts' (1999) 41 *California Management Review* 131.

[184] Lenglet, 'From Internal Control' (n 47).

[185] See www.int-comp.org/Home.

[186] See www.theecoa.org.

compliance officers may also be due to the fact that compliance personnel are drawn from a variety of backgrounds and therefore do not benefit from the unity of similarity in professional training. This observation possibly reinforces the argument above for the need to develop a unifying framework for compliance professionalism based on ethics.

In sum, this section has pointed out the aspects in the professionalism of the compliance function that may undermine its efficacy and the meeting of regulatory expectations. These weaknesses are augmented within the frames of meta-regulation as organisational dominance in the implementation of the compliance function may shape the role, responsibilities, perceptions and values of the compliance function in such a way that may detract from regulatory expectations of what the function can achieve. Any regulatory–professional disjunction may undermine the efficacy of the compliance function in spite of the organisational reforms discussed earlier and indeed can continue to reinforce regulatory–organisational disjunctions. This neglected issue needs to be addressed, and chapters three and four will point out that this issue is also a persistent one in relation to other functions in internal control.

D. CONCLUDING REMARKS

This chapter has discussed the pre-crisis meta-regulatory framework for the compliance function and provides a profile sketch of the compliance function as part of its organisational context as well as a burgeoning profession. The meta-regulatory framework for compliance which has left firms with much discretion in implementation may be defeated in spirit if firms choose to engage in marginalisation of the compliance function while demonstrating cosmetic implementation.

In light of enhanced regulatory expectations for the efficacy of the compliance function, post-crisis reforms have attempted to address the perceived weaknesses of the compliance function. These reforms focus on enhancing the formal powers and organisational positioning of the compliance function in order to improve its efficacy. This book argues that this approach rightly addresses the regulatory–organisational disjunction that has made the compliance function relatively weak in the pre-crisis meta-regulatory framework, but is insufficient overall. Further, firm implementation of such powers in a meta-regulatory framework still needs to be supervised. Regulatory prescriptions in this area may risk micro-managing the firm, or risk introducing one size fits all solutions that are unsuitable for some firms. Regulators need to engage in more empirical and supervisory observation as to what organisational structures, features, governance systems and culture affect the discharge of the compliance function. Regulators need to engage in interdisciplinary understanding especially in relation to research dealing with governance systems and organisational culture, as will be discussed in chapter five. Further, regulatory guidance could be issued to firms individually or selectively, discriminating between different structural aspects of the implementation of the compliance function, in order to provide for countervailing effects against poor or adverse structural features in the organisational implementation of the compliance function. There is arguably a general need for more intelligent forms of regulatory scrutiny[187] to complement the meta-regulatory framework for empowering the organisational position and powers of the compliance function.

Further, the book suggests that the reforms neglect a key issue of the emerging nature of the professional dimension of the compliance function. The strength of professionalism may affect the profession's efficacy in meeting regulatory expectations and could reinforce opportunities for organisational manipulation of the compliance function. The book suggests that there is scope to consider adopting a broad and unifying framework of ethics to complement specific regulatory prescriptions for compliance responsibilities. This approach may help in defining compliance responsibilities with greater clarity and limit the scope for organisational manipulation, therefore realising the achievements of reforms in organisational empowerment discussed above. Chapter eight provides more details of the road map towards enhanced professionalism.

[187] Jodi L Short and Michael W Toffel, 'Making Self-Regulation More than Merely Symbolic: The Critical Role of the Legal Environment' (2010) 55 *Administrative Science Quarterly* 361; Cristie Ford, 'New Governance, Compliance, and Principles-Based Securities Regulation' (2008) 45 *American Business Law Journal* 1.

3

The Role of Risk Management

A. THE DEVELOPMENT AND PURPOSES OF RISK MANAGEMENT

RISK MANAGEMENT IN banks and financial institutions may be described as a 'framework' as well as a 'function' of 'internal control'. The risk management framework in a firm refers to a firm-wide framework that governs the perceptions and evaluations of risk in order to feed into decision-making and action. This is distinguished from the specialist function of risk management[1] (which is referred to as 'risk control' in European Guidelines).[2] Firms are urged to establish a risk management framework generally as risk management is intrinsically bound up in the highest strategic level of decision-making and cascades down to day to day transactional and operational activities. It should not be a responsibility that is viewed as delegated only to a specialist function. Nevertheless, the specialist 'risk control' or 'risk management' function (which is this chapter's preferred term as it is used more widely in practice) is an important centre of the overall framework for firm risk management. This chapter focuses on the risk management function, while the risk management framework will be discussed in chapters five and six in relation to the wider context of corporate governance.

The development of risk management functions in banks and financial institutions is primarily a response to various regulatory obligations. These are in the realm of prudential and securities market regulations. This chapter charts the evolution of the risk management function and discusses the 'failure' of risk management in the global financial crisis of 2008–09. Post-crisis, specific reforms targeted at improving the risk management function and the overall risk management framework in firms (which is dealt with as a matter of corporate governance) have been introduced. The chapter critically analyses the weaknesses of the risk management function in the pre-crisis meta-regulatory framework for internal control, and explores to what extent post-crisis reforms address the weaknesses and what issues may remain.

[1] European Banking Authority, *EBA Guidelines on Internal Governance* (27 September 2011) paras 22, 25.

[2] ibid.

International standards for managing banking risk have been developed in the Basel I Capital Accord[3] (which dealt with credit risk) since 1988, followed by a more comprehensive consideration of banking risks in the Basel II Capital Accord of 2006.[4] However, as the Basel II Capital Accord has recognised, the management of banking risk specific to the profiles of bank assets and trading books cannot be micro-managed by regulatory prescription and significant responsibility lies in banks having robust risk management frameworks and functions, subject to supervision and capital markets accountability.[5] The internal control and risk management functions of banks and financial institutions were developed to deal with international standards for prudential regulation. However, these functions were largely subject to organisational design as pre-crisis European legislation is scant on how they should work. European legislation on credit institutions left it to the regulated firms to define what 'adequate internal control' may be proportionate to the 'nature, scale and complexity' of the firms' activities.[6] The Markets in Financial Instruments Directive 2004 (MiFID) which applied to investment firms mandated the establishment of separate and permanent compliance and internal audit functions in investment firms,[7] but left firms the discretion to decide if a separate risk management function[8] would be necessary and proportionate to the nature, scale and complexity of the firm's business. In the UK, the regulator applied MiFID requirements across the board to authorised financial institutions including banks (that are not insurers, reinsurance

[3] Basel Committee on Banking Supervision, *Basel I: International Convergence of Capital Measurement and Capital Standards* (Basel: BIS, 1998) at www.bis.org/publ/bcbs04A.pdf.

[4] Basel Committee on Banking Supervision, *Basel II: International Convergence of Capital Measurement and Capital Standards: A Revised Framework* (rev November 2005, Basel: BIS, 2004) at www.bis.org/publ/bcbs118.pdf, and www.bis.org/publ/bcbs128.htm.

[5] Pillars 2 and 3 of the Basel II Capital Accord.

[6] European Parliament and Council Directive 2006/48/EC of 14 June 2006 relating to the taking up and pursuit of the business of credit institutions (recast) [2006] OJ L177/1 (Capital Requirements Directive 2006) Art 22.

[7] Commission Directive 2006/73/EC of 10 August 2006 implementing Directive 2004/39/EC of the European Parliament and of the Council as regards organisational requirements and operating conditions for investment firms and defined terms for the purposes of that Directive [2006] OJ L241/26 (MiFID Commission Directive 2006) Arts 6 and 8. The 2004 MiFID Directive has been superseded by Directive 2014/65/EU of the European Parliament and of the Council of 15 May 2014 on markets in financial instruments and amending Directive 2002/92/EC and Directive 2011/61/EU (MiFID II Directive 2014). However, the European Securities and Markets Authority (ESMA) is likely to establish technical standards regarding the risk management function, as specific risk management activities and policies such as in relation to new products are going to be put in place, see ESMA, *Consultation Paper: MiFID II and MiFIR* (22 May 2014) 40.

[8] MiFID Commission Directive 2006, Art 7. Even if firms consider that a separate risk management function is not necessary, Art 7 does require firms to put in place effective and adequate risk management policies and procedures.

underwriting agents or building societies).[9] The relatively skeletal nature of the pre-crisis regulatory framework for risk management is a form of meta-regulation, outlining broadly the option to establish a risk management function, and leaving firms to implement the organisational roles, governance, accountability and objectives of such functions.

The relatively skeletal meta-regulatory framework for the risk management functions of banks and financial institutions was arguably appropriate at that time, as Carey and Stultz point out that banks have already had a long history of instituting risk management systems to meet business needs.[10] For example, formalised systems of interest rate risk management were highly developed before banks needed to respond to the management of credit risk under the Basel I and II Capital Accords. As the banking business has evolved to encompass many forms of financial intermediation business, the management of market risk which is an important financial risk has also developed bottom-up and become a part of bank risk management.[11] Banks and financial institutions have had a long history of initiating the development of risk management systems to manage various aspects of financial risk, and Schroeck argues in 2002 that such initiatives have been taken in order to mitigate solvency concerns. In other words, the development of risk management functions in banks and financial institutions as voluntary initiatives met their own private interests, but such also connected with regulators' prudential concerns aimed at preserving the safety and soundness of banks and financial institutions.[12] The skeletal nature of the meta-regulation of risk management at banks and financial institutions seemed apt as an alignment between the objectives of the institution and regulatory objectives that could be readily achieved.

However, the concept of risk management in banks and financial institutions became gradually moulded by general corporate sector practices. The role of risk management in banks and financial institutions began to evolve with characteristics that ultimately unfortunately contributed to 'risk management failure' at many banks in the global financial crisis of 2008–09.

[9] Financial Conduct Authority and Prudential Regulation Authority (FCA and PRA, formerly FSA) Handbooks, SYSC 1.1A.1.

[10] Mark Carey and René M Stulz, 'Introduction' in Mark Carey and René M Stulz (eds), *The Risks of Financial Institutions* (Chicago, IL: University of Chicago Press, 2006).

[11] Such as the development of 'Value at Risk' methodologies, see Aswath Damodaran, *Strategic Risk Taking: A Framework for Risk Management* (New Jersey: Pearson Education Inc, 2008) ch 7 'Value at Risk', 202. See also people.stern.nyu.edu/adamodar/pdfiles/papers/VAR.pdf.

[12] Gerhard Schroeck, *Risk Management and Value Creation in Financial Institutions* (Chichester: John Wiley & Sons, 2002) 9.

In the corporate sector generally, the concept of risk management has been shaped significantly by obligations to the securities markets. In the 1990s and early 2000s major securities regulation reforms in the UK and EU were rolled out, as well as in the US, following a spate of high profile corporate scandals. The requirements of securities regulation in relation to upholding the integrity of corporate disclosure have since significantly shaped the development of the risk management framework and function at publicly quoted banks and financial institutions.[13]

Since the 1990s, many reforms have been introduced to enhance audit and accounting integrity[14] in the UK and US in response to a spate of corporate scandals such as the collapse of BCCI[15] and Barings in the 1990s and World.com and Enron in the US in the early 2000s.[16] Subsequently, the Turnbull Review in the UK further emphasised the need to have reliable internal and external reporting systems as part of 'internal control' and 'risk management'.[17] The language of 'internal control' used in the Cadbury and Turnbull reports deals with systems that process financial information and reporting and how to ensure that such systems underlie integrity in financial reporting. Although the Turnbull Guidance views internal control as a form of risk management that 'enable[s] [companies] to respond appropriately to significant business, operational, financial, compliance and other risks to achieving the company's objectives',[18] the more precise language surrounding risk management and internal control targets the prevention of accounting fraud and ensuring the integrity of financial reporting. The concept of 'internal control' has very much been fashioned by the securities regulation ideology of supporting transparency to facilitate market discipline. The emphasis placed on accounting and reporting integrity is also found in the US response to Enron's collapse in 2000—the Sarbanes–Oxley Act—although the Act also prescribes certain forms of internal control (such as controls over auditor appointment[19] and mandatory certifications by Chief Financial Officers).[20]

[13] Christoph Van der Elst, 'The Risks of Corporate Legal Principles of Risk Management' (2010) ECGI Law Working Paper 160/2010 at ssrn.com/abstract=1623526; John R Boatright, 'Risk Management and the Responsible Corporation: How Sweeping the Invisible Hand?' (2011) 116 *Business and Society Review* 145.

[14] Marc T Moore, 'The Evolving Contours of the Board's Risk Management Function in UK Corporate Governance' (2010) 10 *Journal of Corporate Law Studies* 279.

[15] Culminating in Sir Adrian Cadbury's review of corporate governance in general and the promulgation of the Cadbury Code of Corporate Governance 1992.

[16] Culminating in the Sarbanes–Oxley Act 2002.

[17] See Financial Reporting Council, *Internal Control: Revised Guidance for Directors on the Combined Code* (October 2005) at www.frc.org.uk/Our-Work/Publications/Corporate-Governance/Turnbull-guidance-October-2005.aspx (Turnbull Guidance).

[18] ibid, para 19.

[19] Sarbanes–Oxley Act 2002, ss 502, 503.

[20] ibid, s 302.

Van der Elst[21] argues that the evolution of 'internal control' as a corporate governance issue in the EU has been led largely by the need for reliable securities disclosure.[22] The drivers that have shaped the rise of internal control and risk management in the corporate sector have also fed into the understanding of risk management by banks and financial institutions. Banks and financial institutions that are listed or publicly traded companies have become sensitive to the obligations of securities transparency and sound corporate reporting. The importance of accountability to shareholders has not only shaped the corporate governance agenda of the corporate sector, but also the financial sector. The 'shareholder primacy' view of corporate governance has permeated the rationale for instituting risk management at firms in the listed sector, and the objective of risk management is therefore seen as mitigating the 'agency' problem between shareholders and management.[23]

Commentators also observe that the shareholder-centric ethos of corporate governance has shaped risk management in banks and financial institutions.[24] Smithson and Simkins conducted a meta-review of empirical studies and concluded that risk management in banks and financial institutions achieve the effect of smoothing out earnings volatility and mitigating agency problems in relation to manager under-investment related to hoarding cash.[25] Further, risk management in banks and financial institutions serves the purposes of shareholder value maximisation.[26] Smithson and Simkins' meta-review of empirical literature concludes that risk management in banks and financial institutions achieves the 'adding of value' for shareholders. Other empirical studies also find a positive

[21] Christoph Van der Elst and Marijn van Daelen, 'Risk Management in European and American Corporate Law' (2009) ECGI Law Working Paper 122/2009 at ssrn.com/abstract=1399647.

[22] The disclosure of 'risk' is required under mandatory disclosure in the Prospectus Directive 2004 (relating to public offers) and in the Transparency Directive 2005 providing for ongoing reporting by listed issuers. However, the disclosure of 'risk' is seen as a qualitative form of disclosure and is therefore not subject to further precision or standardisation.

[23] Henri Servaes, Ane Tamayo and Peter Tufano, 'The Theory and Practice of Corporate Risk Management' (2009) 21 *Journal of Applied Corporate Finance* 60; Söhnke M Bartram, 'Corporate Risk Management as a Lever for Shareholder Value Creation' (2000) 9 *Financial Markets, Institutions & Instruments* 279; Robert E Hoyt and Andre P Liebenberg, 'The Value of Enterprise Risk Management' (2011) 78 *Journal of Risk and Insurance* 795.

[24] See Michael S Pagano, 'How Theories of Financial Intermediation and Corporate Risk-Management Influence Bank Risk-Taking Behavior' (2001) 10 *Financial Markets, Institutions & Instruments* 277 argues that risk management by hedging in banks and financial institutions not only serve to avert loss but to achieve the advantages of mitigating agency costs and smoothing out earnings volatility to gain tax advantages.

[25] Charles Smithson and Betty J Simkins, 'Does Risk Management Add Value? A Survey of the Evidence' (2005) 17 *Journal of Applied Corporate Finance* 8.

[26] Lisa K Meulbroek, 'A Senior Manager's Guide to Integrated Risk Management' (2002) 14 *Journal of Applied Corporate Finance* 56.

relationship between a bank or financial institution's risk management profile or capabilities and stock returns, indicating that shareholders value the risk management in firms and that risk management is perceived to be relevant to shareholder value enhancement.[27] In sum, risk management in banks and financial institutions is shaped by a mixture of factors, from regulatory to corporate governance demands, but the influence of corporate governance demands has arguably been both strong and recent at the turn of the millennium.

The orientation towards the pursuit of shareholder value maximisation has fundamentally changed how banks conduct business. According to Pacces,[28] banks have become obsessed with short-termist corporate profitability due to two factors: first, competition from alternative financial institutions in the maturity transformation business, and second, short-termism, supported by the ideology of 'shareholder value',[29] especially in widely held economies such as the US and UK. Ho,[30] an eminent anthropologist, argues that the business model of banking has changed in embracing 'shareholder value', an ideology which encourages the corporate world to be obsessed with stock market prices and to take a short-termist approach to profitability.[31] Risk management at banks and financial institutions, as infused with shareholder primacy ideology, may not be completely aligned with the solvency objectives underlying prudential risk management. For example, Partnoy[32] writes, pessimistically, on

[27] See Sugato Bhattacharyya and Amiyatosh Purnanandam, 'Risk-taking by Banks: What Did We Know and When Did We Know It?' (2011) at ssrn.com/abstract=1619472; Ryan Baxter et al, 'Enterprise Risk Management Program Quality: Determinants, Value Relevance, and the Financial Crisis' (July 2012) at ssrn.com/abstract=1684807; and for an empirical study of a sample of Indian banks on the same point, see Rudra Sensarma and M Jayadev, 'Are Bank Stocks Sensitive to Risk Management?' (2009) 10 *Journal of Risk Finance* 7.

[28] Alessio M Pacces, 'Consequences of Uncertainty for Regulation: Law and Economics of the Financial Crisis' (2010) 7 *European Company and Financial Law Review* 479.

[29] Alfred Rappaport, *Creating Shareholder Value: The New Standard for Business Performance* (New York: Free Press, 1986). This term has also been associated with Jack Welch, former CEO of General Electric, although he appears to have disavowed his support for it in an interview in 2009, see Francesco Guerrera, 'Welch condemns share price focus' *Financial Times* (12 March 2009). The shareholder value concept is increasingly being questioned in terms of its positive and negative impacts upon corporate purpose. See, eg, Claudio F Loderer et al, 'Shareholder Value: Principles, Declarations, and Actions' (2009) ECGI Finance Working Paper 95/2005 at papers.ssrn.com/sol3/papers.cfm?abstract_id=1099936; Andrew Keay, *The Corporate Objective* (Cheltenham: Edward Elgar, 2011).

[30] Karen Ho, 'Disciplining Investment Bankers, Disciplining the Economy: Wall Street's Institutional Culture of Crisis and the Downsizing of "Corporate America"' (2009) 111 *American Anthropologist* 177.

[31] See also Simon Deakin, 'Corporate Governance and Financial Crisis in the Long Run' in Peer Zumbansen and Cynthia A Williams (eds), *The Embedded Firm: Corporate Governance, Labor, and Finance Capitalism* (New York: Cambridge University Press, 2011).

[32] Frank Partnoy, 'On Rogues, Risk-taking and Restoring Trust in Banks' *Financial Times* (23 September 2011).

the diverging incentives between the firms and regulators concerned with prudential risk management at firms: firms persistently underestimate risk[33] as they pursue aggressive strategies in hyper-competitive financial markets. The business behaviour of banks and financial institutions has therefore affected the way risk management is organised and practised in firms and has ultimately resulted in the 'failure' of risk management for prudential objectives.

Fanto, in two separate articles, argued that the global financial crisis of 2008–09 highlighted a risk management failure in banks and financial institutions. The failures of risk management were in two dimensions, one relating to the limitations of risk management as a professional discipline in its application to financial risk management in firms,[34] and the second relating to the weaknesses in the organisational dimension of the risk management function.[35] Both of these failures have contributed to excessive risk-taking at a significant number of international universal banks.

Excessive risk-taking[36] has been argued by many commentators to be key to the culmination of the systemic crisis that unfolded in 2008–09. Empirical research also supports the link between bank distress and weak risk management frameworks and functions in those firms. A number of empirical studies have shown that financial institutions with a higher quality of risk management (based on variables such as the presence of enterprise risk management systems, the establishment of a risk committee with expertise and time commitment, the profile of a chief risk officer, etc) have not suffered as much in the global financial crisis.[37] On the flip side,

[33] Hans J Blommestein, Lex Hoogduin and JJW Peeters, 'Uncertainty and Risk Management after the Great Moderation: The Role of Risk (Mis)Management by Financial Institutions' (28th SUERF Colloquium, Utrecht, September 2009) at papers.ssrn.com/sol3/papers.cfm?abstract_id=1489826.

[34] James A Fanto, 'Anticipating the Unthinkable: The Adequacy of Risk Management in Finance and Environmental Studies' (2009) 44 *Wake Forest Law Review* 731.

[35] James A Fanto, 'The Role of Financial Regulation in Private Financial Firms: Risk Management and the Limitations of the Market Model' (2009) 3 *Brooklyn Journal of Corporate, Financial & Commercial Law* 29.

[36] See M Brunnermeier, A Crockett, C Goodhart, AD Persaud and Hyun Shin, *The Fundamental Principles of Financial Regulation* (London: Centre for Economic Policy Research, Geneva Reports on the World Economy, 2009); Nouriel Roubini, 'Ten Fundamental Issues in Reforming Financial Regulation and Supervision in a World of Financial Innovation and Globalization' (31 March 2008) at www.roubini.com/analysis/44740; Suzanne McGee, *Chasing Goldman Sachs: How the Masters of the Universe Melted Wall Street Down … And Why They'll Take Us to the Brink Again* (New York: Crown Business, 2010) 124, 126, 128; Gillian Tett, *Fool's Gold: How Unrestrained Greed Corrupted a Dream, Shattered Global Markets and Unleashed a Catastrophe* (London: Abacus Books, 2010); Howard Davies, *The Financial Crisis: Who is to Blame?* (Cambridge: Polity Press, 2010) 142.

[37] See Andrew Ellul and Vijay Yerramilli, 'Stronger Risk Controls, Lower Risk: Evidence from US Bank Holding Companies' (August 2012) at ssrn.com/abstract=1550361 and (2013) 68 *Journal of Finance* 1757.

financial institutions with poorer risk management become entangled in a downward spiral when high risks materialise.[38] Establishing an effective risk management framework as well as function seemed to be key to loss prevention or mitigation, especially in stressed conditions.[39]

Post-crisis reforms have now introduced more prescriptive requirements to enhance the organisational position and power of the risk management function in banks and financial institutions, and have also required the institution of sound and credible risk management frameworks as part of corporate governance in firms. This chapter discusses the reforms in the former aspect while chapters five and six will take up the latter aspect. Sections B and C will analyse the specific weaknesses of 'risk management' in the pre-crisis context and to what extent the post-crisis reforms address these weaknesses. A similar argument will be made here as in chapter two, that the post-crisis reforms focus overwhelmingly on weaknesses in the organisational dimension relating to risk management and although these go some way towards mitigating known weaknesses, the reforms neglect the issue of emerging professionalism on the part of the risk management function. The emerging nature of professionalism will be identified as a key factor that has allowed extensive organisational manipulation of the pre-crisis risk management functions at firms.

However, a query may be raised at this juncture. Can we expect the risk management framework and function to monitor excessive risk-taking at financial institutions when it is uncertain what optimal risk-taking means? In the aftermath of the global financial crisis, do we accept 'optimal risk-taking' as a business decision defined by firms[40] or is 'optimal risk-taking' determined with reference to wider social appetite?[41] If we accept risk-taking as an essentially firm-based decision, then should regulatory

[38] William R Wilson, Laurence C Rose and John F Pinfold, 'Examination of NZ Finance Company Failures: The Role of Corporate Governance' (2010) at papers.ssrn.com/sol3/papers.cfm?abstract_id=1536874, examining the consequences of poor risk management in the financial institutions and banks that failed in New Zealand in the wake of the global financial crisis. See also Kenneth Patrick Vincent O'Sullivan and Stephen Kinsella, 'Financial and Regulatory Failure: The Case of Ireland' (2013) 14 *Journal of Banking Regulation* 1, examining how poor risk management perpetuated a downward spiral in the Anglo-Irish Bank in Ireland.

[39] Peipei Li, 'How Can Corporate Governance Control Enterprise's Financial Risk?' (2009) at papers.ssrn.com/sol3/papers.cfm?abstract_id=1523519; Sean Lyons, 'In Defense of the Corporation' (2009) 66 *Internal Auditor* 1; Justin N Bezis, 'Conceptualizing the Failure of Financial Institutions and the Role of Risk Management in Averting Failure: The CLS Model' (2013) at papers.ssrn.com/sol3/papers.cfm?abstract_id=2196556.

[40] Robert T Miller, 'Oversight Liability for Risk-Management Failures at Financial Firms' (2010) 84 *Southern California Law Review* 47.

[41] Karl S Okamoto, 'After the Bailout: Regulating Systemic Moral Hazard' (2009) 57 *UCLA Law Review* 183 argues that it would be quite impossible to define what optimal risk-taking is from a perspective of social utility.

intervention be made into risk management since risk misjudgements are a necessary learning process for firms?

Moore argues that the post-crisis emphasis on risk management intends to shape risk management towards risk moderation.[42] Hence, regulators' conception of risk management is not merely with reference to business needs, but is shaped by social expectations and mood. In this sense, regulatory expectations of the enhanced risk management function and framework in firms will be based on a public interest perception of what socially optimal risk-taking is at the given point in time. The risk management function in firms, in particular, will need to respond to such enhanced regulatory expectations.

To what extent has financial regulation become more prescriptive in substantive matters of risk decisions for financial businesses? It may be argued that the reforms that enhance the risk management function and framework in firms are meta-regulatory[43] in nature, albeit with more prescriptive requirements than under the pre-crisis regime, and hence regulation does not intervene in the substantive decisions on risk tolerances and preferences that firms will set. Further, it could arguably be unduly stifling for financial businesses if financial regulation reforms become prescriptive over matters of substantive risk-taking decisions. However, increasingly prescriptive prudential regulation, as discussed in chapter one could steer incentives in such a way as to make strategic decision-making in financial business conform to regulators' conception of socially accepted risk appetite. Further, macro-prudential regulation,[44] a new regulatory framework and toolkit introduced in the UK and EU after the global financial crisis, could prescribe intrusive measures[45] that directly curtail the type and volume of risky business firms engage in. In light of the wider framework

[42] Moore, 'The Evolving Contours' (n 14).

[43] It is noted that Enriques and Zetzsche are highly sceptical of the meta-regulation of risk management as such a form of juridification of risk management risks entailing moral hazard on the part of regulators and stakeholders while still being a developing discipline, and juridification tends to encourage standardisation and convergence in order to avoid civil or regulatory liability. Such standardisation may be undesirable as it puts pressure on risk management to be segregated as a formal, compliance issue and risk management may fail to serve its unique purposes for the firm. See Luca Enriques and Dirk Zetzsche, 'The Risky Business of Regulating Risk Management in Listed Companies' (2013) at papers.ssrn.com/sol3/papers.cfm?abstract_id=2344314, and (2013) 103 *European Company and Financial Law Review* 271.

[44] See Mads Andenas and Iris H-Y Chiu, *The Foundations and Future of Financial Regulation: Governance for Responsibility* (Oxford: Routledge, 2014) Part 4.

[45] eg, the powers granted to the Financial Policy Committee of the Bank of England under The Bank of England Act 1998 (Macro-prudential Measures) (No 2) Order [2015]; HM Treasury, *The Financial Policy Committee's Housing Market Tools* (October 2014) on potentially giving the FPC powers to introduce loan-to-value ratios or other measures that may curb an excessively bubbly housing market. These measures would directly affect business activities in the financial sector relating to credit extension and residential mortgage businesses.

of potential regulatory intervention into substantive risk-taking by banks and financial institutions, the risk management function in firms would have to be mindful of the enhanced regulatory expectations of this aspect of internal control in securing regulatory and not just firm objectives.

Sections B and C will therefore highlight the challenges in post-crisis reforms that attempt to make risk management more pronounced and important in firms. The reforms have been introduced mainly in the organisational dimension, and although the organisational position and power of the risk management function will improve under the reforms, there are limitations to what such organisational reforms can achieve. Such limitations are due to (a) the essential regulatory difficulty in governing risk-taking at firms, and (b) the emerging nature of professionalism in the risk management profession. These sections will discuss critically the disjunctions between regulatory expectations and the efficacy of the risk management function at firms, in relation to the pre-crisis context and post-crisis reforms.

The next section now turns to exploring the weaknesses of risk management in the pre-crisis context and points out how organisational weaknesses have caused the failure of risk management. Reforms to address these weaknesses have been introduced and this section will evaluate their achievements and limitations.

B. DISJUNCTIONS BETWEEN REGULATORY EXPECTATIONS AND THE ROLE OF THE RISK MANAGEMENT FUNCTION: ANALYSING THE ORGANISATIONAL DIMENSION

The risk management function sits within but is an important centre of the risk management framework in banks and financial institutions. This section explores the organisational positioning and power of the risk management function at banks and financial institutions in the pre-crisis landscape as well as the post-crisis environment. This section will analyse to what extent post-crisis reforms have changed the organisational dimension for the risk management function, the achievements of such reforms, and what limitations remain.

The Constitution of the Specialist Risk Management Function

The pre-crisis European and UK legislation left the decision whether to install a separate institution of a specialist risk management function to banks and financial institutions according to the nature, scale, size and complexity of their business. Hence, firms could determine for themselves what emphasis they wished to place on risk management as part of the overall strategic direction of the business. It has generally been agreed that risk management functions were 'weak' in the pre-crisis era. Risk management need not reside in a specialist function, but could be seen as a patchwork of bottom-up techniques driven by specific transactions such as hedging or the use of financial derivatives.[46] Patchy and un-integrated forms of risk management have been identified as a key flaw in a number of reflective reports in relation to bank failures and scandals in the crisis.[47] Risk management functions suffered from organisational neglect, many of which were not placed at a sufficiently high level or were endowed with adequate power and resources.

European legislation for banks now provides for the institution of a separate, permanent and independent risk management function.[48] Such a function should also be independent of business influence,[49] a point that will be discussed shortly.

The specialist risk management function is seen as an antidote to overcome certain risk management flaws observed in the banks and financial institutions that suffered in the global financial crisis. Such flaws relate to the low profile or sidelining of the risk management function. Risk management could be carried out narrowly in 'silo' approaches embedded in individual business lines. In UBS' self-reflecting report in 2008, UBS identified the relatively low profile of risk management as a problem relating

[46] There is much evidence relating to transaction-driven risk management, see Pagano, 'How Theories of Financial Intermediation and Corporate Risk-Management Influence Bank Risk-Taking Behavior' (n 24); on active risk management such as buying and selling derivative instruments, see A Sinan Cebenoyan and Philip Strahan, 'Risk Management, Capital Structure and Lending at Banks' (2001) at ssrn.com/abstract=293378 and Consuelo Silva Buston, 'Active Risk Management and Banking Stability' (2012) at ssrn.com/abstract=2049390, two studies that document active risk management in banks and financial institutions, although they present different findings on the benefits of such active risk management. But see Kristine Watson Hankins, 'How Do Financial Firms Manage Risk? Unraveling the Interaction of Financial and Operational Hedging' (2009) at ssrn.com/abstract=936486 for a contrary view.

[47] UBS AG, *Shareholder Report on UBS's Write-Downs* (18 April 2008) at www.ubs.com/1/ShowMedia/investors/share_information/shareholderreport?contentId=140333&name=080418ShareholderReport.pdf, discussed in Paul Rose, 'Regulating Risk by "Strengthening Corporate Governance"' (2010) 17 *Connecticut Insurance Law Journal* 1; House of Commons and House of Lords, Parliamentary Commission on Banking Standards, *An Accident Waiting to Happen: The Failure of HBOS* (2012–13, HL 144, HC 705) paras 19 and 50.

[48] Directive 2013/36/EU of the European Parliament and of the Council of 26 June 2013 on access to the activity of credit institutions and the prudential supervision of credit institutions and investment firms, amending Directive 2002/87/EC and repealing Directives 2006/48/EC and 2006/49/EC (CRD IV Directive) Art 76(5). Supported by *EBA Guidelines* (n 1) paras 24.2, 25. Much of the *EBA Guidelines* are modelled on international best practice recommendations issued by Basel Committee on Banking Supervision, *Principles for Enhancing Corporate Governance* (October 2010) 17ff , para 69ff.

[49] *EBA Guidelines* (n 1) para 25.

to the lack of sufficiently skilled and senior risk managers who were unable to challenge front office decision-makers.[50] A commentator has also discussed the sidelining of risk management in the bankrupt investment bank Lehman Brothers in the US, and the investment bank Merrill Lynch which was rescued by the Bank of America in the nick of time.[51]

Post-crisis, the profile of the separate specialist risk management function would be enhanced by the leadership of a Chief Risk Officer who has sufficient expertise, experience and seniority to challenge an institution's decisions on exposure to risk.[52] EU legislation for banks has endorsed this,[53] but it is not certain if a Chief Risk Officer would be part of the senior management team including the Chief Executive and Financial Officers.[54] Some empirical evidence seems to suggest that giving the Chief Risk Officer a position of seniority, such as to be in the senior management team, could be important for establishing a risk culture as part of the organisational culture in firms.[55] The UK[56] has also provided that where Chief Risk Officers are appointed they should be ensured sufficient authority and stature.[57] The stature of the Chief Risk Officer should be ensured in terms of organisational positioning in peer relation to senior management. Further, the stature of the Chief Risk Officer is also ensured by establishing the new perception that such a person is an expert. McKenna writes that expert power can exert influence within an organisation by virtue of exclusive knowledge or expertise, especially professional expertise.[58] The specialist

[50] Discussed in Rose, 'Regulating Risk' (n 47).

[51] See Jonas Prager, 'The Financial Crisis of 2007/8: Misaligned Incentives, Bank Mismanagement, and Troubling Policy Implications' (2012) at ssrn.com/abstract=2094662.

[52] *EBA Guidelines* (n 1) para 27.3; see also Basel Committee, *Principles for Enhancing Corporate Governance* (n 48) 17ff, para 71ff. The Financial Stability Board also recommends core responsibilities for the Chief Risk Officer especially for systemically important financial institutions, see Financial Stability Board, *Principles for an Effective Risk Appetite Framework* (18 November 2013) para 4.3.

[53] Art 76(5), CRD IV Directive.

[54] This point is also not entirely clear in Art 75(5) of the proposed CRD IV Directive which requires the CRO to be an independent senior executive. However, the international best practice in the Financial Stability Board's recommendation is to give the CRO a sufficiently high stature alongside the CEO and CFO, see Financial Stability Board, *Principles for an Effective Risk Appetite Framework* (18 November 2013).

[55] See Anette Mikes, 'Risk Management and Calculative Cultures' (2007) at ssrn.Com/Abstract=1138636.

[56] Legislative reforms on Chief Risk Officers are in response to David Walker, 'A Review of Corporate Governance in UK Banks and Other Financial Industry Entities: Final Recommendations' (26 November 2009) at webarchive.nationalarchives.gov.uk and www.hm-treasury.gov.uk/d/walker_review_261109.pdf, Recommendation 24.

[57] PRA and FCA (formerly FSA) Handbooks, SYSC, 21.1.2.

[58] Eugene McKenna, *Business Psychology and Organizational Behaviour*, 4th edn (New York: Taylor & Francis Psychology Press, 2006) 423.

risk management function, flanked by stature and expertise,[59] is intended to mitigate the problems of low profile, marginalisation or low quality risk management identified in banks that have suffered losses or scandals in the global financial crisis.

Further, the specialist risk management function provides a central point for the institution of a firm-wide risk management framework[60] and prevents risk management from being narrowly managed in silos or confined to business units. A firm-wide risk management framework is closer to the enterprise-wide risk management model,[61] where risk management is led at the strategic level by the Board, rolls out into all aspects of business and operations, and is considered holistically. EU legislation for banks and investment firms now imposes on Boards the obligation to approve and periodically review the 'strategies and policies for taking up, managing, monitoring and mitigating the risks the institution is or might be exposed to'.[62]

Under a firm-wide risk management framework, Board leadership is needed for the establishment of a 'risk philosophy', the identification of a 'risk taxonomy' and determination of the firm's 'risk appetite' that should govern business decisions. 'Risk philosophy', according to Banks, is a clear statement from the Board and senior management about the firm's values and attitudes towards risk-taking.[63] The Board and senior management must then engage in establishing a 'risk taxonomy' which is a list of risks identified for the business of the firm, that is to say, the comprehensive mapping of the risk environment in which the business of the firm is situated.[64] The establishment of a clear taxonomy of risks also forms the basis of a common language of

[59] Improvements to the stature of the Chief Risk Officer and the expertise profile of the CRO and risk managers are discerned to have taken place, see Ernst & Young and the Institute of International Finance, *Progress in Financial Services Risk Management: A Survey of the Major Financial Institutions* (2012) 5, 30ff.

[60] *EBA Guidelines* (n 1) para 25.3.

[61] Brian W Nocco and René M Stultz, 'Enterprise Risk Management: Theory and Practice' (2006) 18 *Journal of Applied Corporate Finance* 8; Lisa K Meulbroek, 'A Senior Manager's Guide to Integrated Risk Management' in Donald H Chew (ed), *Corporate Risk Management* (New York: Columbia Business School Publishing, 2008); René M Stultz, 'Rethinking Risk Management' in Donald H Chew (ed), *Corporate Risk Management* (New York: Columbia Business School Publishing, 2008); Annetta Cortez, *Winning at Risk* (Chichester: John Wiley & Sons, 2011) 142ff.

[62] Art 76(1), CRD IV Directive; Art 16(2), MiFID II Directive.

[63] Erik Banks, *Risk Culture* (Basingstoke: Palgrave Macmillan, 2012) 11.

[64] ibid, 13; Cortez, *Winning at Risk* (n 61) 15–21 and 23–25; Stephen Bainbridge, 'Caremark and Enterprise Risk Management' (2009) 34 *Journal of Corporation Law* 967; Dan Rosen and Stavros A Zenios, 'Enterprise-Wide Asset and Liability Management: Issues, Institutions, and Models' in SA Zenios and WT Ziemba (eds), *Handbook of Asset and Liability Management* Vol 1 (North Holland: Elsevier, 2006).

risk in the firm which helps in cementing a risk culture.[65] The Board and senior management must then clearly specify the firm's 'risk appetite', ie, the firm's tolerance for risk that can be supported by its capital,[66] so that such clear articulation can be the basis for business decisions taken lower down in the firm. In Banks' words, Boards and senior management need to establish high-level 'risk rules' that must be operationally implemented and be effective.[67] 'Risk rules' refers to the formal codification of rules in the firm related to the allocation of risk-taking rights across the firm, the assignment of monitoring and supervision of risk-taking activities, the penalties for violation of the risk rules, forms of reporting, and transparency and escalation processes.[68] Further, international developments are afoot to provide for some forms of standardisation into how firms can get to grips with instituting a firm-wide risk management framework. The Financial Stability Board (FSB) is introducing an initiative to develop a common risk assessment framework for banks and financial institutions, especially systemically important financial institutions.[69] This initiative would compel firms to set their risk appetites, limits and management policies in a common language and framework in order for regulators to more easily and comparably evaluate the quality of risk management in those institutions. An empirical survey by Ernst & Young documents increased Board attention[70] to the clear articulation of firms' risk appetite and it is observed that changes are taking place in the risk management framework in many firms. The survey also documents many firms perceiving themselves as being on the way to achieving a sound risk culture.[71] In sum, the organisational enhancement of the risk management function seems essential to the institution of a risk and control culture at firms.[72]

[65] Cortez, *Winning at Risk* (n 61) 29; Paul Sweeting, *Financial Enterprise Risk Management* (Cambridge: Cambridge University Press, 2011) ch 2.

[66] Banks, *Risk Culture* (n 63) 12; Cortez, *Winning at Risk* (n 61) 25–31, 126–40; René Stultz, 'Risk Management Failures: What Are They and When Do They Happen?' (2008) 20 *Journal of Applied Corporate Finance* 58 argues that setting the risk appetite for the firm is a highest management responsibility. See FSB, *Principles for an Effective Risk Appetite Framework* (n 54).

[67] Banks, *Risk Culture* (n 63) 11.

[68] ibid. Also see FSB, *Principles for an Effective Risk Appetite Framework: Consultative Document* (n 52) paras 1, 2, 3 and 4.

[69] FSB, *Principles for an Effective Risk Appetite Framework* (n 54); Financial Stability Board, *Guidance on Supervisory Interaction with Financial Institutions on Risk Culture: Consultation Document* (18 November 2013).

[70] Ernst & Young and the Institute of International Finance, *Progress in Financial Services Risk Management* (n 59) 15–16.

[71] ibid, 15–19.

[72] Simon Ashby, Tommaso Palermo and Michael Power, *Risk Culture in Financial Organisations* (Interim Report, November 2012; Research Report, 2014).

The risk management function would be enhanced in its organisational position and profile under a firm-wide risk management framework and would less likely suffer from the marginalisation and weaknesses associated with a silo approach taken by a number of firms in the pre-crisis era. Under the silo approach, risk management functions are partitioned along business lines and serve the needs of the business unit concerned without having a holistic appreciation of firm-wide risks. The silo approach is fragmented and disadvantageous, as such narrowly defined risk management may turn out to be inadequate,[73] and risk becoming too entangled with business perspectives and therefore not independent. Having a silo approach to risk management also undermined cooperation and coordination between business units, and impeded information flows relating to risk across the organisation and upwards to high levels. However, it could be argued that the pre-crisis 'silo' approach is largely due to the structure of prudential regulation.[74] International standards for micro-prudential regulation first addressed only credit risk by providing for a framework of capital adequacy in the Basel I Capital Accord,[75] and then branched out into addressing market risk in light of bottom-up industry developments.[76] Only in 2004 did the Basel II Capital Accord[77] address the suite of credit, market and operational risks as the main risks banks and financial institutions face, although the different risks are treated differently.[78] The approach to managing operational risk is also underdeveloped,[79] and operational risks are regarded as arising out of individual business lines rather than in a holistic and aggregated approach. Moreover, the definition of operational risk excludes reputational and legal risk, and there is an insufficient recognition in the financial sector for risk management related to systemic risk.[80]

[73] Mario Draghi, 'Observations on Risk Management Practices During the Recent Market Turbulence' in Melvin R Turley (ed), *Reforming Risk in Financial Markets* (New York: Nova-Science Publishers, 2009) 119ff; Bainbridge, 'Caremark and Enterprise Risk Management' (n 64) referring to a Towers Perrin survey in 2008 that found a high prevalence of the silo approach in pre-crisis risk management at firms; Ernst & Young and the Institute of International Finance, *Making Strides in Financial Services Management* (2011) cited in Eddy Wymeersch, 'Risk in Financial Institutions: Is it Managed?' (2012) at ssrn.com/abstract=1988926.

[74] Mikes, 'Risk Management and Calculative Cultures' (n 55).

[75] Basel Committee, *Basel I* (n 3).

[76] Basel Committee on Banking Supervision, *Amendment to the Capital Accord to Incorporate Market Risks* (Basel: BIS, 1996) at www.bis.org/publ/bcbs24.pdf?noframes=1.

[77] Basel Committee, *Basel II* (n 4).

[78] Simon Gleeson, *International Banking Regulation* (Oxford: Oxford University Press, 2009) generally.

[79] Andreas A Jobst, 'The Credit Crisis and Operational Risk—Implications for Practitioners and Regulators' (2010) 5 *Journal of Operational Risk* 43; Guy Ford and Maike Sundmacher, 'Leading Indicators for Operational Risk: Case Studies in Financial Services' (2004) at ssrn.com/abstract=963235.

[80] Douglas O Edwards, 'An Unfortunate "Tail": Reconsidering Risk Management Incentives after the Financial Crisis of 2007–2009' (2010) 81 *University of Colorado Law Review*

Draghi, in a post-crisis empirical research, concluded that the key distinguishing risk management feature between successful and unsuccessful banks in the crisis was the practice of enterprise-wide risk management.[81] Enterprise-wide risk management in successful banks enabled them to deal with a more comprehensive suite of risks. Further, banks which practised enterprise-wide risk management were also better able to promptly adapt themselves to changing situations in the face of turmoil in the global financial crisis. The Parliamentary Committee on Banking Standards report on the failure of HBOS in the global financial crisis points out that although HBOS seemed to have a central specialist risk management function, the practice of risk management was very much at a divisional level and such a silo approach marginalised the central risk management function and affected its efficacy.[82] The post-crisis emphasis on the specialist risk management function which occupies a central position in the firm-wide risk management framework is intended to become a more effective monitor of firm-wide risk-taking.

However, it is queried whether the enterprise-wide risk management framework caters to the different technical aspects of specific financial risks. Enterprise-wide risk management does not substitute for the unique technical aspects of managing different types of financial risks and specialist fragmentation in such risk management would need to be managed by the risk management function. Significant differences[83] between risks in terms of nature and time horizons remain and it would be important to develop a balance between holistic management at a high level and differentiated approaches at a more granular level.

Further, as the risk management function sits at the centre of an enterprise-wide risk management framework, there would be a need to reconcile the somewhat competing notions of instituting firm-wide ownership of risk and reliance on the expert and specialist risk management function to manage risk. The risk management function would likely have to manage this dilemma to ensure that there is effective

247; Phillippe Jorion, 'Risk Management Lessons from the Credit Crisis' (2009) 15 *European Financial Management* 923; Wymeersch, 'Risk in Financial Institutions' (n 73); Linda Allen and Anthony Saunders, 'Incorporating Systemic Risk Influences into Risk Measurements: A Survey of the Literature' (2004) 26 *Journal of Financial Services Research* 161.

[81] Draghi, 'Observations on Risk Management Practices' (n 73). See also Michelle Harner, 'Ignoring the Writing on the Wall: The Role of Enterprise Risk Management in the Economic Crisis' (2010) 5 *Journal of Business & Technology Law* 45.

[82] Parliamentary Commission on Banking Standards, *An Accident Waiting to Happen* (n 47) paras 54–61.

[83] Joshua V Rosenberg and Til Schuermann, 'A General Approach to Integrated Risk Management with Skewed, Fat-Tailed Risks' (Federal Reserve Bank of New York Staff Reports, 2004).

diffusion of responsibility in the firm while putting in place an effective and centralised monitoring system for risk-taking.

The book also cautions against adopting the enterprise-wide risk management framework as a panacea against future failures of risk judgements and poor outcomes for financial firms. It would be unrealistic to pitch regulatory expectations at that level, and arguably unfair to find fault with the risk management framework or functions at firms with the benefit of hindsight should poor outcomes occur. It is arguable that regulatory expectations are high for what risk management can achieve in firms, and the book cautions that disjunctions may still occur in spite of organisational enhancement of the risk management framework and functions in firms. This section will point out where disjunctions could occur, and these are largely due to the inherent limitations of the meta-regulatory framework for risk management. Such a critical analysis does not negate the achievements of the reforms in overcoming some sub-optimal problems identified in the global financial crisis. It however points out the limitations of regulation and cautions against excessive regulatory expectations.

The Independence of the Specialist Risk Management Function

Besides instituting the stature and centrality of a specialist risk management function at banks and financial institutions, post-crisis reforms also emphasise the independence of the risk management function.[84] The quality of independence ensures that the specialist risk management function is not compromised or unduly influenced by business interests so that it can provide critical challenge on business decisions on risk exposures. Empirical research conducted to examine the relation between the quality of risk management at banks and financial institutions has used 'independence' as a quality indicator for strong risk management, and has concluded that strong risk management has a positive relationship with the survival and success of banks and financial institutions in the global financial crisis.[85]

There are many factors that shape the quality of independence: the accountability channel; the setting of remuneration for the Chief Risk Officer and risk managers; the appointment and removal of the Chief Risk Officer; the adoption or otherwise of an embedment framework for risk managers in relation to business units; and informal factors such as respect for the specialist risk management function at leadership level and the relations between the risk management function and business unit managers.

[84] Art 76(5), CRD IV Directive.

[85] See Ellul and Yerramilli, 'Stronger Risk Controls' (n 37).

European initiatives provide that the specialist risk management function should not perform tasks that fall within the scope of activities the function is supposed to monitor, or be subordinate to persons performing tasks that the function is supposed to monitor.[86] Further, the remuneration of the risk management function's staff should not be linked to the performance of the activities the function monitors.[87] UK legislation specifically provides that the Chief Risk Officer's remuneration should be decided by the Board.[88] These measures ensure that the risk management function is independent of business considerations.

On accountability, allowing the Chief Risk Officer to report to the Board directly or to the Audit or Risk Committee of the Board is intended to provide the Chief Risk Officer with independence from possible interference from senior management or intimidation from aggressive Chief Executive Officers.[89] In the failed investment bank Lehman Brothers, CEO Richard Fuld, known for his dominating personality, fired the Chief Risk Officer Madelyn Antoncic in 2007 for urging caution in the bank's excessive engagement in the mortgage securitisation business. EU legislation,[90] the EBA Guidelines[91] and UK legislation[92] all provide for accountability for the Chief Risk Officer directly to the Board. Ernst & Young's survey of international banks on this however shows a mixed picture in practice. Many Chief Risk Officers report to the Chief Executive Officer, but some firms institute a system of dual accountability where Chief Risk Officers report to both the Chief Executive Officer and the risk committee of the Board.[93] The survey nevertheless seems to indicate that however the reporting channel is structured, Chief Risk Officers have direct access to Boards[94] and hence the kind of pre-crisis undermining of the independence of Chief Risk Officers is being decisively phased out in practice. The EU and UK legislation also protect the independence of the Chief Risk Officer by ensuring that she or he would not be arbitrarily removed without approval by the Board.[95]

86 *EBA Guidelines* (n 1) para 24.6.
87 ibid.
88 PRA and FCA (formerly FSA) Handbooks, SYSC 21.1.4(1).
89 The CRD IV Directive ensures access to the Board, and removal only by the Board, see Art 76(5).
90 Art 76(5), CRD IV Directive, ibid.
91 *EBA Guidelines* (n 1) para 24.8.
92 PRA and FCA (formerly FSA) Handbooks, SYSC 21.1.3.
93 Ernst & Young and the Institute of International Finance, *Progress in Financial Services Risk Management* (n 59) 30.
94 ibid, 18.
95 *EBA Guidelines* (n 1) para 27.6; Art 76(5), CRD IV Directive; PRA and FCA (formerly FSA) Handbooks, SYSC 21.1.4(2).

Although the institution of a specialist risk management function achieves a form of departmental centralisation, many commentators support the embedment of risk officers or managers in individual business units so that risk managers can be close to the making of business decisions and be in command of business knowledge. This is an area left to firm implementation and not governed by EU or UK regulation. The embedment of risk officers in the front office may create a more efficient working environment as time is not wasted in seeking to bridge the distance between front and back offices.[96] The central risk management function led by the Chief Risk Officer could articulate and roll out risk management policies in a common language across the firm, and lead a team of decentralised risk officers operating in individual business units who should apply risk management policies consistently across the firm.[97] The embedment of risk officers in the front office may improve work efficiency and empower the risk management function with more information (a point that will be discussed below), and also cultivate a greater sense of ownership of risk in the front office.[98] However, the closeness between risk officers and business units may foster sympathy for business perspectives and may affect the application of independent judgement.[99] Hence, the centralised risk management function must be able to effectively manage and monitor decentralised risk officers.

Although commentators mentioned above support the embedment of risk officers in front offices in order to make the risk management function more effective and robust, and to facilitate a keener ownership of the risk culture at every business level, the informal dynamics between the risk management function and business units remain key to how risk management is carried out at the transactional and operational levels. Lam reminds of the importance of a partnership relationship between the risk management function and business units so that risk managers may be seen as a consultancy resource and not as an opposing nemesis.[100] Carrel recommends that the risk management function should engage or train business units in looking at risk factors and scenarios so that business units may not remain detached from risk management but may be able to embrace the importance of risk management as integral to their functions.[101] Sweeting also argues that the Chief Risk Officer should

[96] Philippe Carrel, *The Handbook of Risk Management: Implementing a Post-Crisis Corporate Culture* (Chichester: John Wiley & Sons, 2010) 67.

[97] Joël Bessis, *Risk Management in Banking* (Chichester: John Wiley & Sons, 2011) ch 4.

[98] Carrel, *The Handbook of Risk Management* (n 96) chs 2 and 3; Sweeting, *Financial Enterprise Risk Management* (n 65) ch 2.

[99] Bessis, *Risk Management in Banking* (n 97) ch 4.

[100] James Lam, *Enterprise Risk Management: From Incentives to Controls* (Chichester John Wiley & Sons, 2003) ch 6.

[101] Carrel, *The Handbook of Risk Management* (n 96) chs 2–6.

have regular contact with business units and should manage such relationships in a way that mitigates any offensive-defensive positions.[102] The informal factors regarding the relational dynamics between the risk management function and business units are therefore important in maintaining a sound balance between securing the independence of an effective risk management function and allowing the risk management function to be persuasive and respected by business units.

The Power and Responsibilities of the Specialist Risk Management Function

It could be argued that one of the weaknesses of the risk management function in the pre-crisis era is that there are no specific responsibilities set out in regulation for the risk management function. Hence, the function could be entirely subject to organisational manipulation in terms of the needs it serves.

European initiatives now provide for specific responsibilities for the risk management function in banks. First, the risk management function is specifically asked to monitor transactions with related parties,[103] but such monitoring may be more pursuant to the traditional corporate governance concern of managerial self-dealing and the agency problem. In terms of responsibilities related to prudential risk monitoring, the risk management function is asked to identify material risks arising out of the complexity of the institution's legal structure.[104] The EU and UK are rolling out legislative reforms on recovery and resolution plans,[105] and it would be envisaged that the risk management function would have a role to play in those. The 'recovery plan', more popularly known as the 'living will', is an internationally endorsed measure to facilitate orderly resolution of a financial institution in crisis at minimum social cost.[106] Such 'recovery plans' would be drawn up under the supervision of the regulator. The flip side of the recovery plan is the 'resolution plan', which would involve providing for options in winding down the institution's business while

[102] Sweeting, *Financial Enterprise Risk Management* (n 65) chs 2 and 3.

[103] *EBA Guidelines* (n 1) para 26.6.

[104] ibid, para 26.7.

[105] Directive 2014/59/EU of the European Parliament and of the Council of 15 May 2014 establishing a framework for the recovery and resolution of credit institutions and investment firms and amending Council Directive 82/891/EEC, and Directives 2001/24/EC, 2002/47/EC, 2004/25/EC, 2005/56/EC, 2007/36/EC, 2011/35/EU, 2012/30/EU and 2013/36/EU, and Regulations (EU) No 1093/2010 and (EU) No 648/2012, of the European Parliament and of the Council (BRRD) Arts 4ff and 10ff.

[106] Financial Stability Forum, 'FSF Principles for Cross-border Cooperation on Crisis Management' (2 April 2009) at www.financialstabilityboard.org/publications/r_0904c.pdf, Principle 8.

keeping critical functions operating.[107] Recovery and resolution plans are regulatory responsibilities to be discharged at the highest levels of management.[108] The role of the risk management function in identifying the risks pertaining to the legal structures in the bank or financial institution would not only serve strategic purposes, but also regulatory objectives in discerning the risks that arise out of structure that may affect crisis management and resolution.

Further, the risk management function is tasked to monitor the impact of material changes[109] such as mergers,[110] exceptional transactions or the development of new products or business lines[111] and any new risks[112] that emerge for the institution. In particular, in the development of new products or business lines, banks and financial institutions are asked to implement product governance and approval processes[113] which involves senior management oversight and cross-organisational involvement from all aspects of internal control and relevant business units so that risks may be comprehensively discussed and considered.[114] Product governance for retail banking and investment products is to be more tightly regulated[115] and internal control functions such as risk management would play a key part in ensuring that internal control procedures are adequate for evaluating whether a product developed is appropriate for its target market, whether the product is tested and appropriately distributed and marketed, and whether appropriate reviews for the product and remedial action are prepared for. The involvement of risk management and internal control generally in product governance is seen as necessary to mitigate prudential and conduct risks. Novel products can heighten prudential risks if wholesale sector institutions retain excessive levels[116] of novel and

[107] Basel Committee on Banking Supervision, *Resolution Policies and Frameworks—Progress So Far* (6 July 2011) at www.bis.org/publ/bcbs200.pdf, para 169ff.

[108] Arts 4ff, 10ff, BRRD.

[109] *EBA Guidelines* (n 1) paras 26.8, 26.9.

[110] See also Basel Committee, *Principles for Enhancing Corporate Governance* (n 48) 21, para 89 in relation to the risks posed by mergers and acquisitions upon complexity of structure.

[111] *EBA Guidelines* (n 1) para 23.

[112] ibid, paras 26.12, 26.13.

[113] ibid, paras 23.1–23.4. See also Basel Committee, *Principles for Enhancing Corporate Governance* (n 48) 21, para 88; CRM Policy Group, 'Containing Systemic Risk: The Road to Reform—The Report of the CRMPG III' in Melvin R Turley (ed), *Reforming Risk in Financial Markets* (New York: NovaScience Publishers, 2009) 1.

[114] Already in the *EBA Guidelines* (n 1) 36, para 23, and also to be in ESMA's technical guidelines for investment firms under the MiFID II Directive 2014, see ESMA, *Consultation Paper* (n 7) 46, para 17 dealing with product governance including managing conflicts of interest, understanding risks and returns, and target market.

[115] EBA, *Draft Guidelines on Product Oversight and Governance Arrangements for Retail Banking Products* (November 2014); ESMA, *Final Report: ESMA's Technical Advice to the Commission on MiFID II and MiFIR* (December 2014) 47ff.

[116] Gilles Bénéplanc and Jean-Charles Rochet, *Risk Management in Turbulent Times* (New York: Oxford University Press, 2011) 7ff.

untested securitised products,[117] as in the global financial crisis of 2008–09. Conduct risks could materialise in the form of mis-selling which can subsequently attract reputational and compensation cost.

The risk management function is also tasked to be involved in the establishment of limits such as trading or lending limits in line with the risk appetite of the firm, and would have the power to assess and report violations and recommend remedies.[118] Such power should be supported by a general institutional framework for disciplining breaches and fraudulent behaviour. Kanter argues that the power of 'enforcement' is a source of real power,[119] and hence, giving the risk management function a role in internal enforcement and discipline is important in securing its power.

Commentators have also suggested a couple of areas that should be specifically prescribed as risk management responsibilities so that the risk management function would be co-opted in decision-making and not left out. Lam suggests that the risk management function should monitor for organisational concentrations of power that may be unchecked,[120] while Kross advocates that the risk management function should be especially involved in 'mega' projects as complex and large-scale projects may involve multiple risks over a long time horizon.[121] However, in overall terms, the Ernst & Young survey concluded that there has been a significant expansion in the risk management function's influence and power, particularly on the part of the Chief Risk Officer.[122]

In general, the risk management function has improved in terms of organisational power as the risk management function is overall given a seat at the table of strategic decision-making, to provide information to and advise the Board and senior management.[123] The specification of involvement in strategic decision-making not only expands the responsibility, but also the power of the risk management function. Kanter defines organisational power as 'the ability to get things done and mobilise resources'.[124] The regulatory elevation of the risk management function positions the function for the exercise of power.

[117] Richard E Mendales, 'Collateralized Explosive Devices: Why Securities Regulation Failed to Prevent the CDO Meltdown, and How to Fix it' [2009] *University of Illinois Law Review* 1359.

[118] *EBA Guidelines* (n 1) paras 26.14–26.17.

[119] Rosabeth Moss Kanter, *Men and Women of the Corporation* (New York: Basic Books, 1977, rep 1983) 174.

[120] Lam, *Enterprise Risk Management* (n 100) ch 2. Such monitoring may also mitigate incidents of departmental deviations or rogue trading, as discussed earlier under 'Risk Culture'.

[121] Wilhelm Kross, *Organised Opportunities: Risk Management in Financial Services Operations* (Chichester: John Wiley & Sons, 2007) 131ff.

[122] Ernst & Young and the Institute of International Finance, *Progress in Financial Services Risk Management* (n 59) 30.

[123] *EBA Guidelines* (n 1) paras 26.2, 26.3.

[124] Kanter, *Men and Women* (n 119) 166.

Resources for the Risk Management Function

The organisational positioning, powers and responsibilities of the risk management function have to be supported by an adequate resourcing of the risk management function. The resources for an effective risk management function include human resources in terms of adequate staff count and skilled expertise, a developed information communication system in order to assist the risk management function in gaining access to all relevant information and monitoring of business units, a reporting system to senior management, and a suite of developed information technology resources and databases for use in risk analysis and measurement.

The lack of sufficiently skilled staff in risk management was one of the factors identified by UBS in its self-reflective report[125] regarding its risk management failures, as well as in a critical discussion[126] of the state of internal control at Société Générale where rogue trader Jerome Kerviel caused massive losses. European initiatives now require the risk management function to be adequately staffed and trained.[127] The Ernst & Young survey also reports that in practice, banks and financial institutions have increased skilled headcount in the risk management function significantly even if reductions in numbers have been taking place in other departments.[128] Increased regulation of the risk management framework and function has caused banks and financial institutions to prioritise the development of the risk management function.

Next, it is important for the risk management function to have unfettered access to information so as to be able to conduct risk analysis and measurement robustly.[129] Whether risk analysis and measurement methodologies are themselves robust or not is another question that section C will discuss. The information mechanisms[130] in the firm need to provide a framework for supporting the actual work of risk management. In an enterprise-wide risk management framework, information flows

[125] UBS AG, *Shareholder Report* (n 47) discussed in Rose, 'Regulating Risk' (n 47) 1.

[126] Eric Pichet, 'What Governance Lessons Should Be Learnt from the Societe Générale's Kerviel Affair?' (2008) 3 *La Revue Française de Gouvernance d'Entreprise* 117.

[127] *EBA Guidelines* (n 1) paras 24.7, 24.8.

[128] Ernst & Young and the Institute of International Finance, *Progress in Financial Services Risk Management* (n 59) 30.

[129] See also Basel Committee, *Principles for Enhancing Corporate Governance* (n 48) 22–23, para 92ff.

[130] See Michael Pirson and Shann Turnbull, 'Corporate Governance, Risk Management, and the Financial Crisis: An Information Processing View' (2011) 19 *Corporate Governance: An International Review* 459 for a view emphasising the importance of information transmission and processing to facilitate risk management. The author does not however think that widening the information channels to stakeholders in firm-wide risk management on a regular basis is necessarily ideal.

should be enhanced and open throughout the organisation.[131] Information flows should be fluid both top-down and bottom-up,[132] in respect of the communication of risk philosophy and appetites by the Board and senior management and in respect of reporting from bottom-up as to the state of implementation, monitoring, stress testing and feedback. Banks is of the view that enhanced and open communications throughout the firm creates transparency, responsiveness to problems and respect for risk management, allowing the risk management function to be freer in discussing and challenging issues across levels, enhancing the firm's overall capacity to address problems promptly.[133] Such transparency also facilitates coordination and cooperation across levels in the firm. Enhanced information flows and transparency in a firm may be facilitated by cross-divisional communications such as meetings and interactions and regular reporting to senior management. Carrel is of the view that in such a framework, risk becomes a language to be used 'to receive instructions as much as giving feedback. It is used for benchmarking, performance measurements and forecasting'.[134] Prager discusses how Goldman Sachs, the investment bank that weathered the global financial crisis in a relatively better shape than many other comparable firms, has implemented a successful risk management framework which includes weekly cross committee meetings involving senior management or non-executive director attendance.[135]

For information to be meaningful, it has to be derived from the comprehensive capture of data and robust methods in data processing. Further, information must also be practically accessible. Hence, the role of data and information technology systems play an important part in supporting the information framework for firm-wide risk management.[136] Cortez recommends that data needs to be captured over a sufficiently long period of time, at least for 15 years or as long as the firm has been in operation,[137] and the integrity and completeness of data must be ensured.[138] Godbillon-Camus et al comment that there may be ground

[131] CRM Policy Group, 'Containing Systemic Risk' (n 113); Banks, *Risk Culture* (n 63) 21ff.

[132] Carrel, *The Handbook of Risk Management* (n 96) chs 11–15.

[133] Banks, *Risk Culture* (n 63) 50ff.

[134] Carrel, *The Handbook of Risk Management* (n 96) 198ff.

[135] Prager, 'The Financial Crisis of 2007/8' (n 51).

[136] Kross, *Organised Opportunities* (n 121) 121ff; B Di Renzo, M Hillairet, M Picard, A Rifaut, C Bernard, D Hagen, P Maa and D Reinard, 'Operational Risk Management in Financial Institutions: Process Assessment in Concordance with Basel II' (2007) 12 *Software Process Improvement and Practice* 321.

[137] Cortez, *Winning at Risk* (n 61) 58ff.

[138] Laurent Frésard, Christophe Pérignon and Anders Wilhelmsson, 'The Pernicious Effects of Contaminated Data in Risk Management' (2011) at ssrn.com/abstract=1537244 argue that a lot of data feeding into risk management may be incomplete or contaminated by distorting information and caution should be used in ensuring the integrity of the data to be captured.

level practices not captured in written policies and that effort should also be made to capture such behavioural data in the firm in order to map out a complete picture of firm practices and risk.[139] The Ernst & Young survey also documents an increasing awareness in banks and financial institutions that internal transparency and data systems are crucial for effective risk management.[140] Most firms surveyed are carrying out more investment in information and data systems, capturing more quality and accurate data, and building up aggregation capacities. Further data must be well stored so as to facilitate accessibility, manipulation and use, as well as reporting.[141]

However, it has to be borne in mind that investment in the information and resource infrastructure for effective risk management is costly and many have observed how banks and financial institutions have in the pre-crisis heyday of profit-chasing, undermined cost centres such as the risk management function.[142] Post-crisis, although regulatory reform is an important driver for the overhauling of the risk management framework and function in many firms, Fehle and Psyplakov argue that firms have the tendency to minimise investment in risk management in good times as the transaction costs of risk management are high, and adopt the opposite approach of beefing up risk management in bad times in order to minimise the risk of insolvency.[143] Hence, there may be a natural tendency for firms to adopt a pro-cyclical approach to risk management. It therefore remains an open question whether the organisational frameworks mandated by post-crisis reforms will hold up the effectiveness of risk management in spirit when better times return, or will the regulatory framework for risk management which is meta-regulatory in nature be subject to cosmetic proceduralisation[144] in due course?

This section has provided the context of pre-crisis problems and a critical overview of the reforms made by post-crisis legislation to enhance the organisational dimension of the risk management frameworks and

[139] Brigitte Godbillon-Camus and Christophe J Godlewski, 'Credit Risk Management in Banks: Hard Information, Soft Information and Manipulation' (2005) at ssrn.com/abstract=882027, referring to soft information such as practices in lending based on 'soft' information which are unofficial and subjective perceptions.

[140] Ernst & Young and the Institute of International Finance, *Progress in Financial Services Risk Management* (n 59) 56–59.

[141] Cortez, *Winning at Risk* (n 61) 60.

[142] Michel Crouhy, 'Risk Management Failures During the Financial Crisis' in Robert W Kolb (ed), *Lessons from the Financial Crisis* (New Jersey: John Wiley & Sons 2010); Elizabeth Sheedy, 'The Future of Risk Modelling' in Robert W Kolb (ed), *Lessons from the Financial Crisis* (New Jersey: John Wiley & Sons, 2010).

[143] Frank Fehle and Sergey Psyplakov, 'Dynamic Risk Management: Theory and Evidence' (2005) 78 *Journal of Financial Economics* 3.

[144] eg, see Kimberly D Krawiec, 'Cosmetic Compliance and the Failure of Negotiated Governance' (2003) 81 *Washington University Law Quarterly* 487.

functions in banks and financial institutions. While there is real enhancement to the organisational positioning, profile, independence, power and resources for the risk management function, this section cautions that organisational reforms may be limited in two respects: first, the organisational reforms themselves may be limited by firm implementation within their risk cultures, which may not be optimal; and second, the organisational reforms may not overcome limitations in the substantive capacity and competence of the risk management profession. We next turn to discuss challenges for the risk management function within the overall context of risk culture in firms. The next section will discuss the professional dimension of the risk management function, and whether weaknesses in this dimension will undermine the potential of organisational reforms.

Risk Culture

'Risk culture' is defined by Banks as 'an internal sensibility, reflected in the daily thoughts and actions of all of an institution's employees, that reflects knowledge of and respect for risk'.[145] Cortez defines risk culture as 'a system of values and behaviours present throughout an organization that shape risk decisions. Risk culture influences the decisions of management and employees, even if they are not consciously weighing risks and benefits'.[146] Risk culture is more than just the risk management framework, but refers to an actual practice of risk consciousness and management at all levels in the businesses of the bank or financial institution concerned.

Risk culture could be seen as dependent on the tone at the top,[147] and hence it can be argued that regulatory initiatives to institute Board leadership and the enterprise-wide risk management framework discussed earlier would facilitate the institution of a healthy and optimal risk culture. Indeed, independent research indicates that formal organisational attributes and frameworks such as the power of the risk management function, information systems and flows, and the interaction between the risk management function and senior management all go towards shaping a risk culture in firms.[148] However, this section cautions against

[145] Banks, *Risk Culture* (n 63) 23.

[146] Cortez, *Winning at Risk* (n 61) 145.

[147] Priscilla Burnaby and Susan Hass, 'Ten Steps to Enterprise-Wide Risk Management' (2009) 9 *Corporate Governance* 539; Rosen and Zenios, 'Enterprise-Wide Asset and Liability Management' (n 64) 2; CRM Policy Group, 'Containing Systemic Risk' (n 113) 1, 14–16. See also FSB, *Guidance on Supervisory Interaction with Financial Institutions on Risk Culture: Consultation Document* (n 69) 3.

[148] Ashby, Palermo and Power, *Risk Culture in Financial Organisations* (n 72).

excessive optimism in relying on regulation that supports enterprise-wide risk management and corporate governance (as chapters five and six will explore). Financial institutions are subject to pressures from market competition and sectoral trends which subtly affect the soft practices in firms in relation to risk-taking and management. Further, in large and complex financial institutions, governability may be an issue and tone at the top need not secure a coherent risk culture. Deviant cultures may also exist where there are gaps and vulnerabilities. Finally, it would be mistaken to treat the institution of an enterprise-wide risk management framework as a panacea for securing optimal risk-taking and management outcomes, as trade-offs[149] would still have to be made in decisions regarding business and risk. Genuine mistakes on risk can be made at the strategic level and these cannot be weeded out by having an enterprise-wide risk management framework in place.

The institution of a sound risk culture in firms does not however merely revolve around the implementation of frameworks and procedures such as recommended by the FSB. A Board has to contend with aspects of questionable organisational and sectoral culture in establishing its risk culture. Corporate governance, organisational culture and incentives such as remuneration policies affect risk culture,[150] and the culture of internal control generally, as chapters five and six will discuss in detail. Corporate governance includes how shareholder preferences may affect the risk philosophy and appetites of banks and financial institutions.[151] Further, the risk culture of firms can be shaped by sectoral trends relating to remuneration designs for staff[152] and how performance in financial institutions should be evaluated. Firms embracing a 'risk and win' ethos[153] would define their risk culture that way or merely pay lip service to a prudent risk culture.

149 ibid.

150 Cortez, *Winning at Risk* (n 61) 33, 37; FSB, *Guidance on Supervisory Interaction with Financial Institutions on Risk Culture: Consultation Document* (n 69) 3.

151 Deakin, 'Corporate Governance and Financial Crisis' (n 31); Peter O Mülbert, 'Corporate Governance of Banks after the Financial Crisis—Theory, Evidence, Reforms' (2010) ECGI Law Working Paper 130/2009 at ssrn.com/abstract=1448118; Christopher M Bruner, 'Corporate Governance Reform in a Time of Crisis' (2011) 36 *Journal of Corporation Law* 309; Nicolas Calcina Howson, 'When "Good" Corporate Governance Makes "Bad" (Financial) Firms: The Global Crisis and the Limits of Private Law' (2009) 108 *Michigan Law Review* 44; Reint Gropp and Matthias Köhler, 'Bank Owners or Bank Managers: Who is keen on Risk? Evidence from the Financial Crisis' (2010) European Business School Research Paper 10-02 at ssrn.com/abstract=1555663; Andrea Beltratti and René M Stultz, 'Why Did Some Banks Perform Better during the Credit Crisis? A Cross-Country Study of the Impact of Governance and Regulation' (2009) NBER Working Paper 15180 at papers.ssrn.com/sol3/papers.cfm?abstract_id=1433502; Hanna Westman, 'The Role of Ownership Structure and Regulatory Environment in Bank Corporate Governance' (January 2010) at ssrn.com/abstract=1435041.

152 To be discussed in greater detail in chapter 6.

153 Mark Wexler, 'Financial Edgework and the Persistence of Rogue Traders' (2010) 115 *Business & Society Review* 1.

In Anglo-American jurisdictions, McGee argues that we have witnessed a move from demutualisation to profit-maximisation and empire building in the largest banking groups,[154] a phenomenon described as 'chasing Goldman Sachs', the leading investment bank.[155] In order to generate persistent and higher profits, financial intermediaries innovate and take greater risks, generating the highest fees possible from all kinds of intermediation regardless of the ultimate purpose of capital allocation.[156] Santoro and Strauss also argue that the profit generation by financial intermediaries has become a form of 'profit disjunction' as profits could be generated through complex innovations that do not serve the purposes of social utility and in fact pass risks onto unsuspecting investors.[157] Frenetic profit chasing, the ever-expanding scope of financial intermediation and increased risk-taking have come to characterise the modern banking business model.[158] Such a wider backdrop of industry pressures and market competition[159] may shape the preferences[160] of Boards and senior management such as in risk management. Risk management, if seen to be an obstacle to timely and cost-effective decision-making, could be sidelined or relaxed in implementation.[161] Wilmarth[162] writing in the early 2000s already predicted that behavioural sub-optimalities and 'animal spirits'[163] may govern decision-making at banks and financial institutions, and override the 'braking' tendencies of risk management which could be perceived to slow down decision-making. The same sectoral context of market competition remains post-crisis as financial intermediation continues to be a fiercely competitive business.[164]

[154] Frank H Easterbrook and Daniel R Fischel, *The Economic Structure of Corporate Law* (Cambridge, MA: Harvard University Press, 1996) 35–39 ('Maximands'). See also John Armour, Simon Deakin and Suzanne J Konzelmann, 'Shareholder Primacy and the Trajectory of UK Corporate Governance' (2003) 41 *British Journal of Industrial Relations* 531.

[155] McGee, *Chasing Goldman Sachs* (n 36) generally.

[156] ibid, 97, 120, 150.

[157] Michael A Santoro and Ronald J Strauss, *Wall Street Values: Business Ethics and the Global Financial Crisis* (Cambridge: Cambridge University Press, 2012) ch 2.

[158] McGee, *Chasing Goldman Sachs* (n 36) 124, 126, 128.

[159] The power of competitive pressures is discussed in Kross, *Organised Opportunities* (n 121) 79–98.

[160] Described as both a cognitive failure as well as a moral failure, see Arnold Kling, 'The Financial Crisis: Moral Failure or Cognitive Failure?' (2010) 33 *Harvard Journal of Law & Public Policy* 507.

[161] Edwards, 'An Unfortunate "Tail"' (n 80).

[162] Arthur E Wilmarth, 'The Transformation of the Financial Services Industry: 1975–2000, Competition, Consolidation and Increased Risks' (2002) 2 *University of Illinois Law Review* 215.

[163] Grzegorz Andruszkiewicz, Mark HA Davis and Sebastien Lleo, 'Taming Animal Spirits: Risk Management with Behavioural Factors' (2013) 9(2) *Annals of Finance* 145.

[164] Alternative intermediary outfits such as shadow banks arise to compete for risk allocation business all the time, see Financial Stability Board, *Global Shadow Banking Monitoring Report 2014* (November 2014).

However, it may be argued that healthy risk cultures can be and have been instituted in firms in spite of the industry and market pressures faced by firms. In the global financial crisis, some banks were relatively unscathed. Mikes has carried out an empirical research to compare two financial institutions that have both instituted enterprise-wide risk management, and suffered to significantly different extents in the crisis.[165] The firm that suffered during the global financial crisis had a risk culture shaped by shareholder value maximisation and profit chasing, and adopted a risk management framework reflecting a narrow-minded and business-friendly risk culture. On the other hand, another firm with a risk culture that was more holistic in the balance between solvency concerns and business performance performed better in the global financial crisis. But it may be counter-argued that the soundness or otherwise of a risk culture is unfairly determined with the benefit of hindsight. Boards could make genuinely well-intentioned judgements on risk-taking, which is the business of financial intermediation anyway. Even if Boards and senior management take a serious and committed approach to establishing holistic firm-wide risk management, mistakes in judgements relating to risk philosophy and risk appetite can still be made due to the complexity in financial intermediation business[166] and the very dynamic and competitive nature of the financial intermediation business itself. Miller argues that pre-crisis, many bank Boards have set relatively high-risk appetites in genuine belief of their appropriateness. He argues that, 'the most likely interpretation, in the years leading up to the financial crisis, major financial firms were knowingly, and in exchange for an attractive expected return, taking on very small risks of very large losses, and, unfortunately, these risks materialized'.[167] Stultz also argues that risk judgements could be wrong with the benefit of hindsight, in which case losses suffered by firms should not be attributed to poor risk management as they are really business losses.[168] Even the US court in the shareholder derivative litigation against Citigroup[169] takes a similar line of reasoning by accepting that Citigroup's decisions in relation to risk-taking in the sub-prime mortgage market are protected by the business judgement rule.[170] Banks comments

[165] Mikes, 'Risk Management and Calculative Cultures' (n 55).

[166] Geoffrey P Miller, 'Intellectual Hazard: How Conceptual Biases in Complex Organizations Contributed to the Crisis Of 2008' (2010) 33 *Harvard Journal of Law & Public Policy* 807; Roman Tomasic, 'Corporate Governance Failure: The Role of Internal and External Gatekeepers in UK Banks and Financial Institutions' (2010) 10 *Corporate Governance: International Journal for Enhanced Board Performance* 8, 26.

[167] Miller, 'Oversight Liability' (n 40) 113.

[168] Stultz, 'Risk Management Failures' (n 66).

[169] *In Re Citigroup Inc Shareholder Derivative Litigation* 4 A.2d 106 (Del Ch 2009).

[170] See discussions in Bainbridge, 'Caremark and Enterprise Risk Management' (n 64); Franklin A Gevurtz, 'The Role of Corporate Law in Preventing a Financial Crisis: Some Reflections on *In Re Citigroup Inc Shareholder Derivative Litigation*' in PM Vasudev and Susan Watson (eds), *Corporate Governance after the Financial Crisis* (Cheltenham: Edward Elgar, 2011) 163.

that the failures of MF Global, Dexia and AIG could also be regarded examples of such a situation.[171]

Next, even if the Board and senior management have assumed leadership to establish a risk management framework, the implementation of such a framework may be subject to deviation. Such deviation may be carried out in large and complex financial groups where 'local cultures' may persist in spite of the institution of centralised policies and systems. For example, in the JP Morgan whale loss case, it was pointed out that the firm had an enterprise-wide risk management framework, but the activities of a London unit dominated by a small cluster of trading superstars managed to evade monitoring.[172] The difficulty in securing coherence in the 'local cultures' with the tone at the top has also been highlighted in Barclays, another large multinational banking institution, by the Salz Review[173] commissioned by the bank in the wake of the scandal relating to benchmark manipulation.[174] Further, at a more ad hoc and individual level, rogues in firms may be undetected until severe losses are occasioned, such as the unauthorised trading activities of Kerviel at Société Générale[175] and Adoboli at UBS.[176] A number of commentators observe that in banks and financial institutions, employees at much lower levels may enjoy a significant amount of autonomy to take huge risks.[177] For example, traders on trading floors may be able to take significant risks using leverage, a type of risk termed as 'carry trade risk'.[178] Leverage could magnify returns but could also exacerbate losses. Abuses of such autonomy have been seen in a number of rogue trader scandals[179] but it is neither ideal nor practicable to severely curtail staff discretion or to subject the exercise of discretion to time-consuming and costly monitoring.

Commentators have warned that even with well-intentioned implementation of enterprise-wide risk management led from the top, translation into organisational design is not a clearly charted path and the framework is

[171] Banks, *Risk Culture* (n 63) 87.

[172] United States Senate Permanent Subcommittee on Investigations, *JP Morgan Chase Whale Trades: A Case History of Derivatives Risks and Abuses: Majority and Minority Staff Report* (2012) at www.hsgac.senate.gov/subcommittees/investigations/hearings/chase-whale-trades-a-case-history-of-derivatives-risks-and-abuses, 157–214.

[173] Anthony Salz, *The Salz Review: An Independent Review of Barclays' Business Practices* (April 2013) para 8.23ff.

[174] 'Barclays hit with £290m Fine over LIBOR Fixing' *Telegraph* (27 June 2012).

[175] 'Société Générale uncovers £3.7bn fraud by rogue trader' *Guardian* (24 January 2008).

[176] 'Kweku Adoboli jailed for fraud over £1.4bn UBS loss' *BBCNews* (20 November 2012).

[177] See George Gilligan, 'Jerome Kerviel the "Rogue Trader" of Société Generale: Bad Luck, Bad Apple, Bad Tree or Bad Orchard?' (2011) 32 *Company Lawyer* 355; Kimberly D Krawiec, 'The Return of the Rogue' (2009) 51 *Arizona Law Review* 127.

[178] Okamoto, 'After the Bailout' (n 41).

[179] Gilligan, 'Jerome Kerviel' (n 177) and Krawiec, 'The Return' (n 177).

inevitably bound up with the softer aspects of risk culture in firms.[180] Further, there are concerns that enterprise-wide risk management may be reductionist in nature, forcing risks across diverse businesses to be translated into one language in order to be commensurate, and hence over-simplifying things and introducing secondary level risks to the risk management process itself.

In sum, the regulatory enhancement of the risk management function may still be shaped by a firm's risk culture. The development of risk cultures in firms is still in a fluid state, and risk cultures are neither static nor consistent across firms.[181] The regulatory adoption of a mandatory enterprise-wide risk management framework also does not mean that a firm's risk culture is healthy or optimal, or that strategic decisions relating to risk-taking are never mistaken. The essentially meta-regulatory framework for enterprise-wide risk management and the institution of the risk management function in firms continue to manifest the limitations in meta-regulation discussed in chapter one.

Next, we turn to discuss the inherent limitations in the capacity and competence of the risk management function as an issue in the professional dimension. This discussion is important in order to caution against excessive regulatory expectations hinged upon the achievements in organisational reforms discussed above. The securing of optimal risk management outcomes at firms is dependent on the substantive competencies and capabilities of the risk management profession. We argue that this is an emerging area which is not yet professionally mature and hence regulators should be mindful of having excessive regulatory expectations of what substantive outcomes may be achieved.

C. DISJUNCTIONS BETWEEN REGULATORY EXPECTATIONS AND THE ROLE OF THE RISK MANAGEMENT FUNCTION: ANALYSING THE ORGANISATIONAL DIMENSION

In this section, it is suggested that even if organisational reforms may overcome certain weaknesses in risk management in banks and financial institutions identified in the pre-crisis era, the effectiveness of risk management very much depends on its substantive competence. This section will examine the literature on the professional competencies on the part of risk management personnel and query whether there may be an expectations gap between what risk management professionals see as

[180] See Frank Schiller and George Prpich, 'Learning to Organise Risk Management in Organisations: What Future for Enterprise Risk Management?' (2013) 17 *Journal of Risk Research* 999.

[181] Ashby, Palermo and Power, *Risk Culture in Financial Organisations* (n 72).

their role and the regulatory perception of what risk management professionals could do, especially in securing prudential regulatory objectives. This section will argue that professional competencies in risk management are still developing and this affects the extent to which they could secure effective optimal risk-taking and management at firms. Regulators should be mindful of excessive expectations in terms of the substantive outcomes that risk management can achieve in firms.

The Job Scope of Risk Management Functions

First, this section will argue that the 'job scope' of risk management is not altogether certain. In particular, risk management may embrace a scope of responsibilities that is excessively expansive, and it is questioned whether this reflects an emerging professionalism that is yet ambulatory and could provide opportunities for the organisational manipulation of the risk management function to serve firm needs.

One of the professional associations for risk managers, the Institute of Risk Management has issued guidance relating to ISO Standard 13000 for enterprise-wide risk management and defines the purpose of risk management in the corporate sector generally as 'to achieve maximum sustainable value from all the activities of the organisation. Risk management enhances the understanding of the potential upside and downside of the factors that can affect an organisation'.[182] Corporate risk management is now seen to take on a multitude of purposes regarding performance, value, solvency and sustainability all rolled into one omnibus statement. Some commentators view risk management at banks and financial institutions as being able to meet multiple objectives in managing solvency risks, downside risks as well as seizing opportunities for upside gains and adding value to the firm.[183] In other words, risk management could be positioned to deal with 'pure risks' (ie, risks that have to do with averting disasters so that what is desired to be achieved is a situation of 'no loss')

[182] AIRMIC, ALARM and IRM, 'A Structured Approach to Enterprise Risk Management (ERM) and the Requirements of ISO 31000' (2010) 7.

[183] Pagano, 'How Theories of Financial Intermediation and Corporate Risk-Management Influence Bank Risk-Taking Behavior' (n 24) argues that risk management in financial institutions is both for managing solvency risk as well as for seizing opportunities in capital markets to add value to the firm. Ellul and Yerramilli, 'Stronger Risk Controls' (n 37) examined the relationship between effective risk management and the twin purposes of solvency and performance and found a positive relationship between strong risk management and the twin purposes. This may suggest that the purpose of performance, which is a firm-centric concern, is not misaligned with prudential regulatory objectives. The meta-review of empirical literature carried out in Smithson and Simkins, 'Does Risk Management Add Value?' (n 25) seems to suggest the same conclusion.

as well as 'speculative risks' (ie, risks that present opportunities for an upside as well as a downside).[184] However, the expansive range of responsibilities may cast risk management functions in a chameleonic light, providing opportunities for firms to shape the roles and responsibilities of risk management towards firm-centric objectives.

Some commentators wonder if there is a trade-off between risk management purposed towards value creation and risk management that is purposed towards prudential management. Mikes argues that even if risk management is embedded at a strategic level, risk management may be seen as a 'business partner' and not as 'compliance champion',[185] meaning risk management may take on a substantially business-advisory aspect focused on firm performance and value creation and less emphasis may be placed on regulatory objectives in relation to prudential management and compliance. Blanchard et al argue that risk management is costly and may be seen to affect the financial bottom-line, and hence shareholders and executives rewarded in stock-linked remuneration (whose incentives are similar to shareholders) would always be keen to marginalise the amount of resources that have to be dedicated to risk management.[186] It should not be assumed that risk management functions can simply pursue all aforementioned objectives for the firm as contradictory pursuits may exist within the range of objectives and firms could manipulate the risk management function towards firm value creation, which may not be naturally aligned with prudential regulatory objectives. In 1998, the Basel Committee's recommendations on best practices in internal control for international banks specifically made a distinction between risk management that is firm-centric and risk management that is purposed towards prudential regulatory objectives.[187]

Further, the risk management function in firms could be regarded being bound up in the private paradigms of corporate governance, ie, the purpose of risk management is that it is one of the mechanisms designed to ensure that the agency problem between management and shareholders is mitigated[188] and that shareholder value is protected and enhanced.[189]

[184] Banks, *Risk Culture* (n 63) 1ff.

[185] Anette Mikes, 'Risk Management at Crunch Time: Are Chief Risk Officers Compliance Champions or Business Partners?' (2008) at papers.ssrn.com/abstract=1138615.

[186] Danielle Blanchard and Georges Dionne, 'Risk Management and Corporate Governance' (The Crisis of Corporate Governance: What's Next? conference, Montreal, May 2003).

[187] Basel Committee on Banking Supervision, *Framework for Internal Control in Banking Organisations* (1998) 17, para 20.

[188] Ian Brown, Adam Steen and Julie Foreman, 'Risk Management in Corporate Governance: A Review and Proposal' (2009) 17 *Corporate Governance* 546.

[189] Discussed earlier in section A.

Empirical literature[190] and literature written by risk management practitioners[191] seem to support this perspective and such could shape the consciousness of risk management professionals in relation to their roles and responsibilities within firms. It could be argued that risk management can be manipulated to be essentially firm-centred; the purpose of risk management in corporate governance is to secure shareholder accountability and value maximisation and hence it is not necessarily outward-looking towards securing prudential regulatory objectives.

Next, the institution of risk management in a bank or financial institution could be perceived as forming a legitimate basis for firms to take increased risks in financial intermediation. There is empirical research that indicates that the pursuit of risk management in activities such as active buying and selling of derivatives does not reduce the level of risk-taking in banks and financial institutions.[192] Even if the motivation for risk management by actively selling and buying derivatives may have stemmed from a desire to manage downside risks,[193] the successful management of downside risk may then entail business decisions to be made to expand exposure so that more risks are taken on.[194] Draghi is however of the view that the levels and magnitudes of risks may not pose an issue from the point of view of prudential regulatory concerns so long as they are managed soundly.[195]

The professional objectives of risk management are arguably in a developing stage. Although multiple objectives seem to be endorsed by the Institute of Risk Management, the multiplicity of objectives may obfuscate professional consciousness and provide room for organisational manipulation of the risk management function to serve business objectives[196] such as increasing risk-taking or seeking profits and gains through the application of risk management techniques.

[190] See Pagano, 'How Theories of Financial Intermediation and Corporate Risk-Management Influence Bank Risk-Taking Behavior' (n 24); Smithson and Simkins, 'Does Risk Management Add Value?' (n 25).

[191] See Schroeck, *Risk Management and Value Creation* (n 12) 40ff; David P Belmont, *Value Added Risk Management in Financial Institutions* (Chichester: John Wiley & Sons, 2004) ch 4.

[192] See Sinan Cebenoyan and Strahan, 'Risk Management' (n 46), although see later contrary findings in Buston, 'Active Risk Management' (n 46); Hans Gersbach and Jan Wenzelburger, 'Sophistication in Risk Management, Bank Equity, and Stability' (2010) 10 *International Review of Finance* 63.

[193] Buston, 'Active Risk Management' (n 46) finds a positive relationship between bank stability and active risk management.

[194] Gersbach and Wenzelburger, 'Sophistication in Risk Management' (n 192).

[195] Draghi, 'Observations on Risk Management Practices' (n 73).

[196] Lars Norden, Consuelo Silva Buston and Wolf Wagner, 'Financial Innovation and Bank Behavior: Evidence from Credit Markets' (2011) at ssrn.com/abstract=1800162.

The Professional Competence of the Risk Management Function and its Limitations

Any regulatory expectations placed on the capacity of the risk management framework and function to secure the firm's meeting of prudential regulatory objectives should ultimately be shaped by what the risk management function can do as a matter of professional competence. Commentators have described the risk management function as dealing with the measurement and analysis of risks in the form of 'known' risks ('k'), 'unknown risks' ('u') and 'unknowable' risks ('U').[197] This section will discuss the limitations of risk management in dealing with 'unknown' and 'unknowable' risks and thus cautions against excessive regulatory expectations on what risk management can achieve in terms of substantive outcomes.

'Known risks' refer to risks that can be identified and quantified. Often past data and statistical information are used in analytical models which use mathematical probabilities to generate risk measurements.[198] 'Unknown risks' refer to risks that are not entirely unexpected although the likelihood of occurrence is uncertain, and the magnitude of the materialisation of such risk is also not exactly predictable. Hence, 'unknown risks' present problems of objective measurability, and the risk management function, in analysing and attempting to measure such risks, would often have to engage in making estimations and constructing models.[199] 'Unknowable risks' refer to risks that are unexpected and therefore not measured at all. Often, systemic type events may be regarded as manifestations of 'unknowable risk'.[200] This taxonomy of risks shows that some risks may be more easily measured than others and Kuritzkes et al in an empirical study have found that market risk is the easiest to measure due to the availability of market transparency and is therefore managed to a greater extent in banks and financial institutions.[201] Credit, operational, legal and reputational risks are much harder to measure by comparison.

The failure of many financial institutions in the global financial crisis due to the collapse of asset prices of collaterised debt obligations held by them could be regarded as a materialisation of both the 'unknown risks' and

[197] See Andrew Kuritzkes and Til Schuermann, 'What We Know, Don't Know and Can't Know about Bank Risk: A View from the Trenches' in FX Diebold, N Doherty and RJ Herring (eds), *The Known, The Unknown and The Unknowable in Financial Risk Management* (Princeton, NJ: Princeton University Press, 2010); Richard J Herring, 'The Known, the Unknown, and the Unknowable in Financial Policy: An Application to the Subprime Crisis' (2009) 26 *Yale Journal on Regulation* 391; Jorion, 'Risk Management' (n 80).

[198] Bessis, *Risk Management in Banking* (n 97) xi and sections 4 and 5.

[199] Kuritzkes and Schuermann, 'What We Know' (n 197); Jorion, 'Risk Management' (n 80).

[200] Kuritzkes and Schuermann, 'What We Know' (n 197).

[201] ibid.

'unknowable risks'. Collaterised debt obligations are novel and complex structured finance products which have not been tested, and their volatility could be affected by credit as well as market risk. However, banks did develop crude quantitative methods to attempt to measure such unknown risks,[202] and the risks have been erroneously measured as low by both financial institutions and credit rating agencies. The 'unknown risks' of collaterised debt obligations have been erroneously measured as past data for such novel products is lacking and the subjective estimates applied to the measurement of such risks have been overly optimistic.[203]

Although it could be said that financial institutions and credit rating agencies did not undertake sufficient diligence relating to the underlying credit risk,[204] there was also a general lack of information to support such accurate measurement of those risks. Hence, proxy forms of information and externally generated information such as by credit rating agencies have been used as bases for risk modelling and measurement.[205] Flawed input[206] as a result was used in the subjective estimates of 'unknown risks' which were then built into quantitative models. Reliance on such quantitative models has become almost automatic and risk managers forgot to question the validity of the initial assumptions built into the models.[207] Rebonato is also of the view that that dominant quantitative practice in risk management which is based on the frequentist view of probability is too limited in nature when data is lacking.[208] Further, the over-simplistic models failed to capture the impact of possible systemic events in asset prices failures and institutional failures, although they could arguably be said to be in the realm of 'unknowable' risks.

Nevertheless, the substantive limitations in risk management competence in dealing with unknown and unknowable risks were arguably augmented by behavioural weaknesses. The uncertainties in measuring risk provided room for financial institutions to underestimate such risks when there were strong incentives to engage in the business that could

[202] Douglas Hubbard, *The Failure of Risk Management: Why It's Broken and How Do we Fix it?* (Chichester: John Wiley & Sons, 2009) ch 2.

[203] Fanto, 'Anticipating the Unthinkable' (n 34); Stultz, 'Risk Management Failures' (n 66).

[204] As suggested in *Bathurst Regional Council v Local Government Financial Services* [2012] FCA 1200 where the regional council that suffered losses due to purchases of the toxic collaterised debt obligations successfully sued their investment adviser and Standard & Poor's for misrepresenting the riskiness of the investments due to negligence.

[205] Steven L Schwarcz and Lucy Chang, 'The Custom to Failure Cycle' (2012) 62 *Duke Law Journal* 767; Jorion, 'Risk Management' (n 80).

[206] Hubbard, *The Failure of Risk Management* (n 202) chs 8 and 9.

[207] Edwards, 'An Unfortunate "Tail"' (n 80).

[208] Riccardo Rebonato, *Plight of the Fortune Tellers: Why We Need to Manage Financial Risk Differently* (Princeton, NJ: Princeton University Press, 2007).

generate high returns.[209] Further, the errors in risk measurement were augmented by subjective assumptions made in light of cognitive biases.[210] Risk managers had been underestimating the unknown and unknowable risks due to business pressures, a lack of resources,[211] error of judgement[212] and over-optimism.[213]

Post-crisis, improvements in quantitative modelling[214] are sought via research, expanding modelling methodologies into broader scopes and back testing for validation. Prudential regulatory requirements require more sophisticated risk measurements to be used, and encourage the development of more sophisticated risk management for stressed and complex phenomena.[215] Further, risk professions support the use of qualitative input to support quantitative risk management.

Commentators are of the view that the quantitative approaches are still fundamentally useful but such approaches need to be improved.[216] For example, a more comprehensive suite of risks including low probability but high-impact risks should be taken into account in risk modelling,[217] and risk assumptions that are based on subjective estimates should be made more prudent and subject to regular review.[218] Ray[219] suggests that a completely new framework could be instituted to mine more data and rely less on the traditional frequentist approaches to mathematical probabilities, so that a wider range of causal possibilities could be taken into account. Jorion also suggests that a completely new framework that maps the risks of real-time trading and asset positions should be constructed for risk measurement and analysis in a dynamic manner instead of using the traditional approach based on past returns data.[220]

[209] Kling, 'The Financial Crisis' (n 160); Okamoto, 'After the Bailout' (n 41); Kose John, Anthony Saunders and Lemma W Senbet, 'A Theory of Bank Regulation and Management Compensation' (2000) 13 *Review of Financial Studies* 95 is an early paper that has warned that incentives such as in remuneration fundamentally affect risk-taking at banks and financial institutions.

[210] Rebonato, *Plight of the Fortune Tellers* (n 208) 18ff, 28ff, 43ff, 127ff and 144ff.

[211] Crouhy, 'Risk Management Failures' (n 142), and see the discussion in section B.

[212] Miller, 'Oversight Liability' (n 40).

[213] Schwarcz and Chang, 'The Custom to Failure Cycle' (n 205).

[214] Johannes Wernz, *Bank Management and Control: Strategy, Capital and Risk Management* (Heidelberg: Springer, 2014).

[215] eg, the Basel III Capital Accord that requires VaR measurements for market risk be based on stressed scenarios.

[216] See Bénéplanc and Rochet, *Risk Management in Turbulent Times* (n 116) 194ff.

[217] Rosenberg and Schuermann, 'A General Approach to Integrated Risk Management' (n 83); William W Lang and Julapa A Jagtiani, 'The Mortgage and Financial Crises: The Role of Credit Risk Management and Corporate Governance' (2010) 38 *Atlantic Economic Journal* 123.

[218] Rebonato, *Plight of the Fortune Tellers* (n 208) 196ff.

[219] Christina Ray, *Extreme Risk Management: Revolutionary Approaches to Evaluating and Measuring Risk* (New York: McGraw-Hill, 2010) 1ff, 52ff, 153ff, 167ff, 176ff and 206ff.

[220] Jorion, 'Risk Management' (n 80).

Many risk management commentators are also of the view that quantitative approaches to risk management should be flanked by qualitative approaches. The qualitative approach to risk management refers to the element of critical scrutiny of assumptions and inherent limitations of quantitative approaches so that they can be regularly reviewed, updated and adjusted to meet changing conditions. In other words, although quantitative approaches remain fundamental and primary to generating risk measurements and analyses, the robustness of such measurements and analyses for the purposes of feeding into decision-making at strategic and operational levels needs to be supported by qualitative information and the application of critical scrutiny of quantitatively generated results. Commentators are of the view that enterprise-wide risk management provides the platform for a more comprehensive and qualitative approach to risk management.[221] The galvanisation of enterprise-wide coordination within a firm may provide a better chance of mitigating flaws in the primary quantitative approaches to risk management in terms of comprehensiveness, underlying assumptions and identification of correlations.[222] Hence, it could be argued that the organisational reforms discussed earlier could be crucial to feeding into the enhancement of risk management competence.

Further, mandatory requirements imposed on banks and financial institutions to carry out stress testing may indeed improve the substantive competence of risk management at firms. Regulators in the EU and UK have now introduced mandatory requirements of stress testing upon banks and financial institutions so that they could put their quantitative approaches to risk management to regular back testing and forward-looking stress testing[223] and mitigate any flaws discovered in the process.

In the UK, stress testing applies to all financial institutions that meet certain thresholds in terms of assets under management, the value of assets on their balance sheet or revenue.[224] Stress testing allows a firm to take stock of its prudential soundness and provides information to regulators in terms of the needs for supervisory monitoring. The regulator adopts an integrated stress testing approach which includes firms' own reverse stress testing and accountability, selective stress testing by the regulator

[221] See Carrel, *The Handbook of Risk Management* (n 96); Sweeting, *Financial Enterprise Risk Management* (n 65) generally.

[222] Edwards, 'An Unfortunate "Tail"' (n 80); Boatright, 'Risk Management' (n 13).

[223] Also supported in Hubbard, *The Failure of Risk Management* (n 202) ch 10; CRM Policy Group, 'Containing Systemic Risk' (n 113); Miller, 'Intellectual Hazard' (n 166); Schwarcz and Chang, 'The Custom to Failure Cycle' (n 205).

[224] FSA, 'Stress and Scenario Testing: Feedback on CP08/24 and final rules' (December 2009) PS 09/20 at www.fsa.gov.uk/pubs/policy/ps09_20.pdf; PRA and FCA Handbooks (as of 30 April 2013, formerly FSA Handbook) SYSC 20.

for 'high-impact' firms, and system-wide stress testing taking into account the wider economic context.[225] Reverse stress testing requires firms to identify scenarios and possible adverse circumstances that may cause the firm to become unviable, and firms have to carry out stress tests to determine how they may weather these hypothetical situations. The results of such stress tests are submitted to the regulator who may then require a firm to implement measures to enhance its resilience and/or make adjustments to its recovery and resolution plans according to the results of the stress tests.[226]

The framework of stress testing undertaken by firms has the potential to improve accountability to regulators, assist regulatory supervision, and overcome the weaknesses in information asymmetry associated with the meta-regulation of micro-prudential and risk management in financial institutions.[227] The production of such information for reflection and scrutiny may also force the risk management function to develop substantive methodologies that are aligned with securing prudential regulatory objectives, and hence become less influenced by firm manipulation. Further, it may be argued that meeting the regulatory obligations of stress testing could encourage risk management professionals to become more aligned with the objective of securing the firm's meeting of prudential regulatory objectives.

However, it may be argued that stress testing can still be subject to firm manipulation and the risk management function can be co-opted into firm-centric purposes for cosmetic compliance. As regulated firms determine the content of stress tests (ie, what the hypothetical scenarios are and how they are going to meet such challenges), they could be perversely incentivised to design scenarios and mechanisms that are geared towards future regulatory evasion.[228] It is also argued that stress testing needs to be based on extreme but nonetheless plausible scenarios.[229] Scenario framing in stress testing is usually done with the benefit of hindsight, and can be limited and backward looking. Scenario planning is not yet

[225] Such as those based on a wide survey/reflection undertaken each year by the regulator and covering macro- and micro-prudential risks and conditions (eg, FSA, 'Prudential Risk Outlook 2011' (2011) at www.fsa.gov.uk/pubs/other/pro.pdf.

[226] PRA and FCA Handbooks 2013 (formerly FSA Handbook) SYSC 20.2.6. See, eg, 'Bank of England announces results of UK stress test' (18 December 2014) which saw the Co-operative Bank failing its stress test and being required to submit a remediation plan to boost its safety and soundness.

[227] Til Schuermann, 'Stress-Testing Banks' (2012) at papers.ssrn.com/sol3/papers.cfm?abstract_id=2041579.

[228] DN Ghosh, 'Quirks of the Market Regulator' (2004) 39 *Economic and Political Weekly* 1550; Onnig H Dombalagian, 'Requiem for the Bulge Bracket? Revisiting Investment Bank Regulation' (2010) 85 *Indiana Law Journal* 777.

[229] Mario Quagliariello (ed), *Stress Testing the Banking System: Methodologies and Applications* (Cambridge: Cambridge University Press, 2011) generally.

well developed in either the regulatory toolkit or the reverse stress testing principles, leaving it largely to firms to figure out. This aspect of delegation to firms may entail weaknesses in scenario planning that are favourable for firms. Further, it may remain unclear to the regulator whether the scenarios are sufficiently robust and whether all scenarios have been considered. This problem is especially acute in respect of systemically important financial institutions that may have cross-border operations.[230] Such firms need to plan for a range of scenarios but regulators may not be able to check the comprehensiveness and credibility of scenario planning across varied international businesses. Stress testing, subject to a meta-regulatory approach, can therefore be susceptible to firm manipulation. That said, burgeoning literature[231] on stress testing indicates developments towards quantitative standardisation of stress testing methodologies and this may also be a signal of the development of independent and substantive competencies in the risk management profession.

A Professional Body for Risk Management

The Institute of Risk Management (IRM) is arguably the best known body for risk management professionals.[232] Being established in 1986, it is a relatively young professional body and its role lies in professional education and certification of risk managers, as well as in networking and coalescing a coherent professional identity in risk management. For example, the Institute has played an important part in the development of ISO 31000[233] for the general corporate sector. The standard provides for a framework of risk management in the mould of enterprise-wide risk management. The state of professionalism in risk management is arguably emerging in nature.

However, as much of substantive risk management competence is developed in quantitative training, increased professionalism could be developed as risk management expertise becomes more mature as a body of learning and knowledge. Some commentators are of the view that the sharing of information and expertise in professional communities can help

[230] Basel Committee on Banking Supervision, *Global Systemically Important Banks: Assessment Methodology and the Additional Loss Absorbency Requirement* (Rules text) (Basel: BIS, 2011) at www.bis.org/publ/bcbs207.pdf; Rosa Lastra, 'Systemic Risk, SIFIs and Financial Stability' (2011) 6 *Capital Markets Law Journal* 197; Nassim Nicholas Taleb and Charles S Tapiero, 'The Risk Externalities of Too Big to Fail' (2009) NYU Poly Research Paper at papers.ssrn.com/sol3/papers.cfm?abstract_id=1497973.

[231] Craig Friedman and Yangyong Zhang, 'A Method to Find Diverse and Manageable Sets of Plausible yet Severe Financial Scenarios' (2014) at ssrn.com/abstract=2379083.

[232] At www.theirm.org.

[233] At www.iso.org/iso/home/standards/iso31000.htm.

build up the capacity and competence of risk managers generally.[234] Ray, for example, recommends that risk management professionals should collectively develop scenarios for stress testing, pool together risk management expertise in order to build up a body of knowledge, and develop databases of risk management data and intelligence (which she terms MARKINT) that can be used in the processes of constructing more robust and credible quantitative models.[235] The IRM has developed a professional platform for information sharing, training and development and provides professional training leading to various forms of certification for levels of risk management competence and sector-specific risk management competence.

The work of professional bodies such as the Institute will go some way towards the gradual development of a more distinct professional identity for risk managers. It is envisaged that substantive training will become more mature and this will greatly enhance the perception of risk managers as experts within their organisation, as they may more likely be able to take advantage of the organisational reforms discussed earlier and resist organisational manipulation of their functions.

However, it can be argued that the development of professional knowledge and competence in risk management can be better and more quickly helped by the generation of more independent substantive content for sharing and learning. Many financial institutions develop their own proprietary quantitative models and the lack of knowledge sharing in this area may have contributed to the undetected weaknesses in many proprietary models, resulting in the lack of learning and slowness in the development of risk management competencies. Gerding recommends, in relation to credit rating agencies assessing product risk, that risk assessments can be enhanced via the development of open technical standards in rating methodologies.[236] This argument borrows from the idea of 'open source' in software developments that open participation in information pooling and technical development by any interested party can help shape and build a robust product. The ethics in open source lie in no one being able to claim proprietary rights over any final product. Applying the argument in the context of risk management methodologies, financial institutions could perhaps benefit from more open sharing of risk management methodologies which could be used constructively to build up more robust risk management techniques and approaches. However, unlike the ethos in 'open source', financial institutions may not be willing to give away their proprietary systems voluntarily.

[234] See Hubbard, *The Failure of Risk Management* (n 202) ch 11; Sweeting, *Financial Enterprise Risk Management* (n 65) ch 5.

[235] Ray, *Extreme Risk Management* (n 219) 217ff, 232ff.

[236] Erik F Gerding, 'Code, Crash and Open Source' (2009) 84 *Washington Law Review* 127.

Finally, it is also queried whether the professional competence of the risk management function may be affected by the ethical dimension. Chapter two has discussed the role of professional ethics in shaping the compliance function in banks and financial institutions, and the potential that ethics can provide a unifying framework to cement professional identity and consciousness. Where risk management is concerned, Lam writes in 2003 that its professional stature is a developing area,[237] and this is in fact seen in that professional organisations for risk managers are focused on education, training and accreditation[238] but not on developing codes of ethics and discipline, unlike the established professions of lawyers or auditors. Alfieri queries if the language of risk management broadly speaking is too technical and rational and is deprived of an ethical dimension.[239] The American Treadway Commission which has produced a set of guidelines for enterprise-wide risk management has also affirmed the role of ethics in shaping risk management, viz,

> [t]he effectiveness of enterprise risk management cannot rise above the integrity and ethical values of the people who create, administer, and monitor entity activities. Integrity and ethical values are essential elements of an entity's internal environment, affecting the design, administration, and monitoring of other enterprise risk management components.[240]

The ethical dimension could be an important missing piece that would enhance both the professional competence of the risk management function as well as its effectiveness in the organisational fabric in firms.

D. CONCLUSION

The importance of the risk management framework and function in banks and financial institutions has been flagged up in the global financial crisis. Post-crisis, regulators have carried out reforms to institute a mandatory enterprise-wide risk management framework at banks and financial institutions and to enhance the effectiveness of the specialist risk management function that occupies an important position in the framework.

This chapter has pointed out the pre-crisis context of organisational weaknesses in relation to the specialist risk management function and

[237] Lam, *Enterprise Risk Management* (n 100) ch 19.

[238] Such as the Institute of Risk Management at www.theirm.org and the Professional Risk Managers' International Association at prmia.org/index.php?page=aboutus.

[239] Anthony V Alfieri, 'Big Law and Risk Management: Case Studies of Litigation, Deals, and Diversity' (2011) 24 *Georgetown Journal of Legal Ethics* 991.

[240] Committee of Sponsoring Organizations of the Treadway Commission, *Enterprise Risk Management- Integrated Framework* (September 2004) 29–30.

the specific reforms intended to address these weaknesses and empower the risk management function to more effectively monitor a firm's securing of prudential regulatory objectives. However, regulatory expectations placed on the risk management function must be mindful of the inherent limitations of the function as it operates within an overall risk culture in firms, a product of the firm's values, ethos, real practices and attitudes towards risk-taking and management. Regulation cannot prescribe for the exact characteristics of a risk culture. Further, the efficacy of the risk management function depends on its professional capacity and competence. The limits in this area could affect substantive outcomes to be achieved, and could also give rise to room for organisational manipulation to serve firm-centric needs.

The chapter discusses the emerging professionalism of the risk management profession and suggests that although there are developments in strengthening the professional training and qualifications of risk managers led by the Institute of Risk Management, and the increasingly credible professional profile of the Institute as a professional body, the professionalism of risk management is in an emerging state. The profession needs to over time articulate the parameters of its roles and responsibilities and its approach to professional ethics. The chapter is however optimistic that regulatory responsibilities imposed on risk management such as in stress testing, prudential compliance and product governance could go some way in clearly defining the roles, responsibilities and expertise of the profession in contributing to a stronger professionalism. Such a stronger professionalism is desirable in order to resist organisational manipulation, a weakness highlighted in the global financial crisis, but also important for setting realistic regulatory expectations in terms of the extent to which risk management, as a form of internal control, can contribute to the governance of firms in securing prudential regulatory objectives.

4

The Role of Internal Audit

A. SKETCHING THE PROFILE OF INTERNAL AUDIT

THE INTERNAL AUDIT function may be regarded as a 'third line of defence',[1] in the infrastructure of internal control at banks and financial institutions. The internal audit function is envisaged to have residual oversight of internal control generally and to act as a gatekeeper after the first line of defence, which is senior management and front office, and the second lines of defence which are compliance and risk management. This perspective has recently been endorsed as part of the international[2] and EU regulatory frameworks.[3]

This chapter will first provide an overview of the development of the internal audit function in the financial sector. Unlike the compliance and risk management functions, internal audit was not regarded to have 'failed' in the financial institutions hit by the global financial crisis of 2008–09. However, its role was nevertheless considered by policymakers and enhanced as part of the general regulatory reforms to internal control. This also means that there may be heightened regulatory expectations surrounding the role of the internal audit function, as the final gatekeeper that could monitor risk-taking and wrongdoing in the firm. This chapter will critically discuss the achievements of the regulatory reforms to the internal audit function. These reforms, in the same vein as those applicable to the compliance and risk management functions, have focused on organisational empowering and improvement of the internal audit function. This chapter will also discuss whether the professional dimension of the internal audit function supports enhanced regulatory expectations of what internal audit can achieve.

[1] Peter Hughes, 'Bank Internal Audit—Third Line of Defence or First Line of Attack?' in *Interim Management* (ICAEW, August 2011).

[2] Basel Committee on Banking Supervision, *The Internal Audit Function in Banks* (Final Report) (Basel: BIS, June 2012) Principle 13, para 60ff.

[3] European Banking Authority, *EBA Guidelines on Internal Governance* issued on 27 September 2011 at www.eba.europa.eu/News-Communications/Year/2011/The-EBA-has-published-today-its-Guidelines-on-Inte.aspx.

The gatekeeping role of the internal audit function serves the firm's needs in providing reasonable assurance that the first and second lines of defences in the firm are duly discharging their responsibilities. Sarens et al observe that the financial sector has had the longest history of instituting internal audit functions, and hence the internal audit institution predates regulatory imposition.[4] Financial institutions have had a long history of regarding internal audit as a necessary feature to safeguard organisational needs and purposes, taking on a capacity of monitoring, assurance, checking and verifying the reliability of the functions of other parts of the organisation. Such monitoring and assurance is intended to assist management in achieving the intended productivity and efficiencies of the organisation,[5] as Davies puts it, 'a protective and constructive role to assist management'.[6] The internal audit function may generally be seen as an internal mechanism to check the agency problems at every level of operations in the organisation, including other internal control functions, in order to assist the organisation in achieving its goals. The gatekeeping role of the internal audit function in banks and financial institutions, as section C will discuss in greater detail, has first developed from branch auditing[7] as a mechanism to check agency problems between head office and branches. It has now evolved to become a mechanism that addresses agency problems in the corporate governance paradigm, ie, financial reporting and accountability generally to shareholders.[8] The UK has emphasised the role of the internal audit function in relation to financial assurance since 1992,[9] only affirming a wider remit of monitoring risk management in the last decade or so.[10] Although the remit of the internal audit function has expanded since the turn of the millennium, the internal

[4] Gerrit Sarens, Marco Allegrini, Giuseppe D'Onza and Robert Melville, 'Are Internal Auditing Practices Related to the Age of the Internal Audit Function? Exploratory Evidence and Directions for Future Research' (2011) 26 *Managerial Auditing Journal* 51.

[5] Early writings such as DR Carmichael, 'Hypotheses of Internal Control' (1970) 45 *The Accounting Review* 235; James B Bower and Robert E Schlosser, 'Internal Control—Its True Nature' (1965) 40 *The Accounting Review* 338.

[6] MBT Davies, 'The Objectives of Internal Auditing' (1956) 31 *The Accounting Review* 227.

[7] Esther M Shont, *Internal Bank Auditing* (New York: John Wiley & Sons, 1982) ch 1.

[8] Mohammed Al-Shetwi, Shamsher Mohamed Ramadili, Taufiq Hassan, Shah Chowdury and Zulkarnain Muhamad Sori, 'Impact of Internal Audit Function (IAF) on Financial Reporting Quality (FRQ): Evidence from Saudi Arabia' (2011) 5 *African Journal of Business Management* 11189; Shu Lin, Mina Pizzini, Mark Vargus and Indranil Bardhan, 'The Role of Internal Audit Function in the Disclosure of Material Weaknesses' (2010) at ssrn.com/abstract=1592593; Gerrit Sarens and Mohammad J Abdolmohammadi, 'Monitoring Effects of the Internal Audit Function: Agency Theory versus other Explanatory Variables' (2011) 15 *International Journal of Auditing* 1.

[9] Sir Adrian Cadbury, *Report of the Committee on the Financial Aspects of Corporate Governance* (1992).

[10] ICAEW, *Internal Control: Guidance for Directors on the Combined Code* (the Turnbull Report) (1999, 2005 rev).

audit function has always been a firm-centric function that is intended to meet firm objectives and needs.

Pre-crisis, a meta-regulatory framework has been in place for organisational matters within financial institutions such as the internal audit function. European legislation required all investment firms to establish a separate and independent internal audit function that is able to review the effectiveness of the firm's internal control framework and functions.[11] This has been applied to all banks and investment firms in the UK.[12] As the internal audit function is one that firms would have instituted anyway, what is sought to be achieved by bringing the function under the meta-regulatory framework for internal control in financial institutions?

It is arguable that policymakers have subjected the internal audit function to a meta-regulatory framework so as to introduce regulatory expectations in relation to the internal audit's role, viz, to ensure that the other internal control functions secure the regulatory objectives of regulatory compliance and sound risk management. It may be surmised that such regulatory expectations may be perceived as not to have been met in the global financial crisis. Post-crisis, regulatory authorities have now more clearly articulated the scope of their expectations for the internal audit function.

In the wake of the global financial crisis, the Basel Committee has overtly referred to 'supervisory expectations' in relation to the internal audit function in the following respects: how the internal audit function is constituted and discharges its responsibilities, as well as the intelligence role of the internal audit function in assisting regulatory supervision.[13] The Basel Committee envisages that the internal audit function should engage in regular discussions with regulators about the risk profiles and weaknesses of the bank or financial institution concerned, including areas such as:

1. Application and effectiveness of risk management procedures and risk assessment methodologies, as applied to credit risk, market risk, liquidity risk, operational risk (including information technology and business continuity management), and other risks relevant to the Basel capital adequacy Pillar 2 requirements.
2. Contingency planning.
3. Outsourcing arrangements.

[11] Commission Directive 2006/73/EC of 10 August 2006 implementing Directive 2004/39/EC of the European Parliament and of the Council as regards organisational requirements and operating conditions for investment firms and defined terms for the purposes of that Directive [2006[OJ L241/26 (MiFID Commission Directive 2006) Art 8.

[12] The PRA and FCA Handbooks, SYSC 6.2.

[13] Basel Committee, *The Internal Audit Function* (n 2) 15–18, Principles 16–20.

4. Fraud risk.
5. The integrity of financial reporting in respect of matters such as measurement (including fair values) and impairment of financial instruments; significant transactions in financial instruments with a regulatory impact; other judgemental accounting areas, including estimates.
6. Matters of regulatory concern in business or market conduct issues as identified through the audit of the compliance function, such as transaction reporting; adherence to rules for dealing with client assets; anti-money laundering processes and controls; and management of conflicts of interest.[14]

In order to empower the internal audit function in its 'supervisory' and monitoring role, much of post-crisis legislative reforms relate to organisational aspects of the internal audit function. Once again we see that reforms have taken place largely in the organisational dimension to boost the position, profile and powers of the internal audit function in order to support its role in securing the firm's meeting of regulatory objectives. The chapter will critically discuss what may be achieved by such reforms.

The intelligence role of the internal audit function arguably serves the purpose of providing for direct engagement between regulators and internal audit. Such dynamics support a sense of accountability on the part of internal audit to regulators and more overt regulatory expectations of internal audit's role in securing the firm's meeting of regulatory objectives. Further, the Basel Committee envisages that regulators should be able to evaluate the effectiveness of the internal audit function and take appropriate action by requiring senior management of banks and financial institutions to take remedial actions in respect of any internal audit deficiencies.[15] This means that the regulator has a direct interest in the role and functions of internal audit in meeting its objectives and can intervene to secure the effectiveness of the function according to the regulator's point of view. Compared with the compliance and risk management functions, the regulatory expectations imposed on internal audit are much more overt.

This chapter critically discusses the regulatory expectations of the internal audit function's intelligence and regulatory accountability role, and queries whether this role is supported by the professional understanding and ethos of the internal audit profession. This chapter is cautious of undue regulatory expectations of what internal audit can deliver in securing the firm's meeting of regulatory objectives. The internal audit

[14] ibid, 17, Principle 17.
[15] ibid, 18, Principles 18–20.

profession seems much more developed than compliance or risk management, and its representative professional body, the Institute of Internal Auditors, has been established since 1948 and was granted a royal charter in 2010. The professional stature of internal audit may create an impression regarding its gatekeeping potential, though unlike external auditors, it operates from within and carries out a similar verification and assurance function. However, section C will discuss the professional development of internal audit and point out its highly procedural and meta-level nature and its intimate dependence on the organisational context. Further, the professional perception of the internal audit's role is firm-centric. The chapter is of the view that the effectiveness of internal audit is heavily shaped by its organisational purposes (as will be discussed in section B) in serving organisational needs and objectives. Hence, regulatory expectations of what the internal audit function can achieve may be misplaced given the direction of development in internal audit professionalism.

The next section will turn to the organisational reforms designed to enhance and empower the internal audit function in its internal 'supervisory' and monitoring role.

B. DISJUNCTIONS BETWEEN REGULATORY EXPECTATIONS AND THE ROLE OF THE INTERNAL AUDIT FUNCTION: ANALYSING THE ORGANISATIONAL DIMENSION

In the pre-crisis context, European legislation provided a skeletal meta-regulatory framework for the internal audit function, only requiring that investment firms institute a 'separate and independent' internal audit function.[16] Although internal audit did not come under as much scrutiny as the risk management function in relation to prudential failures at banks in the global financial crisis, or the compliance function in relation to conduct failures that are ongoing, post-crisis reforms have provided for enhancement to the organisational profile and power of the internal audit as part of the overall reforms to internal control.

This section will discuss the achievements and limitations of such reforms. One of the concerns is that the internal audit function has always been a staunchly firm-centric function. Hence, organisational reforms to empower its 'supervisory' or monitoring role may introduce cognitive dissonance to the function's understanding of its role and responsibilities, or merely reinforce its firm-centric focus. Sarens et al find that organisational factors affect the internal audit function's adherence to professional standards

[16] MiFID Commission Directive 2006, Art 8.

such as the Institute of Internal Auditors standards.[17] Organisational factors seem to play a significant part in shaping the professionalism of the internal audit function.

Independence of the Internal Audit Function

One of the key organisational attributes prescribed for the internal audit function in regulation is the independence of the function.[18] The purpose of safeguarding the independence of the internal audit function is to ensure that its assurance role may be performed objectively and is reliable both for the firm and regulators. One commentator opines that '[Internal Audit] needs to be professionally sceptical, politely suspicious, alert to detection, and accept that role means never fully integrated into the organisation'.[19] The perceived ability to keep a distance from the organisation has become a key indicator for the effective discharge of the internal audit role in terms of healthy scepticism and irregularity detection. This is also the key attractive quality to regulators in viewing internal audit as an extension of regulatory governance mechanisms operating from the inside of the organisation. Hence, independence is a structural feature that proxies for objectivity. Post-crisis reforms have introduced in some detail prescriptive requirements to protect the structural independence of the internal audit function. This section will critically review these.

The Basel Committee recommends that independence be achieved by insulating the internal audit function from the subjects of its monitoring. For example, the internal audit function should not be involved in designing or selecting internal control measures (although the input of internal audit can be sought by senior management). The internal audit function should also report directly to the Board. The internal audit function should be protected from conflicts of interest through mandatory job rotation, and the remuneration of internal audit officers should not be linked to business performance or any particular business lines. The Institute of Internal Auditors (IIA) also supports organisational structures that support the independence of internal audit, viz, independence from other internal control functions, accountability to the audit committee, the

[17] Gerrit Sarens and Mohammad J Abdolmohammadi, 'Factors Associated with Best Practices in Internal Auditing: Emerging vs Developed Countries' (2009) at ssrn.com/abstract=529017, based on findings in the Institute of Internal Auditors' survey the Common Body of Knowledge, see IIA, *Core Competencies for Today's Internal Auditor* (2010) Executive Summary, 2–3.

[18] *EBA Guidelines* (n 3) 44, para 29.4; Basel Committee, *The Internal Audit Function* (n 2) 4–5, Principle 2, paras 12–16.

[19] See Tomas Brytting, Richard Minogue and Veronica Morino, *The Anatomy of Fraud and Corruption* (Farnham: Gower Publishing, 2011) 172.

appointment of the Chief Internal Auditor by the audit committee, and the determination of remuneration for the Chief Internal Auditor by the audit committee.[20]

Reporting to the Board, and in particular the audit committee, may safeguard the internal audit function from interference and intimidation by senior management. Cahill discusses how in the early 1990s the failure of an Irish bank exposed weaknesses in the bank's internal audit function in terms of its reporting accountability, a crucial factor culminating in the failure of the bank.[21] The Northern Irish Bank had an internal audit function which reported on flaws and misgivings regarding bogus current accounts opened in branches. However, such reporting stopped at senior management and was not made available to the audit committee. The Board was thus unaware of the internal control failures until too late. Accountability to the audit committee thus allows internal audit findings to be reported to the highest level so that agency problems at the senior management level may not compromise the ability of the Board to deal with irregularities. European initiatives now support the accountability of the internal audit function directly to the Board or audit committee of the Board.[22]

However, reporting to the audit committee may frame the internal audit function's role more narrowly towards financial assurance. Further, as chapter six will discuss, post-crisis reforms require banks and financial institutions to establish Board risk committees to be dedicated to monitoring risk-taking. There is a need to rationalise the relationship between internal audit and the risk committee as well, since the role of internal audit in banks and financial institutions is also to provide an assurance role on internal control and risk management.[23] Further, the relationship between the audit and risk committees would need to be rationalised in order to provide an overall coherent framework for leadership in internal control. These points will be taken up further in chapter six.

In terms of safeguarding the internal audit function from being tainted with conflicts of interest, the Basel Committee proposes that the remuneration for internal auditors should be decoupled from the firm's financial performance.[24] The IIA proposes that remuneration for the Chief Internal Auditor should be set by the audit committee, so that senior management would not have undue influence over internal audit. The Basel Committee

[20] *Financial Services Code* (UKIIA, 2011) paras 12ff.

[21] Edward Cahill, 'Audit Committee and Internal Audit Effectiveness in a Multinational Bank Subsidiary: A Case Study' (2006) 7 *Journal of Banking Regulation* 160.

[22] *EBA Guidelines* (n 3) 44, para 29.6.

[23] *Financial Services Code* (UKIIA, 2011) para 15 leaves the issue open as to whether the internal audit function should report to the audit or risk committee.

[24] Basel Committee, *The Internal Audit Function* (n 2) 5, Principle 2, para 16.

also proposes that job rotation may be necessary to secure the objectivity of the internal audit function as job rotation provides freshness of perspective for internal auditors and mitigates the hazards associated with repetitive continuity in the discharge of the function.[25] However, caution should be exercised in implementing job rotation. Empirical research has shown that the internal audit function is sometimes used as a management training ground, ie, as part of the training of would-be senior executives and management.[26] The use of internal audit as a management training ground boosts the profile of internal audit so that it is not seen as a graveyard posting. However, Christ et al[27] and Rose et al[28] warn that the use of internal audit as a management training ground is likely to compromise the objectivity of internal auditors who may become sympathetic to business perspectives or become keen to please senior management in order to be moved to more attractive management positions in the firm. Further, managers who have become familiar with the procedures of internal audit may be able to devise ways of circumvention. Although it is important for internal audit to understand business perspectives to be in a better position to exercise critical judgement in their audit function, there may be an inevitable trade-off with objectivity.

It may also be queried whether an internal audit function would be more independent and objective if it is outsourced. Although European initiatives do not specify that the internal audit function should be in-house,[29] the Basel Committee's guidelines seem to prefer a predominantly in-house outfit with the possibility of some elements of outsourcing.[30] There is empirical research that indicates that outsourced internal audit functions are seen to be more objective and more relied on by external auditors.[31] But there is equally contrary empirical research showing that in-house internal audit may be more proximate to detecting irregularities and hence

[25] ibid, 5, Principle 2, para 15.

[26] See William A Messier, J Kenneth Reynolds, Chad A Simon and David A Wood, 'The Effect of Using the Internal Audit Function as a Management Training Ground On The External Auditor's Reliance Decision' (2011) at ssrn.com/abstract=1313806.

[27] Margaret H Christ, Adi Masli, Nathan Y Sharp and David A Wood, 'Using the Internal Audit Function as a Management Training Ground: Is the Monitoring Effectiveness of Internal Auditors Compromised?' (2012) at ssrn.com/abstract=1946518.

[28] Anna M Rose, Jacob M Rose and Carolyn S Norman, 'Is the Objectivity of Internal Audit Compromised when the Internal Audit Function is a Management Training Ground?' (2013) 53 *Accounting & Finance* 1001.

[29] *EBA Guidelines* (2011) 31–32, para 18.

[30] See Basel Committee, *The Internal Audit Function* (n 2) 11, Principle 8, para 47; 7, Principle 3, para 27.

[31] See Steven M Glover, Douglas F Prawitt and David A Wood, 'Internal Audit Sourcing Arrangement and the External Auditor's Reliance Decision' (2007) at ssrn.com/abstract=898800.

more effective.[32] However, such research is in relation to the financial assurance role of the internal audit and may not apply to the other roles in relation to internal control assurance. Prawitt et al also comment generally that in-house internal audit enjoys the advantages of greater proximity to information but may be compromised by such proximity.[33] Outsourced internal audits may suffer from less proximity to information but are generally regarded as more objective and competent.

Positioning and Power of the Internal Audit Function

Like the risk management and compliance functions discussed in chapters two and three, the organisational positioning and power of the internal audit function can affect its effectiveness. Post-crisis reforms emphasise the securing of sufficient authority for the internal audit function. The Basel Committee requires that the role and power of internal audit is to be set out in a Charter which includes:

— The purpose and scope of the internal audit function.
— The key features of the internal audit function.
— The obligation of the internal auditors to communicate the results of their engagements and a description of how and to whom this should be done (reporting line).
— The criteria for when and how the internal audit function may outsource some of its engagements to external experts.
— The terms and conditions according to which the internal audit function can be called upon to provide consulting or advisory services or to carry out other special tasks.
— The responsibility and accountability of the head of internal audit.
— A requirement to comply with sound internal auditing standards.
— Procedures for the coordination of the internal audit function with the statutory or external auditor.[34]

The Charter is to be agreed between the Chief Internal Auditor and the Board. This prevents senior management from influencing the Charter and affecting the power and authority of the internal audit function. The IIA recommends that the audit committee in particular agrees the

[32] See Paul Coram, Colin Ferguson and Robyn Moroney, 'Internal Audit, Alternative Internal Audit Structures, and the Level of Misappropriation of Assets Fraud' (2006) at ssrn.com/abstract=1021611.

[33] Douglas F Prawitt, Nathan Y Sharp and David A Wood, 'Internal Audit Outsourcing and the Risk of Misleading or Fraudulent Financial Reporting: Did Sarbanes–Oxley get it Wrong?' (2011) at ssrn.com/abstract=1333710.

[34] Basel Committee, *The Internal Audit Function* (n 2) 7, Principle 5, para 27.

objectives and powers of internal audit with the Chief Internal Auditor.[35] On the one hand, this means that the role and positioning of internal audit is endorsed at the highest level in the organisation and is therefore more secure from interference by senior management; but on the other hand, it also means that the role and positioning of the internal audit function is negotiated between the internal audit function and the organisation. It is queried as to whether organisational manipulation of the internal audit function's role could nevertheless take place. However, such a scope may be minimised where there is regulatory prescription for the responsibilities of internal audit and where the internal audit function is able to define its role and responsibilities clearly by reference to professional understanding. Section C will query to what extent the internal audit profession has a strong form of professionalism. It is also noted that European initiatives do not prescribe to a large extent the role and responsibilities of the internal audit function, unlike initiatives taken in relation to the risk management and compliance functions. For example, the internal audit function may be tasked to oversee internal reporting and whistle-blowing procedures in particular.[36]

The appointment of a Chief Internal Auditor who is sufficiently senior in the organisation is a further measure that supports the power and authority of the internal audit function.[37] The Basel Committee recommends that the internal audit function be adequately staffed with persons of sufficient qualifications and skills, and that resources be provided to ensure continuous training and development of internal auditors' expertise.[38] Generally speaking, the IIA notes[39] a general trend of firms hiring of more and more qualified internal auditors in the corporate sector, and hence the underinvestment of resources or sidelining of internal audit seems unlikely to be a concern in the immediate future.[40]

Further, European initiatives and the Basel Committee recommendations emphasise the importance of ensuring that the internal audit function obtains unfettered and comprehensive access to information so that it can

[35] *Financial Services Code* (UKIIA, 2011) para 17.

[36] *EBA Guidelines* (n 3) 30, para 17.2.

[37] *Financial Services Code* (UKIIA, 2011) para 12.

[38] Basel Committee, *The Internal Audit Function* (n 2) 5–6, Principle 3, paras 18–19.

[39] IIA, *Characteristics of an Internal Audit Survey* Executive Summary (2010).

[40] Although there is empirical research that indicates that it is still important to look at the driving factors for empowering or disempowering internal audit in an organisation. Internal factors to the organisation such as the expertise and influence of the audit committee and the risk control culture are important in determining the level of investment in internal audit, while external factors such as industry trends, firm size and stakeholder demand could also play a role, see Abhijit Barua, Dasaratha V Rama and Vineeta Sharma, 'Audit Committee Characteristics and Investment in Internal Auditing' (2010) 29 *Journal of Accounting and Public Policy* 503 discussing their own research and a review of existing empirical literature.

effectively perform an assurance role.[41] However, ease of access to a wide range of information needs to be supported by sound technological systems and so the quantity and quality of information available to the internal audit function would depend on firm implementation of information systems.[42] Further, Maxwell et al warn that given the wide remit of assurance that internal audit has to perform, such as in relation to operational risk management, internal audit functions can be subject to information overload.[43] Silo approaches can often be taken so as to keep the workload of the internal audit function manageable. In such a case, the assurance role of the internal audit function may be affected if it is not able to gain a synthesised or comprehensive view of the firm's operations and processes.

Next, it is queried whether the internal audit function should be in a position to exercise 'enforcement' power, ie, the power to deal with irregularities in terms of issuing remediation instructions or further upwards reporting. Kanter argues that the power of 'enforcement' is a source of real power[44] and such may further secure the authority of internal audit in an organisation. However, the European initiatives and Basel Committee recommendations are silent on this.

Organisational reforms post-crisis have enhanced protections for the independence of the internal audit function and boosted the power and positioning of the function. However, as internal audit was not flagged up for criticism in the crisis, the post-crisis reforms were also rather modest, leaving many aspects to firm implementation, notably in terms of key responsibilities. Regulatory expectations of what the internal audit function can do, however, seem to have ramped up as evidenced in the Basel Committee's recommendations to make the internal audit function effective monitors within firms and intelligence providers to regulators. We argue that such regulatory expectations are not matched by the effects achieved by the organisational reforms, as organisational reforms can only go so far in securing a certain formal positioning of the internal audit function. The efficacy of the function still crucially depends on its intra-firm dynamics within the firm's context and the professionalism of the internal audit function. The following discusses what limitations may be faced by the internal audit function within the firm's risk culture, highlighting the essential weaknesses in the nature of the meta-regulatory framework.

[41] *EBA Guidelines* (n 3) 44, para 29.2; Basel Committee, *The Internal Audit Function* (n 2) 4, Principle 1, para 11.

[42] eg, see Gun Ho Lee, 'Rule-based and Case-based Reasoning Approach for Internal Audit of Bank' (2008) 21 *Knowledge-Based Systems* 140.

[43] Andrew Maxwell, Michael Eichhorn, Hamid Seddighi and Peter Smith, 'Measuring Operational Risk in the Context of Basel II: How can the Internal Audit Function Strengthen its Role?' (2012) *Journal of International Banking Law and Regulation* 161.

[44] Rosabeth Moss Kanter, *Men and Women of the Corporation* (New York: Basic Books, 1977) 174.

Wider Contextual Factors

Is internal audit a key architect of the firm's control culture or is it subject to the firm's control culture? Sarens et al find that in Belgium, one of the key factors affecting the profile of the internal audit function in organisations is the overall ethical culture in the organisation.[45] Organisations that are more committed to an ethical and control culture have larger internal audit outfits, showing that more investment and commitment is made to raise the profile and effectiveness of internal audit, and the internal audit function in turn is able to carry out its assurance functions within the organisation context to be consonant with organisational culture. The importance of organisational culture in general for internal control will be discussed in chapter six.

Evidence is however mixed on the effect of corporate governance upon internal audit. Sarens et al find that corporate governance variables such as ownership concentration, audit committee characteristics and leverage (creditor monitoring) are not relevant for the profile and effectiveness of internal audit.[46] However, others have found that corporate governance variables are more important in jurisdictions characterised by more diffused ownership, stronger securities market regulation and demand for market transparency.[47] Contextual factors such as an ethical culture in firms and certain corporate governance characteristics are important for the firm implementation of the internal audit function. Although this is an inherent weakness in the nature of any meta-regulatory framework, the efficacy of the internal audit function is also shaped by the strength of professionalism brought to the function. The next section discusses the professional dimension of the internal audit function and argues that although the professionalism of internal audit is more advanced than the risk management or compliance professions, such professionalism has been shaped by firm-centric needs. Hence, disjunctions may exist between regulatory expectations of the governance role of internal audit, and the role of internal audit as perceived in professional understanding.

[45] Sarens and Abdolmohammadi, 'Monitoring Effects of the Internal Audit Function' (n 8).

[46] ibid.

[47] Laura Sierra García, Emiliano Ruiz Barbadillo and Manuel Orta Ruiz Pérez, 'Audit Committee and Internal Audit and the Quality of Earnings: Empirical Evidence from Spanish Companies' (2012) 16 *Journal of Management & Governance* 305; Barua, Rama and Sharma, 'Audit Committee Characteristics' (n 40); and see chapter 5.

C. DISJUNCTIONS BETWEEN REGULATORY EXPECTATIONS AND THE ROLE OF THE INTERNAL AUDIT FUNCTION: ANALYSING THE PROFESSIONAL DIMENSION

This section charts the evolution of the internal audit function and profession in financial institutions. The internal audit profession is relatively mature compared with the emerging compliance and risk management functions, and such an appearance of professionalism may be the basis for regulatory expectations of the governance role of the internal audit function.

The Institute for Internal Auditors is the flagship professional body for internal auditors. The UK Chartered Institute was founded in 1948 and has received a royal charter, indicating the consolidation of its identity as the key professional and accrediting organisation for internal auditors. Empirical research also shows that internal auditors are generally regarded as having a common body of professional competencies. There is a rich amount of literature on evaluating the quality of the internal audit.[48] Such empirical research is not only based on organisational factors which may be proxied for internal audit effectiveness (such as independence, discussed in section B)[49] but also based on external auditors' evaluation of the knowledge, skills and experience of internal auditors and their adherence to professional codes of conduct.[50] Mohamed et al report that external auditors are able to assess the effectiveness of internal auditors by looking at the tenure of the internal audit function in the organisation, the staff training internal auditors receive, internal auditors' skills in information technology and computing, and internal auditors' expertise in auditing and accounting.[51] Bame-Aldred et al also find that external auditors evaluate internal auditors by referring to the organisational status and policies

[48] See Barbara Arel, Cathy A Beaudoin and Anna M Cianci, 'The Impact of Ethical Leadership, the Internal Audit Function, and Moral Intensity on a Financial Reporting Decision' (2011) at ssrn.com/abstract=1756284; Mina Pizzini, Shu Lin, Mark Vargus and Douglas Ziegenfuss, 'The Impact of Internal Audit Function Quality and Contribution on Audit Delays' (2011) at ssrn.com/abstract=1673490; Zulkifflee Mohamed, Mazlina Mat Zain, Nava Subramaniam and Wan Fadzilah Wan Yusoff, 'Internal Audit Attributes and External Audit's Reliance on Internal Audit: Implications for Audit Fees' (2012) 16 *International Journal of Auditing* 268.

[49] Glover, Prawitt and Wood, 'Internal Audit Sourcing Arrangement' (n 31) on outsourcing as a proxy for objectivity; Vikram Desai, Robin W Roberts and Rajendra Srivastava, 'An Analytical Model for External Auditor Evaluation of the Internal Audit Function Using Belief Functions' (2006) at ssrn.com/abstract=938183 however posit that it is difficult to evaluate precise skills and competence and hence external auditors evaluate internal auditors using the proxy indicator of objectivity and independence.

[50] See Charles W Bame-Aldred, Duane M Brandon, William F Messier, Larry Rittenberg and Chad M Stefaniak, 'A Summary of Research on External Auditor Reliance on the Internal Audit Function' (2012) at ssrn.com/abstract=2035087; Mohamed, Zain, Subramaniam and Fadzilah, 'Internal Audit Attributes' (n 48).

[51] Mohamed, Zain, Subramaniam and Fadzilah, 'Internal Audit Attributes' (n 48).

supporting the objectivity of the internal audit function, the accounting professional qualifications, and information technological competence of internal auditors.[52] Hence, besides organisational skills, there seems to be some consensus around internal auditors' expertise in accounting and information technology. However, one may say that such research is skewed towards evaluating internal auditors in their financial assurance role and is therefore rather limited in nature. That said, there is much less literature on the evaluation of the effectiveness of the internal audit function in relation to other areas of work beyond financial assurance.[53] Sarens, for example, maps out a list of underexplored issues for future research in relation to the measurability of internal audit effectiveness in relation to corporate governance and risk management, and the profile of a competent internal auditor.[54]

It is queried if regulatory expectations of the internal audit function are based on the impression of internal audit's professional profile, rather than what the profession is able to achieve. This section will explore the nature of internal audit professionalism, and critically cautions against excessive regulatory expectations of substantive outcomes that may be achieved by the internal audit's monitoring role. This section argues that the long history of bottom-up developments in the remit of the internal audit function in serving firm needs has shaped the professional understanding of the internal audit function. Internal audit functions are firm-centric in nature, and they are likely to remain so even if they respond to changes in the remit of their work. In particular, the internal audit function sees itself as growing into management advisory roles in the future. It is argued that there may be significant disjunctions between regulatory expectations of the governance role of the internal audit function as a distinct and almost aloof internal monitor of the firm, and the perception of the professional trajectory of internal audit. Further this section argues that as the remit of the internal audit function grows more expansively in the future, the assurance role of the internal audit function is likely to become more broad level and procedural in nature. The procedural nature of the internal audit function's work is more aligned with firm needs in controlling for agency problems, than with regulatory expectations in securing certain substantive outcomes in firm compliance and risk management.

[52] Bame-Aldred, Brandon, Messier, Rittenberg and Stefaniak, 'A Summary of Research' (n 50).

[53] See, eg, Audrey A Gramling, Irem Nuhoglu and David A Wood, 'A Descriptive Study of Factors Associated with the Internal Audit Function having an Impact: Comparisons between Organizations in a Developed and an Emerging Economy' (2012) at ssrn.com/abstract=1947393, but the work of the internal audit function is described more generally and does not distil precise competencies that are required for various assurance work.

[54] Gerrit Sarens, 'Internal Auditing Research: Where are we Going? Editorial' (2009) 13 *International Journal of Auditing* 1.

Development of Internal Audit in Financial Assurance

Early practice-oriented literature on the internal audit function in banks and financial institutions highlights the key role of branch auditing. Traditional writings such as Davies' article in 1956 refer to the internal audit's role in the 'safeguarding of organisational assets'.[55] This is a protective role, seeking to ensure that organisational assets are not misused. This protective role may be understood as dealing with fraud prevention, fraud detection and perhaps even the handling of discovered fraudulent activity. Shont[56] writes that branch auditing is the earliest traditional role of the internal audit function and provides detailed descriptions of internal audit procedures and checklists[57] with respect to verifying financial flows at the end of each banking business day in terms of the ledger and securities in vaults. The main responsibility of the internal audit function was error detection and the deterrence of employee fraud.[58]

The contemporary internal audit function continues with the protective remit to safeguard the organisation and detect error and fraud, shaped by two driving factors: the rise in the importance of financial reporting to the securities market, and the regulatory framework for micro-prudential regulation. Both regulatory developments have compelled banks and financial institutions to shape the role of the internal audit function as a protective one against mis-disclosure and prudential mismanagement. Although these roles of the internal audit function have been developed due to regulatory demands, they were firm-centric in nature and sought to protect the firm against non-compliance.

The integrity of financial reporting, as discussed in earlier chapters, became an acute issue in the general corporate sector from the 1990s in the UK with the fall of Polly Peck and BCCI and more internationally in the early 2000s with the fall of American energy giant Enron which prompted reforms in the form of the Sarbanes–Oxley Act 2002. In the UK, the Cadbury review which took place after the fall of the BCCI, framed the integrity of financial reporting within a broader context of sound corporate governance.[59] Management fraud in the BCCI and Polly Peck, two large public companies with significant operations in the UK, had collapsed, and these scandals engaged policymakers with the reality of the agency problem. The integrity of financial reporting was adversely affected by a broader malaise of agency problems in corporate governance. The

[55] Davies, 'The Objectives of Internal Auditing' (n 6); Carmichael, 'Hypotheses of Internal Control' (n 5).

[56] Shont, *Internal Bank Auditing* (n 7) ch 1.

[57] ibid, chs 4 and 5.

[58] John Trethowan, "Financial Controls in the Northern Bank Group" in Ray Kinsella (ed), *Internal Controls in Banking* (Chichester: John Wiley & Sons, 1995) 67.

[59] *Report of the Committee on the Financial Aspects of Corporate Governance* (n 9).

Cadbury Committee therefore recommended a model of good corporate governance for companies, including Board composition with non-executive directors, the formation of independent committees of the Board and the more engaged role of shareholders, in order to secure the monitoring of accurate financial reporting at the highest levels. Non-executive directors would also be part of a Board's audit committee that is dedicated to monitoring the integrity of financial reporting. In the US, the fall of Enron also triggered corporate governance reforms in relation to boosting the integrity of financial reporting. The Sarbanes–Oxley Act 2002 imposes mandatory requirements such as: the institution of audit committees[60] that should consist of largely independent directors tasked with overseeing the external auditor; the personal responsibility of the Chief Financial Officer in signing off financial reports,[61] and the institution of internal control which should be assessed and reported by management.[62]

Corporate governance reforms provide the backdrop for shaping the role of the internal audit function in the general corporate sector. It would be a function that provides assurance to the audit committee and the Board on the integrity of the processes and systems that generate and report financial information in the organisation.[63] The financial assurance role of internal audit is observed in many jurisdictions as one of the staple functions of internal audit[64] or the only staple function.[65] This role has also been well studied in empirical literature and many commentators have provided evidence of how the institution of an internal audit function has improved the integrity of financial reporting.

First, the existence of an internal audit function could have a deterring effect upon fraudulent or irregular behaviour that affects the integrity of financial information in the organisation. Such deterrence stems from the possibility that internal audit may detect or question irregularities.[66] Further, higher-level irregularities at the senior management level such as earnings management practices may also be mitigated by the presence of internal audit.[67] Next, internal audit's role in monitoring the integrity

[60] s 301, Sarbanes–Oxley Act 2002.

[61] ibid, s 302.

[62] Ibid, s 404.

[63] Gerrit Sarens, Ignace De Beelde and Patricia Everaert, 'Internal Audit: A Comfort Provider to the Audit Committee' (2009) 41 *The British Accounting Review* 90.

[64] Dominic SB Soh and Nonna Martinov-Bennie, 'The Internal Audit Function: Perceptions of Internal Audit Roles, Effectiveness, and Evaluation' (2011) 26 *Managerial Auditing Journal* 605.

[65] Marika Arena and Kim J Jeppesen, 'The Jurisdiction of Internal Auditing and the Quest for Professionalization: The Danish' (2011) 14 *International Journal of Auditing* 111.

[66] Arel, Beaudoin and Cianci, 'The Impact of Ethical Leadership' (n 48).

[67] DF Prawitt, JL Smith and DA Wood, 'Internal Audit Quality and Earnings Management' (2009) 84(4) *Accounting Review* 1255. For a contrary finding, see R Davidson, J Goodwin-Stewart and P Kent, 'Internal Governance Structures and Earnings Management' (2005) 45 *Accounting & Finance* 241. A group of other researchers in Spain however found

of financial information and reporting also improves the chances of fraud or irregularity detection. Several studies in general organisation literature show that the existence of internal audit in firms entails more self-reported irregularities, less detection of errors by external auditors[68] and more effective actual detection of financial fraud.[69] Coram et al[70] and Lin et al[71] have carried out empirical research to show that internal audit is able to capture irregularities and weaknesses at an early stage leading to effective self-reporting of incidences.

The role of the internal audit function in the general corporate sector in financial assurance is therefore well established, and internal audit in banks and financial institutions which are listed or publicly quoted would likely take on a similar role.[72] The establishment of a reporting line for internal audit to the audit committee (discussed earlier) further reinforces the remit of the internal audit function in financial assurance. This assurance role has also extended to a form of corporate governance assurance.[73] Such corporate governance assurance is in part derived from financial reporting assurance that serves to support Board accountability to shareholders, but also extends more generally to providing assurance on the governance quality in an organisation such as in relation to Board competence and oversight, adherence to corporate codes of conduct and stakeholder relations.

The Role of Internal Audit in Relation to Micro-Prudential Regulation

Although the internal audit function may be dominated by its financial assurance role in the general corporate sector, the internal audit function

that an actively engaged Audit Committee on the Board represented by higher numbers of meetings correlates with less earnings management, see García, Barbadillo and Pérez, 'Audit Committee and Internal Audit' (n 47).

[68] W Wallace and R Kreutzfeldt, 'Distinctive Characteristics of Entities with an Internal Audit Department and the Association of the Quality of Such Departments with Errors' (1991) 7 *Contemporary Accounting Research* 485.

[69] Al-Shetwi, Ramadili, Hassan, Chowdury and Sori, 'Impact of Internal Audit Function' (n 8); S Nestor, 'The Impact of Changing Corporate Governance Norms on Economic Crime' (2004) 11 *Journal of Financial Crime* 347.

[70] Coram, Ferguson and Moroney, 'Internal Audit' (n 32).

[71] Lin, Pizzini, Vargus and Bardhan, 'The Role of Internal Audit Function' (n 8).

[72] Barclay Simpson, *An Introduction to Internal Auditing in Banking*, para 5.6 at www.barclaysimpson.com/document_uploaded/Intro%20IA%20Banking%20publication.pdf.

[73] Georges Selim, Sally Woodward and Marco Allegrini, 'Internal Auditing and Consulting Practice: A Comparison between UK/Ireland and Italy' (2009) 13 *International Journal of Auditing* 9; Sarens and Abdolmohammadi, 'Factors Associated with Best Practices in Internal Auditing' (n 17); Gramling, Nuhoglu and Wood, 'A Descriptive Study of Factors' (n 53).

in banks and financial institutions is also significantly involved in micro-prudential compliance. In response to the micro-prudential regulatory framework led by the Basel Committee, the internal audit function has been developed to engage with monitoring prudential risk management in banks and financial institutions. Kinsella[74] and Quinn[75] argued in the mid-1990s that internal audit is responsible for checking on the expanding range of micro-prudential regulatory controls instituted at banks to match the range of risks undertaken in credit and market activities.

Capital adequacy is the mainstay of micro-prudential regulation and has been developed and refined in the Basel I, II and now III Accords. Under Basel I, a framework was developed to assign credit risk weightings to different categories of debt, so that banks could set aside capital against the possibility of default.[76] Basel I focused on credit risk, and subsequently, the Basel Committee started work on market risk in 1996.[77] Other categories of risk are increasingly being recognised in the face of changes to business models in the financial sector, particularly in terms of conglomeration and the rise of financial 'supermarkets'.[78] In 1996, the Basel Committee recognised that banks' trading books, particularly in foreign exchange and commodities, could also present a significant source of risk and recommended that market risk be taken into account in capital adequacy provision.[79] The Basel Committee then issued a new Capital Accord in 2004 incorporating changes to credit risk computation and its work on market risk. The Basel II Accord also recognised operational risk as another significant source of risk for financial institutions.[80] Operational risk is defined as the risk of loss resulting from inadequate or failed internal processes, people and systems, or from external events. This definition includes legal risk, but excludes strategic and reputational risk.

Further, as chapter one has discussed, the Basel II Capital Accord provides that firms may use proprietary approaches to calculate certain

[74] Ray Kinsella, 'Introduction: Internal Controls in Banking' in Ray Kinsella (ed), *Internal Controls in Banking* (Chichester: John Wiley & Sons 1995) 1.

[75] Brian Quinn, 'The Bank of England and the Development of Internal Control Systems' in Ray Kinsella (ed), *Internal Controls in Banking* (Chichester: John Wiley & Sons 1995) 35.

[76] Basel Committee on Banking Supervision, *Basel I: International Convergence of Capital Measurement and Capital Standards* (Basel: BIS, 1998) at www.bis.org/publ/bcbs04A.pdf.

[77] Basel Committee on Banking Supervision, *Amendment to the Capital Accord to Incorporate Market Risks* (Basel: BIS, 1996) at www.bis.org/publ/bcbs24.pdf?noframes=1.

[78] Jeremy W Markham, 'Super-Regulator: A Comparative Analysis of Securities and Derivatives Regulation in the US, UK and Japan' (2003) 28 *Brooklyn Journal of International Law* 319; Arthur E Wilmarth, 'The Transformation of the Financial Services Industry: 1975–2000, Competition, Consolidation and Increased Risks' (2002) 2 *University of Illinois Law Rev* 215.

[79] Basel Committee, *Amendment to the Capital Accord to Incorporate Market Risks* (n 77).

[80] Basel Committee on Banking Supervision, *Basel II: International Convergence of Capital Measurement and Capital Standards: A Revised Framework* (rev November 2005, Basel: BIS, 2004) at www.bis.org/publ/bcbs118.pdf.

aspects of credit, market and operational risks if approved by regulators. The risk management functions would be responsible for developing and implementing these proprietary approaches, but the role of the internal audit function would be to provide assurance for risk management and internal control generally.[81] Further, the Basel Committee envisages that the internal audit function oversees risk management functions, such as in relation to operational risk.[82]

The role of internal audit in providing assurance for the risk management of financial risks such as credit, market, interest rate, exchange rate and sovereign risks as well as widely defined 'operational risks' is a challenging one in terms of the width of the remit. Can the professional competencies of the internal audit function cope with the width of the remit? Further, in relation to providing assurance over firm proprietary approaches, the internal audit function may face difficulties as there is a lack of standardised guidelines to fall back on. In relation to operational risk in particular, this area of risk management remains rather fluid and inchoate, and providing assurance over operational risk management may be particularly challenging.

Fernandez-Laviada et al find in an empirical survey in 2007 that the operational risk management departments in banks and financial institutions are still emerging in nature but the internal audit function is required to provide assurance of the quality of operational risk management to senior management and the Board.[83] Jobst argues that banks have not devoted sufficient resources or undertaken significant efforts in defining and determining the range of operational risks to be managed.[84] The challenges surrounding the identification and measuring operational risk at the primary level would affect how internal audit could provide a reasonable assurance of operational risk management. Maxwell et al also find that internal audit is in need of improvement in its assurance role relating to operational risk management, particularly in relation to technical knowledge and being able to more accurately judge the quality of control effected by the operational risk management department.[85] These difficulties may be mitigated as the Basel Committee moves towards a

[81] Basel Committee, *The Internal Audit Function* (n 2) 4, Principle 1, paras 10–11.

[82] ibid, 78, Principle 13, para 60ff.

[83] Ana Fernandez-Laviada, 'Internal Audit Function Role in Operational Risk Management' (2007) *Journal of Financial Regulation and Compliance* 143.

[84] Andreas A Jobst, 'The Credit Crisis and Operational Risk—Implications for Practitioners and Regulators' (2010) 5 *Journal of Operational Risk* 43.

[85] Andrew Maxwell, Michael Eichhorn, Hamid Seddighi and Peter Smith, 'Measuring Operational Risk in the Context of Basel II: Are Internal Audit Functions on the "Right" Hymn Sheet?' (2010) *Journal of International Banking Law and Regulation* 543; Maxwell, Eichhorn, Seddighi and Smith, 'Measuring Operational Risk' (n 43) (on the organisational weaknesses of the internal audit function).

more standardised approach to measuring operational risks.[86] Although a challenging pursuit, the internal audit function has been shaped to meet a growing number of firm needs.

However, in providing assurance for micro-prudential risk management, the internal audit function not only has to engage with certain rather technical areas, but has to determine how to judge the application of firm discretion in such risk management.[87] This section will argue that the internal audit function has coped with the challenges of its assurance remit by taking a largely broad level and procedural approach. This approach characterises the professional competencies of internal audit in a certain way, and questions will be raised as to whether regulatory expectations of the governance role of the internal audit function are appropriate given the nature of its professional competencies.

Expanding Remit of Internal Audit's Role and Implications

The width of the assurance remit of the internal audit function has been further extended in the Basel Committee's post-crisis articulation on the role of internal audit. The Basel Committee provides that '[e]very activity (including outsourced activities) and every entity of the bank should fall within the overall scope of the internal audit function'[88] and that the internal audit function should establish audit plans that cover the monitoring of the risk management framework and function (as discussed in chapter three), micro-prudential risk management, financial information and regulatory reporting, the compliance function, and the corporate governance framework in banks and financial institutions.[89] The European initiatives in contrast are more modest, focusing the work of the internal audit function on monitoring the risk control/management and compliance functions.[90] However, the Financial Stability Board (FSB) proposes to expand the internal audit's assurance role in relation to the setting of risk appetite, the establishment of quantitative risk limits and metrics and the monitoring of risk management.[91] The IIA (embracing the Basel Committee's recommendations) sets out unequivocally in its new

[86] Basel Committee on Banking Supervision, *Consultative Document: Operational Risk—Revisions to the Simpler Approaches* (October 2014).

[87] The scope for firm discretion is being reduced as policymakers move towards standardisation and enhanced supervision of what remaining scope for discretion there is left. This is discussed in chapter 1, section B.

[88] Basel Committee, *The Internal Audit Function* (n 2) 7–8, Principle 6, paras 29–31.

[89] ibid, 8–10, Principle 7, paras 32–45.

[90] *EBA Guidelines* (n 3) 40, para 29.

[91] Financial Stability Board, *Principles for an Effective Risk Appetite Framework: Consultative Document* (17 July 2013) para 4.6.

Financial Services Code (which provides guidelines for internal audit in the financial sector) that 'internal audit's scope shall be unrestricted'.[92]

Even in the general corporate sector, the trend of involving internal audit in an assurance role in corporate governance[93] and risk management generally[94] has taken off and has resulted in an ever-expanding remit of the internal audit function. Although this is partly exogenously driven by regulatory and soft law reforms, the internal audit profession is supportive of its expanding assurance remit.[95] The Institute of Internal Auditors, which is recognised as the professional body for internal auditors,[96] has issued a new definition of 'internal audit' in 2011, viz,

> [i]nternal auditing is an independent, objective assurance and consulting activity designed to add value and improve an organization's operations. It helps an organization accomplish its objectives by bringing a systematic, disciplined approach to evaluate and improve the effectiveness of risk management, control, and governance processes.[97]

The expanding remit of the internal audit function is welcomed by the internal profession, perhaps in order to prevent their marginalisation as other internal control functions are being empowered and revamped.

However, the expanding remit of internal audit raises two questions: the first, is whether internal auditors can cope with new demands in terms of their professional competence; and the second, is whether the expansion of remit puts internal audit into a position where it becomes more intimately wrapped up in firm-centric perspectives and needs at every level. The internal audit function could become shaped to be a general 'protector' of the firm, such as envisaged in the 'Corporate Defence Mechanism' vision put forward by Lyons.[98] Such a role moves the internal audit function closer to the firm and further from a more aloof monitoring role, as regulators may prefer. The Price Waterhouse Coopers survey of the internal audit profession in 2013 also opines that the profession needs

[92] *Financial Services Code* (UKIIA, 2013) para 3 at www.iia.org.uk/resources/sector-specific-standards-guidance/financial-services/financial-services-code.

[93] Cristina Boţa-Avram, 'Main Coordinates of Internal Audit Practices in the Context of Corporate Governance at European Level' (2012) at ssrn.com/abstract=2129421; Sarens and Abdolmohammadi, 'Monitoring Effects of the Internal Audit Function' (n 8).

[94] Laura Spira and Michael Page, 'Risk Management: The Reinvention of Internal Control and the Changing Role of Internal Audit' (2003) 16 *Accounting, Auditing and Accountability Journal* 640; Jan Cattrysse, 'Reflections on Corporate Governance and the Role of the Internal Auditor' (2005) at ssrn.com/abstract=485364, 32ff; Marika Arena and Giovanni Azzone, 'Identifying Organizational Drivers of Internal Audit Effectiveness' (2009) 13 *International Journal of Auditing* 43.

[95] See Sean Lyons, 'Enterprise Defense Management—Internal Auditors to the Fore' (2013) at papers.ssrn.com/sol3/papers.cfm?abstract_id=2304665.

[96] See *EBA Guidelines* (n 3) para 29.5, explanatory note.

[97] Institute of Internal Auditors, 'Definition of Internal Auditing' (2011) at www.theiia.org/guidance/standards-and-guidance/ippf/definition-of-internal-auditing.

[98] Lyons, 'Enterprise Defense Management' (n 95).

to continue to make itself relevant to firms, and one measure of internal audit effectiveness lies in whether the function has become more proactive in assisting management in internal control design.[99]As will be pointed out shortly, such a proactive role further reinforces the closeness between the internal audit function and management, and this could affect the objectivity that regulators wish to protect on the part of internal audit to serve a governance and monitoring role.

Professional Competencies

The wide assurance remit of the internal audit function immediately raises the question as to whether the function has all the necessary professional competencies to provide assurance over such a broad range of matters. For example, how would internal audit monitor the effectiveness of the compliance function? McCormick, in discussing the range of legal risks faced by banks, explains the expanding range of contemporary legal risks that have to be understood and navigated by legal and compliance departments in banks.[100] To this end, legal and compliance departments need to identify, assess and advise on various legal (transactional) and regulatory risks. Is the internal audit function in a position to evaluate how robustly the compliance function has dealt with legal and regulatory risks? In terms of anti-money laundering compliance, prescriptions in the law and severe penalties[101] have necessitated the institution of specific systems in banks and financial institutions to deal with customer due diligence, thresholds for alerts and money laundering reporting.[102] Mulig et al argue that the internal audit function has also had to keep up with the developments in anti-money laundering laws in order to verify and ensure that anti-money laundering controls at banks and financial institutions adequately meet the requirements under law.[103] Constant adjustment of skills and expertise on the part of the internal audit function is required. The regular survey of the internal audit profession carried out by the IIA also points out that internal auditors feel that they are in constant need of bridging skills

[99] Price Waterhouse Coopers, *2013 State of the Internal Audit Profession Study* (2014) at www.pwc.com/en_US/us/risk-assurance-services/publications/assets/pwc-2013-state-of-internal-audit-profession-study.pdf.

[100] Roger McCormick, *Legal Risk in Financial Markets*, 2nd edn (Oxford: Oxford University Press, 2010) chs 24 and 25 in particular.

[101] See s 327ff, UK Proceeds of Crime Act 2002.

[102] Tim Bennett, *Money Laundering Compliance*, 2nd edn (W Sussex: Tottel Publishing, 2007) ch 14. Procedures and systems have been developed based on the Joint Money-Laundering Steering Group guidance at www.jmlsg.org.uk/jmlsg-guidance and the Wolfsberg Group of Anti-Money Laundering Principles and Compliance.

[103] Elizabeth E Mulig and L Murphy Smith, 'Understanding and Preventing Money Laundering' (2004) 19 *Internal Auditing* 22.

gaps, such as in enterprise risk management.[104] Further, as the UK IIA has now placed much emphasis on internal audit's role in overseeing the risk management framework and function in financial institutions,[105] it is also queried as to what extent internal audit should be in possession of quantitative skills and training in order to provide assurance on the effectiveness or otherwise of the risk management function.

The IIA[106] and the Basel Committee[107] have articulated the broad level qualities internal audit must possess, ie, objectivity, professionalism and integrity. The IIA has left it open as to what specialist skills are required on the part of internal auditors.[108] The Institute's standard of Proficiency requires that internal auditors need to have adequate knowledge to audit the task undertaken but not at the level of the expert primarily responsible for the task.[109] Further, competencies, knowledge and skills are regarded as a collective term that may be appropriately certified but must be appropriate to the task at hand. The Standard of Professional due care requires that internal auditors consider the needs of the organisation, the materiality and complexity of the task undertaken, the adequacy of procedures and systems used, the cost–benefit of the assurance undertaken and the appropriateness of technology and data analysis techniques used.[110] Literature on the practice of internal auditing seems to focus on internal audit as putting in place frameworks for planning, engagement with other departments and general oversight, evaluation and reporting of internal control.[111] It seems that the professional competencies of internal auditing are not defined in relation to distinct bodies of substantive knowledge, but in relation to skills that are coordinative and procedural in nature. Soh et al argue that the role of the internal audit function is one of meta-oversight, and this is increasingly becoming recognised as its staple role.[112]

The key responsibilities of the internal audit function thus lie in instituting procedures and systems in implementing control and in monitoring, reviewing and adjusting such procedures. In discussing how internal audit verifies bank compliance with regulatory requirements such as customer-facing legal duties and regulatory duties to combat money laundering

[104] IIA, *Core Competences* (n 17) Executive Summary, 2.

[105] *Financial Services Code* (UKIIA, 2013) paras 4 and 10 at www.iia.org.uk/resources/sector-specific-standards-guidance/financial-services/financial-services-code.

[106] Desai, Roberts and Srivastava, 'An Analytical Model' (n 49); Standards 1100, 1200, The Institute of Internal Auditors, *International Standards for the Professional Practice of Internal Auditing (Standards)* at www.theiia.org.

[107] Basel Committee, *The Internal Audit Function* (n 2) Principles 2, 3 and 4, para 12ff.

[108] IIA, *International Standards* (n 106) Standards 1210 and 1220 on Proficiency and Due Professional Care respectively).

[109] ibid, Standard 1210 on Proficiency.

[110] ibid, Standard 1220 on Due Professional Care.

[111] KH Spencer Pickett, *The Essential Guide to Internal Auditing*, 2nd edn (Chichester, John Wiley & Sons, 2011).

[112] Soh and Martinov-Bennie, 'The Internal Audit Function' (n 64).

and financial crime, Shont provides a snapshot of how the internal audit function designs procedures to ensure that all customer due diligence has been achieved, to record customer needs, to make relevant disclosures and warnings, and to accomplish all relevant paperwork.[113] This snapshot may be a typical representation of how the internal audit function works. In other words, proceduralisation may be an essential characteristic of the professional competence of internal audit. Eden et al also provide an example of internal audit procedures in auditing bank branches in compliance with management policies and rules.[114] Proceduralisation occurs in the verification of written records; the analysis of policies adopted by the audited department; the evaluation of the logic and completeness of the department's procedures; and in ensuring that internal services and staffing are efficient and appropriate to serve the organisation's policies.

Proceduralisation, according to Power, is a way of manifesting the orderliness and rationality of a professionalised work system, such orderliness and rationality providing the basis on which the internal audit function provides assurance.[115] The work of the internal audit function may be characterised by the implementation of systems and procedures to verify and check that various organisational and operational processes have been completed or that information recording or reporting has been achieved.[116] Spira and Page have pointed out that the internal audit function has always adopted a technocratic, almost scientific approach to its role, and proceduralisation is central to its administration.[117] Proceduralisation provides an impression of credibility and order to the role of the internal audit function. Chapter one has warned of the pros and cons of proceduralisation, in particular, in relation to whether proceduralisation may become ritualistic, ossified and reduced to 'box-ticking' exercises. Can effective meta-oversight of a range of specialist functions be provided via broad-level proceduralisation without necessarily drawing on substantive knowledge and skills? This issue is particularly relevant to banks and financial institutions where transaction and financial flows may be complex and difficult to monitor.[118] Leese, writing in the mid-1990s, is

[113] Shont, *Internal Bank Auditing* (n 7) chs 4 and 5.

[114] Dov Eden and Leah Moriah, 'Impact of Internal Auditing on Branch Bank Performance: A Field Experiment' (1996) 68 *Organizational Behavior and Human Decision Processes* 262.

[115] Michael Power, *Organized Uncertainty* (Oxford: Oxford University Press, 2008).

[116] Lee, 'Rule-based and Case-based Reasoning Approach for Internal Audit of Bank' (n 42); Lin, Pizzini, Vargus and Bardhan, 'The Role of Internal Audit Function' (n 8).

[117] Spira and Page, 'Risk Management' (n 94).

[118] Gillian Tett, 'The Banks that are too Complex to Exist' *Financial Times* (8 June 2012) citing Henry TC Hu, 'Too Complex to Depict? Innovation, "Pure Information" and the SEC Disclosure Paradigm' (2012) 90 *Texas Law Review* 1601. Complexity in information has been empirically researched as one of the key reasons for internal control failure, see Jan Pfister, *Managing Organizational Culture for Effective Internal Control* (Berlin: Physica-Verlag, 2009) ch 4.

already of the view that it is challenging for the internal audit function to catch up with the rapidly changing business conditions of banks in order to remain relevant and useful to the organisation.[119] One may view procedural meta-oversight as a superficial form of assurance. However, it may be argued that such a form of procedural meta-oversight is sufficient for the needs of the firm as the internal audit function's key role is to monitor that agency problems do not subsist in internal control functions. Such agency problems can be detected through procedural approaches, as deviation from policies is often a sign of agency problems.[120] However, regulators should be cautious not to place undue regulatory expectations on the internal audit function to deliver substantive outcomes such as fraud or failure prevention.

Further, the procedural nature of internal audit's work means that the effectiveness of the internal audit function is highly dependent on the organisational context. The organisational context conditions the procedures that would be designed and implemented by the internal audit function. The Institute of Internal Auditors regular survey, the Common Body of Knowledge, also points out that organisational factors affect the extent of adherence and implementation of the Institute's professional standards in an organisation.[121] Resource limitations, size of the internal audit and management support are all key factors affecting the extent of convergent adoption of the Institute's standards, and this means that organisational factors affect the extent of professionalism of the internal audit function in an organisation. The importance of organisational factors to the professional effectiveness of internal audit may give rise to opportunities for organisational manipulation. Although the post-crisis reforms have become more prescriptive in the organisational dimension and such may reduce the scope for organisational manipulation, section B has pointed out issues that remain open. The internal audit profession's embrace of its management consultant role, that will shortly be discussed, further makes it susceptible to organisational manipulation.

Further, given the expansive remit for the internal audit function, the priorities of the internal audit function may have to be determined according to a risk-based approach, as equal intensity in meta-oversight across all business and control functions in the firm may be impracticable. The Basel Committee acknowledges that the internal audit function's meta-oversight as applied across an organisation can only be carried out in a

[119] Graham Leese, 'The Role of Group Audit' in Ray Kinsella (ed), *Internal Controls in Banking* (Chichester: John Wiley & Sons, 1995) 47.

[120] Cahill, 'Audit Committee and Internal Audit Effectiveness' (n 21); Eric Pichet, 'What Governance Lessons Should Be Learnt from the Societe Générale's Kerviel Affair?' (2008) 3 *La Revue Française de Gouvernance d'Entreprise* 117.

[121] IIA, *Core Competencies* (n 17) Executive Summary, 3.

risk-based approach,[122] ie, selectively determining the higher-risk areas in which to concentrate critical scrutiny and adopting more superficial checks on areas of low-risk.[123] Risk-based approaches have been affirmed at the European level.[124] This approach accords with the framing of internal audit's role as a high-level architect of the firm's control culture,[125] and not as policemen of substantive decisions made by business departments or other internal control functions.

In sum, the professional competencies of an internal auditor relate to navigating an organisation and being able to provide critical and objective reflection on the systems, frameworks and procedures in the organisation. The role of the internal audit function is one of general meta-oversight[126] and not a specific duplication of effort in order to detect errors. Hence, regulatory expectations should not extend to particular substantive outcomes, as such meta-oversight is not insurance against substantive risk management or compliance deficiencies.

The Role of Internal Audit as Management Consultant

The IIA regards the internal audit function as being able to act as a monitoring and feedback mechanism, providing recommendations of best practice to management, acting as a catalyst for improvement.[127] Empirical evidence suggests that the internal audit function increasingly sees itself as being in a consulting role,[128] helping to design systems and frameworks and being consulted upon in respect of particular tasks and projects. Selim et al observe from empirical survey that the internal audit function is being used in a consultative capacity in respect of designing a wide range of systems, and in mergers and acquisitions planning, contingency planning

[122] Basel Committee on Banking Supervision, *The Internal Audit Function in Banks* (Consultation Paper, December 2011).

[123] Sidney A Shapiro and Robert L Glicksman, *Risk Regulation at Risk* (Stanford, CA: Stanford University Press, 2003) on risk-based approaches to regulation, but gives a generally good account of how risk-based approaches work. Power, *Organized Uncertainty* (n 115) argues that public sector adoption of risk-based approaches has been inspired by and borrowed from private sector approaches anyway.

[124] *EBA Guidelines* (n 3) 44, para 29.5.

[125] Shont, *Internal Bank Auditing* (n 7) ch 6.

[126] Pfister, *Managing Organizational Culture* (n 118) ch 2, arguing that the concept of 'internal control' is an enterprise-wide or comprehensive business view that captures how every function exercised within the organisation is exercised within the parameters of organisational principles, policies and culture.

[127] Chartered Institute of Internal Auditors, *What is Internal Auditing*? at www.theiia.org.

[128] See Soh and Martinov-Bennie, 'The Internal Audit Function' (n 64) 605; Boţa-Avram, 'Main Coordinates of Internal Audit Practices' (n 93); Price Waterhouse Coopers, *2013 State of the Internal Audit Profession Study* (n 99).

and disaster recovery, project management, inventory management, management of information systems, security management, outsourcing and cost reviews, risk management reviews, and even strategic management and change management.[129] Thunuguntla also argues that the internal audit function can act as management consultants, assisting management in solving problems and acting as management coaches.[130]

The profession may be in favour of expanding towards management consulting as such a role seems more in line with 'adding value'[131] to the organisation and therefore does not assume a more unfavourable position of being a cost centre. Further, Burton et al find in empirical research that internal auditors still suffer from an image problem and are being regarded as second-class citizens in the firm.[132] Internal auditors are often regarded as problem detectors and 'nit-pickers', or as watchdogs in an organisation and hence suffer from an unpopular disposition. This unpopular disposition has resulted in the lack of enthusiasm on the part of employees to be hired or posted to an internal audit position. The profession's 're-branding' of internal audit as a management consulting position may thus boost the profile of the profession, elevate its organisational position (such as becoming a rotational post for management training) and enable the function to be staffed with better qualified candidates. Further, the consulting role of the internal audit function may also provide internal audit with more access to information and proximity to management and operational departments, assisting in its assurance role.

However, there are certain consequences associated with turning into management consultants, chief of which is compromising the objectivity of the internal audit function. Gramling et al's empirical research indicates that where internal auditors have been involved in designing systems, they are generally ill-disposed to audit such systems subsequently, showing a reduced tendency to be objectively critical or sceptical in their audit.[133] Internal audit's management consulting role will tend to undermine the overall effectiveness of the function in policing and monitoring. It may be argued that internal audit personnel should only review and monitor systems that they have not been involved in designing. However, the general ethos of being involved in management consulting could still have an overall impact upon the objectivity of internal audit, even if formal independence is instituted.

[129] Selim, Woodward and Allegrini, 'Internal Auditing and Consulting Practice' (n 73).

[130] Jagannadham Thunuguntla, 'Standards on Internal Audit- Codifying the Best Practices' (2011) at ssrn.com/abstract=1754776.

[131] Price Waterhouse Coopers, *2013 State of the Internal Audit Profession Study* (n 99).

[132] F Greg Burton, Matthew Starliper, Scott L Summers and David A Wood, 'Recruiting Internal Auditors: The Effects of Using the Internal Audit Function as a Management Training Ground and Performing Consulting Services' (2012) at ssrn.com/abstract=2162611.

[133] Audrey A Gramling, Arnold Schneider and Lori B Chefchik, 'Effects of Prior Internal Audit Work on Internal Control Evaluations' (2012) at ssrn.com/abstract=2162959.

The independence and objectivity of the internal audit function arguably forms the basis for regulatory expectations of the internal monitoring and governance role of the function that ensures the securing of the firm's adherence to regulatory objectives. European initiatives expressly prohibit banks and financial institutions from involving the internal audit function in designing or selecting models or risk management tools,[134] but there is no blanket prohibition against management consulting in general. However, it is queried if the internal audit function acting as management consultant would be able to shape the control culture of the firm in a more powerful and persuasive manner. If so, the management consultant role would not be contrary to regulatory expectations of internal audit's role. Hansen et al's empirical research suggests that internal audit is usually sensitive to the tone at the top, but there is little evidence to suggest that it may be able to influence the tone at the top.[135] In sum, there is the potential that the professional understanding of internal auditors may diverge from regulatory expectations, and regulators may wish to take a balanced approach in the meta-regulation of the internal audit function and be mindful of undue regulatory expectations of its role.

Professional Ethics and Ethical Assurance?

Finally, it is queried whether there is a role for the internal audit function to contribute to the development of an ethical control culture by virtue of its professional stature. Such a role may be aligned with meeting regulatory expectations while mitigating any undue expectations of the achievement of substantive outcomes. The IIA provides a brief Code of Ethics for internal auditors based on the four principles of integrity, objectivity, confidentiality and competence.[136] Integrity refers to honesty, diligence and responsibility in discharging functions and in securing regulatory and legal compliance, and compliance with the ethical principles of the organisation; objectivity refers to the lack of bias in performing the audit and avoidance of conflicts of interest; confidentiality refers to prudent use of information and avoidance of abuse; and competence refers to possessing reasonable knowledge and skills for auditing the task at hand and engagement in continuing professional development and training.[137]

134 *EBA Guidelines* (n 3) 44, para 29.4.

135 James Hansen, Nathaniel M Stephens and David A Wood, 'Entity-Level Controls: The Internal Auditor's Assessment of Management Tone at the Top' (2008) at ssrn.com/abstract=1297362.

136 IIA, *Code of Ethics* at na.theiia.org/standards-guidance/mandatory-guidance/pages/code-of-ethics.aspx, and www.iia.org.uk/resources/global-guidance/code-of-ethics.

137 These ethical principles are reflected in the Basel Committee, *The Internal Audit Function* (n 2) 4–6, Principles 2, 3 and 4, paras 13–25.

This book suggests that the professionalism of the internal audit function could be understood as the infusion of professional ethics into the ethical control culture at firms. Such understanding may go some way towards protecting the professionalism of the internal audit function from being submerged in firm-centric perspectives. Such understanding could also provide a sounder basis for more practical regulatory expectations for the role of the internal audit function.

D. CONCLUSION

The internal audit function, as a third line of defence, is perhaps most overtly relied on by regulators as an architect of firm control culture that gate-keeps the firm from missing or falling short of regulatory objectives. Regulatory expectations may also be based on the relatively more mature profile of the professionalism of the internal audit function.

Post-crisis regulatory reforms have enhanced certain organisational attributes of the internal audit function, notably in protecting its independence and objectivity in banks and financial institutions. These attributes are arguably important for securing regulatory expectations of the internal audit function in being able to 'supervise', monitor and report on issues within the firm. However, the chapter argues that the professional understanding of the roles and responsibilities of the internal audit function may be somewhat contrary to regulatory expectations. The chapter argues that the evolution of the internal audit function predates regulation and has always taken on a firm-centric emphasis. Even as the remit of the internal audit function has changed and grown in response to modern regulatory demands, the profession sees itself as meeting firm needs and adding value to the firm. Its largely procedural approaches and increasing importance as management consultant may to a certain extent diverge from regulatory expectations.

However, it remains to be seen to what extent national financial regulators may adopt the Basel Committee's recommendation that internal audit should directly engage with regulators. Such engagement would define the internal audit function along the lines of intelligence provision to regulators, and would introduce a new channel of accountability, ie, to regulators. Direct accountability to regulators will likely change internal auditors' view of their professionalism and may influence the manner in which they carry out their roles and responsibilities. European legislation has hitherto not taken this step.

5

The Contextual Frameworks of Corporate Governance and Organisational Culture

A. INTERNAL CONTROL AS SITUATED WITHIN THE FRAMEWORKS OF CORPORATE GOVERNANCE AND ORGANISATIONAL CULTURE

THE META-REGULATION OF internal control functions discussed in chapters two to four is purposed towards achieving firm adherence to regulatory objectives. The chapters have also pointed out the common post-crisis approach of enhancing the organisational positioning, profile, power, resources and accountability of internal control functions in order to make them more effective. As internal control functions are situated within an organisational fabric, the question arises as to whether it is adequate just to reform the organisational dimensions relating to internal control functions. Should wider organisational aspects such as corporate governance and even culture or sub-cultures[1] be subject to regulatory governance?

Corporate governance may be defined as 'a system by which companies are directed or controlled'.[2] The OECD defines corporate governance as

> [p]rocedures and processes according to which an organisation is directed and controlled. The corporate governance structure specifies the distribution of rights and responsibilities among the different participants in the organisation—such as the board, managers, shareholders and other stakeholders—and lays down the rules and procedures for decision-making.[3]

Corporate governance relates to the framework for the exercise of powers in decision-making in companies, and revolves around the dynamics

[1] Edgar H Schein, *Organizational Culture and Leadership* (NY: Jossey-Bass, 2010) 55ff.

[2] Adrian Cadbury, *Report of the Committee on the Financial Aspects of Corporate Governance* (December 1992) (Cadbury Report) para 2.5.

[3] *OECD Principles of Corporate Governance* (2004) at www.oecd.org/corporate/oecd principles-ofcorporategovernance.htm.

of Board–shareholder relations[4] in the 'agency' paradigm.[5] The agency paradigm is an important one even in many continental European corporate governance systems where stakeholders other than shareholders assume powers in corporate decision-making.[6] Organisational culture may be defined as 'a set of shared mental assumptions that guide interpretation and action in organizations by defining appropriate behaviour for various situations'.[7] Such mental assumptions could be based on a variety of interacting factors such as the organisation's power and control structures, mission, values, rituals, symbols, myths and stories.[8] The G-30 regards corporate governance as a form of 'hardware' in the firm in terms of an organising framework for decision-making but organisational culture may be regarded as 'software' in terms of implementing actual corporate practices.[9] Corporate governance is important in the shaping of an overall organisational culture but is not the only factor for the development of organisational culture or organisational change.[10]

The corporate governance framework of a firm and its organisational culture therefore provide the 'hardware' and 'software' for the overall risk and control culture within which internal control functions are located.[11] The effectiveness of internal control functions is shaped by the overall risk and control culture at firms.[12] As corporate governance and organisational culture are important contextual forces that shape the implementation of internal control functions, certain aspects of corporate governance are now subject to express regulatory requirements. The regulation of aspects of corporate governance, which will be discussed in detail in chapter six, is purposed towards facilitating an optimal control culture in firms. It is

[4] 'Governance and the Code' in the UK Corporate Governance Code 2012 at www.frc.org.uk/Our-Work/Publications/Corporate-Governance/UK-Corporate-Governance-Code-September-2012.aspx, para 7.

[5] M Jensen and W Meckling, 'Theory of the Firm: Managerial Behavior, Agency Costs and Ownership Structure' (1976) 3 *Journal of Financial Economics* 305.

[6] European Company Law Experts, Paul Davies, Guido Ferrarini, Klaus Hopt, Alain Pietrancosta, Rolf Skog, Stanislaw Soltysinski, Jaap Winter, Eddy Wymeersch, 'Response to the European Commission's Green Paper "The EU Corporate Governance Framework"' (2011) at europeancompanylawexperts.files.wordpress.com/2012/04/ssrn-id1912548.pdf.

[7] D Ravasi and M Schultz, 'Responding to Organizational Identity Threats: Exploring the Role of Organizational Culture' (2006) 49 *Academy of Management Journal* 433.

[8] Generally, see Edgar H Schein, *Corporate Culture: What it is and How to Change it* (Classic reprint) (Forgotten Books, 2012); Mats Alvesson, *Understanding Organizational Culture* (London: Sage, 2012).

[9] G-30, *Towards Effective Governance in Financial Institutions* (2012) at www.group30.org/rpt_64.shtml.

[10] Thomas G Cummings and Christopher G Worley, *Organization Development and Change*, 8th edn (Boston, MA: South-Western College Publishing, 2004).

[11] G-30, *Towards Effective Governance* (n 9).

[12] Deepa Govindarajan, 'Corporate Risk Appetite: Ensuring Board and Senior Management Accountability for Risk' (2011) at ssrn.com/abstract=1962126.

less certain whether aspects of organisational culture may be susceptible to regulation to any extent.[13]

This chapter first discusses why aspects of corporate governance and organisational culture are salient to the risk and control cultures in which internal control functions are situated. With the benefit of hindsight, many such perspectives have been developed in the wake of the global financial crisis of 2008–09. Chapter six will take on where this chapter leaves off and explore the post-crisis reforms into corporate governance and organisational culture which are intended to enhance the risk and control cultures at banks and financial institutions.

B. THE SALIENCE OF CORPORATE GOVERNANCE AT BANKS AND FINANCIAL INSTITUTIONS

Where there are corporate failures in the UK, it has become almost customary to look into the governance of the firms concerned to discern if corporate governance failures have contributed to firm failure.[14] This approach was also taken in the wake of the global financial crisis and post-mortem examinations of the corporate governance of banks were commissioned in the UK and at the international level.[15] However, many commentators have cautioned against over-eagerness in looking for problems in corporate governance and in making normative conclusions about the link between governance and corporate failures in banks and financial institutions.[16] Caution also has to be exercised as to the extent to which lessons regarding corporate governance in banks and financial institutions may be generally applied to the corporate sector.

A piece of empirical research predating the global financial crisis found that most global banks in the period from 1990 to 2003 have put in place

[13] Tania Duarte, 'Culture, Regulation and Reputation' (10 January 2014) at blogs.lse.ac.uk/conductcosts/2014/01/10/culture-regulation-and-reputation; but see 2010 speech by then Financial Services Authority Chief Hector Sants who said that regulators should look into culture, see Hector Sants, 'Can Culture be Regulated?' (4 October 2010) at www.fsa.gov.uk/library/communication/speeches/2010/1004_hs.shtml.

[14] eg, in relation to the failure of Barings Plc in 1995, several directors were disqualified for not having instituted sufficient oversight systems and controls throughout the banking group. See *Re Barings plc* (No 5) [1999] 1 BCLC 433. In relation to the Equitable Life scandal of failure to pay out on guaranteed annuities, see Lord Penrose's report which criticised the governance and the role of directors in the mutual, see news.bbc.co.uk/1/hi/business/3543549.stm, where the report is available in full.

[15] David Walker, 'A Review of Corporate Governance in UK Banks and other Financial industry Entities: Final Recommendations' (26 November 2009) at webarchive.nationalarchives.gov.uk and www.hm-treasury.gov.uk/d/walker_review_261109.pdf (the Walker Review); Basel Committee on Banking Supervision, *Principles for Enhancing Corporate Governance* (October 2010); OECD, *Corporate Governance and the Financial Crisis: Key Findings and Main Messages* (June 2009).

[16] Discussed below.

optimal corporate governance according to the best practices recognised then.[17] Adams[18] and Cheffins[19] also conducted empirical research on the corporate governance of US financial institutions and US and UK financial firms respectively, in the years leading up to the global financial crisis. They found that well-accepted corporate governance best practices were reasonably robust in financial institutions. Therefore, it appears that there were no marked 'corporate governance failures' at many banks and financial institutions. However, corporate governance best practices are developed largely to combat the agency problem, so one has to bear in mind that optimal corporate governance refers to procedures and systems that appear to secure the alignment of management with shareholders' interests, not necessarily to the securing of an optimal control environment in terms of prudential and regulatory compliance. Hence, the lack of 'corporate governance failures' only narrowly relates to the agency paradigm.

Moreover, it may be argued that mainstream corporate governance best practices are irrelevant or even contrary to the objective of averting financial institution failure. The agency paradigm may not have been relevant to the corporate failure of certain financial institutions. Gupta, Krishnamurti and Tourani-Rad find that, even where there have been sub-optimalities in mainstream corporate governance in banks, such corporate governance practices were not causal factors of bank or financial institution failure or adverse performance.[20] Further, as will be discussed shortly, certain mainstream corporate governance best practices such as shareholder engagement[21] could be adverse to the public interest of financial stability. In other words, mainstream corporate governance best practices may give rise to unintended but perverse effects in the risk control and management at banks and financial institutions. If so, a different view of corporate governance in banks and financial institutions may need to be taken. Indeed, certain mainstream corporate governance sub-optimalities may be useful for financial institutions. Empirical research found that conventional corporate governance sub-optimalities, such as the duality of Chief Executive Officers or less independent Boards, may improve the efficacy of decision-making in a financial institution during a crisis and serve completely

[17] See Oya Altınkılıç, Robert S Hansen and Emir Hrnjić, "Investment Bank Governance" (2007) at papers.ssrn.com/sol3/papers.cfm?abstract_id=785544.

[18] Renee Adams, 'Governance and the Financial Crisis' (2009) ECGI Finance Working Paper 248/2009 at ssrn.com/abstract=1398583.

[19] Brian R Cheffins, 'Did Corporate Governance "Fail" During the 2008 Stock Market Meltdown? The Case of the S&P 500' (2009) ECGI Law Working Paper 124/2009 at ssrn.com/abstract=1396126.

[20] Kartick Gupta, Chandrasekhar Krishnamurti and Alireza Tourani-Rad, 'Is Corporate Governance Relevant during the Financial Crisis? Cross-Country Evidence' (March 2011) at ssrn.com/abstract=1792948.

[21] See, eg, Christopher M Bruner, 'Conceptions of Corporate Purpose in Post-Crisis Financial Firms' (2012) 36 *Seattle University Law Review* 527 and discussion later.

different (and useful) purposes in non-stressed times.[22] One commentator has even suggested that sub-optimal conventional corporate governance practices such as remuneration that is less sensitive to corporate performance could be beneficial to banks and financial institutions in view of the public interest need for financial stability.[23] The application of mainstream corporate governance standards to financial institutions should perhaps be more carefully examined. This also means that bank corporate governance may be 'special' and the financial regulation of aspects of corporate governance would be unique and not necessarily transferable to other areas of corporate regulation. Hopt argues that regulatory intervention in the corporate governance of financial institutions is based on the systemic risks that may be posed by financial institution failure, and hence does not apply to corporate governance generally in the corporate sector.[24]

The most salient cause of financial institution failure in the global financial crisis of 2008–09 that bears some relationship to corporate governance is the high level of risk-taking that those institutions engaged in. Excessive levels of risk-taking[25] coupled with poor risk management[26] at banks have been opined to be key factors in the failure of a number of financial institutions.[27] Even after the immediate aftermath of the global financial crisis, the failure of MF Global in October 2011 was also due to excessive

[22] See Marc van Essen, Peter-Jan Engelen and Michael Carney, 'Does "Good" Corporate Governance Help in a Crisis? The Impact of Country- and Firm-Level Governance Mechanisms in the European Financial Crisis' (2013) 21 *Corporate Governance* 201.

[23] See Alessio M Pacces, 'Regulation of Banking and Banks Governance: When Liquidity Drives Financial Behavior' (2010) at ssrn.com/abstract=2202735.

[24] KJ Hopt, 'Corporate Governance of Banks after the Financial Crisis' in E Wymeersch, KJ Hopt and G Ferrarini (eds), *Financial Regulation and Supervision: A Post-Crisis Analysis* (Oxford: Oxford University Press, 2012).

[25] David H Erkens, Mingyi Hung and Pedro Matos, 'Corporate Governance in the 2007–2008 Financial Crisis: Evidence from Financial Institutions Worldwide' (2012) 18 *Journal of Corporate Finance* 389; Steven A Ramirez, 'Lessons from the Subprime Debacle: Stress Testing CEO Autonomy' (2009) 54 *Saint Louis University Law Journal* 1. But what is 'excessive' is difficult to pinpoint as Miller points out that taking low but severe risks could turn out to be 'excessive' and not calculated after all, see Robert T Miller, 'Oversight Liability for Risk-Management Failures at Financial Firms' (2010) 84 *Southern California Law Review* 47 and Okamoto and Edwards warn that it is impossible to define what is socially optimal risk-taking for banks. See Karl S Okamoto and Douglas O Edwards, 'Risk-Taking' (2010) 32 *Cardozo Law Review* 159.

[26] Poor risk management at firms has been argued to be an important contributing factor to firm failure and financial instability: see M Brunnermeier, A Crockett, C Goodhart, AD Persaud and Hyun Shin, *The Fundamental Principles of Financial Regulation* (London: Centre for Economic Policy Research, Geneva Reports on the World Economy, 2009); Grant Kirkpatrick, 'The Corporate Governance Lessons from the Financial Crisis' (2009) 96 *OECD Financial Market Trends* 1; Michael E Murphy, 'Assuring Responsible Risk Management in Banking: The Corporate Governance Dimension' (2011) 36 *Delaware Journal of Corporate Law* 121.

[27] Brunnermeier et al, *The Fundamental Principles of Financial Regulation* (n 26); Gabriele Sabato, 'Financial Crisis: Where Did Risk Management Fail?' (2009) at papers.ssrn.com/sol3/papers.cfm?abstract_id=1460762; Anette Mikes, 'Risk Management at Crunch Time: Are Chief Risk Officers Compliance Champions or Business Partners?' (2008) at papers.ssrn.com/sol3/papers.cfm?abstract_id=1138615; Hans J Blommestein, Lex Hoogduin and JJW

risk-taking led by then Chief Executive Officer Jon Corzine.[28] Sub-optimal levels of risk-taking and materialisation of losses have continued to dog the financial sector, such as in the case of the UK Co-operative Bank in 2013.[29] Excessive risk-taking in banks and financial institutions may be regarded as an issue in corporate governance[30] as such risk-taking is either strategically driven by the Board and senior management or carried out by the delegates of senior management who are inadequately monitored as to their excesses. Hence, the aspect of corporate governance that may be salient to the safety and soundness of financial institutions is not the agency problem as such but the nature of the firm's prudential management framework and culture shaped by its corporate governance.

The Basel Committee is of the view that '[s]upervisors have a keen interest in sound corporate governance as it is an essential element in the safe and sound functioning of a bank and may adversely affect the bank's risk profile if not implemented effectively'.[31] Although any risk-taking may only be characterised as 'excessive' with the benefit of hindsight, as levels of risk-taking are business judgements and are not susceptible to ex ante prescription towards 'social optimality',[32] the risk and control culture at failed institutions have now come under scrutiny and the role of corporate governance called into question. The contextual frameworks of corporate governance and organisational culture have become relevant for examining how they may affect the risk and control cultures at banks and financial institutions.

Seeking solutions in corporate governance has been an established way of policymaking in the UK in order to address grievances against the corporate sector. As discussed in earlier chapters, the Cadbury Committee that was commissioned to look into how firms could maintain the integrity of their financial reporting turned to solutions in corporate governance. The Cadbury committee took a broader and more thorough view of

Peeters, 'Uncertainty and Risk Management after the Great Moderation: The Role of Risk (Mis)Management by Financial Institutions' (28th SUERF Colloquium, Utrecht, September 2009) at papers.ssrn.com/sol3/papers.cfm?abstract_id=1489826; Michel Crouhy, 'Risk Management Failures During the Financial Crisis' in Robert W Kolb (ed), *Lessons from the Financial Crisis* (New Jersey: John Wiley & Sons, 2010) 283; Elizabeth Sheedy, 'The Future of Risk Modelling' in Robert W Kolb (ed), *Lessons from the Financial Crisis* (New Jersey: John Wiley & Sons, 2010) 301; Frank Partnoy, 'On Rogues, Risk-taking and Restoring Trust in Banks' *Financial Times* (23 September 2011).

[28] According to the bankruptcy trustee's report in the US, reported in 'Corzine Blasted in MF Global Autopsy' *The Wall Street Journal* (4 April 2013).

[29] 'Crisis-torn Co-op Bank suffers cash breakdown' *Telegraph* (2 June 2013).

[30] Paul Rose, 'Regulating Risk by "Strengthening Corporate Governance"' (2010) 17 *Connecticut Insurance Law Journal* 1; Hussein Tarraf, 'The Role of Corporate Governance in the Events Leading up to the Global Financial Crisis: Analysis of Aggressive Risk-Taking' (2011) 5 *Global Journal of Business Research* 93.

[31] Basel Committee, *Principles for Enhancing Corporate Governance* (n 15) para 15.

[32] Okamoto and Edwards, 'Risk-Taking' (n 25).

how the integrity of financial reporting could be affected and came to the conclusion that the governance of the company was integral to a sound financial reporting process, and that internal governance and controls had to be in place before integrity in the output of financial reporting could be secured. Hence, much of the Cadbury Report dealt with a model of good governance for companies, including Board effectiveness, Board composition including non-executive directors, the formation of independent committees of the Board, the appointment of auditors and how audit services should be provided, and the role of shareholders. The Cadbury Report gave rise to the institution of the first Corporate Governance code in the UK. In 1995 the issue in the spotlight was executive remuneration, as public outcry mounted against excessive executive remuneration in privatised utilities companies, while witnessing staff reductions and pay restraint for staff in such companies.[33] The Committee led by Sir Richard Greenbury to look into this issue produced a report which again recommended changes to corporate governance, viz more robust guidelines for the structure and operation of independent remuneration committees on the Board, and also advocated greater shareholder engagement with remuneration issues. Reaching into corporate governance is seen as the apt avenue for addressing public concerns over financial reporting, pay gaps and social disparity, as it is an arguably proportionate way of governing business in the UK, balancing the interests of the constituents of the company in a private contractarian paradigm[34] with the interests of wider society. Through corporate governance reforms, the business sector would be able to redeem itself by demonstrating self-governance and 'bottom-up' responsible behaviour in the corporate sector.[35] However, as the problems that surfaced in the 1990s related to management misconduct and excesses, corporate governance best practices have been aimed at combating the agency problem, and the agency paradigm has thus come to characterise what optimal corporate governance is about.

Although the global financial crisis has been a more severe crisis than the events that triggered corporate governance reforms in the 1990s, the UK continues to reach into the corporate governance of banks and financial institutions by instituting the Walker Review in 2009 to seek remediation solutions going forward that can be implemented at firm level.[36] The EU has further taken the step of expressly regulating certain aspects

[33] Richard Greenbury, *Report: Directors' Remuneration*, paras 1.6–1.7 (17 July 1995) (the Greenbury Report).

[34] The 'nexus of contracts' conception of the company, see discussion in Iris H-Y Chiu, 'Institutional Shareholders as Stewards: Toward a New Conception of Corporate Governance' (2012) 6 *Brooklyn Journal of Corporate, Financial & Commercial Law* 387, section A.

[35] Dignam terms this as 'negotiated regulation' between policymakers and the corporate sector, see A Dignam, 'Capturing Corporate Governance: The End of the UK Self-regulating System' (2007) 4 *International Journal of Disclosure and Governance* 24.

[36] To be discussed in detail in chapter 6.

of corporate governance in the interests of legislative harmonisation in prudential regulation.[37] Chapter six will discuss the reforms in detail, but this chapter will note for now that although the corporate governance reforms are purposed towards addressing sub-optimal risk and control cultures at banks and financial institutions, they have been nevertheless shaped in a path-dependent manner by the dominant agency paradigm. This chapter will now turn to the specific aspects of corporate governance in banks and financial institutions that relate to prudential management. Chapter six will then assess to what extent these aspects have indeed been addressed in post-crisis reforms.

Aspects of Corporate Governance Relevant to Risk-Taking, Monitoring and Control

There has been a flurry of academic commentary and empirical research on what aspects of corporate governance relate to sub-optimal levels of risk taking and management. Post-crisis insights have been developed with regard to previously undiscovered or underemphasised aspects of corporate governance in relation to the risk and control culture at firms. In general, commentators have identified problems with Board leadership as a key corporate governance issue that contributes to sub-optimal risk decisions culminating in adversity or poor performance. There are two aspects to this: Board characteristics that contribute to excessive risk-taking, and Board characteristics that fail to monitor risk-taking although not necessarily driving excessive risk-taking.

The Board characteristics that contribute to excessive risk-taking as summarised from literature review are as follows:

a. Boards were focused on growth and short-termist results, an issue also linked to shareholder value maximisation and the cherished central position of shareholders in mainstream corporate governance paradigms (to be discussed shortly).
b. Boards inadequately considered issues of risk appetite setting and control.

[37] See European Parliament and Council Directive 2011/61/EU of 8 June 2011 on Alternative Investment Fund Managers and amending Directives 2003/41/EC and 2009/65/EC and Regulations (EC) No 1060/2009 and (EU) No 1095/2010 [2011] OJ L174/1 (AIFM Directive) Arts 13, 15 and 18; European Parliament and Council Regulation (EC) 1060/2009 of 16 September 2009 on credit rating agencies [2009] OJ L302/1, Art 6, Annex I; Directive 2013/36/EU of the European Parliament and of the Council of 26 June 2013 on access to the activity of credit institutions and the prudential supervision of credit institutions and investment firms, amending Directive 2002/87/EC and repealing Directives 2006/48/EC and 2006/49/EC (CRD IV Directive) Arts 88, 91–95; Directive 2014/65/EU of the European Parliament and of the Council of 15 May 2014 on markets in financial instruments and amending Directive 2002/92/EC and Directive 2011/61/EU (MiFID II Directive) Arts 9 and 10.

c. Boards were dominated by powerful and long-tenured Chief Executive Officers in favour of aggressive and risk-taking strategies.
d. Boards were staffed with financial experts that encourage greater risk-taking as a strategic approach.
e. Other Board composition features.

Dallas has written extensively on the phenomenon of short-termism in the investment economy and how that has affected corporate and financial sector practices.[38] Short-termism has become a structural economic phenomenon and bank Boards pursuing short-termist achievements in growth and earnings may take risks that meet short-term objectives but compromise longer term corporate stability. Bhagat et al's empirical research indicates that bank Boards do take high risks in terms of leverage or growth such as through acquisitions in order to generate short-termist achievements in growth and earnings.[39] These measures however do not produce sustained longer-term profitability. Such results are echoed in another empirical research.[40] Although bank Boards in the UK are expressly subject to a directors' duty to promote the success of the company in the long term,[41] and the UK Corporate Governance Code refers to Board effectiveness for the sustainable success of an entity over the longer term,[42] it is highly difficult to impeach a Board decision for being short-termist, especially if short-term performance is delivered to the satisfaction of shareholders, in sync with the primacy of accountability to shareholders.[43] It is unlikely that shareholder derivative litigation regarding short-termism can be sustained especially if short-term performance is secured, and also unlikely that any substantive allegations of breaches of directors' duties may be maintained.

Where (b) is concerned, Boards may not regard setting risk appetites and controls to be key to their strategic function and may delegate and marginalise this aspect, or Boards may regard risk control as an obstacle to the pursuit of growth and profit and may thus subordinate risk considerations to aggressive business strategies. Such a strategic direction may indeed be consistent with the Boards' primary accountability to shareholders. As such, Boards' apparently legitimate pursuit of risk-taking for

[38] Lynne Dallas, 'Short-Termism, the Financial Crisis, and Corporate Governance' (2012) 37 *Journal of Corporation Law* 265.

[39] Sanjai Bhagat, Brian Bolton and Jun Lu, 'Size, Leverage, and Risk-taking of Financial Institutions' (2012) at ssrn.com/abstract=2122727.

[40] See Angelica Gonzalez and Paul André, 'Board Effectiveness and Short Termism' (2012) at ssrn.com/abstract=1979751.

[41] s 172, Companies Act 2006.

[42] 'Governance and the Code' (n 4) para 4.

[43] Also in s 172, Companies Act 2006. The short-termist demands of the equity market have been extensively studied in BIS, The Kay Review of UK Equity Markets and Long-Term Decision Making (Final Report, 23 July 2012); George Cox, Overcoming Short-termism within British Business: The Key to Sustained Economic Growth (2013) at www.yourbritain.org.uk/uploads/editor/files/Overcoming_Short-termism.pdf.

profit augmentation, even if risk moderation is traded off, is likely to be regarded as falling within the existing directors' legal duties which are very much framed within the agency paradigm.[44]

It has therefore been suggested that corporate governance reforms need to fundamentally recalibrate the agency-based legal duties imposed on directors, and introduce legal duties that address directors' accountability to a wider slate of constituents that would be affected by bank safety and soundness. Commentators such as Vasudev suggest that minimum Board responsibilities with respect to risk management need to be prescribed:

> [R]eviewing, approving, and monitoring fundamental financial and business strategies and the performance of the company relative to those strategies; assessing major risks facing the company; and ensuring that reasonable processes are in place to maintain the integrity of the company and the corresponding accountability of senior management.[45]

The Parliamentary Commission on Banking Standards has also made a far-reaching suggestion: to impose a duty on individual directors to safeguard bank safety.[46] This suggestion will be discussed in chapter six although it is not ultimately taken up in legislation. Mülbert also suggests, due to the moral hazard effects of deposit insurance and potential bank bail-outs, that directors should owe a duty to the Financial Services Compensation Scheme and to stakeholders like depositors and creditors.[47] Brittan, writing in the *Financial Times*,[48] also calls for banks bailed out by the state to incorporate a public purpose objective. This was consulted upon by the Department for Business, Innovation & Skills and ultimately dropped.[49]

The problem with recalibrating directors' duties for bank Boards towards optimal risk control is that 'optimal risk control' is not merely judged with reference to shareholders' wealth maximisation interests. Bank Boards would have to take into account a wider slate of interests that may be affected by the safety and soundness of the bank. Bank directors may argue that it would be difficult for them to pursue and balance multiple objectives such as institutional and financial stability and shareholder value.[50] Bank Boards may indeed become uncertain as to the nature of

[44] Boards' strategic decisions in good faith towards the financial success of the company are unlikely to be impeached, see *Re Smith and Fawcett Ltd* [1942] Ch 304.

[45] PM Vasudev, 'Credit Derivatives and Risk Management: Corporate Governance in the Sarbanes–Oxley World' [2009] *Journal of Business Law* 331, 351.

[46] House of Lords and House of Commons, Parliamentary Commission on Banking Standards, *Changing Banking for Good* Vol I (2013–14, HL 27-I, HC 175-I) para 110.

[47] Peter O Mülbert, 'Corporate Governance of Banks after the Financial Crisis—Theory, Evidence, Reforms' (2010) ECGI Law Working Paper 130/2009 at ssrn.com/abstract=1448118.

[48] Samuel Brittan, 'Use the UK's state bank holdings to speed a recovery' *Financial Times* (22 September 2011).

[49] BIS, *Transparency and Trust: Enhancing the Transparency of UK Company Ownership and Increasing Trust in UK Business* (April 2014) at www.gov.uk/government/uploads/system/uploads/attachment_data/file/304297/bis-14-672-transparency-and-trust-consultation-response.pdf, paras 249, 258.

[50] Which was discussed in the BIS report, ibid, para 258.

legal duties imposed on them if we move away from the certainty of the agency-based paradigm for directors' duties. However, as banks and deposit-taking financial institutions are financed to a large extent by depositors and creditors, shareholder primacy arguments are weaker in the context of banks.[51] That said, micro-prudential reforms internationally and in the EU are now making shareholders more important than ever to banks and financial institutions as they are a source of increased capital and would be liable for bail-in if a firm goes under distress.[52] The recalibration of the directors' legal duty in prudential management for the benefit of a wide slate of constituents has not taken place in hard and soft law reforms. There is a reluctance to move away from the fundamental agency-based ideology in corporate governance even where special policy reasons may exist for the financial sector. Chapter six will argue that post-crisis reforms tend to address aspects of corporate governance and organisational culture avoiding fundamental recalibrations in the agency-based ideology in corporate governance. This may be due to the fear of introducing unintended ramifications in terms of stakeholder enforcement and uncertain parameters of firm and directorial liability. Further, fundamental reforms to financial institution corporate governance may also cause ripple effects in the mainstream corporate sector.

Next, Boards may be tolerant of excessive risk-taking if they are dominated by powerful and aggressive Chief Executive Officers (even if the Chairman and Chief Executive are different persons). Chen and Zheng show that long-tenured Chief Executive Officers who succeed in maintaining information asymmetry about their capabilities are able to convince the Board to engage in increased risk-taking according to their preferences.[53] The domineering Chief Executives of Lehman Brothers and MF Global who underestimated risk-taking and led their institutions to their demise are real life examples that support empirical research such as Chesney et al's that show a link between CEO risk-taking and large-scale write-downs incurred by financial institutions in the global financial crisis.[54] Ramirez argues that CEO dominance has led to empire building

[51] Simon Deakin, 'Corporate Governance and Financial Crisis in the Long Run' in Cynthia A Williams and Peer Zumbansen (eds), *The Embedded Firm: Corporate Governance, Labor and Finance Capitalism* (New York: Cambridge University Press 2011).

[52] Basel III Accord, as implemented by the CRD IV Directive 2014 and bail-in provisions in Directive 2014/59/EU of the European Parliament and of the Council of 15 May 2014 establishing a framework for the recovery and resolution of credit institutions and investment firms and amending Council Directive 82/891/EEC, and Directives 2001/24/EC, 2002/47/EC, 2004/25/EC, 2005/56/EC, 2007/36/EC, 2011/35/EU, 2012/30/EU and 2013/36/EU, and Regulations (EU) No 1093/2010 and (EU) No 648/2012, of the European Parliament and of the Council (Recovery and Resolution Directive 2014) putting shareholder capital at risk could further justify the importance of shareholders in corporate governance.

[53] Dong Chen and Yudan Zheng, 'CEO Tenure and Risk-Taking' (2013) at ssrn.com/abstract=2038064.

[54] Marc Chesney, Jacob Stromberg and Alexander F Wagner, 'Risk-taking Incentives, Governance, and Losses in the Financial Crisis' (2010) Swiss Finance Institute Research Paper Series 10-18 at ssrn.com/abstract=1595343.

and complacency in misjudgements about risk, such as in the Royal Bank of Scotland where Fred Goodwin underestimated the risks of a sparse due diligence in the acquisition of ABN-AMRO which then infected RBS with toxic collaterised mortgage-based assets.[55] Similarly in Northern Rock where Adam Applegarth underestimated the risks of excessive reliance on wholesale credit in funding ambitious plans to secure an ever greater market share of the UK residential mortgage market. As the UK Corporate Governance Code already requires the separation of the Chairman from the CEO, CEO duality is not the cause for dominance. Reforms targeted at this issue will be discussed in chapter six. They deal mainly with improving the Board's monitoring expertise so as not to be captured by the CEO. However, Board dynamics and dynamics with the CEO are issues of governance and organisational culture that may not easily be susceptible to being shaped by regulatory frameworks.

Finally, some aspects of Board composition may contribute to excessive risk-taking. Some empirical research suggests that largely independent Boards may contribute to excessive risk-taking and worse financial performance.[56] Conventional corporate governance best practices champion independent Boards as independence is a quality related to monitoring the agency problem. However, as will be discussed later, shareholder primacy may entail adverse effects upon risk-taking and hence independent directors who are protective of shareholder primacy may contribute towards greater risk-taking tolerated by Boards. However, it is noted that contrary empirical evidence is also found showing that independent directors contribute to better financial performance,[57] in some cases due to less risk-taking and better risk management and control. Another issue with Board composition is whether financial literacy and expertise on Boards is essential to avert poor risk decisions. A significant amount of empirical research supports the increase of directors with financial expertise on the Board for better monitoring purposes,[58] but a contrary piece of empirical research suggests that Boards with greater numbers of independent directors with financial expertise are prone to higher risk-taking

[55] Ramirez, 'Lessons from the Subprime Debacle' (n 25).

[56] See Erkens, Hung and Matos, 'Corporate Governance in the 2007–2008 Financial Crisis' (n 25); Edyta M Dorenbos and Alessio M Pacces, 'Corporate Governance of Banks: Is More Board Independence the Solution?' (2013) at papers.ssrn.com/sol3/papers.cfm?abstract_id=2260341.

[57] Yin-Hua Yeh, Huimin Chung and Chih-Liang Liu, 'Committee Independence and Financial Institution Performance during the 2007–08 Credit Crunch: Evidence from a Multi-country Study' (2011) 19 *Corporate Governance* 437; Emilia Peni and Sami Vähämaa, 'Did Good Corporate Governance Improve Bank Performance during the Financial Crisis?" (2011) 41 *Journal of Financial Services Research* 19.

[58] See Harold Hau and Marcel Thum, 'Subprime Crisis and Board (In-)Competence: Private vs Public Banks in Germany' (2009) 24 *Economic Policy* 701; John Holland, 'Banks, Knowledge and Crisis: A Case of Knowledge and Learning Failure' (2010) *Journal of Financial Regulation and Compliance* 87.

due to the confidence directors have in their financial expertise.[59] It may be inconclusive as to whether reform in this aspect of corporate governance relating to Board expertise, which is eagerly championed in UK and EU policymaking, will significantly contribute to a more optimal risk culture. There is also research to suggest that large size Boards relate to poorer performance[60] but contrary conclusions suggest that this is again an area of mixed evidence.[61]

We turn now to discuss other Board characteristics discussed in post-crisis literature considered to have undermined effective risk oversight and monitoring. The characteristics of Boards relating to weak risk monitoring are as follows:

a. Failure of Board leadership in giving risk management a sufficiently high-level profile for Board attention and strategic direction.
b. Lack of Board emphasis on risk management as being a concern distinct from compliance or audit.
c. Lack of information and knowledge of risk profiles of departments.
d. Limited Board ability to engage in risk monitoring of highly complex businesses in large banking groups.

Boards in the pre-crisis years have been roundly criticised for not having prioritised the monitoring of risk-taking and management. Larcker and Tayan opine that Boards focus on strategy and seldom see risk management as part of setting strategic direction.[62] Risk management has often been regarded as a specialist task delegated to the risk management function. The lack of attention given to the importance of risk management at the highest levels of management has been regarded as a key contributing factor to financial institution failures in the global financial crisis of 2008–09.[63] Ellul and Yerramilli's empirical research shows that the quality of risk management and internal control matters to the viability and performance of bank holding companies in the crisis.[64] Further, poorer quality risk

[59] See Bernadette Minton, Jérôme PA Taillard and Rohan Williamson, 'Do Independence and Financial Expertise of the Board Matter for Risk Taking and Performance?' (2011) at www.ssrn.com/abstract=1661855.

[60] See Marina Brogi, 'Regulation, Corporate Governance and Risk Management in Banks and Insurance Companies' (2008) at ssrn.com/abstract=1710086.

[61] See Hugh Grove, Lorenzo Patelli, Lisa M Victoravich and Pisun (Tracy) Xu, 'Corporate Governance and Performance in the Wake of the Financial Crisis: Evidence from US Commercial Banks' (2011) 19 *Corporate Governance* 418; Narjess Boubakri, 'Corporate Governance and Issues from the Insurance Industry' (2011) 78 *Journal of Risk and Insurance* 501.

[62] David Larcker and Brian Tayan, *Corporate Governance Matters: Closer Look at Organisational Choices and their Consequences* (New Jersey: Pearson, 2011) ch 6.

[63] Basel Committee, *Principles for Enhancing Corporate Governance* (2010) 38; Govindarajan, 'Corporate Risk Appetite' (n 12); Klaus Hopt, 'Better Governance of Financial Institutions' (2012) at ssrn.com/abstract=2212198.

[64] Andrew Ellul and Vijap Yerramilli, 'Stronger Risk Controls, Lower Risk: Evidence from US Bank Holding Companies' (2010) at ssrn.com/abstract=1550361 and (2013) 68 *Journal of Finance* 1757.

management is also indicated by narrow conceptions of risk management such as silo-based risk management according to business lines.[65] Many commentators have observed that, in the banks that failed in the crisis, risk management was largely undertaken on a silo-based approach, ie, each department separately managed their distinct risks according to their lines of business.[66] Such narrow conceptions of risk management reinforce the lack of priority given to risk management at the highest levels of management. Such narrow-minded approaches do not encourage a holistic appreciation of risks and have contributed to the lack of communication of risks to the highest levels of management. More integrated risk control frameworks such as the Turnbull Guidance in the UK[67] or the enterprise-wide risk management framework recommended by the US COSO[68] require engagement in risk management at the highest levels of management, ie, the Board, in order to institute a holistic and comprehensive framework for objective setting, risk identification and assessment, risk response, control activities, communications and monitoring.[69] We observe a history of Boards being passive movers in taking leadership in risk management, and have only been driven to take risk issues on board after public scrutiny into corporate failures. This was so in the 1990s when financial reporting integrity, as discussed earlier, became an issue of concern in the UK, and similarly in the US where the Sarbanes–Oxley Act 2002 forced senior management to take responsibility for financial reporting in the wake of the collapse of energy giant Enron.[70]

The lack of pre-crisis engagement by Boards in risk management at the strategic level is also due to a lack of competence in this area.[71] A number of commentators opine that the lack of Board competence or expertise has been correlated with failures and adverse performance at banks and financial institutions. Mehran, Morrison and Shapiro provide a literature review showing that empirical evidence points to a correlation between

[65] Discussed in chapter 3.

[66] See Michelle Harner, 'Ignoring the Writing on the Wall: The Role of Enterprise Risk Management in the Economic Crisis' (2010) 5 *Journal of Business & Technology Law* 45; Michelle Harner, 'Barriers to Effective Risk Management' (2010) 40 *Seton Hall Law Review* 1323; House of Commons and House of Lords, Parliamentary Commission on Banking Standards, *An Accident Waiting to Happen: The Failure of HBOS* (2012–13, HL 144, HC 705) paras 54–61.

[67] Financial Reporting Council, *Internal Control: Revised Guidance for Directors on the Combined Code* (October 2005) at www.frc.org.uk/Our-Work/Publications/Corporate-Governance/Turnbull-guidance-October-2005.aspx.

[68] Committee of Sponsoring Organizations of the Treadway Commission (COSO), *Enterprise Risk Management- Integrated Framework* (September 2004); Christoph Van der Elst and Marijn van Daelen, 'Risk Management in European and American Corporate Law' (2009) ECGI Law Working Paper 122/2009 at ssrn.com/abstract=1399647.

[69] Kirkpatrick, 'The Corporate Governance Lessons from the Financial Crisis' (n 26).

[70] s 302, Sarbanes–Oxley Act 2002.

[71] Murphy, 'Assuring Responsible Risk Management in Banking' (n 26); Ian Brown, Adam Steen and Julie Foreman, 'Risk Management in Corporate Governance: A Review and Proposal' (2009) 17 *Corporate Governance* 546.

a lack of meaningful leadership in banks and financial institutions and poorer quality risk management.[72] Hau and Thum's empirical study finds correlations between the lack of financial expertise and experience on the part of supervisory boards in German financial institutions and larger losses suffered by those institutions in the global financial crisis.[73] However, the lack of emphasis on Board competence in risk management is understandable. The pre-crisis years have featured corporate failures that are largely due to management fraud and the mainstream wisdom for monitoring management fraud advocates independence on Boards for effective monitoring[74] and auditing expertise[75] on Boards and audit committees to improve detection. Although the OECD criticises the corporate sector for failing to prioritise risk management, which had been mentioned as a best practice as early as in the OECD's 2004 Principles,[76] the importance of risk management was arguably an area tucked away in corporate governance when other issues were alive. The importance of risk management at Board level is now re-emphasised with a vengeance and hardened in EU legislation[77] for banks and financial institutions, which will be elaborated upon in chapter six.

It is also queried whether Boards had not been sufficiently incentivised to adequately monitor risk control as it is uncertain that directorial liability may result. It is to be noted that there is empirical research showing that enhancement in director liability regimes (whether or not actual success in enforcement is achieved) could improve Board effectiveness in monitoring risk control issues.[78] Hence, holding directors to a greater standard of care where risk governance in banks is concerned could entail behavioural

[72] Hamid Mehran, Alan Morrison and Joel Shapiro, 'Corporate Governance and Banks: What have we Learned from the Financial Crisis?' (June 2011) Federal Reserve Bank of New York Staff Report No 502 at ssrn.com/abstract=1880009.

[73] Hau and Thum, 'Subprime Crisis' (n 58). Note however that Mehran warns that directors with financial expertise and experience may also favour greater risk-taking and hence could exacerbate risk-taking tendencies in banks and financial institutions. See Mehran, Morrison and Shapiro, 'Corporate Governance and Banks' (n 72).

[74] MS Beasley, 'An Empirical Analysis of the Relation between the Board of Director Composition and Financial Statement Fraud' (1996) 71 *Accounting Review* 443; H Uzun, SH Szewczyk and R Varma, 'Board Composition and Corporate Fraud' (2004) 60 *Financial Analysts Journal* 33; ST Petra, 'Do Outside Independent Directors Strengthen Corporate Boards?' (2005) 5 *Corporate Governance* 55; Yang Ni and Lynette Purda, 'Does Monitoring by Independent Directors Reduce Firm Risk?' (2012) at northernfinance.org/2012/program/papers/405.pdf.

[75] Husam Aldamen, Keith Duncan, Simone Kelly, Ray McNamara and Stephan Nagel, 'Audit Committee Characteristics and Firm Performance during the Global Financial Crisis' (2012) 52 *Accounting & Finance* 971; Chaudhry Ghafran and Noel O'Sullivan, 'The Governance Role of Audit Committees: Reviewing a Decade of Evidence' (2012) *International Journal of Management Review* 1; Lawrence A Cunningham, 'Rediscovering Board Expertise: Legal Implications of the Empirical Literature' (2008) 77 *University of Cincinnati Law Review* 465.

[76] OECD, *Principles of Corporate Governance 2004* (n 3) Principle VI.D.1.

[77] CRD IV Directive 2014, Arts 88, 91.

[78] See Tobias Körner, 'Board Accountability and Risk Taking in Banking: Evidence from a Quasi-Experiment' (2012) at ssrn.com/abstract=1996520.

change. However, even if directors are asked to monitor risk control more intensely, the suggestion above does not capture how this higher standard of care is to be applied when compared with other directorial decisions. Further, how would directors be evaluated for effective management of risk control where implementation of risk frameworks are delegated?[79] This is the key issue that the Court in the US could not overcome when it dismissed the shareholder derivative litigation against the directors of Citigroup.[80] How should directors be judged in terms of the quality of Board supervision over delegation of functions such as risk management? The UK Companies Act 2006 already requires directors generally to act with due care, skill and diligence.[81] As the regulatory framework for risk management is meta-regulatory in nature, as long as directors adduce evidence of implementation in the form of systems and arrangements, such could be sufficient to show discharge of the duty of diligence. Would courts be able or willing to make judgements on the quality of systems and procedures and the monitoring carried out at Board level?[82]

It has also been suggested that the Boards of failed banks, such as Bear Stearns and Lehman Brothers in the US and Northern Rock and HBOS in the UK, were not well informed of risky profiles and operations and hence could not have provided leadership in considering the strategic impact of risk management.[83] Due to the inherent challenges in managing large complex financial enterprises where risk issues and transformations take place so rapidly, it may be unrealistic to expect Boards that meet a few times in a year to be able to keep on top of things.[84] There are issues in terms of increased time commitment, going full-time[85] or enhancing the Chairman's leadership that need to be addressed,[86] but there is also a question of whether large and complex global financial institutions are

[79] Simon Deakin, 'What Directors Do (and Fail to Do): Some Comparative Notes on Board Structure and Corporate Governance' (2010/11) 55 *New York Law School Law Review* 525.

[80] *In Re Citigroup Inc Shareholder Derivative Litigation* 4 A.2d 106 (Del Ch 2009), based on the standard in *In re Caremark International Inc Derivative Litigation* 698 A.2d 959 (Del Ch 1996).

[81] Companies Act 2006 (UK), s 174.

[82] Nathalie Janson, 'A Radical Proposal for Reforming the Banking System' (March 2011) at ssrn.com/abstract=1773917; Alec E Orenstein, 'A Modified *Caremark* Standard to Protect Shareholders of Financial Firms from Poor Risk Management' (2011) 86 *New York University Law Review* 766.

[83] Kirkpatrick, 'The Corporate Governance Lessons from the Financial Crisis' (n 26); Michael Pirson and Shann Turnbull, 'Corporate Governance, Risk Management, and the Financial Crisis: An Information Processing View' (2011) 19 *Corporate Governance: An International Review* 459; Holland, 'Banks, Knowledge and Crisis' (n 58).

[84] Roman Tomasic and Folarin Akinbami, 'Towards a New Corporate Governance after the Global Financial Crisis' (2011) *International Company and Commercial Law Review* 237; Christoph Van der Elst, 'The Risks of Corporate Legal Principles of Risk Management' (2010) ECGI Law Working Paper 160/2010 at ssrn.com/abstract=1623526.

[85] Samuel R Foreman, 'Bored Boards: The Directorial Disengagement Dilemma' (2010) 50 *Washburn Law Journal* 174.

[86] The Walker Review (n 15), to be discussed in chapter 6.

inherently unmanageable. This point has been raised in the wake of JP Morgan's whale loss,[87] an episode attributed to flaws in internal monitoring despite having enterprise-wide monitoring structures and appropriate leadership for risk management in place. This issue will again be critically discussed in chapter six when the reforms to corporate governance are analysed in terms of what they can achieve.

Aspects of Conventional Best Practices in Corporate Governance that may be Unsuitable for Banks and Financial Institutions

It may also be argued that excessive risk-taking in banks and financial institutions in the years leading up to the global financial crisis has ironically been shaped by certain conventional best practices in corporate governance that are actually unsuitable in the context of banks and financial institutions. Hence, financial sector corporate governance needs to be treated in a unique manner. This chapter has earlier alluded to the prospect of ideological shifts away from the agency-based corporate governance paradigm for the financial sector, but such an approach seems unsupported in policy and law reforms. In the absence of such a radical move, specific prescriptions have been introduced to regulate aspects of corporate governance as chapter six will discuss in detail. The achievement of these prescriptions may however be limited as the agency-based assumptions in corporate governance have not changed.

The classic agency paradigm in corporate governance is centred upon the Board's accountability to shareholders, as open-ended 'residual claimants' in supplying equity capital.[88] This is very much the paradigm reflected in UK corporate law and governance, and to a lesser extent in certain countries in the EU whose corporate governance frameworks have been shaped by the political power gained by labour as a key stakeholder.[89] However, since the 1990s, a discernible move towards embracing shareholder rights and primacy has taken place in an age of 'finance capitalism'.[90] Hansmann and Kraakman famously declared that the international convergence upon shareholder centricity in corporate law marks the end of history in

[87] United States Senate Permanent Subcommittee on Investigations, *JP Morgan Chase Whale Trades: A Case History of Derivatives Risks and Abuses: Majority and Minority Staff Report* (2012) at www.hsgac.senate.gov/subcommittees/investigations/hearings/chase-whale-trades-a-case-history-of-derivatives-risks-and-abuses, 157–214.

[88] Chiu, 'Institutional Shareholders' (n 34) section A and citations therein.

[89] K Hopt, 'Labor Representation on Corporate Boards: Impacts and Problems for Corporate Governance and Economic Integration in Europe' (1994) 14 *International Review of Law and Economics* 203.

[90] John W Cioffi, *Public Law and Private Power. Corporate Governance Reform in the Age of Finance Capitalism* (Ithaca, NY: Cornell University Press, 2010).

corporate law.[91] The authors argued that this convergence has been brought about as the world witnessed the failures of alternative corporate law ideologies centred upon managerial primacy, co-determination and state-controlled corporations. The success of American and British corporations that are based on the shareholder-centric model in corporate governance would provide a driver to export this successful model to the rest of the international corporate world. Other commentators have also argued that political preferences have shifted towards the development of strong investment economies supported by a shareholder-centric ideology in corporate law in light of global trade and competition.[92] The shift in such political preferences has also been discerned in European countries hitherto dominated by left-leaning political ideologies that favour bank-based finance and concentrated ownership.[93] It is arguably not incorrect to broadly agree with Hansmann and Kraakman that the shareholder-centric ideology dominates in corporate governance and law in most of the developed world, although the legal institutions regarding shareholder power and rights remain varied and fragmented[94] even in jurisdictions that broadly embrace the same shareholder-centric ideology.

Nevertheless, the shareholder-centric ideology in corporate law has affected the business practices of banks and financial institutions as for-profit corporations.[95] In chapter three, it is mentioned that a number of commentators draw the connection between the shareholder-centric ideology and excessive risk-taking in high growth financial institutions. Ho, an anthropologist, argues that the business model of banking has been shaped by embracing 'shareholder value',[96] an ideology which encourages

[91] Henry Hansmann and Reinier Kraakman, 'The End of History for Corporate Law' (2000–01) 89 *Georgetown Law Journal* 439. See critique in Paddy Ireland, 'Shareholder Primacy and the Distribution of Wealth' (2004) 68 *Modern Law Review* 49. Hansmann and Kraakman have maintained that their thesis holds in fact and can be also supported by efficiency claims ten years after the publication of the original piece, see 'Reflections on the End of History for Corporate Law' (2011) at papers.ssrn.com/sol3/papers.cfm?abstract_id=2095419.

[92] See Alan Dignam and Michael Galanis, *The Globalization of Corporate Governance* (Aldershot: Ashgate, 2009).

[93] Laura Horn, 'Corporate Governance in Crisis? The Politics of EU Corporate Governance Regulation' (2012) 18 *European Law Journal* 83; Roger M Barker, *Corporate Governance, Competition, and Political Parties: Explaining Corporate Governance Change in Europe* (Oxford: Oxford University Press, 2010).

[94] The often clumped-together Anglo-American corporate governance model actually exposes differences in shareholder rights to a vast extent, see Christopher M Bruner, *Corporate Governance in the Common Law World: The Political Foundations of Shareholder Power* (Cambridge: Cambridge University Press, 2013); Priya P Lele and Mathias M Siems, 'Diversity in Shareholder Protection in Common Law Countries' (2007) at ssrn.com/abstract=988409; Mathias Siems, 'Convergence in Corporate Governance: A Leximetric Approach' (2010) 35 *Journal of Corporation Law* 729.

[95] David Bholat and Joanna Gray, 'Organizational Form as a Source of Systemic Risk' (2012) at ssrn.com/abstract=2121649.

[96] Karen Ho, 'Disciplining Investment Bankers, Disciplining the Economy: Wall Street's Institutional Culture of Crisis and the Downsizing of "Corporate America"' (2009) 111 *American Anthropologist* 177.

the corporate world to be obsessed with stock market prices and to take a short-termist approach to profitability.[97] Pacces also argues that banks have been driven towards obsession with short-termist corporate profitability due to competition from alternative financial institutions in the maturity transformation business.[98] Further, an increase in financial sector liberalisation and competition has taken place since the 1990s.[99] The deregulation championed by the US Financial Modernization Act 1999, which lifted restrictions on banks engaging in investment activities, has been the major driving force behind financial empire building and the growth of the financial sector in the US and globally.[100] A number of economists warned, in the early part of the twenty-first century, that liberalisation which entails competition in the financial sector, would result in greater risk-taking behaviour generally by banks as the generation of profits becomes more challenging under competitive pressure.[101]

Empirical research carried out to discern the relationship between corporate governance and bank failures or performance in the global financial crisis has given credibility to the argument that the shareholder-centric ideology that dominates the management of banking and financial institutions contributes to excessive risk-taking and greater propensity for institutional failure. Beltratti and Stultz found that shareholder-friendly Boards were correlated with worse financial performance.[102] This result is consistent with Gropp and Köhler's[103] and Westman's[104] findings that shareholder-aligned Boards—either because of the operation of a better shareholder rights protection legal regime or due to the presence of a controlling shareholder—led their banks into larger losses during the crisis. The results indicate that the risks taken, pursuant to these shareholder risk-taking preferences, have generally been greater and the

[97] See also Deakin, 'Corporate Governance and Financial Crisis' (n 51).

[98] Alessio M Pacces, 'Consequences of Uncertainty for Regulation: Law and Economics of the Financial Crisis' (2010) 7 *European Company and Financial Law Review* 479.

[99] Giving further effect to the abolition of currency and credit controls in the 1980s, see the discussion in Mads Andenas, 'Harmonising and Regulating Financial Markets' in Mads Andenas and Camilla Andersen (eds), *Theory and Practice of Harmonisation* (Cheltenham: Edward Elgar, 2012) 7–10.

[100] Sandra Suarez and Robin Kolodny, 'Paving the Road to "Too Big to Fail": Business Interests and the Politics of Financial Deregulation in the United States' (2011) 39 *Politics & Society* 74.

[101] See, eg, Wilko Bolt and Alexander F Tieman, 'Banking Competition, Risk and Regulation' (2004) 106 *The Scandinavian Journal of Economics* 783; Thomas F Hellmann, Kevin C Murdock and Joseph E Stiglitz, 'Liberalization, Moral Hazard in Banking, and Prudential Regulation: Are Capital Requirements Enough?' (2000) 90 *The American Economic Review* 197.

[102] Andrea Beltratti and René M Stultz, 'Why Did Some Banks Perform Better during the Credit Crisis? A Cross-Country Study of the Impact of Governance and Regulation' (July 2009) NBER Working Paper 15180 at papers.ssrn.com/sol3/papers.cfm?abstract_id=1433502.

[103] Reint Gropp and Matthias Köhler, 'Bank Owners or Bank Managers: Who is keen on Risk? Evidence from the Financial Crisis' (January 2010) European Business School Research Paper 10-02 at ssrn.com/abstract=1555663.

[104] Hanna Westman, 'The Role of Ownership Structure and Regulatory Environment in Bank Corporate Governance' (January 2010) at ssrn.com/abstract=1435041.

materialisation of risks leading to losses has been more extensive. Shareholder alignment could occur in financial institutions with dispersed and concentrated ownership. Erkens, Hung and Matos find that dispersed institutional shareholders exhibit higher risk-taking preferences and their influence upon Boards has not been salutary in the financial crisis: banks with institutional shareholders have recorded greater losses and worse stock performance.[105] However Boubaker et al find that banks with multiple large owners exhibit high risk-taking behaviour too.[106] However a single concentrated owner has a moderating influence upon risk-taking in financial institutions. On the contrary, Rauch's study finds that dispersed ownership exerts a risk-controlling effect upon banks and financial institutions in terms of both liquidity and solvency risk.[107] A study that sought to measure the correlation between shareholder-insulated Boards and bank bail-outs using data in the global financial crisis has found that US investment banks with management insulated from shareholder pressures (based on the ease with which shareholders may gain control over the Board) have not been as vulnerable to seeking bailouts.[108] This study may provide a form of corroboration for the above studies on the impact of shareholder primacy upon risk-taking at banks.

The relatively high risk preferences of shareholders may be explained by the unique corporate governance model of most banks and financial institutions that are financed much more by debt than equity. Gualandri et al argue that banks in particular are financed dominantly by borrowing from depositors and other creditors, less so by equity finance.[109] The significantly heavier reliance on leverage means that depositors and creditors share a substantial amount of residual risk which in conventional corporate governance models would fall upon shareholders. White argues that given the highly leveraged nature of banks and financial institutions, the risk-bearing capacity of residual losses is extended to stakeholders (such as creditors and depositors) to a greater extent than shareholders in the conventional paradigm of corporate governance.[110] The opportunity to shift

[105] Erkens, Hung and Matos, 'Corporate Governance in the 2007–2008 Financial Crisis' (n 25).

[106] Sabri Boubaker, Pascal Nguyen and Wael Rouatbi, 'Large Shareholders and Firm Risk-Taking Behavior' (2012) at ssrn.com/abstract=2026038.

[107] Christian Rauch, 'The Good—or the Bad and the Ugly? Corporate Governance and Risk Taking in Banking' (2011) at ssrn.com/abstract=1928899.

[108] Daniel Ferreira, David Kershaw, Tom Kirchmaier and Edmund-Philipp Schuster, 'Shareholder Empowerment and Bank Bailouts' (2012) at papers.ssrn.com/sol3/papers.cfm?abstract_id=2170392.

[109] Elisabetta Gualandri, Aldo Stanziale and Enzo Mangone, 'Internal Corporate Governance and the Financial Crisis: Lessons for Banks, Regulators and Supervisors' (2011) at ssrn.com/abstract=1971659.

[110] Lawrence J White, 'Corporate Governance and Prudential Regulation of Banks: Is there any Connection?' in James R Barth, Chen Lin and Clas Wihlborg (eds), *Research Handbook on International Banking and Governance* (Cheltenham: Edward Elgar, 2012).

risks to stakeholders while gaining the upsides of corporate performance incentivises shareholders to prefer higher risk-taking. Hence, Ciancanelli and Gonzalez argue that the agency paradigm is much more complex in the banking sector, in that the main issue is risk-shifting between shareholders and stakeholders such as depositors and creditors.[111] Further, the potential of state bail-out puts the state in the position of key stakeholder,[112] mitigating shareholder and creditor risk. The unique nature of banks and financial institutions allows shareholders to prefer more short-termist risk-taking to maximise shareholder returns while being apathetic to longer-term viability. If these incentives are reinforced by a general shareholder-centric ideology in corporate governance and law, then levels of risk-taking preferred by shareholder-friendly management could be adverse to other stakeholders. In this way, the conventional best practice in corporate governance relating to shareholder centricity may be adverse to the corporate stability needs of financial institutions and wider financial stability objectives. Although corrective regulatory reforms seek to put shareholders more at risk through greater equity capital requirements in micro-prudential regulation[113] and bail-in provisions[114] in the EU harmonised legal framework for recovery and resolution of banks and financial institutions, it is arguable that depositor, creditor and state exposure remain high, especially in a systemic crisis. These interests are not addressed in the conventional agency-based corporate governance paradigm.

This section has taken stock of the aspects of corporate governance relevant to risk control weaknesses in banks and financial institutions, a key problem in the global financial crisis of 2008–09. Certain weaknesses in the corporate governance in banks and financial institutions that have adversely affected the risk control culture in firms seem to be addressed in post-crisis reforms that subject aspects of corporate governance to regulation. Mülbert and Citlau support externally imposed regulation on aspects of corporate governance in order to govern financial institutions towards the financial stability objective.[115] Commentators are also of the view that the complex agency relationships in banks and the opacity of financial intermediation activities make private monitoring difficult[116] and so corporate governance should be subject to some regulation in order to facilitate

[111] Penny Ciancanelli and Jose Antonio Reyes Gonzalez, 'Corporate Governance in Banking: A Conceptual Framework' (2000) at papers.ssrn.com/paper.taf?abstract_id=253714.

[112] Chiu, 'Institutional Shareholders' (n 34).

[113] Basel III Capital Accord and CRD IV Directive 2014.

[114] Recovery and Resolution Directive 2014, Arts 43ff.

[115] Peter O Mülbert and Ryan D Citlau, 'The Uncertain Role of Banks' Corporate Governance in Systemic Risk Regulation' (2011) ECGI Working Paper at ssrn.com/abstract=1885866.

[116] See Dirk Heremans and Katrien Bosquet, 'The Future of Law and Finance after the Financial Crisis: New Perspectives on Regulation and Corporate Governance for Banks' (2011) 5 *University of Illinois Law Review* 1551.

enhanced private and regulatory monitoring. However, chapter six will point out that regulation does not challenge the fundamental agency-based premise for conventional best practices in corporate governance. For example, one of the post-crisis developments is the move in the UK and US towards encouraging more shareholder monitoring and engagement in the financial sector as well as the corporate sector generally.[117] This development, questioned by several commentators,[118] will be further discussed in chapter six.

The next section turns to the drivers for the rise of the modern banking culture and takes stock of how organisational culture at banks and financial institutions has developed and shaped risk control.

C. ORGANISATIONAL CULTURE AS THE CONTEXT FOR RISK AND CONTROL

Organisational culture is regarded as the 'software', reflecting the actual practices adopted by the people who run or operate a bank or financial institution.[119] This is distinguished from the 'hardware' of governance frameworks which could be more broad-based and standardised in nature. Organisational culture may be regarded as a ubiquitous 'glue' of shared[120] perceptions in a firm or assumptions and beliefs[121] underlying organisational work practices in the firm or units in the firm,[122] the 'way' everyday life is carried out in an organisation.[123] This 'software' aspect of how things are done in banks and financial institutions has come under scrutiny since the global financial crisis of 2008–09, as risk-taking practices, as well as post-crisis business conduct scandals such as benchmark manipulation and product mis-selling, can only be understood in the context of the organisational culture of the firm. This section will argue that the organisational culture at many banks and financial institutions is affected by the rise of modern banking culture as a sectoral phenomenon. Modern banking culture is characterised by keen competition and empire-building, especially in large universal banking groups and behavioural tendencies such as herding. That said, individual organisational cultures

[117] UK Stewardship Code 2012; Bruner, 'Conceptions of Corporate Purpose' (n 21).

[118] See Christopher M Bruner, 'Corporate Governance Reform in a Time of Crisis' (2011) 36 *Journal of Corporation Law* 309; Pacces, 'Regulation of Banking and Banks Governance' (n 23); Usha Rodrigues, 'Corporate Governance in an Age of Separation of Ownership from Ownership' (2011) 95 *Minnesota Law Review* 1822.

[119] G-30, *Towards Effective Governance* (n 9).

[120] Joanne Martin, *Organisational Cultures: Mapping the Terrain* (London: Sage, 2001) however argues that what is regarded as 'shared' is often very debatable, see chapter 3 generally.

[121] Schein, *Organizational Culture and Leadership* (n 1) 6.

[122] Peter T Van den Berg and Celeste PM Wilderom, 'Defining, Measuring, and Comparing Organisational Cultures' (2004) 53 *Applied Psychology: An International Review* 570.

[123] Martin, *Organisational Cultures* (n 120) 5.

also play a significant part in shaping the unique risk and control cultures in banks and financial institutions.

Modern Banking Culture as a Sectoral Phenomenon

Many post-crisis commentaries and writings describe the modern banking culture, especially in large universal financial groups, as a 'trading culture'. The Archbishop of Canterbury has also described modern banking culture as 'a culture of entitlement'.[124] The Parliamentary Commission on Banking Standards has further found a broadly prevailing 'culture of fear' that adversely affects risk and control culture in UK banks and financial institutions.[125] These general cultural themes seem to have pervaded modern banking institutions.

The rise of a trading culture at banks and financial institutions is due to their engagement in trading business. Banks engage in market trading not only in the capacity of intermediaries. The practice of proprietary trading which allows banks and financial institutions to risk their own capital in the markets may be seen as the quintessential representation of the trading culture. The rise of the trading culture is a response to the increasing competitive pressures in the financial intermediation market where banks compete for maturity transformation and intermediation services with non-bank financial institutions and shadow banks.[126] Inevitably, the advent of a trading culture has changed the banking sector's risk and control practices and the nature of the relationships between the sector and its users.[127] The trading culture emphasises profit-seeking,[128] and such profit-seeking is often short-termist in nature and has become a mantra of investment banking. The trading culture has also affected retail parts of financial institutions, producing a form of short termism[129] in chasing sales and market

[124] 'Archbishop of Canterbury criticises bankers for 'culture of entitlement' *Guardian* (27 April 2013).

[125] *Changing Banking for Good* Vol I (n 46) para 138ff; and House of Lords and House of Commons, Parliamentary Commission on Banking Standards, *Changing Banking for Good* Vol II (HL 27-II, HC 175-II) chapter 7.

[126] Arthur E Wilmarth, 'The Transformation of the Financial Services Industry: 1975–2000, Competition, Consolidation and Increased Risks' (2002) 2 *University of Illinois Law Review* 215; Pacces, 'Consequences of Uncertainty' (n 98).

[127] Pointed out by former Citigroup CEO John Reed, see 'Culture clash means banks must split, says former Citi chief' *Financial Times* (9 September 2013).

[128] House of Lords and House of Commons Parliamentary Commission on Banking Standards, *Proprietary Trading* (2012–13, HL 138, HC 1034) paras 30–31.

[129] Ho, 'Disciplining Investment Bankers' (n 96); Peter Folkman et al, 'Working for Themselves: Financial Intermediaries and Present Day Capitalism' (2007) 49 *Business History* 552; Deakin, 'Corporate Governance and Financial Crisis' (n 51); Dallas, 'Short-Termism' (n 38); David Oakley, 'Financial System Waiting for Next Crisis' *Financial Times* (6 June 2013) on John Kay's characterisation of the modern financial sector as being dominated by an unhealthy trading culture.

share that is further incentivised by remuneration packages designed around yearly bonuses.[130] In particular, pre-crisis remuneration packages have been designed to overly emphasise bonuses in order to stimulate risk-taking and individual performance[131] in response to the need for frenetic profit seeking in a landscape of intense competition. Behavioural drivers in hyper-competitive financial institutions persistently underestimate risk in order to pursue more aggressive growth and higher gains.[132] The Salz Review has observed the impact of high yearly bonuses upon the culture of Barclays in relation to the investment banking arm. The review opined that the investment banking arm of Barclays is pervaded by a 'winning culture' that emphasises short-term and individualistic performance.[133] The effect of this is that individualistic behaviour is encouraged, giving rise to a 'culture of entitlement' described by the Archbishop of Canterbury mentioned above. Schroeder describes the impact of high bonuses upon individual employees as creating an 'eat-what-you-kill' mentality, entailing selfish behaviour that becomes obsessed with individual performance and wealth accumulation in order to be more impressive than one's fellow employee.[134]

Further, such a culture of entitlement reinforces selfish and individualistic behaviour that is increasingly divorced from notions of social utility and the wider good of the purposes of banking.[135] Santoro and Strauss argue that modern banking culture causes profit generation to become disengaged from the generation of social utility, unlike in the days of relationship-based financial services which are highly dependent on serving clients' best interests.[136] Another commentator opines that a 'tough-guy macho' culture generally persists in the banking and financial sector, characterised by high risk-taking, individualistic behaviour, short-termism, blindness to stakeholders, and a lack of cooperation.[137] The culmination of the 'trading culture' and the 'culture of entitlement' is a generally predatory modern banking culture.[138]

A predatory culture[139] manifests a good number of the following characteristics: a lack of ethics; a focus on narrow yardsticks for profitable success,

[130] Tamara C Belinfanti, 'Beyond Economics in Pay for Performance' (2012) 41 *Hofstra Law Review* 91 argues that such yearly bonuses under-incentivise performance that is based on longer-term wealth creation.

[131] Demetra Arsalidou, 'The Regulation of Executive Pay and Economic Theory' (2011) 5 *Journal of Business Law* 431; Felix Suntheim, 'Managerial Compensation in the Financial Service Industry' (2010) at ssrn.com/abstract=1592163.

[132] Blommestein et al (n 27).

[133] Anthony Salz, *The Salz Review: An Independent Review of Barclays' Business Practices* (April 2013) para 8.23ff.

[134] Jeanne L Schroeder, 'Mad Money: Wall Street's Bonus Obsession' (2012) 33 *Cardozo Law Review* 2307.

[135] Michael A Santoro and Ronald J Strauss, *Wall Street Values: Business Ethics and the Global Financial Crisis* (Cambridge: Cambridge University Press, 2012) chs 2, 5.

[136] ibid, ch 5.

[137] See Eugene McKenna, *Business Psychology and Organizational Behaviour*, 4th edn (New York: Taylor & Francis Psychology Press, 2006) 516.

[138] Jerome Want, *Corporate Cultures* (New York: St Martin's Press, 2006).

[139] ibid.

sometimes at the expense of organisational values; incidents of individual fraudulent activities; short-termist mindsets; a lack of rules of conduct, rituals or rites; a lack of employee commitment, customer satisfaction and/or investor confidence; blindness to stakeholders and to the consequences of one's actions; exploitation of stakeholders; punitive and alienating work environments; high turnover rates among employees and management; and an unwillingness to adopt cultural changes unless and until imposed externally. Gapper[140] and Leadsom,[141] writing in the *Financial Times* in the wake of the Barclays LIBOR fixing scandal of 2012, lament the selfish and unethical culture that has developed in contemporary banks, especially investment banks.

The modern banking culture in the pre-crisis years is arguably incompatible with a culture of control that is cognisant of wider stability concerns. Berson et al discussed three dominant categories of organisational cultures, viz innovative cultures characterised by leadership that drives and supports original and individualistic thinking; bureaucratic cultures characterised by values revolving around security, order and predictability; and supportive cultures characterised by a predominant concern for employees and stakeholders.[142] Their empirical research finds that innovative cultures generally drive sales growth and financial performance but are negatively associated with bureaucratic cultures that emphasise control and stability, or supportive cultures that emphasise concern for others. Büschgens et al's subsequent meta-analytical review of organisational behaviour literature also confirms the same point, ie, organisational cultures that sustain more innovation seem to be diametrically opposed to cultures that facilitate control and order.[143] Modern banking culture that has developed to meet modern banking needs in a fiercely competitive landscape may be incompatible with control and stabilising tendencies. Such a finding would pose significant issues for the efficacy of internal control in banks and financial institutions as internal control appears to be riding against the prevailing cultural tide. Further, innovative cultures are also arguably inherently opposed to more communitarian perspectives,[144] and hence banks and financial institutions are likely unable to take into account the collective systemic risk impact of their behaviour.[145]

140 John Gapper, 'Trading Floor Culture no longer Acceptable' *Financial Times* (5 July 2012).

141 Andrea Leadsom, 'How an Old Hand would Change Barclays' *Financial Times* (5 July 2012).

142 Yair Berson, Shaul Oreg and Taly Dvir, 'CEO Values, Organizational Culture and Firm Outcomes' (2008) 28 *Journal of Organizational Behavior* 615.

143 Thorsten Büschgens, Andreas Bausch and David B Balkin, 'Organizational Culture and Innovation: A Meta-Analytic Review' (2013) 30 *Journal of Product Innovation Management* 1.

144 David Knights and Majella O'Leary, 'Reflecting on Corporate Scandals: The Failure of Ethical Leadership' (2005) 14 *Business Ethics: A European Review* 359 argue that too much emphasis has been placed on individual winning characteristics in business management and there is a need to look for communitarian narratives.

145 Richard Windram, 'Risk-Taking Incentives: A Review of the Literature' (2005) 19 *Journal of Economic Surveys* 65.

A state of weakness in the internal control at many banks and financial institutions in the pre-crisis years has been observed by many commentators who explain how the aggressive profit chasing and growth cultures at banks have persistently undervalued[146] the importance of risk management and the devotion of resources to sound risk management.[147] According to an empirical study, resource constraints are frequently a driver for lower quality risk management in firms.[148]

The undermining of internal control at banks and financial institutions in the pre-crisis years has further given rise to a culture of fear. The Parliamentary Commission on Banking Standards describes the 'culture of fear' prevalent in banks and financial institutions as a culture of silence, tolerance of questionable practices and failure to report upwards.[149] There is generally little tolerance for contrary opinions that tend towards being prudent or conservative,[150] and little or no whistle-blowing culture exists at most banks and financial institutions. In this context, the Parliamentary Commission has found a generally complicit internal control culture that is based on procedural box-ticking, and subscribing to management theories that are friendly to business objectives.[151] Such is the case even if formal independence of internal control functions is maintained. This means that the pervasive 'trading' and 'predatory' cultures at banks and financial institutions have in reality undermined the efficacy of internal control to exert countervailing and checking forces upon business activities and behaviour. This is in spite of formal attributes in organisational structures that may promote independent and objective internal control efficacy.

Organisational Cultures at Banks and Financial Institutions

The above has discussed the evolution of a modern banking culture has become a sectoral phenomenon especially in relation to large universal banking groups. Individual organisational cultures and sub-cultures are however also key to distinguishing between healthy banks and banks that experienced failure or greater stress in the global financial crisis

[146] See Donald C Langevoort, 'Chasing the Greased Pig Down Wall Street: A Gatekeeper's Guide to the Psychology, Culture and Ethics of Financial Risk-taking' (2011) 96 *Cornell Law Review* 1209.

[147] Crouhy, 'Risk Management Failures' (n 27); Sheedy, 'The Future of Risk Modelling' (n 27).

[148] See Ryan Baxter et al, 'Enterprise Risk Management Program Quality: Determinants, Value Relevance, and the Financial Crisis' (July 2012) at ssrn.com/abstract=1684807.

[149] *Changing Banking for Good* Vol II (n 125) para 128ff.

[150] 'HBOS executives "threatened" colleagues who questioned risk-taking' *Guardian* (30 October 2012).

[151] *Changing Banking for Good* Vol II (n 125) paras 141–42.

of 2008–09 or between banks afflicted with conduct scandals and those otherwise.[152]

For example, the trading cultures at some banks may be more aggressive than in others in undermining internal control and risk management. Such has been identified in UBS, Merrill Lynch, Lehman Brothers and the Royal Bank of Scotland. In UBS' self-reflecting report in 2008, UBS identified the relatively low profile of risk management as a problem. The bank failed to appoint sufficiently skilled and senior risk managers who were ultimately unable to challenge front office decision-makers.[153] A commentator has also discussed the sidelining of risk management in the bankrupt investment bank Lehman Brothers in the US, and the investment bank Merrill Lynch which has been rescued by the Bank of America in the nick of time.[154] The Parliamentary Commission[155] also identified domineering Chief Executive Officers who drove aggressive trading and growth cultures in firms and neglected concern for control and wider systemic impact—the examples being Fred Goodwin of the Royal Bank of Scotland and Jon Corzine of the bankrupt American brokerage giant MF Global. Organisational theorists have consistently argued that 'tone at the top' is highly important to the development of culture as culture revolves around the stances taken by leaders[156] and those who are in a position to display power and persuasion.[157] The undermining of control cultures generally leads to a 'culture of fear' as discussed above, resulting in internal control inefficacy in reining in excesses and maintaining control. This was observed in Bank of America and Lehman Brothers in the US.[158] On the contrary, a healthy respect for a control culture alongside a robust appetite for risk-taking has shaped the success of investment bank Goldman Sachs.[159]

However, the Parliamentary Commission has also recognised that leadership is not the only driver for cultural change and development.[160] Morgan opines that although leadership can drive changes in values and management practices, the culture and sub-cultures in firms are living and evolving and can deviate from the rules, frameworks and management fads that are

[152] Rüdiger Fahlenbrach, Robert Prilmeier and René M Stulz, 'This Time is the Same: Using Bank Performance in 1998 to Explain Bank Performance during the Recent Financial Crisis' (2012) 67 *Journal of Finance* 2139.

[153] Discussed in Rose, 'Regulating Risk' (n 30).

[154] See Jonas Prager, 'The Financial Crisis of 2007/8: Misaligned Incentives, Bank Mismanagement, and Troubling Policy Implications' (2012) at ssrn.com/abstract=2094662.

[155] *Changing Banking for Good* Vol II (n 125) para 774ff.

[156] Schein, *Organizational Culture and Leadership* (n 1) ch 10, 223ff.

[157] Tim Hallett, 'Symbolic Power and Organizational Culture' (2003) 21 *Sociological Theory* 128.

[158] *Changing Banking for Good* Vol II (n 125) para 774.

[159] ibid, para 811.

[160] ibid, paras 761ff.

overtly put in place.[161] Leadership may not always be able to change the mindsets and perceptions of employees.[162] The practices of middle management and the existence of sub-cultures in certain business units of the organisation, particularly in large and complex organisations, can cement cultures that are distinct or deviate from the tone at the top. The Salz Review observed distinct sub-cultures in the investment banking arm of Barclays and in its American business units, showing that in large and complex universal banks, contrary cultural developments may take place and 'local' cultures may evolve distinctly and be immune from central control.[163] Such local cultures may develop due to distinct organisational practices that are allowed to persist, the consolidation of power by leaders in such business units or distinct values shaped by remuneration practices. The development of local cultures could also culminate in rogue trader scandals in spite of an overall framework for scrutiny and control. The London whale loss at JP Morgan could also be attributed to the unchecked activities of a small elite group of traders in the Chief Investment Office who have become less and less accountable beyond the general frameworks of control.[164]

The general undermining of internal control by aggressive trading cultures in organisations is now addressed both by the organisational enhancement of internal control functions (discussed in chapters two to four) and by the regulation of certain aspects of corporate governance that seek to steer leadership towards the maintenance of healthy control cultures. Is culture susceptible to regulation or enforcement?[165] Would culture change in response to regulatory reforms that change incentives in governance? Chapter six will argue that corporate governance reforms institute certain frameworks for oversight and accountability that may change practices and have an impact upon the organisational culture at firms. However, this may be a slow and gradual process.[166] That said, the regulation of financial sector remuneration and structural reforms at large banking groups may change the incentives of financial sector personnel and usher in changes in overall culture.[167] The development of more precise supervisory metrics on the part of regulators to assess the risk and

[161] Gareth Morgan, *Images of Organization* (London: Sage Publications, 2006) 138.

[162] ibid, 143.

[163] *The Salz Review* (n 133) para 8.21ff.

[164] United States Senate Permanent Subcommittee on Investigations, *JP Morgan Chase Whale Trades: A Case History of Derivatives Risks and Abuses* (n 87) 157ff.

[165] Hector Sants, 'Do Regulators have a Role to Play in Judging Culture and Ethics?' (speech at Chartered Institute of Securities and Investments Conference, 17 June 2010) at www.fsa.gov.uk/pages/Library/Communication/Speeches/2010/0617_hs.shtml.

[166] 'Banks need a generation to change culture, report says' *Financial Times* (26 November 2014).

[167] To be discussed in chapter 6.

control cultures[168] at firms may also incentivise firm leadership to take culture seriously and accelerate the pace of change.

D. CONCLUSION

This chapter has discussed corporate governance and organisational culture as broader contexts shaping the risk and control cultures in banks and financial institutions and affecting the role and efficacy of internal control. This chapter takes stock of the post-crisis commentary in relation to aspects of corporate governance and organisational culture that are salient to shaping the risk and control cultures at firms. The discussion raises fundamental questions such as whether post-crisis reforms into corporate governance can significantly change risk culture even if fundamental agency-based ideologies in corporate governance remain unchallenged, and whether the regulation of aspects of corporate governance, financial sector remuneration and structural reforms could indeed affect organisational and risk cultures at firms. The next chapter will discuss the post-crisis reforms targeted at aspects of corporate governance. It will also discuss the extensive reforms in regulating financial sector remuneration and structural reforms for large banking groups which may change incentives and, therefore, change organisational and risk cultures at firms.

[168] See, eg, Simon Ashby, Tommaso Palermo and Michael Power, *Risk Culture in Financial Organisations* (Interim Report, November 2012; Research Report, 2014) which discusses the importance of looking into the nature of trade-offs in risk decisions, frameworks and systems for information flows, systems for interaction and not just accountability, the use of external advisers and perceptions of regulatory expectations.

Part II

Making Internal Control Effective in Banks and Financial Institutions

6

Regulating Aspects of Corporate Governance and Organisational Culture as a Broader Framework for Internal Control

AS DISCUSSED IN Part I, internal control functions in banks and financial institutions have been enhanced by regulatory reform and are positioned to meet increased regulatory expectations of their internal governance role. Although internal control functions have had a long history of being internal gatekeepers for individual corporations as such, the gatekeeping role is now fashioned more towards securing the firm's meeting of regulatory objectives, becoming more outward-facing and aligned with regulators' interests.

This part of the book now addresses the key regulatory strategies designed to make internal control functions at banks and financial institutions effective as internal gatekeepers who serve regulatory expectations in securing the firm's meeting of regulatory objectives. This chapter focuses on the reforms introduced to corporate governance and broader organisational aspects in order to support the institution of a robust risk and control function in which internal control functions are located. This chapter will address to what extent the organisational reforms discussed in relation to each of the internal control functions in chapters two to four are being flanked by the corporate governance and general organisational reforms here and what issues may remain. Chapter seven then discusses the regulatory strategies directed at the personal and individual liability of internal control personnel. However, the discussion on enforcement in chapter seven will highlight the need for regulators to consider the disjunction between regulatory expectations and professional perceptions of the relevant internal control role (the regulatory–professional disjunction), and to what extent such disjunction has been mitigated or overcome by the organisational reforms specific to the relevant internal control function and generally. Chapter eight will argue that although much has been achieved by the organisational reforms relevant to each internal control function, the expectations gap between regulators and internal control professions may continue to affect perceptions of internal control efficacy and shape the liability regimes for internal control personnel. There is a need for the internal control professions and regulators to engage in better dialogue in order to shape both regulatory expectations and the professionalism of internal control professions so that internal control functions can be truly effective in their organisations, and clarity and fairness can be achieved with respect to the expectations of their roles and responsibilities.

This chapter will now examine the extent of regulatory intervention into the governance frameworks within the firm. This is an area that is to a certain extent unique to the financial sector as the reasons for such regulatory intervention, based on public interest, are not often applicable to the corporate sector generally.[1] This chapter argues that the objective of EU regulatory intervention into corporate governance is to establish structural features that generate more senior oversight and monitoring of strategic risk decisions and risk management generally. These are mandatory and not enabling (ie, allowing opting out) in nature but are meta-regulatory. The chapter will critically discuss what such corporate governance regulation achieves. To a certain extent, the corporate governance reforms do address Board weaknesses in relation to marginalising or inadequately overseeing risk governance. However, some aspects of corporate governance regulation are merely path dependent in terms of hardening conventional best practices in corporate governance and are not necessarily related to the specific raison d'etre of regulating corporate governance in the financial sector.

This chapter will also discuss the UK's unique regime of regulatory vetting and approval of key personnel before appointment to a bank or financial institution. The UK has ushered in reforms to subject senior personnel to enhanced liability regimes.[2] These reforms which target individual incentives may usher in behavioural change that will shape organisational and risk cultures at firms. Further, regulatory reforms to control financial sector remuneration,[3] and structural reforms to the

[1] Klaus Hopt, 'Better Governance of Financial Institutions' (2012) at ssrn.com/abstract=2212198; KJ Hopt, 'Corporate Governance of Banks after the Financial Crisis' in E Wymeersch, KJ Hopt and G Ferrarini (eds), *Financial Regulation and Supervision: A Post-Crisis Analysis* (Oxford: Oxford University Press, 2012) and Part B in (2013) 13 *Journal of Corporate Law Studies* 219.

[2] House of Lords and House of Commons, Parliamentary Commission on Banking Standards, *Changing Banking for Good* Vol 1 (2013–14, HL 27-I, HC 175-I) para 110ff; *Changing Banking for Good* Vol II (2013–14, HL 27-II, HC 175-I) para 1170 (12 June 2013); Financial Services (Banking Reform) Act 2013 amending Financial Services and Markets Act 2000 by inserting s 64Aff.

[3] European Parliament and Council Directive 2010/76/EU of 24 November 2010 amending Directives 2006/48/EC and 2006/49/EC as regards capital requirements for the trading book and for re-securitisations, and the supervisory review of remuneration policies [2010] OJ L329/3 (Capital Requirements Directive 2010) Art 22(1); Directive 2013/36/EU

banking sector[4] will be discussed as to their impact upon organisational and risk cultures at firms. Soft law measures such as an increased demand for banking professionalism[5] and encouraging shareholders to act as risk monitors[6] of their investee firms will also be critically discussed.

A. REGULATING THE BOARDS OF BANKS AND FINANCIAL INSTITUTIONS: STRUCTURAL ASPECTS IN CORPORATE GOVERNANCE

As discussed in chapter five, the key corporate governance concerns that arose in the global financial crisis related to the strategic marginalisation of risk management and the lack of Board leadership and oversight of risk management[7] in the banks and financial institutions that failed or experienced severe stress. EU legislation in the Directive applying to credit institutions (CRD IV Directive) that will be discussed below, and in the Directive applying to investment firms and market operators (MiFID II Directive 2014), have now introduced reforms[8] to make explicit the Board's role in risk management, to prescribe certain aspects of conduct on the part of executive and non-executive directors and to regulate certain aspects of Board composition. Mandatory intervention into organisational features are often only seen as necessary if organisational initiatives

of the European Parliament and of the Council of 26 June 2013 on access to the activity of credit institutions and the prudential supervision of credit institutions and investment firms, amending Directive 2002/87/EC and repealing Directives 2006/48/EC and 2006/49/EC (CRD IV Directive) Arts 92–94; PRA and FCA Remuneration Codes, SYSC 19A.

[4] Independent Commission on Banking, *Final Report* (London: ICB September, 2011) at www.hm-treasury.gov.uk/d/ICB-Final-Report.pdf; HM Treasury, *Banking Reform: Delivering Stability and Supporting a Sustainable Economy* (White Paper, Cm 8356, June 2012) (Treasury White Paper 2012) resulting in the Financial Services (Banking Reform) Act 2013 at s 142Aff; Erkki Liikanen, *High-level Expert Group on Reforming the Structure of the EU Banking Sector* (Final Report, October 2012).

[5] *Changing Banking for Good* Vol II (n 2) para 763ff. Richard Lambert, *Banking Standards Review: Final Report* (19 May 2014) at www.bankingstandardsreview.org.uk/assets/docs/may2014report.pdf. proposing to establish an independent body funded by the private sector to establish a principles-based code of ethics for the banking industry.

[6] David Walker, 'A Review of Corporate Governance in UK Banks and other Financial Industry Entities: Final Recommendations' (26 November 2009) at webarchive.nationalarchives.gov.uk; www.hm-treasury.gov.uk/d/walker_review_261109.pdf (Walker Review 2009); UK Stewardship Code 2012 at www.frc.org.uk/Our-Work/Codes-Standards/Corporate-governance/UK-Stewardship-Code.aspx.

[7] Viral V Acharya, Jennifer N Carpenter, Xavier Gabaix, Kose John, Matthew Richardson, Marti G Subrahmanyam, Rangarajan K Sundaram and Eitan Zemel, 'Corporate Governance in the Modern Financial Sector' in Viral Acharya and Matthew Richardson (eds), *Restoring Financial Stability: How to Repair a Failed Financial System* (Chichester: Wiley Finance, 2009) 185.

[8] EU legislative reforms will be discussed shortly but this approach is being internationalised under the initiatives of the Basel Committee, see Basel Committee on Banking Supervision, *Guidelines: Corporate Governance Principles for Banks* (Consultation Paper, October 2014).

are unlikely to be taken due to inertia or lack of incentives.[9] These measures are intended to prevent Boards from marginalising the importance of risk management and drive greater Board oversight of risk decisions. In particular, the prescriptions in corporate governance for banks and market operators mirror each other, with investment firms subject to a lesser extent. This means that the EU regards banks and market operators, ie, operators of stock exchanges and investment firms that operate electronic trading facilities, as being equivalent in terms of systemic importance and hence subject to the same extent of corporate governance prescriptions to safeguard prudential management. The UK has also made regulatory vetting and approval of key personnel a more stringent process, in excess of EU requirements, and has introduced more severe personal responsibility and liability regimes. Such measures intend to provide enhanced incentives for senior personnel to take ownership of their responsibilities.

The Functions of the Board

The functions of the Board of regulated credit institutions[10] and investment firms[11] in the EU are now expressed comprehensively to comprise of: (a) the overall responsibility for strategic objectives, risk strategy and internal governance; (b) the responsibility to ensure integrity in accounting and financial reporting; (c) the responsibility to ensure compliance with laws and regulations; (d) the oversight of disclosure and communications in the firm; (e) the responsibility to provide effective oversight of senior management; and (f) periodic review of all governance arrangements.[12]

Risk governance has now been raised in profile to sit alongside the Board's usual role in strategic management.[13] Although the OECD[14] and the US COSO[15] have earlier recognised the importance of the Board's

[9] See Timothy F Malloy, 'Regulation, Compliance and the Firm' (2003) 76 *Temple Law Review* 451.

[10] CRD IV Directive, Art 88(1).

[11] Directive 2014/65/EU of the European Parliament and of the Council of 15 May 2014 on markets in financial instruments and amending Directive 2002/92/EC and Directive 2011/61/EU (MiFID II Directive 2014) Art 9 contains similar provisions on oversight of effective and prudent management and the Board's responsibility to set an appropriate remuneration policy.

[12] These are also consistent with the international best practices recommended in the Basel Committee on Banking Supervision, *Principles for Enhancing Corporate Governance* (October 2010); Basel Committee, *Guidelines* (n 8).

[13] See also Basel Committee, *Guidelines* (n 8) Principle 1.

[14] OECD, *Principles of Corporate Governance* (2004) at www.oecd.org/corporate/oecdprinciplesofcorporategovernance.htm, Principle VI.D.1; Grant Kirkpatrick, 'The Corporate Governance Lessons from the Financial Crisis' (OECD Report 2009) at www.oecd.org/dataoecd/32/1/42229620.pdf.

[15] Committee of Sponsoring Organizations of the Treadway Commission (COSO), *Enterprise Risk Management- Integrated Framework* (September 2004).

role in overseeing risk governance in the corporate sector generally, the deployment of hard law to secure this Board function shows the determination of policymakers to ensure that Board priorities are aligned with the public interest in banks and financial institutions. In the general corporate sector, the profile of risk governance has also been raised to Board level[16] but general corporate sector Boards seem to be subject to a lesser requirement for annual review that seems less stringent than the constant engagement with risk governance that is required for financial institution Boards. Further, the Financial Stability Board (FSB) is recommending a set of best practices to assist Boards in setting a risk appetite, risk limits and establishing risk management policies and frameworks.[17] EU legislation (in the form of the CRD IV Directive and the MiFID II Directive 2014) has also raised the profile of compliance with laws and regulations as a Board function[18] and in effect, this compels the Board to engage with internal control at the highest level. Further, the Basel Committee, in its endeavours at the harmonisation of international banking regulation,[19] suggest that the Board should be responsible for the institution and oversight of an effective internal audit function, therefore making the Board responsible for the effectiveness for all three lines of defence in a banking institution. This does not in the author's view allow Boards to influence internal control and shape their roles in a business friendly way as the EU legislation provides an overarching requirement that banks and investment firms be 'effectively and *prudently* managed'. Further, Boards are made responsible for ensuring that frameworks that would secure effective internal control are instituted and overseen at the highest level, ie, the Board responsibilities referred to in (d), (e) and (f) above. Effective oversight of information flows[20] and senior management functions facilitate the Board's engagement with the overall control culture in the firm; such engagement is to be reinforced by the requirement imposed on Boards to regularly review governance arrangements. In sum, the Board is imposed with the responsibility to ensure leadership in instituting robust internal control.

One may argue that the emphasis placed on the risk governance responsibility of the Board is effectively rhetorical in nature. The Board's leadership in risk governance sits alongside its strategic responsibilities and trade-offs would still need to be made between risk moderation and

[16] UK Corporate Governance Code C.2.1.

[17] Financial Stability Board, *Principles for an Effective Risk Appetite Framework: Consultative Document* (17 July 2013).

[18] This has already been expressly provided in UK legislation: see PRA and FCA Handbooks, SYSC 4.3.1. See also Basel Committee, *Guidelines* (n 8) Principle 1, 9.

[19] Basel Committee, *Guidelines* (n 8) Principle 10.

[20] Michael Pirson and Shaan Turnbull, 'Corporate Governance, Risk Management, and the Financial Crisis: An Information Processing View' (2011) 19 *Corporate Governance: An International Review* 459; Basel Committee, *Principles for Enhancing Corporate Governance* (n 12) Principle 8; Basel Committee, *Guidelines* (n 8) Principle 8.

business objectives. However, as specific risk setting and management responsibilities are now recommended to be imposed on the Board by the Financial Stability Board,[21] the Board is compelled to engage with processes that show how and why risk decisions are taken. Such processes could augment the sense of ownership of risk decisions at the highest levels and improve accountability, thus having an impact upon directorial incentives in decision-making. Nevertheless, the American experience with the post-crisis *Citigroup* litigation[22] shows the difficulties in challenging the Board's role in risk governance: such a role is high level in nature and allegations of inadequate discharge of responsibility would be highly difficult to prove.

On a more general note, Bovens is of the view the collective responsibility could generate a situation of absence of real responsibility.[23] So if the Board is collectively responsible for overseeing risk governance, then cosmetic engagement with processes can be undertaken and no ownership of responsibility may be taken by any Board member. Although EU legislation does not address this issue, the UK's senior persons regime which will be discussed shortly arguably addresses the personal responsibility of individual Board members who are tasked with different responsibilities. The drawbacks of such an approach will also be discussed.

The Responsibilities of Executive Directors, in Particular the Chairman

EU legislation has now introduced certain prescriptions that incentivise bank directors to devote sufficient dedication to their roles and hence enhance their general oversight and monitoring capacity. Although the EU legislation does not differentiate between executive and non-executive directors to a significant extent in terms of how they should discharge their roles, executive directors are prohibited from holding another executive directorship elsewhere and not more than two other non-executive directorships.[24] Non-executive directors on the other hand are allowed

[21] FSB, *Principles for an Effective Risk Appetite Framework: Consultative Document* (n 17) para 4.

[22] *In Re Citigroup Inc Shareholder Derivative Litigation* 4 A.2d 106 (Del Ch 2009); Franklin A Gevurtz, 'The Role of Corporate Law in Preventing a Financial Crisis: Some Reflections on *In Re Citigroup Inc Shareholder Derivative Litigation*' in PM Vasudev and Susan Watson (eds), *Corporate Governance after the Financial Crisis* (Cheltenham: Edward Elgar, 2011) 163.

[23] Mark Bovens, *The Quest for Responsibility: Accountability and Citizenship in Complex Organisations* (Cambridge: Cambridge University Press, 1998) 45ff.

[24] CRD IV Directive, Art 91(3)(a), also applied to investment firms in Art 9, MiFID II Directive 2014. Market operators are also subject to the same corporate governance prescriptions: see Art 45, MiFID II Directive 2014.

to hold up to four other non-executive directorships elsewhere.[25] These provisions are to ensure that members of the Board are able to devote sufficient time and commitment to the management of the relevant bank or financial institution.

The UK Walker Review in particular called for the Chairman of the Board to devote at least two-thirds of his time to the management of the relevant bank or financial institution,[26] but this has not been legislated by the UK financial regulators the Prudential Regulatory Authority (PRA) and the Financial Conduct Authority (FCA). The Walker Review also suggested special responsibility on the part of the Chairman to provide leadership and to facilitate meaningful and adequate Board discussions and communications between executive and non-executive directors for decision-making on strategy and risk.[27] This has been generally adopted in the UK Corporate Governance Code.[28]

One of the key legislative endorsements[29] of conventional corporate governance best practices in EU legislation relates to the separation of the Chairman and Chief Executive Officer.[30] This is to ensure that senior management, including the Chief Executive Officer (CEO), is duly subject to Board oversight. As discussed in chapter five, the dominance of an aggressive CEO favouring risk-taking has overshadowed Board oversight to adverse outcomes in the failed banks of RBS, Lehman Brothers and MF Global. The legislative endorsement of the separation of Chairman from CEO is a path dependent approach consistent with prevailing best practices in conventional corporate governance standards, but may nevertheless emphasise the Chairman's and the Board's oversight role. However, all the failed banks mentioned above had separate Chairmen from CEOs. Hence, the structural feature of separation may not be sufficient to facilitate adequate and effective oversight by the Board. Further, UK legislation requires the CEO to be responsible for instituting adequate internal control.[31] Although the Board has oversight of internal control generally, the efficacy of such oversight may depend on Board dynamics and dynamics with senior management. Hence, whether or not the Chairman is separate from the CEO, the dynamics between the Board and the CEO in instituting internal control and governance could affect the efficacy of internal

[25] CRD IV Directive, Art 91(3)(b), also applied to investment firms in Art 9, MiFID II Directive 2014. Market operators are also subject to the same corporate governance prescriptions: see Art 45, MiFID II Directive 2014.

[26] Walker Review 2009 (n 6) Recommendation 7.

[27] The Chairman's leadership role is also highlighted in the Basel Committee, *Principles for Enhancing Corporate Governance* (n 12) Principle 3, paras 44–45.

[28] UK Corporate Governance Code A.3.

[29] CRD IV Directive, Art 88(1)(e).

[30] UK Corporate Governance Code A.2.1; see also A.3.1 relating to limiting succession opportunities for the Chief Executive to Chairmanship.

[31] PRA and FCA Handbooks, SYSC 4.4.5.

control functions. Perhaps it would be more meaningful to legislate for separate accountability of internal control functions to the Board in order to preserve direct and meaningful Board oversight of this now key responsibility. The Parliamentary Commission on Banking Standards has therefore proposed that internal control functions be made sufficiently senior[32] and report directly to the Board.[33] In chapters two to four, we note that the accountability channels of internal control functions vary slightly and it remains to be seen if this issue would need to be addressed by further regulatory prescription in the future.

Although policymakers are determined to 'harden' conventional best practices in corporate governance such as the separation of Chairman from the CEO in order to preserve the Board's risk oversight role,[34] chapter five has mentioned empirical research suggesting that the duality of Chairman and CEO may not always be adverse to the risk profile of a financial institution, and could in fact deliver benefits in providing consistent leadership in stressed times.[35] This point may raise a more general issue in relation to the concern that regulation of aspects of corporate governance merely falls within the agency-based conventional standards in corporate governance and does not adequately grapple with unique financial sector concerns.

The Special Role of Non-Executive Directors

EU legislation now requires all directors of banks and investment firms to possess sufficient knowledge, skills and experience for the business although the Board should still feature a range of diverse skills and competencies to meet the needs of the business.[36] As discussed in chapter five, much has been said about enhancing the financial expertise of the Board in order to provide leadership in optimal risk-taking, but it is noted that there is empirical research that points out a correlation between increased risk-taking and financial expertise.[37] This is because directors' financial expertise may allow them to feel more comfortable about taking higher

[32] Discussed also in chapters 2–4.

[33] *Changing Banking for Good* Vol II (n 2) para 729ff.

[34] CRD IV Directive, Art 88(1)(e); Basel Committee, *Principles for Enhancing Corporate Governance* (n 12) Principle 3, para 46.

[35] See Marc van Essen, Peter-Jan Engelen, and Michael Carney, 'Does "Good" Corporate Governance Help in a Crisis? The Impact of Country- and Firm-Level Governance Mechanisms in the European Financial Crisis' (2013) 21 *Corporate Governance* 201.

[36] CRD IV Directive, Art 91(1), (7) and MiFID II Directive 2014, Art 9(1).

[37] See Bernadette Minton, Jérôme PA Taillard and Rohan Williamson, 'Do Independence and Financial Expertise of the Board Matter for Risk Taking and Performance?' (2011) at www.ssrn.com/abstract=1661855; A Sinan Cebenoyan and Philip Strahan, 'Risk Management, Capital Structure and Lending at Banks' (2001) at ssrn.com/abstract=293378.

levels of risk and employing sophisticated risk mitigation techniques, and the resulting risk profile for firms may actually be rather high. It is noted that regulatory prescription has not gone as far as to specify financial expertise to be represented in certain proportions on Boards.

All directors are also required to act with independence of mind to critically oversee and challenge senior management.[38] This is a move away from insisting on formal independence as such,[39] although an empirical study finds that formal independence matters for mitigation of risk-taking in financial firms.[40] Although no distinction is made between executive and non-executive directors in EU legislation, the UK seems to support the view that non-executive directors (who are more likely to be also independent) have a particular role to play in acting as critical and constructive challengers of executive decision-making.[41] This view is endorsed by the G-30 recommendations for improving corporate governance in banks and financial institutions.[42] Moore argues that the UK's position is that non-executive directors are expected to play a role in risk moderation in constructively challenging executive decisions on risk management.[43] The Walker Review has also paid particular attention to beefing up non-executive directors' knowledge of the business, time commitment and access to advice,[44] and has expressly articulated expectations for non-executive directors to 'challenge and test proposals on strategy put forward by the executive. They should satisfy themselves that board discussion and decision-taking on risk matters is based on accurate and appropriately comprehensive information'.[45] The UK Prudential Regulatory Authority (PRA) and Financial Conduct Authority (FCA) regulatory handbooks, which are important pieces of subsidiary legislation, have however not made particular prescriptions as to the role of non-executive directors, preferring to incorporate general best practices in the UK Corporate

[38] CRD IV Directive, Art 91(8) and MiFID II Directive 2014, Art 45 that applies to market operators. The provisions applicable to the management body of investment firms generally in Art 9 are less specific.

[39] Also argued in Terry McNulty, Chris Florackis and Phillip Ormrod, 'Boards of Directors and Financial Risk during the Credit Crisis' (2013) 21 *Corporate Governance* 58 that formal independence as such is no guarantee for the substantive qualities of critical monitoring and constructive challenge that are derived from Board dynamics that mitigate against groupthink.

[40] See Minton, Taillard and Williamson, 'Do Independence and Financial Expertise of the Board Matter for Risk Taking and Performance?' (n 37).

[41] Walker Review 2009 (n 6) Recommendation 6.

[42] G-30, *Towards Effective Governance in Financial Institutions* (2012) at www.group30.org/rpt_64.shtml.

[43] Marc T Moore, 'The Evolving Contours of the Board's Risk Management Function in UK Corporate Governance' (2010) 10 *Journal of Corporate Law Studies* 279.

[44] Walker Review 2009 (n 6) Recommendations 1–3, 5–6.

[45] ibid, Recommendation 6.

Governance Code.[46] The Code does attribute a particular role in constructive and critical challenge to non-executive directors.[47]

EU legislation[48] also supports adequate induction and training for directors[49] although the UK Walker Review has focused on such training for non-executive directors in particular.[50] In sum, the UK and EU regulatory regimes have continued to embrace the assumptions in conventional corporate governance best practices in relation to the monitoring role and capacity of non-executive or independent directors, perceiving them as aptly placed to deal with conventional agency problems as well as risk moderation.

This chapter will shortly further discuss individual directorial liability for executive and non-executive directors under new incentive-based reforms intended to change behaviour.[51]

Regulating Board Composition

EU legislation requires the Board as a whole to possess a range of skills, expertise and experience adequate for the bank or financial institution's business,[52] and it would be the role of the nomination committee of the Board to ensure that such a balance is achieved in the Board recruitment processes and policies.[53] This is however not completely down to the nomination committee's discretion, as technical guidelines on the balance of skills and expertise for the Board are envisaged to be issued by the European Banking Authority and the European Securities and Markets Authority (EBA and ESMA, respectively). As questions have arisen over the suitability of Chairmen with diverse backgrounds (such as in zoology) in one of the UK's failed banks in the global financial crisis,[54] regulatory prescription into the balance of skills and expertise on bank and financial institution Boards may go some way towards responding to the concerns of populating Bank boards with renowned but inadequate trophy directors.

[46] PRA and FCA Handbooks, SYSC 3.1.2A.

[47] UK Corporate Governance Code A.4.

[48] CRD IV Directive, Art 91(9); MiFID II Directive 2014, Art 45(3) applying to market operators.

[49] The importance of training and induction for directors in financial institutions is discussed in P Schwizer, R Casiraghi and V Stefanelli, 'Boards at Work: Why and How Induction and Training Could Enhance Directors' Effectiveness in the Boardroom' (2011) 11 *International Journal of Regulation and Governance* 1.

[50] Walker Review 2009 (n 6) Recommendations 1–3.

[51] See below, the senior persons regime.

[52] CRD IV Directive, Art 91(7); MiFID II Directive 2014, Art 45(4)ff for market operators; see also Basel Committee, *Principles for Enhancing Corporate Governance* (n 12) Principle 1; Basel Committee, *Guidelines* (n 8) Principle 2.

[53] CRD IV Directive, Arts 88(2)(a), 91(10); MiFID II Directive 2014, Art 45(5).

[54] Matt Ridley, Chairman of Northern Rock, 2004–07.

In the UK where regulatory pre-vetting takes place before the approval of individuals to take up Board positions in financial institutions,[55] the regulator may have significant control over Board composition. However, such control may sometimes backfire if approved appointments subsequently turn out to be questionable.[56] It is however unlikely that regulatory liability may be attracted for approving bank Board appointments as chapter five has observed that the literature review yields a mixed picture in terms of the relationship between Board composition and bank performance or failure.

Next, EU legislation requires the nomination committees of Boards in banks and market operators (including investment firms with such operations) to promote diversity on Boards in particular in relation to the under-represented gender.[57] The move towards increasing the number of female directors on corporate Boards is not limited to the financial sector, as there is a broader movement in the EU to champion this cause.[58] However, in the financial sector, research on the effect of the male hormone testosterone on risk-taking on trading floors may have become rather important to the cause of championing for diversity.[59] Perhaps the 'moderating' influences of female directors upon bank and financial institution Boards would be necessary for overall risk governance. Further, it is believed that gender diversity on Boards would enhance critical and constructive challenge in Board discussions.[60] A number of commentators however caution against viewing the issue of gender diversity on Boards as a merely instrumental issue towards improving efficacy on Boards.[61] This is because although

[55] PRA and FCA Handbooks, FIT module.

[56] 'Ex-Co-op Bank chairman Paul Flowers charged with drug offences' *Financial Times* (16 April 2014).

[57] CRD IV Directive, Art 88(2)(a); MiFID II Directive 2014, Art 45(4)(a).

[58] European Commission, 'Proposal for a Directive of the European Parliament and of the Council on improving the gender balance among non-executive directors of companies listed on stock exchanges and related measures' (November 2012).

[59] John M Coates, Mark Gurnell and Zoltan Sarnyai, 'From Molecule to Market: Steroid Hormones and Financial Risk-Taking' (2010) 365 *Philosophical Transactions of the Royal Society B: Biological Sciences* 331; John M Coates and Joe Herbert, 'Endogenous Steroids and Financial Risk Taking on a London Trading Floor' (2008) 105 *Proceedings of the National Academy of Science* 6167; John Coates, *The Hour Between Dog and Wolf. Risk Taking, Gut Feelings, and the Biology of Boom and Bust* (New York: Penguin Press, 2012).

[60] Melsa Ararat, Mine H Aksu and Ayse Tansel Cetin, 'The Impact of Board Diversity on Boards' Monitoring Intensity and Firm Performance: Evidence from the Istanbul Stock Exchange' (2010) at papers.ssrn.com/sol3/papers.cfm?abstract_id=1572283 on Turkish banks; MA Gulamhussen and Silva Maria Santos, 'Women in Bank Boardrooms and their Influence on Performance and Risk-Taking' (April 2010) at papers.ssrn.com/sol3/papers.cfm?abstract_id=1615663 argues that gender diversity on bank Boards improves risk moderation.

[61] See John M Conley, Lissa L Broome and Kimberley D Krawiec, 'Dangerous Categories: Narratives of Corporate Board Diversity' (2011) 89 *North Carolina Law Review* 759, 760; James A Fanto, Lawrence M Solan and John M Darley, 'Justifying Board Diversity' (2011) 89 *North Carolina Law Review* 901.

empirical results on proving such efficacy may be elusive,[62] there may be a good normative reason for championing such a cause from the social equality point of view. Social equality should not be regarded as an alien concept to the corporate sector. Viewed in this light, the regulation of Board composition in terms of gender diversity on financial sector Boards is part of a broader movement to introduce socially motivated regulation into corporate governance. This is not necessarily unwarranted and this book will not delve more into gender diversity as a social cum corporate governance issue. One must however note that this aspect of regulating corporate governance in banks and financial institutions shows the pervasiveness of wider agendas and objectives in corporate governance.[63] This also means that the regulation of aspects of corporate governance in the financial sector are not necessarily related to the issues of risk governance pointed out in chapter fived. If the European Commission's general proposal for regulating gender diversity on EU corporate Boards does not come through, we may be left with the anomalous situation that such regulation is only expressly found in relation to the financial sector,[64] and is arguably only tenuously related to the issue of risk and control at financial institutions.

Finally it is to be noted that there is no particular emphasis on formal proportions of independent[65] or non-executive directors in the EU legislation.[66] The focus on independence on Boards arose in the 1990s through to the 2000s due to the then prevailing problem of accounting fraud and the lack of Board oversight in that area. Independence on Boards and the role of the audit committee were then championed to be necessary countervailing corporate governance features to combat collusive executives in relation to accounting fraud, earnings management and other

[62] Renee B Adams and Daniel Ferreira, 'Women in the Boardroom and their Impact on Governance and Performance' (2012) at papers.ssrn.com/sol3/papers.cfm?abstract_id=1107721; Deborah Rhode and Amanda K Packel, 'Diversity on Corporate Boards: How Much Difference Does Difference Make?' (2010) at papers.ssrn.com/sol3/papers.cfm?abstract_id=1685615.

[63] See Laura Horn, 'Corporate Governance in Crisis? The Politics of EU Corporate Governance Regulation' (2012) 18 *European Law Journal* 83.

[64] Although soft law in the general corporate sector encourages Boards to reflect on the balance of gender diversity and make disclosure with regard to the Board's evaluation, see UK Corporate Governance Code 2012 B.6, which incorporated the recommendations of the UK's Davies Report on gender diversity on Boards: see E Mervyn Davies, *Women on Boards* (February 2011) at www.bis.gov.uk//assets/biscore/business-law/docs/w/11-745-women-on-boards.pdf.

[65] Some empirical research however indicates that independence matters, see Yin-Hua Yeh, Huimin Chung and Chih-Liang Liu, 'Committee Independence and Financial Institution Performance during the 2007–08 Credit Crunch: Evidence from a Multi-country Study' (2011) 19 *Corporate Governance* 437.

[66] Although the Basel Committee still seems to view sufficient independence on the Board as being important especially for critical questioning: see Basel Committee, *Principles for Enhancing Corporate Governance* (n 12) Principle 1, para 38.

sub-optimal financial reporting practices.[67] McNulty et al have rightly argued that the banking crisis raised problems not in relation to fraud oversight and monitoring, but in relation to the oversight of risk and complexity.[68] Effective oversight in risk and complexity depended more on preparedness for meetings, background knowledge and skills and ability to embrace cognitive conflict in discussions, rather than on the attribute of independence as such.[69] These cannot be prescribed by regulation but it may be argued that the overall framework discussed above in relation to Board responsibilities and time commitment of directors go some way towards facilitating such critical engagement with risk governance. In this light, the UK Walker Review's recommendation of yearly Board evaluation,[70] which has been adopted generally into the UK Corporate Governance Code,[71] may be relevant to help focus on the quality of Board dynamics, and the results of Board evaluation could also be a window into the Board for the purposes of regulatory supervision.[72]

The EU has focused on introducing a structural framework for internal control and corporate governance, perhaps because such is easily susceptible to legal convergence and this assists in the EU's agenda for forging a common rule book in financial regulation. It may be queried whether corporate governance regulation on Board member profiles and Board composition would be meaningful from the point of view of securing robust risk governance. Further, the G-30 warns that there may be benefits in allowing a diversity of governance practices to flourish.[73] Boards and shareholders may then be forced to more meaningfully engage in considering governance structures that are compatible with risk strategies and considerations. A caveat against the convergent rule book sought by the EU may be the danger of discouraging engagement by Boards and shareholders with risk management as a living, breathing issue, relying instead on the convergent prescriptions as a set of practices for comfort and security.

Next we turn to the role of shareholders in corporate governance. Post-crisis reforms have embraced a path dependent perspective of shareholders consistent with the agency-based paradigm, and have proceeded to give

[67] Chaudhry Ghafran and Noel O'Sullivan, 'The Governance Role of Audit Committees: Reviewing a Decade of Evidence' (2012) *International Journal of Management Review* 1; Husam Aldamen, Keith Duncan, Simone Kelly, Ray McNamara and Stephan Nagel, 'Audit Committee Characteristics and Firm Performance during the Global Financial Crisis' (2012) 52 *Accounting & Finance* 971; Narjess Boubakri, 'Corporate Governance and Issues from the Insurance Industry' (2011) 78 *Journal of Risk and Insurance* 501.

[68] McNulty, Florackis and Ormrod, 'Boards of Directors' (n 39).

[69] ibid.

[70] Walker Review 2009 (n 6) Recommendations 12–13.

[71] UK Corporate Governance Code B.6.

[72] Endorsed by the G-30, *Towards Effective Governance* (n 42).

[73] G-30, *Towards Effective Governance* (n 42).

shareholders an enhanced role in monitoring their investee firms. Instead of addressing the perverse corporate governance role that shareholders could play in incentivising increased risk-taking, as commentators discussed in chapter five have pointed out, shareholders have been encouraged to take more engaged positions in their corporate governance role.

B. SHAREHOLDERS' ROLE

The UK PRA is keen to enrol shareholders in the governance landscape to act as gatekeepers in risk management supervision of financial institutions.[74] Policymakers have also generally considered the corporate governance role of shareholders as being relevant to monitoring risk management in UK banks and financial institutions. In the wake of the global financial crisis, institutional shareholders have been accused of having been 'asleep'.[75] The critique is that institutional shareholders have been uncritical of risky business practices in their investee banks and should have monitored Board risk management. Although the European Commission Green Paper acknowledges that the lack of critical scrutiny by institutional shareholders in financial institutions may be a 'special case' due to the complexity of banking businesses,[76] the Green Paper nevertheless points out that shareholder apathy is a chronic problem in listed companies with dispersed ownership.

The Walker Review also suggests that shareholder engagement is relevant to corporate governance reforms in bank and financial institutions in the wider interest of risk management and financial stability.[77] The Review is of the view that shareholder monitoring should take on a character of 'stewardship' in order to contribute to the governance potential of corporate governance, viz:

> The potentially highly influential position of significant holders of stock in listed companies is a major ingredient in the market-based capitalist system which needs to earn and to be accorded an at least *implicit social legitimacy*. As counterpart to the obligation of the board to the institutional shareholders, this implicit legitimacy can be acquired by at least the larger fund manager through

[74] Bank of England (Prudential Regulation Authority), 'Our Approach to Banking Supervision' (May 2011) at www.bankofengland.co.uk/publications/Documents/other/financialstability/uk_reg_framework/pra_approach.pdf, Part 4, para 37.

[75] Jennifer Hughes, 'FSA Chief Lambasts Uncritical Investors' *Financial Times* (11 March 2009); Kate Burgess, 'Myners Lashes out at Landlord Institutional shareholders' *Financial Times* (21 April 2009). Also Helia Ebrahimi, 'Institutional Institutional Shareholders Admit Oversight Failure on Banks' *Daily Telegraph* (27 January 2009).

[76] Commission, 'Green Paper on the EU Corporate Governance Framework' COM (2011) 164 final, para 2.

[77] Walker Review 2009 (n 6).

> assumption of a reciprocal obligation involving attentiveness to the performance of investee companies over a long as well as a short-term horizon. On this view, those who have significant rights of ownership and enjoy the very material advantage of limited liability should see these as complemented by *a duty of stewardship. This is a view that would be shared by the public, as well as those employees and suppliers* who are less well-placed than an institutional shareholder to diversify their exposure to the management and performance risk of a limited liability company.[78]

Further, the Walker Review emphasises the importance of institutional monitoring in no uncertain terms:

> Experience in the recent crisis phase has forcefully illustrated that while institutional shareholders enjoy limited liability in respect of their investee companies, in the case of major banks the taxpayer has been obliged to assume effectively unlimited liability. This further underlines the importance of discharge of the responsibility of institutional shareholders as owners, which has been inadequately acknowledged in the past (emphasis added).[79]

The role of shareholders as monitors in the risk management of financial institutions, providing a form of co-governance, is an idea that is embraced at many policymaking levels in the UK. However, it may be argued that shareholder primacy does not help in improving prudential risk management. As underlined earlier in chapter five, empirical research tends to suggest that shareholder incentives are aligned with excessive risk-taking.[80] Some commentators argue that looking to shareholders to provide a form of governance is fundamentally wrong. These arguments are not premised on the weaknesses of shareholder monitoring and how to overcome such weaknesses (the position taken in the Stewardship Code), but rather on the fundamental unsuitability of shareholders to provide a form of governance through their monitoring. It is argued that shareholder incentives are incompatible with acting as a force for governance, and encouraging shareholder monitoring/activism may possibly be completely irrelevant to banks and financial institutions or, worse, harmful to bank and financial institution governance.

These arguments would seem to indicate that the reliance placed on shareholder monitoring/activism is impracticable and may indeed be fundamentally incompatible with governance objectives. However, policy makers in the UK are not endorsing shareholder primacy as such, but

[78] ibid, para 5.7.

[79] ibid.

[80] See Simon Deakin, 'Corporate Governance and Financial Crisis in the Long Run' in Cynthia A Williams and Peer Zumbansen (eds), *The Embedded Firm: Corporate Governance, Labor, and Finance Capitalism* (New York: Cambridge University Press 2011); Peter O Mülbert, 'Corporate Governance of Banks after the Financial Crisis—Theory, Evidence, Reforms' (2010) ECGI Law Working Paper 130/2009 at ssrn.com/abstract=1448118.

shareholder stewardship. This may suggest that shareholders are enrolled in governance only insofar as they subscribe to the notion of stewardship. We turn now to examine what stewardship means.

The UK Stewardship Code 2010 has been rolled out in response to the Walker Review, to apply to institutional shareholders on a comply-or-explain basis. The key notions in 'stewardship' seem to be long-termism and taking a more holistic view of the well-being and performance of the company. This chapter argues that the notion of stewardship is ambivalent. It does not seem to merely reiterate agency-based concepts of shareholder monitoring, but it does not offer an alternative vision in express terms. In light of the lack of clarity of what 'stewardship' means, this chapter is of the view that the implementation of 'stewardship' is likely to follow path dependent lines in relation to the agency-based paradigm of corporate governance. In the absence of fundamental paradigm shifts in corporate governance, shareholders are likely to implement 'stewardship' in convenient and least costly ways that are not fundamentally different from current practices.

The UK Stewardship Code[81]

The Code requires that as a matter of stewardship, institutional shareholders should 'monitor' their investee companies.[82] Such 'monitoring' includes seeking to be satisfied that corporate governance arrangements are robust, carrying out meetings with company directors and/or the Chairman of the Board, maintaining records of such meetings, considering the use of voting power and attendance at general meetings. 'Monitoring' also includes the 'escalation' of shareholder engagement by, for example, intensifying meetings with Board members, making public statements and even requisitioning general meetings, where it is appropriate to do so to protect and enhance shareholder value.[83] 'Monitoring' is couched in terms of protecting and, under Principle 4, 'enhancing' shareholder value. In this sense, it may be argued that the 'monitoring' in the Code is an outworking of private interest, reaffirming the well-accepted private corporate governance role of shareholders in the agency paradigm. So does 'stewardship' imply an active shareholders' role in monitoring investee financial institutions for prudent risk management? The Principles discussed so far do not couch shareholder monitoring in terms of specific interests such as the safety and soundness of banks. The Code seems to

[81] 2010, amended as of 2012.
[82] Stewardship Code (UK) (n 6) Principle 3.
[83] ibid, Principle 4.

provide a template for legitimate shareholder behaviour without articulating if such behaviour is to be rooted in wider common interests.

It may be argued that there are a few features of the Code that encourage shareholders to be cognisant of wider public interest in their role, and therefore move away from traditional shareholder monitoring in the private agency-based corporate governance paradigm. First, Principle 5 of the Code envisages that institutions may step up engagement in collective terms, especially 'at times of significant corporate or wider economic stress, or when the risks posed threaten the ability of the company to continue'.[84] Collective institutional shareholder engagement may represent a type of market governance mindful of wider social concerns, beyond the atomistic concerns of investment purposes. The reference to 'wider economic stress' likely refers to a concern for public interest.[85] Principle 5 thus seems to have the effect of framing shareholder engagement within normative expectations that are consistent with public interest objectives. Principle 5 also seems to disavow collective activism in the interests of private gain or 'shareholder value'.[86] It is premised upon the context of wider corporate or economic stress, but its chief weakness is that it is not an overt reference to the public interest either.

Further, Principles 1, 2 and 6 require institutions to make public their general stewardship policy, their conflicts of interest management policy and their voting policy. Such disclosure does not merely target the beneficiaries of institutions. It is suggested that public disclosure encourages policymakers and regulators to scrutinise the stewardship activities of institutions in order to consider the governance potential of institutional shareholders. Given the context and rhetoric surrounding the Code, the Principles in the Code seem to endorse notions of the wider good. However, the public-interest aligned perspective of stewardship is ideologically weak as it is still unclear to whom shareholders are accountable as stewards. If accountability is to beneficiaries, they are probably too indifferent and dispersed to hold institutions to account and, in any case, such accountability does not apparently add anything to the legal trusteeship duties already owed. However, if shareholders' 'accountability'

[84] ibid, Principle 5.

[85] Walker Review 2009 (n 6) Part I, which discusses stewardship as part of the social legitimacy of shareholding.

[86] However, if institutions choose to act collectively for a group purpose that is not representative of the wider good for other shareholders or stakeholders, there is no way of preventing institutions from using Principle 5 to do so. This critique may be drawn from Aviv Pichadze, 'Institutional Investors as Blockholders' in PM Vasudev and Susan Watson (eds), *Corporate Governance after the Financial Crisis* (Cheltenham: Edward Elgar, 2011), 145, who argues that institutions can behave as blockholders where it is opportunistic to do so and that this creates an agency problem akin to the majority–minority shareholder divide in closely-held or family-held companies.

as 'stewards' means something more, then the Code arguably does not clearly articulate to whom institutions are accountable.

One of the reasons for this perceived weakness in articulating the accountability channels may be that too much deference is still paid to the private agency-based paradigm of corporate governance. Policymakers may be too keen to avoid overtly introducing stakeholderist or communitarian models into corporate governance,[87] as both the theoretical and legal landscape could change dramatically. But if we cannot pinpoint for whom institutions should act as stewards, it becomes difficult to judge the exercise of stewardship, and institutions may then dominate the definition of stewardship. Thus, it may be argued that the stewardship concept is likely to be weakly implemented as it is ideologically confused. The stewardship concept seems to infuse some concern for the wider good into the dominant shareholder-centred agency model of corporate governance, without being bold enough to embark on progressive theoretical changes. Institutions may implement stewardship by perhaps narrowly extending the criteria of assessment that they use in evaluating their asset managers, although well-established criteria based on short-term financial performance are difficult to overhaul.[88] Further, 'stewardship' evaluation may also become proceduralised and subjective, ie, institutions may look for the existence of corporate policies dealing with social responsibility and stakeholder engagement instead of critically considering the corporation's substantive business vision and strategy. Narrow-minded interpretations of stewardship could undermine any wider ideological embrace of public interest notions in shareholders' corporate governance role.

A number of commentators have argued that the conventional agency paradigm is too simplistic when applied to the banking and finance sector.[89] Ciancanelli and Gonzalez argue that the agency paradigm is much more

[87] See discussion of these alternative corporate governance models in Iris H-Y Chiu, 'Institutional Shareholders as Stewards: Toward a New Conception of Corporate Governance' (2012) 6 *Brooklyn Journal of Corporate, Financial & Commercial Law* 387.

[88] Amit Goyal and Sunil Wahal, 'The Selection and Termination of Investment Management Firms by Plan Sponsors' (2008) 63 *Journal of Finance* 1805; CFA Centre for Financial Integrity/Business Roundtable Institute for Corporate Ethics, 'Breaking the Short-Term Cycle: Discussion and Recommendations on How Corporate Leaders, Asset Managers, Investors and Analysts Can Refocus on Long-term Value' (2006) at www.corporate-ethics.org/pdf/Short-termism_Report.pdf; Aspen Institute, *Overcoming Short-termism: A Call for a More Responsible Approach to Investment and Business Management* (9 September 2009) at www.aspeninstitute.org/publications/overcoming-short-termism-call-more-responsible-approach-investment-business-management. See also Simon CY Wong, 'Why Stewardship is Proving Elusive for Institutional Investors' [2010] *Butterworths Journal of International Banking and Financial Law* 406.

[89] See Kern Alexander, 'UK Corporate Governance and Banking Regulation: The Regulator's Role as Stakeholder' (2004) 33 *Stetson Law Review* 991; Christopher M Bruner, 'Corporate Governance Reform in a Time of Crisis' (2011) 36 *Journal of Corporation Law* 309.

complex in the banking sector.[90] As banks are highly geared to depending on deposits and wholesale funding to form a large part of their working capital, depositors and creditors share a substantial amount of residual risk. The development of bail-in regimes[91] would put unsecured senior and junior bondholders and unsecured depositors at risk too and greatly raise their residual claimant status. The potential of state bail-out also puts the state in the position of key stakeholder.[92] Hence, the agency paradigm in the banking sector is not a simple binary shareholder–management model, but should also take into account key stakeholders, such as the state, depositors, and wholesale and repo market creditors.

The Stewardship Code, by putting shareholders in the central monitoring role, may be endorsing the simple agency paradigm in corporate governance and this may be retrograde given the Code's governance aspirations following the global financial crisis.[93] However, on the other hand, the Code is reliably based on well-accepted paradigms in corporate governance and gives rise to the perception of improved corporate governance without disturbing the dominant agency-based foundations. Given that the crisis provides a fitting opportunity for reform, it is curious to find such reluctance to introduce bolder shifts in the corporate governance paradigm in the banking sector. Bruner also argues that the re-emphasis placed on shareholders in the Stewardship Code is path dependent rather than imaginative.[94]

In sum, the Stewardship Code seems to exhort institutional shareholders to take on a more explicit governance role, but there may be misplaced implicit assumptions that private shareholders' interests are aligned with certain notions of public interests. This chapter is sceptical that such assumptions can be robustly made. In the absence of fundamental ideological changes in corporate governance articulated in relation to shareholder stewardship, it is likely that shareholders would implement stewardship in path dependent terms, not deviating from the dominant agency-based

[90] Penny Ciancanelli and Jose Antonio Reyes Gonzalez, 'Corporate Governance in Banking: A Conceptual Framework' (2000) at papers.ssrn.com/paper.taf?abstract_id=253714.

[91] See Directive 2014/59/EU of the European Parliament and of the Council of 15 May 2014 establishing a framework for the recovery and resolution of credit institutions and investment firms and amending Council Directive 82/891/EEC, and Directives 2001/24/EC, 2002/47/EC, 2004/25/EC, 2005/56/EC, 2007/36/EC, 2011/35/EU, 2012/30/EU and 2013/36/EU, and Regulations (EU) No 1093/2010 and (EU) No 648/2012, of the European Parliament and of the Council (Recovery and Resolution Directive 2014) Art 43ff. Martin Sandbu, 'Flexibility Decided by States is a Wrong Move for Europe's Banks' *Financial Times* (26 June 2013) voicing concerns about the balance of precision and flexibility in bail-in priorities.

[92] Chiu, 'Institutional Shareholders as Stewards' (n 87).

[93] Deakin, 'Corporate Governance and Financial Crisis' (n 80).

[94] Bruner, 'Corporate Governance Reform' (n 89).

paradigm.[95] This chapter is of the view that shareholders' monitoring role will continue to be punctuated by the contrary incentives that commentators have earlier discussed, and that 'stewardship' has not provided an answer to the corporate governance problem that shareholders could pose for the safety and soundness of banks and financial institutions.

Practical Challenges and Ideological Weaknesses in the Notion of Stewardship

On the practical front, the asset managers who manage institutional portfolios may not be willing to step into the position of 'governance' through corporate governance.

Institutions such as pension funds manage investments by outsourcing, relying on the skills and aptitude of investment managers to create returns.[96] The competition between asset managers for the management mandate of institutions allows institutions to regularly hire and fire asset managers. Commentators have found that such 'manager tournaments' entail regular replacement[97] of asset managers on the basis of performance, although other reasons also exist.[98] Hence, asset managers have little incentive to engage in shareholder activism to improve the longer-term value of investee companies. Further, a pervasive emphasis on numbers exists in the institutional fund industry and this has given rise to general scepticism regarding unquantifiable matters such as good corporate governance or risk management. Mitchell also argues that the modern investment economy has fundamentally changed from one that holds stock for the longer term, in order to gain dividends based on the actual operating profit of companies, to one that holds stock in order to make quick capital gains based on market movements.[99] Smith and Walter argue that institutional investors have become dull in terms of providing discipline in the marketplace due to their own short-termism and conflicts of interests.[100] According to Mitchell, shareholder gains are divorced from

[95] Iris H-Y Chiu, 'Turning Institutional Investors into "Stewards"—Exploring the Meaning and Objectives in "Stewardship"' (2013) *Current Legal Problems* 443.

[96] Anton van Nunen, *Fiduciary Management: Blueprint for Pension Fund Excellence* (Hoboken, NJ: Wiley Finance, 2008).

[97] See Paul Cox, Stephen Brammer and Andrew Millington, 'Pension Fund Manager Tournaments and Attitudes towards Corporate Characteristics' (2007) 34 *Journal of Business Finance & Accounting* 1307.

[98] See Goyal and Wahal, 'The Selection and Termination of Investment Management Firms' (n 88).

[99] Lawrence E Mitchell, 'The Legitimate Rights of Public Shareholders' (2009) 66 *Washington and Lee Law Review* 1635.

[100] Roy C Smith and Ingo Walter, *Governing the Modern Corporation* (Oxford: Oxford University Press, 2006) 121, 276.

actual operations, products and services provided by investee companies and so shareholders are not incentivised to behave as owners. The backdrop of the political economy and the attitudes of investment managers cannot easily be reformed by the mere rhetoric of 'stewardship'.[101]

The investment management industry is however endeavouring to show that they are engaging with the concept of stewardship.[102] The implementation of 'stewardship' is largely incremental,[103] and the prevalent practice of outsourcing voting to proxy advisory and voting agencies (such as ISS, Manifest or PIRC) raises questions of whether 'stewardship' is indeed meaningfully discharged.[104] Cheffins also points out that given the high foreign ownership of UK listed companies, the stewardship of institutions, if any, could have a relatively insignificant influence upon the corporate landscape.[105]

The corporate governance reforms discussed in the last two sections highlight a mixture of approaches in the post-crisis regulatory agenda. Although some reforms—such as in relation to Board structures discussed in section A—deal with the problems identified in relation to the risk and control culture at banks and financial institutions, some reforms have

[101] Wong, 'Why Stewardship is Proving Elusive for Institutional Investors' (n 88). In this light see BIS, *The Kay Review of UK Equity Markets and Long-Term Decision Making* (Final Report, 23 July 2012) which presents recommendations for more radical structural changes to the asset management industry in order to encourage 'stewardship'. See critical comments in Chiu, 'Turning Institutional Investors into "Stewards"' (n 95).

[102] Financial Reporting Council, *Developments in Corporate Governance 2012: The Impact and Implementation of the UK Corporate Governance and Stewardship Codes* (December 2012) is of the view that institutions are signing up to the Code, developing policies to reduce conflicts of interest, attending and voting at general meetings and increasing collective activism. Also see David Oakley, 'Biggest UK Investors Plan Joint Move on Excess' *Financial Times* (16 June 2013) highlighting the establishment of Investor Forum, a platform for collective activism to deal especially with remuneration scrutiny.

[103] Financial Reporting Council, *Developments in Corporate Governance 2012* (n 102).

[104] See also David Oakley, 'Spotlight on Shareholder Advice Groups' *Financial Times* (9 June 2012); ESMA, 'Discussion Paper: An Overview of the Proxy Advisory Industry. Considerations on Possible Policy Options' (22 March 2012) ESMA/2012/212 at www.esma.europa.eu/system/files/2012-212.pdf, where ESMA highlights concerns over the power that proxy voting agencies wield over institutional shareholders who tend to follow their advice. Although no regulation is recommended, ESMA recommends that a code of conduct be promulgated for the proxy voting and advisory industry, see ESMA, 'ESMA recommends EU Code of Conduct for proxy advisor industry' (19 February 2013) at www.esma.europa.eu/news/ESMA-recommends-EU-Code-Conduct-proxy-advisor-industry?t=326&o=home. Albert Verdam also explores the powerful position of market leader ISS: see Albert Verdam, 'An Exploration of the Role of Proxy Advisors in Proxy Voting' (2006) at papers.ssrn.com/sol3/papers.cfm?abstract_id=978835. He raises concerns regarding box-ticking adopted by ISS; de-contextualisation from national contexts; and selective focus on corporate disclosure, conflicts of interest and mistakes made. See also Stephen J Choi, Jill E Fisch and Marcel Kahan, 'The Power of Proxy Advisors: Myth or Reality?' (2010) 59 *Emory Law Journal* 869 arguing that the ISS wields significant corporate governance monitoring powers as it is very influential with institutions.

[105] Brian R Cheffins, 'The Stewardship Code's Achilles' Heel' (2010) 73 *Modern Law Review* 1004.

merely taken a path dependent approach to affirm established conventional corporate governance standards even if they bear a tenuous relationship with the issue of the risk and control culture at firms.

Next we turn to a suite of reforms and measures that bear some relationship to changing banking culture. First, we discuss the UK's unique approach of approving individuals and imposing individual responsibilities and liabilities. The spotlight on individual conduct makes it hard for individuals to hide behind a façade of organisational responsibility, and may introduce incentives to change behaviour and culture at firms.

C. THE REGULATION AND APPROVAL OF INDIVIDUALS IN BANKS AND FINANCIAL INSTITUTIONS: THE UK REGIME

The EU has stopped short of requiring regulatory approval of key personnel in banks and financial institutions although reporting on corporate governance will be enhanced so as to provide insight for supervisory monitoring.[106] The UK has always operated a unique system of pre-vetting and approving key personnel appointments at banks and financial institutions in excess of European legislative requirements.[107] Such a system perhaps compensated for the lack of a regulatory framework for financial sector corporate and organisational governance in the pre-crisis era. The approval regime is based on certain general criteria applicable to all key appointments whether or not in senior management or the Board. Post-crisis, the UK has further developed its regulatory regime for individual persons and their responsibilities in the Financial Services (Banking Reform) Act 2013.[108] The regulatory regime now operates in two tiers: one applicable to senior persons and the other to other personnel performing functions such as client-facing functions, anti-money laundering functions and business leadership functions.

The UK regulators have hitherto required any person performing a 'controlled function' in a financial institution to be separately licensed by the regulators for taking on such appointment.[109] Controlled functions include functions of significant responsibility in the firm, customer-facing functions and functions that deal with customer property.[110] Post-crisis, UK regulators would focus pre-vetting only on senior managers, leaving firms to assess the fitness and proprietary of other staff. The Act defines senior management as persons who are responsible for one or more aspects

[106] CRD IV Directive, Art 97; but an equivalent provision is not found in the MiFID II Directive 2014.

[107] Financial Services and Markets Act 2000, s 59; PRA and FCA Handbooks APER and FIT.

[108] s 64Aff, Financial Services and Markets Act 2000 as amended.

[109] s 65A, Financial Services and Markets Act 2000 as amended.

[110] s 59, UK Financial Services and Markets Act 2000.

of the business and are in a position to make decisions with risk of serious consequences for the business.[111] Such persons may only be approved upon regulatory agreement with a statement of specific responsibilities[112] attached to the application; such statement may be varied in due course with agreement of the regulator if the duties of such person change. Hence, a new approval system for Senior Managers would be instituted, and persons performing certain defined functions prescribed by the PRA and FCA would fall within that category. Other staff not falling within the senior managers regime would not need pre-vetting and approval, but would be subject to firm assessment of propriety according to prescribed regulatory criteria, ie, the 'Certification' regime. Firms would also be required to reassess these persons every year according to the prescribed regulatory criteria. The regulators thus move from pre-vetting for all controlled functions to intensive and selected pre-vetting of senior managers, while placing the responsibility on firms to ensure fitness and propriety of other staff. However, all senior managers and licensed staff would be subject to an enhanced ex post system of discipline and enforcement,[113] with senior managers attracting a significantly higher amount of continuous scrutiny of their fitness and propriety.

The criteria for assessing the fitness and propriety of the persons in the 'Certification' regime are based on the former criteria for 'controlled functions' set out in the regulators' subsidiary legislation.[114] These criteria would also be used for regulatory approval of senior persons. These are: honesty, integrity and reputation, competence and capability, and financial soundness. In terms of honesty, integrity and reputation, the regulators will take into account previous convictions, disciplinary proceedings and previous refusals of registrations.[115] In 2014, the FCA regarded the former Managing Director of BlackRock, Jonathan Burrows, to be unfit for reasons of dishonesty as he had persistently dodged paying the correct amount of train fares over a number of years in his commute to work.[116] Although Burrows' settlement with the train company did not relate to his work in the financial sector, the overall integrity of a person may be judged according to any relevant evidence that suggested a lack of propriety in personal behaviour. In terms of financial soundness, regulators would look for records of bankruptcy or judgement debts in order to ascertain the personal financial soundness of applicants. For competence and capability, the regulators are asked broadly to consider the 'training

[111] s 59ZA, Financial Services and Markets Act 2000 as amended.

[112] ibid, ss 60(2A) and 62Aff.

[113] PRA and FCA, *Strengthening Accountability in Banking: A New Regulatory Framework* (July 2014).

[114] PRA and FCA Handbooks, FIT 2 generally.

[115] ibid, FIT 2.1.

[116] Final Notice against Jonathan Burrows, 15 December 2014 at www.fca.org.uk/your-fca/documents/final-notices/2014/jonathan-paul-burrows.

and experience' of the relevant person. This is a criterion that regulators have not given much attention to in the pre-crisis years, as there has been no corresponding movement of banking professionalism as such. One notes that the EBA has prescribed slightly different non-binding guidelines for regulatory approvals of Board members.[117]

The UK Walker Review recommended that the regulators extend vetting and approval to take into account the balance of skills and expertise on the Boards of banks and financial institutions, with a particular focus on the skills and expertise related to risk strategy.[118] This may mean that approval decisions for Board appointments should not be based on individual profiles, but based on how individual profiles may fit and work together. It is queried whether too much is being asked of the regulatory vetting process and the false senses of assurance and security that may entail from such regulatory vetting and approval of Board members. This has not been formally incorporated into the UK's regulatory text. Further, the Walker Review suggested that regulators vet non-executive directors of large systemically significant banks and financial institutions carefully in terms of whether they are able to grapple with the complexity of the business.[119] This suggestion may be captured by regulatory vetting in relation to training and competence. However, given the EU legislation's deliberate reluctance to prescribe that Board members should have specific expertise such as financial expertise, care should be taken so that regulatory vetting for training and competence does not funnel into narrowly eligible criteria.

Personal Responsibility and Liability

As discussed earlier, the UK regulator has always maintained an approval regime for persons performing controlled functions, one of which is the directorship of a bank or financial institution, whether in the capacity of executive or non-executive director. Approved persons are subject to continuing conduct obligations in a broadly worded code known as APER (Code of Practice for Approved Persons) in the regulator's Handbook. In the wake of the global financial crisis of 2008–09, the Parliamentary Commission on Banking Standards proposed a new regime of personal responsibility and liability for senior management in the financial sector which is now adopted in legislation. The development of personal responsibility

[117] EBA, *Guidelines on the Assessment of the Suitability of Members of the Management Body and Key Function Holders* (22 November 2012).

[118] Walker Review 2009 (n 6) Recommendation 4.

[119] ibid, Recommendation 5.

and liability regimes may be characterised differently from the structural aspects of corporate governance hitherto dealt with by regulatory reforms. Personal responsibility and liability regimes very much relate to incentives and aim at changing conduct at the micro level in order to support changes in overall firm culture. There is empirical research that finds that behavioural changes take place in favour of more engagement in risk oversight and monitoring under an enhanced director liability regime whether or not enforcement figures are high.[120] Hence, incentive-based regulation such as the introduction of enhanced directorial liability may be important in supporting the structure-based corporate governance regulation discussed earlier.

The reforms now provide for differentiated treatment between senior managers and other key appointment holders in terms of personal liability.[121] Senior managers are now subject to an enhanced conduct regime that attracts enhanced regulatory and criminal liability.[122] These conduct rules are regulatory requirements and breaches of such requirements entail regulatory enforcement such as the imposition of a fine, disqualification from working in the financial services sector, or both, and in some circumstances to criminal liability. The regulatory conduct requirements imposed on senior managers are in addition to general directors' duties under company law, and senior persons may regard the regulatory regime as much more threatening than civil liability regimes in directors' duties. We will now examine the regulatory regime of APER and the reforms to senior persons' liability introduced in 2013.[123]

Liability Under APER

APER provides for seven high level principles in terms of how an approved person should conduct himself/herself, and the regulator is entitled to take action to fine, suspend or ban an approved person who is considered to be in breach of the principles in APER. The following sets out the principles in APER:

Statement of Principle 1
An approved person must act with integrity in carrying out his accountable functions.

[120] See Tobias Körner, 'Board Accountability and Risk Taking in Banking: Evidence from a Quasi-Experiment' (2012) at ssrn.com/abstract=1996520.

[121] ss 66A, 66B, Financial Services and Markets Act 2000 as amended by the Financial Services (Banking Reform) Act 2013; s 29 Financial Services (Banking Reform) Act 2013.

[122] PRA and FCA, *Strengthening Accountability in Banking* (n 113).

[123] ss 66A, 66B, Financial Services and Markets Act 2000 as amended by the Financial Services (Banking Reform) Act 2013; s 29 Financial Services (Banking Reform) Act 2013.

Statement of Principle 2
An approved person must act with due skill, care and diligence in carrying out his accountable functions.

Statement of Principle 3
An approved person must observe proper standards of market conduct in carrying out his accountable functions.

Statement of Principle 4
An approved person must deal with the FCA, the PRA and other regulators in an open and cooperative way and must disclose appropriately any information of which the FCA or the PRA would reasonably expect notice.

Statement of Principle 5
An approved person performing an accountable significant-influence function must take reasonable steps to ensure that the business of the firm for which he is responsible in his accountable function is organised so that it can be controlled effectively.

Statement of Principle 6
An approved person performing an accountable significant-influence function must exercise due skill, care and diligence in managing the business of the firm for which he is responsible in his accountable function.

Statement of Principle 7
An approved person performing an accountable significant-influence function must take reasonable steps to ensure that the business of the firm for which he is responsible in his accountable function complies with the relevant requirements and standards of the regulatory system.

The then Financial Services Authority (FSA) has taken enforcement actions against directors of relatively small investment firms where decision-making could be more easily attributable to directorial responsibility, but less rarely against directors of large financial institutions. For example, this chapter will briefly discuss the enforcement against Michael Lee Thommes.[124] Thommes was the sole shareholder and managing director of a small firm, General Finance Centre Limited that was carrying on the business of mortgage broker. Two whistle-blowers highlighted to the regulator that the firm was committing mortgage fraud by failing to check the income, occupation and personal information of mortgage applications and tolerated misleading and inconsistent information supplied by applicants. The firm nevertheless proceeded to broker mortgages with lending institutions. The regulator took enforcement action against Thommes for failing to establish controls and systems to ensure compliance with laws

[124] 15 Jan 2013 at www.fsa.gov.uk/static/pubs/final/michael-lee-thommes.pdf.

and regulations and therefore fined and banned Thommes from performing a controlled function in the financial services industry due to unfitness and impropriety evidenced by his conduct and responsibility for the firm's mortgage fraud. Thommes referred the matter to the Upper Tribunal, but the regulator's decision was upheld.

However, in the wake of the global financial crisis, a high-profile enforcement action was carried out against the director of corporate finance at Halifax Bank of Scotland (HBOS), Peter Cummings.[125] Further, Principles 6 and 7 were used as the basis to indict three directors at Swinton Group Ltd[126] for failing to institute a sales culture that would prevent unsuitable and predatory sales of add-on insurance products to retail customers. The then FSA was able to carry out significant enforcement actions against financial firm executives under APER before the reforms in 2013 came into force.

Peter Cummings[127] was the director of the Corporate Division of HBOS which needed government rescue in the global financial crisis of 2008–09. In late 2008, HBOS had suffered losses due to impairment of assets up to £7 billion out of which £4.7 billion were incurred by the Corporate Division. The massive losses made by the Corporate Division were due to excessive risk-taking by making loans that were highly risky, subordinated or sub-investment grade. Cummings pursued an aggressive growth strategy for the Corporate Division and was expanding HBOS' exposure to corporate credit although huge risks were taken. This would have required Cummings to institute and oversee a robust risk control and management system commensurate with the high-risk growth strategy. The then FSA alleged that Cummings was in breach of Principle 6 of APER, ie, discharging his functions without due care, skill or diligence. Although the then FSA acknowledged that Cummings was not solely responsible for the growth of the Corporate Division which had been ongoing under the leadership of Cummings' predecessor, Cummings failed to ensure that an adequate system of control and risk management was in place to monitor the high levels of risk incurred. Hence, the then FSA meted out a fine of £500,000 and banned Cummings for life from taking on controlled functions in the financial services sector.

The deterrence objective was also evident in high-profile enforcement against directorial personnel at Swinton Group Limited in 2014.[128] Swinton

[125] At www.fsa.gov.uk/static/pubs/final/peter-cummings.pdf.
[126] At fca.org.uk/news/former-swinton-executives-fined-and-banned-misselling.
[127] At www.fsa.gov.uk/static/pubs/final/peter-cummings.pdf.
[128] At fca.org.uk/news/former-swinton-executives-fined-and-banned-misselling.

Group Limited provided basic insurance products for retail customers, such as accidental personal injury insurance, home insurance and motor vehicle cover. The FCA found that there was a persistent sales culture of pushing add-on products to retail customers, such as vehicle recovery cover, accidental injury cover for partners and dependants, and home emergency repair cover. The add-on products were often offered to retail customers with free premiums for a few initial months before additional premiums would become payable. The Group was fined in July 2013 by the FCA for failing to ensure that the add-on products were sold fairly to customers. In November 2014, the Authority took disciplinary action against the Chief Executive Peter Halpin, finance director Anthony Clare and director Nicholas Bowyer as being the person mainly responsible for instituting incentive structures to promote add-on sales. Peter Halpin was fined in the region of over £400,000 and banned from carrying on significant functions in any other financial institution for failing to ensure that compliance programmes such as call monitoring were carried out, and that adequate information on sales practices were passed on to be evaluated by compliance departments. Anthony Clare was fined £206,000 and similarly banned for the failure to ensure adequate compliance oversight of the sales processes while being in the position of having oversight of compliance, risk management and finance. Nicholas Bowyer was fined £306,000 and similarly banned for having instituted the questionable sales incentive schemes and hence being responsible for a culture of unsuitable and predatory sales practices at the firm.

Personal liability for directors and senior management under APER is a formidable strategy in regulating key decision-makers in a financial institution. CEOs of large financial groups such as UBS and Mitsui Sumitomo have also been subject to enforcement actions. In the Mitsui Sumitomo case, the Chief executive Yohichi Kumagai was fined £100,000 and banned for life from working in the UK financial services industry.[129] The FSA alleged that he had breached Principles 5 and 7 by failing to institute adequate committees on the Board and to ensure that sufficiently senior persons were responsible for certain high-level executive functions. He had also allowed the level of capital adequacy to fall below the threshold level required by regulation. Kumagai had assumed position of Chief Executive in 2009 and had taken on responsibility for growing the non-life insurance business in the UK. By 2011, the FSA had several meetings with Kumagai to point out deficiencies in the corporate governance of

[129] At www.fsa.gov.uk/static/pubs/final/yohichi-kumagai.pdf.

Mitsui Sumitomo and worrying levels of capital adequacy. However, the regulator was ultimately of the view that Kumagai failed to adequately address these issues and appreciate their importance and severity.

However, in relation to John Pottage, Chief Executive of UBS who was alleged to have also failed to ensure that the business of the firm was organised in a controlled and compliant manner as required under Principle 7, Pottage referred the FSA's decision to the Upper Tribunal[130] and secured a victory overturning the FSA's case against him. Pottage assumed position as Chief Executive at a time when he was aware of risk management and control deficiencies at UBS in terms of operational risk, implementation of the lines of defence at UBS, inadequate information flows of risk between departments and to the executive level, and breaches in the conduct of client money handling. Pottage was of the view that he had instituted an overhaul review, made new appointments and installed systems, and had personal engagement with issues via discussion in frequent meetings. However, the FSA alleged that UBS' failings were to be attributed to Pottage's oversight responsibility which was inadequate. The Upper Tribunal agreed with Pottage that he had done enough as was required to address the problems brought to his attention and had instituted reforms in processes and systems. The failure of ground implementation could not fully be attributed to Pottage, and not every defect discovered warranted costly inquiries and overhaul as the FSA had expected Pottage to undertake. The FSA had also relied excessively on an expert opinion report that pointed out what Pottage ought to have done, and the Tribunal disagreed with many aspects, considering the demands excessive. Pottage was therefore cleared by the Upper Tribunal. The decision in favour of Pottage is however in the minority as the majority of Tribunal decisions upheld the regulator's enforcement.

The APER regime before the reforms of 2013 has been robustly used to carry out enforcement against directors and senior executives in the financial sector. However, in the wake of public outcry against the seemingly lack of large-scale enforcement against bankers who seemed to have walked away scot-free after running banks into near failure, legislators and regulators felt compelled to modify the regulatory regime in order to introduce enhanced personal liability for senior managers. The reforms in the Financial Services (Banking Reform) Act 2013 have thus provided for enhanced obligations and liability for senior persons.

[130] *John Pottage v FSA* (20 April 2012) at www.tribunals.gov.uk/financeandtax/Documents/decisions/John_Pottage_v_FSA_decision.pdf.

Enhanced Senior Persons Liability Under Senior Persons Regime

The Parliamentary Commission on Banking Standards proposed enhanced regulatory liability for senior persons and employees performing any function that 'could harm the bank'[131] as well as a special criminal liability regime for senior persons who have recklessly mismanaged a bank. The Financial Services (Banking Reform) Act 2013 has adopted much of the Parliamentary Commission's recommendations and provides for senior persons to be subject to enforcement for misconduct if such persons contravene the Conduct Rules applicable to them, or are knowingly involved in a regulatory contravention by the financial institution concerned, or are holding an office with responsibility related to a regulatory contravention.[132] Further, senior management must be approved with a statement of responsibilities and the failure to carry on such responsibilities also means that specific liability will be attached to the relevant senior person.

The Conduct Rules that the PRA and FCA will put in place for senior persons retains much of the former APER. Two new provisions are now added:

SM3: You must take reasonable steps to ensure that any delegation of your responsibilities is to an appropriate person and that you oversee the discharge of the delegated responsibility effectively.

SM4: You must disclose appropriately any information of which the FCA or PRA would reasonably expect notice.[133]

Senior persons are subject to enhanced liability as compared with other employees. They are subject to regulatory liability not only for breaches of the Code of Conduct or for knowing involvement in the firm's contravention of regulatory requirements, but also where the firm has breached a regulatory requirement, and the senior person happens to be responsible for that area. The latter seems to be a form of strict liability and is intended to incentivise meticulous monitoring and oversight. Although the Parliamentary Commission on Banking Standards initially recommended that an individual senior person would only be able to defend against liability if she or he proves to the court's satisfaction that all reasonable steps have been taken to mitigate the effects of a specified failing, the Act seems to provide for strict liability, leaving negligence liability for the more serious criminal offence of mismanaging a financial institution into failure. The PRA and FCA indicate that in implementing the senior persons regime, they would take the approach of presuming responsibility when breach of the Conduct Rules or failure of designated responsibilities occurs; such

[131] *Changing Banking for Good* Vol II (n 2) paras 632–34.

[132] ss 66A, 66B, Financial Services and Markets Act 2000 as amended by the Financial Services (Banking Reform) Act 2013.

[133] PRA and FCA, *Strengthening Accountability in Banking* (n 113).

presumption may be rebutted upon evidence that all reasonable steps to prevent the breach or failure have been taken.[134]

Although such strict liability is secondary liability, ie, that the individual is liable on account of the firm's primary contravention of regulatory requirements, secondary liability usually serves a deterrent purpose in order to motivate the individual to prevent the firm's primary contravention. The threat of strict secondary liability for senior persons may incentivise them to act or make decisions in such a way as to secure effective internal control and regulatory compliance, and in due course cement a healthy compliance culture in the firm. However, less beneficial effects could also entail, such as in fostering defensiveness and risk or blame shifting in organisational culture.

Although senior persons cannot evade liability by delegation, it would arguably be improbable that every regulatory contravention would automatically attract senior person liability, as the consequence of disqualification is very severe indeed. As the Upper Tribunal in Pottage's case discussed above has shown, the Tribunal is willing to accept that a certain extent of personal attention and involvement is reasonable enough and that excessive demands on the part of the regulators would be rejected. However, what would be uncertain is the extent of personal endeavour that would be needed for a senior person to have peace of mind. This book is concerned that such uncertainty is likely to result in risk averse and defensive personal behaviour on the part of senior persons. For example, senior persons may engage in excessively precise and narrow delineations of scope of responsibility. This may result in many more office holders in narrowly defined posts in order to limit personal risk. Such may also result in more silo and defensive approaches which may be unhealthy for the risk and control cultures of the organisation as a whole. Senior persons may also engage in excessive proceduralisation in order to ensure a trail of auditable personal endeavours that may discharge the individual of liability, and such inward-looking and defensive preoccupations may draw attention away from the important tasks of strategically managing the business. Further, there is concern whether non-executive directors who are usually tasked to chair committees of the Board such as the audit or risk committees may bear a disproportionate amount of liability for being in that position, albeit in a non-executive capacity. This could disincentivise individuals from taking up such positions and also encourage firms to 'game the regime' by designing personal risk and blame shifting strategies onto non-executive directors in order to protect executive directors and officers. The PRA and FCA sought to address this concern by specifying only certain non-executive directors to whom the senior persons regime would apply; other non-executive directors would be treated

[134] ibid.

as falling within the scope of certified functions.[135] The small scope of non-executive directors under the senior persons regime would be the Chairman, Senior Independent Director, Chairs of the Risk, Remuneration and Audit Committees and Chair of the Nomination Committee (for FCA approved persons only). The PRA and FCA will also expect the statements of responsibility for such senior persons to be narrow and not as extensive as those applying to executive senior persons, hence mitigating the sting of being subject to the senior persons regime.

The Parliamentary Commission on Banking Standards also proposed to enact a special criminal offence for senior persons of recklessly mismanaging a bank.[136] This is intended to reflect the need for a severe and credible public interest position in bank safety and soundness, but such prosecution would likely only be undertaken rarely in the most severe of cases and is not likely to be used to punish directors of small institutions. The Parliamentary Commission on Banking Standards believed that requiring the mens rea of recklessness is apt as strict criminal liability would be overly inclusive. An individual must be proved beyond a reasonable doubt to be in a mental state of 'recklessness' in managing the bank, the definition of such a mental state being well established in general criminal law jurisprudence.[137] The offence of reckless mismanagement of a bank would only be alleged against an individual under such circumstances as bank failure with substantial costs to the taxpayer, lasting consequences for the financial system, or failures that have caused serious harm to customers.[138] Further, in order to ensure consistency and independence in the carrying out of enforcement in financial regulation, the Parliamentary Commission on Banking Standards proposed that all enforcement functions are to be housed in an independent body nested with the FCA but appointed by both the PRA and FCA.[139]

The 2013 Act however has deviated from the Commission's proposals.[140] It allows the PRA, FCA, Secretary of State or Director of Public Prosecutions to institute criminal proceedings against senior management who have knowingly taken a decision for the business, being aware that a risk of failure could ensue, and in so doing has fallen below the standard of a reasonable person in his or her shoes. Such a decision must also have caused the failure of the financial institution. This means that a threshold slightly

[135] PRA and FCA, *Approach to Non-Executive Directors in Banking and Solvency II Firms & Application of the Presumption of Responsibility to Senior Managers in Banking Firms* (February 2015) at fca.org.uk/static/documents/consultation-papers/cp15-05.pdf.

[136] *Changing Banking for Good* Vol II (n 2) paras 1174–86.

[137] ibid, paras 1176–79.

[138] ibid, para 1183.

[139] ibid, paras 1187–202.

[140] s 29, Financial Services (Banking Reform) Act 2013.

above negligence has been instituted for liability instead of recklessness. However, the Act provides that causation needs to be proved and so a strict liability standard is not applied. On balance the Act's position may be sounder as criminal recklessness is hard to prove where decisions taken in an organisation may be subject to herding behaviour, copying other successful institutions, or under myopic pressures pursuing profits and competitive edges. Such decisions could nevertheless be objectively negligent.

Individual liability regimes can provide incentives for individuals to take ownership of their responsibilities but such regimes can also incentivise the development of complex systems of verification, recording and reporting, paper trails and box-ticking. One may look to the US in relation to directors' *Caremark* liability for some lessons in relation to avoiding negligence-based liability for directors.

Under Delaware law, directors are duty bound to monitor activities of control that they have delegated to be executed by others. However, personal liability for the failure to discharge such duty can only be established if no adequate systems of internal control have been put in place. Where systems of corporate internal control such as information transmission and reporting have been established, directors would be regarded to have done their best in discharging the duty to monitor.[141] Hence, the personal responsibilities of senior persons in terms of care, skill, diligence, adequate monitoring of delegation and adequate institution of control may arguably be regarded as discharged if satisfactory systems and procedures are instituted such as under the *Caremark* standard. The new enhanced liability regimes may incentivise more proceduralisation in order to protect senior persons, and it remains to be seen if changed control cultures may result.

Finally, the UK has introduced reforms to allow the Secretary of Business to take disqualification proceedings against directors of failed companies which have been implicated in breaches of duty, misfeasance, breaches of legislation and/or sectoral regulation such as financial sector regulation.[142] Further, directors guilty of criminal misconduct overseas may also be subject to disqualification proceedings here. This means that directors should be mindful that, in addition to sectoral sanctions that may apply to them, such as disqualification from working in the financial services sector, the Secretary of Business could ask for a general disqualification

[141] *In re Caremark International Inc Derivative Litigation*, 698 A.2d 959 (Del Ch 1996).

[142] BIS, *Transparency & Trust: Enhancing the Transparency of UK Company Ownership and Increasing Trust in UK Business* (April 2014) 55, para 223, culminating in the Small Business, Enterprise and Employment Act 2015.

to apply to them.[143] A general power to allow sectoral regulators to apply blanket disqualifications across sectors is however not supported.

The personal liability and responsibility of Board members in the financial sector has moved well beyond the private realms of company law, from enforcement led by shareholders' actions to enforcement led by public authorities. Director disqualification proceedings are rooted in public interest[144] in order to protect the general public from persons unsuitable to conduct business in the wider economy. However, it may be argued that if banks are not allowed to 'fail' then the disqualification actions may not arise. Nevertheless, some commentators have argued that the artificial avoidance of failure by nearly-failed banks in the UK should not take these situations out of the scope of disqualification proceedings.[145] This book however sounds a note of caution in terms of taking non-executive directors to task, as disqualifications may send a disproportionately chilling signal and adversely impact upon the recruitment of a broad range of individuals.

In sum, the personal liability regimes for individual senior persons in the UK have the potential to change incentives and behaviour due to the likelihood of strong and robust regulatory enforcement. However, unintended consequences may entail from such strong personal liability regimes, which regulators should continue to monitor. We turn next to the other reforms that are aimed towards changing banking culture.

D. REFORMING BANKING CULTURE

In the immediate aftermath of the global financial crisis, the then Chief Executive of the UK regulator the FSA stated in no uncertain terms that regulators need to be judging culture in financial institutions that impedes the achievement of regulatory objectives.[146] Chapter five has discussed the aspects of sub-optimal culture that have persisted in a number of banks and financial institutions in the pre-crisis years. This chapter will examine the reforms aimed at changing culture. These reforms have a common theme: the enhancement of a sense of responsibility on the part of

[143] Although it may be argued that disqualification proceedings only arise upon insolvency and banks are not allowed to become insolvent, as resolution processes are carried out before that prospect arises. Hence, the general disqualification sanctions may not apply to financial institution directors.

[144] *Secretary of State for Trade & Industry v Deverell* [2000] 2 BCLC 133.

[145] See Rod Edmunds and John Lowry, 'The Failure of RBS and HBOS: Holding Banking Directors to Account via the Disqualification Regime' in Iris H-Y Chiu and Michael McKee (eds), *The Law of Corporate Governance in Banks and Financial Institutions* (Cheltenham: Edward Elgar, 2015) at ch 3.

[146] Hector Sants, 'Can Culture be Regulated?' (4 October 2010) at www.fsa.gov.uk/library/communication/speeches/2010/1004_hs.shtml.

banking sector personnel for the wider impact of banking and finance, going beyond incentive-based regulation. This section will examine the remuneration reforms that call for more skin in the game and soft reforms to banking ethics. Section E will examine the impact of structural reforms to large banking groups upon bank culture.

Remuneration Reforms

A major initiative that attempts to change incentives for risk-taking behaviour has been introduced in the form of financial sector remuneration regulation.[147] The impact of financial sector remuneration upon prudential stability is the reason why regulatory oversight in this area has been introduced. The structure of financial sector remuneration has arguably given rise to a number of perverse incentives[148] on the part of financial sector employees and management, including short-termism and excessive risk-taking. There is also the issue of the sheer size of remuneration packages, which has become a source of social discontent.[149] Further, remuneration incentives may be linked to mis-selling and other forms of adverse conduct.[150] Regulating financial sector remuneration may be seen as a way to change incentives for behaviour, which, in the aggregate and over the long term, could engender a more optimal risk control and perhaps ethical culture in financial sector firms.

The regulation of financial sector remuneration in the EU and UK has developed in two stages. First, the 2010 amendments made to the Capital Requirements Directive 2006 introduced a general principle of aligning remuneration policies to sound and effective risk management[151] and provided some prescriptive detail on the composition of remuneration.[152] These, together with the guidelines issued by the Committee of European

[147] Also see Basel Committee, *Guidelines* (n 8) Principle 11.

[148] M Brunnermeier, A Crockett, C Goodhart, AD Persaud and Hyun Shin, *The Fundamental Principles of Financial Regulation* (London: Centre for Economic Policy Research, Geneva Reports on the World Economy, 2009); Financial Stability Board, 'Thematic Review on Compensation: Peer Review Report' (30 March 2010) at www.financialstabilityboard.org/publications/r_100330a.pdf; Bernard S Sharfman, 'How the Strong Negotiating Position of Wall Street Employees Impacts the Corporate Governance of Financial Firms' (2011) 5 *Virginia Law & Business Review* 350.

[149] Alan Dignam refers to 'snarky' social language surrounding bankers' pay. See Alan Dignam, 'Understanding the Financial Crisis: Pay, Risk and Responsibility in the 21st Century' ('Current Legal Problems' lecture at Bentham House, University College, London, 4 November 2010).

[150] FCA, *Commercial Insurance Intermediaries—Conflicts of Interest and Intermediary Remuneration: Report on the Thematic Project* (May 2014) 6ff; FSA, *Final Guidance: Risks to Customers from Financial Incentives* (January 2013) 13ff.

[151] Capital Requirements Directive 2010, Art 22(1).

[152] ibid, Annex V, para 11.

Banking Regulators (CEBS, which is now the European Banking Authority (EBA)), have been transposed into the UK regulator's Remuneration Code.[153] Subsequently, the recast Capital Requirements Directive 2013 (CRD IV Directive) was enacted and the Directive preserved much of the Remuneration Code but added tighter controls over the composition of financial sector remuneration.[154] It is to be noted that the UK Remuneration Code applies to both banks and investment firms above a certain prudential threshold[155] but the reforms in the CRD IV Directive apply only to banks. The UK transposition of the CRD IV Directive has widened its application to investment firms.

The emphasis placed on regulating the composition of financial sector remuneration stems from concerns over excessive bonuses or variable pay awarded to financial sector employees. Thannasoulis argues that much of financial sector remuneration is variable remuneration so that financial institutions can 'insure' themselves against poor performance, paying out only where there is performance to be rewarded.[156] A number of commentators argue that variable pay incentivises optimal levels of risk-taking so that financial sector intermediaries would not be too conservative and under-invest, allowing opportunities to create wealth to slip by.[157] The variable pay component of financial sector remuneration is therefore an implementation of a more well-accepted general principle of pay for performance.

However, the application of pay for performance generally in executive pay has come under much critique and the same problems that have occurred in the application of pay for performance in executive pay have played out in the financial sector, on a larger scale not limited to executive pay. Financial sector employees have managed the definition of 'performance' in such a way that eligibility criteria for bonuses may be readily met. Bender and Moir observe that much of executive remuneration, generally across sectors, is structured around performance measures that are readily measurable, such as earnings, profits, returns on equity,

[153] PRA and FCA Handbooks (as of 30 April 2013, formerly FSA Handbook) SYSC 19A.

[154] CRD IV Directive, Arts 92–95.

[155] The investment firm providing a full suite of investment services and is categorised as a 730k firm for the purposes of complying with prudential requirements, see PRA and FCA Handbooks, SYSC 19A.1.1, and *General Guidance on Proportionality: Remuneration Code* (20 October 2014) at www.fca.org.uk/your-fca/documents/finalised-guidance/remuneration-code.

[156] John Thannasoulis, 'The Case for Intervening in Bankers' Pay' (2012) 67 *The Journal of Finance* 849.

[157] See Kent Matthews and Owen Matthews, 'Controlling Bankers' Bonuses: Efficient Regulation or Politics of Envy?' (2010) *Institute of Economic Affairs* 72; Kevin J Murphy, 'Regulating Banking Bonuses in the European Union: A Case Study in Unintended Consequences' (2013) at ssrn.com/abstract=2235395.

largely accounting measures.[158] In the financial intermediation business, remuneration is also structured around 'hard' targets, such as assets under management and the volume of sales of financial products. Commentators have also commented extensively on how executives 'game' the system surrounding the definition of performance by undertaking manipulative measures to achieve such performance.[159] For example, stock-linked compensation could be enhanced by efforts to engineer a spike in share price so as to cash out stock options, or long-term investment decisions could be delayed so that earnings are boosted in order to boost earnings-linked variable pay.[160]

Where the financial sector is concerned, if performance is defined around sales volumes, such a performance measure incentivises sales of products, but does not take into account the risk or investment performance of the product actually sold. There is arguably a mismatch between the measures of performance related to remuneration and 'performance' in terms of the purpose or quality of outcomes in financial intermediation activities. An investment manager's performance may be measured according to yardsticks—such as total assets under management or returns on investment calculated on a yearly basis—and a bank manager may be remunerated according to his or her performance in loan sales. However, the ex post performance of the financial product does not feed back into the measurement of financial sector employees' performance. This results in a short-termist and myopic view of what 'performance' means in financial intermediation. It also leads to a decoupling of the notion of 'performance' for the purposes of reward from the actual performance of the financial product sold or financial service rendered. Short-termism may be an expression of the efficiency of our times, led by technological advances in the expansion of markets and speed of execution of transactions. However, it may also be queried whether this is indeed a market disease or a 'failure' that gradually dislodges reward from purpose.[161]

Performance benchmarks in the financial sector may also be structured in such a way as to incentivise certain behaviour. As mentioned above, if performance benchmarks are based on total assets under management, then investment managers are incentivised to increase investment volume,

[158] Ruth Bender and Lance Moir, 'Does "Best Practice" in Setting Executive Pay in the UK Encourage "Good" Behaviour?' (2006) 67 *Journal of Business Ethics* 75.

[159] See Lucian Bebchuk and Jesse M Fried, *Pay without Performance: The Unfulfilled Promise of Executive Compensation* (Boston, MA: Harvard University Press, 2006) generally.

[160] Erica Beecher-Monas, 'The Risks of Reward: The Role of Executive Compensation in Financial Crisis' (2011) 6 *Virginia Law & Business Review* 101.

[161] Richard Lambert, 'Sir Ralph's lessons on short-termism' *Financial Times* (22 May 2011).

without necessarily paying attention to suitability.[162] This may also apply to the sale of loans, as a number of commentators have observed how remuneration incentives have propelled predatory lending in the sub-prime market.[163] In sum, the performance benchmarks used by the industry, and measures based on short-termism in general, are likely to result in a dislocation of reward from purpose in financial intermediation activities. The UK Remuneration Code now prohibits variable remuneration to be awarded based on performance benchmarks such as sales revenue or turnover,[164] requiring holistic measurements of profit to be the yardstick. The reform of performance incentives is also advocated at a lower level[165] in relation to retail sales of investment and insurance products so that malpractices in mis-selling may be averted. The FCA has carried out reviews and issued guidance to explicitly highlight undesirable incentive schemes and encourage changes to be made.

Financial sector remuneration regulation now attempts to address the weaknesses in the pay for performance model in variable pay by: (a) defining performance more tightly; (b) exerting controls on the amount and composition of variable pay; and (c) introducing mandatory deferrals of variable pay. This section suggests that although the above measures address to a certain extent the problems that have surfaced in relation to the manipulation of the 'performance' criteria for variable pay, other agency problems may entail in response to the changes and there may not be a genuine change in terms of mindsets or organisational culture. This section will however argue that the approach of *malus* and clawback, which has been adopted in the EU legislation of 2013, also instituted in the US, may impose a greater sense of personal responsibility and skin in the game for financial sector employees and could be more promising in terms of changes in behaviour and organisational culture generally.

[162] See European Parliament and Council Directive 2004/39/EC of 21 April 2004 on markets in financial instruments amending Council Directives 85/611/EEC and 93/6/EEC and Directive 2000/12/EC of the European Parliament and of the Council and repealing Council Directive 93/22/EEC [2004] OJ L145/1 (Markets in Financial Instruments Directive) (MiFID) Art 19; FCA Handbook (as of 30 April 2013, formerly FSA Handbook) COBS 9 generally. 'Suitability' obligations apply to a greater extent to retail clients rather than sophisticated clients, but sophisticated clients can still expect that investment advisers would have a duty to ensure that they understand the investment risks of any particular recommendation; see Commission Directive 2006/73/EC of 10 August 2006 implementing Directive 2004/39/EC of the European Parliament and of the Council as regards organisational requirement and operating conditions for investment firms and defined terms for the purposes of that Directive [2006] OJ L241/26 (MiFID Commission Directive 2006) Art 35; FCA Handbook (as of 30 April 2013, formerly FSA Handbook) COBS 9.2.

[163] See Philip Bond, David K Musto and Bilge Yilmaz, 'Predatory Lending in a Rational World' (2005) FRB Philadelphia Working Paper 06-2 at papers.ssrn.com/sol3/papers.cfm?abstract_id=875621.

[164] PRA and FCA Handbooks, SYSC 19A.3.25, 26.

[165] FCA, *Commercial Insurance Intermediaries* (n 150) 6ff; FSA, *Final Guidance: Risks to Customers from Financial Incentives* (January 2013) 13ff.

Perhaps more robust use of the *malus* and clawback mechanisms could incentivise real behavioural and cultural change in due course.

The UK Remuneration Code which transposes the relevant EU legislation applies to

> senior management, risk takers, staff engaged in control functions and any employee receiving total remuneration that takes them into the same remuneration bracket as senior management and risk takers, whose professional activities have a material impact upon the firm's risk profile.[166]

The Code also imposes a reporting obligation on financial institutions with respect to compliance with and breaches of the remuneration rules.[167] The regulator may carry out enforcement and disciplinary actions against firms in breach and, where applicable, the regulator could order firms to pursue civil recovery for wrongfully paid remuneration above certain thresholds.[168]

The general principles for remuneration design are that remuneration policies should be risk aligned and promote the long-term interest of the financial institution.[169] In relation to mitigating remuneration incentives promoting adverse conduct, remuneration design should also be in avoidance of conflicts of interest.[170] However, most of the principles for remuneration design revolve around prudential risk management rather than conduct adjustment as such.

In relation to the design of variable remuneration, the EU legislation and UK Remuneration Code deal with how 'performance' criteria should be established, as well as how variable remuneration should be structured and proportioned as part of the total remuneration package. Individual performance should be based on measures[171] that are consistent with sound risk measurement, a range of quantitative and qualitative metrics[172] including non-financial metrics,[173] and compatibility with the maintenance of a sound capital base for the institution,[174] assessed on a multi-year framework[175] over the long term,[176] taking into account current and future risks[177] and the performance of the business unit as a whole.[178] The Code attempts to change metrics used by the industry, such as

[166] CRD IV Directive, Art 92(2); PRA and FCA Handbooks, SYSC 19A.3.4, 19A.3.6 further provides a list of office holders likely to fall within the scope of the Code.
[167] PRA and FCA Handbooks, SYSC 19A.3.4.
[168] ibid, SYSC 19A3.34, and Annex 1, para 5R.
[169] CRD IV Directive, Art 92(2).
[170] ibid; PRA and FCA Handbooks, SYSC 19A.3.9.
[171] PRA and FCA Handbooks, SYSC 19A.3.7, 3.35.
[172] ibid, SYSC 19A.3.23.
[173] ibid, SYSC 19A.3.37.
[174] CRD IV Directive Art 94(1)(a), (c) and (d); PRA and FCA Handbooks, SYSC 19A.3.18.
[175] PRA and FCA Handbooks, SYSC 19A.3.38.
[176] CRD IV Directive, Art 94(1)(b); PRA and FCA Handbooks, SYSC 19A.3.8.
[177] CRD IV Directive, Art 94(1)(j), (k); PRA and FCA Handbooks, SYSC 19A.3.13, 22.
[178] CRD IV Directive, Art 94(1)(a); PRA and FCA Handbooks, SYSC 19A.3.36.

revenue-based measures or returns on equity, in order that performance may not be measured merely by readily attainable benchmarks.[179] The reference to the long-term, present and future risks also attempts to introduce a longer-term perspective to measuring performance. These measures could be seen as ways of dealing with short-termist incentives and the reward/purpose mismatch. However, the implementation of changed metrics in remuneration design is very much dependent on each financial institution's Board remuneration committee's efforts and oversight.[180]

Variable remuneration based on performance has habitually been structured in such a way as to be aligned with the conventional measures of financial performance of a firm—such as earnings or returns on equity which measures value creation by reference to stock price performance. Such measures of performance are fundamentally rooted in shareholder primacy. As chapter five has pointed out, the primacy of shareholders may perhaps not be an appropriate corporate governance paradigm for banks as they are extremely highly geared and rely more on debt and deposits for finance. However, in the absence of a well-accepted alternative corporate governance paradigm for banks and financial institutions, the values of shareholder primacy pervade the definition of financial performance. Remuneration policies structured around such financial performance thus incentivise risk-taking aligned with shareholder preferences for higher risk-taking to maximise returns.[181] Shareholder preferences for risk-taking are argued to be higher than socially optimal levels of risk-taking.[182] In fact, research suggests that shareholder incentives may exacerbate risk-taking tendencies, as they also pursue short-term returns on equity and tolerate high levels of risk-taking in business models.[183] In this light, it can

[179] PRA and FCA Handbooks, SYSC 19A.3.23. The PRA and FCA may disallow outright RoE, EPS and TSR to be used as sole metrics for variable remuneration, demanding a risk-adjusted balance scorecard approach to be used: see PRA and FCA, *Strengthening the Alignment of Risk and Reward: New Remuneration Rules* (July 2014).

[180] CRD IV Directive, Art 95; PRA and FCA Handbooks, SYSC 19A.3.10–12.

[181] Lucian Bebchuk and Holger Spamann, 'Regulating Bankers' Pay' (2010) 98 *Georgetown Law Journal* 247; Mülbert, 'Corporate Governance of Banks after the Financial Crisis' (n 80).

[182] Francesco Vallascas and Jens Hagendorff, 'CEO Remuneration and Bank Default Risk: Evidence from the US and Europe' (2013) *Financial Markets, Institutions & Instruments* 47, arguing that remuneration linked to stock incentivises CEOs of banks to prefer greater risk-taking.

[183] Ing-Haw Cheng, Harrison G Hong and Jose A Scheinkman, 'Yesterday's Heroes: Compensation and Creative Risk-Taking' (2010) NBER Working Paper 16176 at papers.ssrn.com/sol3/papers.cfm?abstract_id=1502762, arguing that shareholder short-termist incentives facilitated excessive risk-taking by banks during the global financial crisis; Andrea Beltratti and René M Stultz, 'Why Did Some Banks Perform Better during the Credit Crisis? A Cross-Country Study of the Impact of Governance and Regulation' (2009) NBER Working Paper 15180 at papers.ssrn.com/sol3/papers.cfm?abstract_id=1433502, also seems to suggest that banks in shareholder-friendly jurisdictions performed the worst during the global financial crisis; Reint Gropp and Matthias Köhler, 'Bank Owners or Bank Managers: Who is Keen on Risk? Evidence from the Financial Crisis' (2010) European Business School Research Paper 10-02 at ssrn.com/abstract=1555663.

be argued that absent regulatory control, financial institutions would not have the incentives to overhaul the metrics for variable remuneration.[184]

However, the development of modified metrics for variable remuneration in the financial sector may take some time, and it remains uncertain if alternative credible and well-accepted metrics may be put in place instead of the conventional return on equity.[185] There is also the hazard that risk-infused metrics may create complexity and opacity in remuneration metrics, making it more difficult for remuneration committees and regulators to discern the soundness of remuneration policies. That said, there is some commentary on the development of sustainability-based metrics in financial sector remuneration policies in Germany required under law, suggesting that discernible changes are underway in financial sector remuneration.[186] Markham however is of the view that financial institutions will continue to develop performance definitions and criteria that will pander to the needs of short-termism which is a structural problem in the corporate and financial sector.[187]

In terms of regulatory control over the amount and composition of variable pay, the EU position favours a balance between fixed and variable remuneration in such a way that the fixed component is sufficiently high and that the variable component does not form an excessive proportion of total remuneration.[188] The pre-crisis years have seen bankers' remuneration sky-rocket in terms of the variable component, and the levels of remuneration have far outstripped many other sectors.[189] The EU now requires that variable remuneration awarded in banks be capped at the amount of the fixed component but can be raised to up to twice the amount of the fixed component upon shareholder approval at a general meeting.[190] On the one hand, such an absolute cap may exert an effect on moderating risk-taking. On the other hand, it may also be queried whether regulatory control over variable remuneration is based on broader social concerns of inequality and the perceived unfairness of rewards for failure.

However, one perverse consequence of the EU bonus cap is that remuneration design in the financial sector now aims at skirting the legislative

[184] Simone M Sepe, 'Making Sense of Executive Compensation' (2011) 36 *Delaware Journal of Corporate Law* 189.

[185] The use of 'return on assets' is mooted by a number of influential commentators: see *Changing Banking for Good* Vol II (n 2) para 853.

[186] Emilie Matthieu, 'Beyond Wall Street: Germany, the United States, and Executive Compensation' (2013) 38 *Brooklyn Journal of International Law* 579.

[187] Jerry W Markham, 'Regulating Excessive Executive Compensation—Why Bother?' (2010) at ssrn.com/abstract=1705686.

[188] Capital Requirements Directive 2010, Annex V, para 11; PRA and FCA Handbooks, SYSC 19A.3.44 on an appropriate balance.

[189] Jeanne L Schroeder, 'Mad Money: Wall Street's Bonus Obsession' (2012) 33 *Cardozo Law Review* 2307.

[190] CRD IV Directive, Art 94(1)(g); PRA and FCA Handbooks, SYSC 19A.3.44(3).

restrictions while not affecting real amounts of pay for bankers. It is observed that the fixed component in financial sector salaries has risen.[191] High fixed components in pay would mean a loss of elasticity and responsiveness to performance, which in spite of the problems surrounding the definition of performance, could be a worse consequence in terms of disincentivising optimal risk-taking[192] and innovation.[193] Further, instituting higher proportions of fixed pay may be contrary to the move towards making remuneration more risk aligned (which demands flexibility in pay design) and prematurely truncates efforts that may be developed in that area.[194] Banks and financial institutions have also reportedly designed a 'grey' form of payment known as 'role-based allowances' for staff whose variable remuneration may be affected by the cap. Such 'role-based allowances' are not tied to individuals or to their performance, but are tied to certain roles. However, they are not included in basic pay, are not pensionable and are discretionary in nature. The EBA is of the view that these are not fixed remuneration and ought to be subject to the cap.[195] The UK is however resistant to interference with banking pay structures, and tensions between the PRA and EBA remain despite the failure of the UK challenge to the bonus cap in the Court of Justice.[196]

However, regulatory controls such as prohibiting guaranteed bonuses may be sound as guaranteed bonuses are not consistent with the ethos of 'pay for performance'. The EU legislation[197] and Remuneration Code provide for a clampdown on guaranteed bonuses unless for new staff and only in the first year of employment or for exceptional performance,[198] and where the institution has a strong and sound capital base.

A number of commentators have remarked, in light of the headline-grabbing attention generated by the regulatory control over bonuses, that regulatory control over variable remuneration is highly motivated by social concerns.[199] The political will to deal with remuneration regulation is boosted by social demand, and regulatory control therefore

[191] Thannasoulis, "The Case for Intervening in Bankers' Pay' (n 156); 'Higher Bank Salaries Poised to Offset Brussels Bonus Cap' *Financial Times* (17 July 2013).

[192] Kevin J Murphy, 'Regulating Banking Bonuses in the European Union (n 157).

[193] Matthews and Matthews, 'Controlling Bankers' Bonuses' (n 157).

[194] Guido Ferrarini, Niamh Moloney and Maria-Cristina Ungureanu, 'Executive Remuneration in Crisis: A Critical Assessment of Reforms in Europe' (2010) 10 *Journal of Corporate Law Studies* 73.

[195] October 2014, at www.eba.europa.eu/documents/10180/534414/EBA+Report+on+the+principles+on+remuneration+policies+and+the+use+of+allowances.pdf.

[196] 'Britain Abandons Banker Bonus Fight after EU Court Blow' *Bloomberg* (21 November 2014).

[197] CRD IV Directive, Art 94(1)(e).

[198] PRA and FCA Handbooks, SYSC 19A.3.40R.

[199] See Ferrarini, Moloney and Ungureanu, 'Executive Remuneration in Crisis' (n 194); Eilis Ferran, 'New Regulation of Remuneration in the Financial Sector in the EU' (2011) at ssrn.com/abstract=1825167.

serves to give the impression of credibility of action. Some still doubt that remuneration regulation plays any key role in risk control in a bank or financial institution.[200] However, the author wonders if the very fact that policymakers are willing to take on remuneration control may incentivise financial institutions to become more attentive towards compliance and risk management, so that remuneration controls may have a more lasting cultural influence. The Parliamentary Commission on Banking Standards arguably takes on this point specifically by suggesting that remuneration control may engender a lasting cultural influence. Further, exceptional controls on variable remuneration are put in place where a financial institution receives state aid: there should be no bonuses paid to members of the management body, ie, Board and senior management, and bonuses paid to employees have to be strictly limited and not be inconsistent with maintaining sound capital adequacy and timely exit from government support.[201]

Further, the EU also controls the extent of cash bonuses that may be awarded, insisting that at least 50 per cent of variable remuneration be awarded in stock that should be held for minimum periods in order to avoid quick cash outs and short-termism.[202] There is research that supports a correlation between cash bonuses and short-termist excessive risk-taking.[203] Cash bonuses that could be attained relatively quickly incentivise risk-taking behaviour to maximise the bonus and could therefore encourage blindness to longer-term effects of such behaviour. However, there is also contrary research that shows that cash bonuses may incentivise senior executives to be more prudent with risk (unless the institution is close to distress in which case risk-taking may be exacerbated irrationally).[204] Nevertheless, rewarding in stock should arguably not be regarded as a better alternative as there is already a significant amount of literature on the malpractices[205] associated with executive stock options that could similarly feature in relation to stock options awarded to financial sector employees. Empirical research also shows that stock-based remuneration has not succeeded in imposing a long-term perspective on managerial behaviour, as managers at the failed banks Lehman Brothers

[200] Guido Ferrarini and Maria Cristina Ungureanu, 'Economics, Politics, and the International Principles for Sound Compensation Practices: An Analysis of Executive Pay at European Banks' (2011) 64 *Vanderbilt Law Review* 432.

[201] CRD IV Directive, Art 93; PRA and FCA Handbooks, SYSC 19A.20, 21.

[202] CRD IV Directive, Art 94(1)(l); PRA and FCA Handbooks, SYSC 19A.3.47R.

[203] See Demetra Arsalidou, 'The Regulation of Executive Pay and Economic Theory' (2011) 5 *Journal of Business Law* 431; Felix Suntheim, 'Managerial Compensation in the Financial Service Industry' (2010) at ssrn.com/abstract=1592163.

[204] See Vallascas and Hagendorff, 'CEO Bonus Compensation and Bank Default Risk' (n 182).

[205] Bebchuk and Fried, *Pay without Performance* (n 159); Vallascas and Hagendorff, 'CEO Bonus Compensation and Bank Default Risk' (n 182).

and Bear Stearns cashed out stock options regularly before the failure of the banks.[206] Thus, there may not be a discernible difference between the incentives shaped by stock-based remuneration and cash bonuses.[207]

Finally, remuneration controls also include mandatory deferral of remuneration. EU legislation as transposed in the Remuneration Code provides for mandatory deferral of at least 40 per cent of variable remuneration[208] (subject to ongoing performance review and not to vest until review)[209] and 60 per cent where the variable remuneration is a particularly high amount, as well as the deferred vesting of long-term stock-linked remuneration plans.[210] The deferral period under the EU harmonised regime is 3–5 years, but the PRA and FCA propose to extend this to 5–7 years for senior managers.[211]

The mandatory deferral of a significant amount of variable remuneration serves to align financial sector employees' incentives with long term performance, compelling them to consider the long-term performance of their intermediation activities. However, it may be argued that 3–5 years is relatively near term and the performance of some financial products may not be discerned until a medium or long term has elapsed.[212] For this reason, the UK Parliamentary Commission on Banking Standards recommends that the regulator should have the power to intervene and require deferred remuneration of up to 10 years.[213] Belinfanti's behavioural research points out that deferral of remuneration generally results in behaviour that seeks to compensate for the deferral in the present and so this may not mitigate risk-taking tendencies.[214] However, over a sufficiently long period of time, the discounting tendency decreases and deferral may be able to achieve its intended behavioural modification effects of incentivising more prudent risk-taking. In accordance with this research, the Parliamentary Commission's recommendation seems to be more supportable than the current position of deferral of up to five years. However, Feess at al warn that mandatory deferral of compensation could provide

[206] See Lucian Bebchuk, Alma Cohen and Holgar Spamann, 'The Wages of Failure: Executive Compensation at Bear Stearns and Lehman 2000–2008' (2010) 27 *Yale Journal on Regulation* 257.

[207] It remains to be seen whether strict long-term requirements on vesting and selling may work: see Lucian A Bebchuk and Jesse M Fried, 'Paying for Long Term Performance' (2009) 158 *University of Pennsylvania Law Review* 1915.

[208] CRD IV Directive, Art 94(1)(m); PRA and FCA Handbooks, SYSC 19A.3.49R.

[209] CRD IV Directive, Art 94(1)(n); PRA and FCA Handbooks, SYSC 19A.3.51R.

[210] CRD IV Directive, Art 94(1)(m); PRA and FCA Handbooks, SYSC 19A.3.24.

[211] PRA and FCA, *Strengthening the Alignment of Risk and Reward* (n 179).

[212] *Changing Banking for Good* Vol II (n 2) para 813.

[213] ibid, para 881.

[214] Tamara C Belinfanti, 'Beyond Economics in Pay for Performance' (2012) 41 *Hofstra Law Review* 91.

perverse incentives to reallocate risky projects, and thus distort the financial intermediation role of banks and financial institutions.[215] Hence, the impact of remuneration regulation upon incentives and remuneration design needs to be monitored. On stock-linked compensation plans, EU legislation has not provided further guidance on retention periods and design in order to incentivise long-termist considerations and behaviour. Bebchuk and Fried point out that careful design in terms of retention, staggered offloading and prevention of manipulative tactics such as backdating are needed in order to achieve an optimal design for long-term vesting of stock-linked remuneration.[216]

Malus or Clawback

Although regulatory control over financial sector remuneration has been stepped up, the above has pointed out that there is scepticism over what regulating the fixed/variable structure of remuneration can achieve. Deferral may encourage longer-term perspectives of risk-taking and performance, but it remains uncertain whether financial sector employees may develop other means to 'game' the system, or remain unmoved to embark on behavioural change. Further, commentators warn that such remuneration regulation is targeted at each pay package and fails to take into account of correlations with and impact upon the risk behaviour in other activities and the risk profile of the organisation as a whole.[217] This section suggests that the power to enforce *malus* or clawback may create more incentives for bankers to have 'skin in the game' in terms of the ultimate performance of their risk and allocation decisions, and hence align reward and purpose.[218] EU legislation has now provided for a power of up to 100 per cent clawback or *malus* of variable remuneration for banks where significant losses have occurred or where the employee concerned has not met the standards of propriety and fitness.[219] The UK Remuneration Code provides that all financial institutions should put in place a power to claw back bonuses where subdued or negative financial

[215] Eberhard Feess and Ansgar Wohlschlegel, 'Mandatory Deferral of Banker Compensation and Misallocation of Risky Projects' (2012) at papers.ssrn.com/sol3/papers.cfm?abstract_id=2118560.

[216] Bebchuk and Fried, 'Paying for Long Term Performance' (n 207).

[217] See Arantxa Jarque and Edward S Prescott, 'Banker Compensation and Bank Risk Taking: The Organizational Economics View' (2013) at papers.ssrn.com/sol3/papers.cfm?abstract_id=2228910.

[218] Supported in Jesse M Fried and Nitzan Shilon, 'Excess Pay Claw-backs' (2011) 36 *Journal of Corporation Law* 722.

[219] CRD IV Directive, Art 94(1)(n).

performance ensues.[220] Such powers are now recognised as an integral part of risk management in banks and in prudential regulation.[221]

Clawback refers to recouping variable remuneration where employee misconduct has occurred or where significant losses have been incurred, while *malus* refers to the deduction of deferred variable remuneration in the two situations mentioned.[222] These powers will be mandatorily inserted into employees' contracts and so firms do not have the option to disapply them; firms however have the power to determine when the power should be applied and to what extent. Although the Parliamentary Commission on Banking Standards agrees that powers of clawback or *malus* have to be contractually framed, it also moots the possibility of regulatory intervention to examine if such powers should be exercised. Leaving banks and financial institutions to define and implement clawback and *malus* may result in them succumbing to weak and negligible implementation. This is the key weakness in meta-regulatory regimes that co-opt a significant amount of firm discretion in implementation as discussed in chapter one.[223]

This book is of the view that the clawback and *malus* mechanisms are able to introduce 'skin in the game' incentives for financial sector employees in their risk-taking decisions, as they may be called to account for their decisions, compelling them to consider if 'they are putting their money where they mouth is'.[224] Such imposition of personal responsibility at a micro-level could be important in influencing risk-taking behaviour,[225] and could also have a collective impact upon the sector. The book also supports the Liikanen proposal[226] to compel the bail-in of outstanding variable remuneration due to financial sector employees in cases of institutional failure. This approach introduces incentives to encourage employees to regard the preservation of the viability of the institution as key to

220 PRA and FCA Handbooks, SYSC 19A.3.27. See *Changing Banking for Good* Vol II (n 2) para 883.

221 Basel Committee, *Guidelines* (n 8) Principle 11.

222 Clawback can take place up to 7 years after payout, but the PRA and FCA propose extending it to 10 years if the firm or regulator conducts an inquiry into potential misconduct. See PRA and FCA, *Strengthening the Alignment of Risk and Reward* (n 179).

223 Cristie Ford, 'New Governance in the Teeth of Human Frailty: Lessons from Financial Regulation' (2010) *Wisconsin Law Review* 441.

224 Fried and Shilon, 'Excessive Pay Clawbacks' (n 218).

225 Dowd and others are of the view that personal liability was more pronounced in the early days and bankers were also more prudent and conservative, see Kevin Dowd et al, 'Capital Inadequacies: The Dismal Failure of the Basel Regime of Bank Capital Regulation' (July 2011) *Cato Institute Policy Analysis* No 681 at ssrn.com/abstract=1961708; Frank A Sloan et al, 'Liability, Risk Perceptions, and Precautions at Bars' (2000) 43 *Journal of Law and Economics* 473 arguing generally that legal liability rules have a direct impact upon risk perception by regulated entities, such as bar owners, and will influence the prudence of their behaviour.

226 Liikanen, *High-level Expert Group on Reforming the Structure of the EU Banking Sector* (n 4) para 5.5.3.

their own private benefit, and therefore supports micro-prudential regulation objectives. However, for the clawback, *malus* or bail-in approaches to work, the variable remuneration component of employees' remuneration may ironically have to be of a sufficient proportion, or else they would not be motivated to consider the clawback, *malus* or bail-in as a significant factor in behavioural change. Therefore, prescriptive rules such as capping variable remuneration to the amount of yearly basic salary as enacted in the EU mentioned above may actually be counterproductive. In dealing with the weaknesses of remuneration design in the financial sector, the EU seems to have embarked on all possible avenues of attack but may have failed to consider how the different measures may affect or undercut each other.

It is also queried whether a broader power for *malus* and clawback could be ordered in relation to misconduct such as mis-selling. Mis-selling may result in losses for the financial institution concerned in terms of loss of clientele and in payment of regulatory fines. The EU Directive may be read widely enough to accommodate this interpretation but the Remuneration Code focuses specifically on financial losses. The range of circumstances that could result in *malus* and clawback would need to be more clearly defined, or firms and regulators may risk counterclaims from affected individuals.[227]

In the US, the Dodd–Frank Act provides for clawback and *malus* that can be undertaken by the resolution authority, the FDIC, in cases where a financial institution needs to be liquidated.[228] This book also suggests that the regulator should have the power to enforce *malus* or clawback where state aid is rendered to a failing institution or in the case of resolution or liquidation. Such powers would be beyond contract and in the public interest, although there may be arguments against such powers due to the broad nature of its likely retrospective application. However, where a bank or financial institution has received state aid, or is being resolved or liquidated, the modification of private contractual interests should be an expected outcome. It is well accepted in the recovery and resolution regime that private contractual and property rights would be affected.[229] Although the jurisprudence on resolution is still being developed in terms of certainty, the legitimacy of altering private contractual rights by *malus* or clawback should be acceptable. Further, an institution receiving state

[227] It is uncertain to what extent contractual promises such as guaranteed bonuses would be subject to malus or clawback, and the decision against Commerzbank may remain unresolved under the new regime. See 'Commerzbank must pay €50m of bonuses after losing legal battle' *Financial Times* (16 April 2013).

[228] Joshua Mitts, 'Recoupment under Dodd–Frank: Punishing Financial Executives and Perpetuating "Too Big To Fail"' (2012) 122 *Yale Law Journal* 507.

[229] Banking Act 2009, ss 16–72; Recovery and Resolution Directive 2014.

aid should be more cognisant of public interest, and the social dimension of not perpetuating reward for failure clearly resonates with the citizenry.

This book believes that *malus* or clawback has a great potential to induce behavioural and culture change in the financial sector but robust enforcement in deserved circumstances is needed. The current EU position leaves to firms to undertake the relevant *malus* and clawback based on widely defined circumstances in legislation. This position suffers from two key weaknesses due to its meta-regulatory nature. First, the range of circumstances is widely framed at the moment and there is a lack of clarity in how to apply it to individual cases. Such a lack of clarity would encourage challenge by affected individuals and could undermine the enforcement of those powers. Second, the enforcement action is to be taken by the firms concerned, not the regulator, and firms may be disincentivised to take such actions if the criteria for the exercise of powers are unclear and susceptible to litigious challenge. This book proposes that the framework for the exercise of powers in *malus* and clawback should be enhanced by more clearly defining the range of circumstances to which the power applies. Further, regulators should be given powers to direct such *malus* or clawback or take actions directly, especially in the case of institutions receiving state aid, or based on principles of subrogation in relation to other institutions. The framework for regulatory intervention can be enhanced to realise the potential of *malus* or clawback as an incentive-changing mechanism.

It is to be noted that commentators studying the uptake of clawback provisions in the US mandated under the Dodd–Frank Act have found that the introduction of clawback provisions in contracts results in incentives to seek higher pay, perhaps in mitigation of the future risk of clawback.[230] Further, clawback provisions may disincentivise organisational loyalty as individuals 'watch their own backs'. The commentators have reported higher executive turnover post-organisational uptakes of clawback clauses. Hence, although clawback and *malus* provisions may introduce stronger risk-aligned incentives in decision-making, the impact upon individual defensiveness and changes in behaviour needs to be monitored.

Banking Ethics

The Parliamentary Commission on Banking Standards is of the view that cultural overhaul in banking institutions could be achieved through subjecting individuals to regulatory regimes in terms of professional

[230] See Illona Babenko, Benjamin Bennett, John M Bizjak and Jeffrey L Coles, 'Clawback Provisions' (2012) at papers.ssrn.com/sol3/papers.cfm?abstract_id=2023292.

competence and in terms of ethical behaviour.[231] As discussed earlier, the PRA and FCA have avoided being overly prescriptive in terms of the competence criteria for approval of individuals in the FIT module. This approach is consistent with industry concerns that it would be impracticable to impose regulatory requirements in order to standardise the banking professional qualification and banking ethics, as there are too many diverse aspects in the banking business.[232] Although some of the testimonies provided to the Parliamentary Commission on Banking Standards acknowledged that although a general decline in banking standards in terms of competence could be observed,[233] it would still be likely to be up to the voluntary efforts of professional or quasi-professional bodies to forge qualifications requirements.[234]

In terms of ethics, although representations were made to the Parliamentary Commission for bankers' membership bodies to take up the challenge of establishing a code of ethics and provide disciplinary oversight of bankers, the Parliamentary Commission on Banking Standards was unconvinced of the efficacy of self-regulatory discipline administered by bankers' membership bodies.[235] It was thus recommended that the regulator draws up a comprehensive Banking Standards Code that applies to all financial sector personnel, and that deals largely with ethics and standards of conduct.[236] Such a Code would lead the way for cultural change starting with behavioural changes on the part of financial sector personnel. It is envisaged that the Code will provide the compliance and ethical backdrop to compel behavioural changes, as well as incentivise individual behavioural changes through the use of enforcement of personal liability.[237] The Parliamentary Commission is of the view that a 'culture of professionalism' can change culture not only at the top but also at middle and lower levels, pervading all levels of personnel.[238] However, the ultimate provision in the Banking Reform Act 2013 is much more nuanced in terms of ethics and pays more attention to management competence, due oversight and personal integrity and diligence.

The PRA and FCA's ultimate approach highlights the difficulty in regulating for 'ethics'.[239] It may be argued that ethical behaviour is a form of

[231] *Changing Banking for Good* Vol II (n 2) chapter 6 generally.

[232] John Gapper, 'There is no such thing as the banking profession' *Financial Times* (12 February 2014).

[233] *Changing Banking for Good* Vol II (n 2) para 575.

[234] ibid, para 599.

[235] ibid, para 601.

[236] ibid, 612ff.

[237] Already discussed above.

[238] *Changing Banking for Good* Vol I (n 233)I at para 758.

[239] ACCA Global, *Culture v Regulation: What is Needed to Improve Ethics in Finance* (2014) at www.accaglobal.com/content/dam/acca/global/PDF-technical/corporate-governance/pol-tp-cvr.pdf, 3.

responsible behaviour to self and others that is not merely compelled by compliance; it is usually a form of beyond-compliance behaviour. Hence, making ethics subject to regulation is counterproductive to instilling an ethical culture. However, it may also be argued that as ethics is essentially self-regulatory, promoting such effective self-regulation may ironically have to be sought through the language of regulation and compliance, as such language carries strong normative connotations that incentivise behaviour change, having the potential to overcome the 'market failures' associated with non-compliance-based paradigms.[240]

The area of professional and ethical banking standards remains soft law in nature and may devolve to the Banking Standards Review Council, established from mid-2014.[241] The Council is to be an independent body but supported by the banking industry to champion ethical standards, engage with the industry such as through an annual meeting with the non-executive directors of banks, engage with stakeholders such as consumers and professional bodies to develop a high-level principles-based code of ethics and complement the regulatory roll out of the certified and senior persons regimes. The Council's role is arguably one that is intended to shape culture, as the development of a 'right culture' is a continuous process and not quite susceptible to rule-based definitions and regulatory enforcement. As the Council has been established in the context of public and regulatory distrust of the financial sector, it aims to be perceived as an independent institution that encourages cultural change. In sum, the regulability of ethics and professionalism remains in question, but the power and incentives for persuasion in the soft law initiatives of the Council remain to be seen.

E. STRUCTURAL REFORMS AND THEIR IMPACT UPON BANKING CULTURE

Policymakers in the UK have ushered in structural reforms to the banking sector in order to force large banking groups to structurally separate and protect their retail operations from the risks in other lines of business.[242] These reforms are aimed at achieving a few contemporaneous objectives: improving safety and soundness by reducing systemic risk; allowing retail banks to focus on consumer protection, thereby changing culture and enhancing the social utility of retail banks; and promoting easier

240 Wayne Norman, 'Business Ethics as Self-Regulation: Why Principles that Ground Regulations should be Used to Ground Beyond-Compliance Norms as Well' (2012) 102 *Journal of Business Ethics* 43.

241 Lambert, *Banking Standards Review: Final Report* (n 5).

242 s 142H, Financial Services and Markets Act 2000 as amended by the Financial Services (Banking Reform) Act 2013.

resolution of structurally separated banks. The Vickers Independent Commission on Banking Reform established by the UK Coalition Government in April 2010 first recommended structural reforms and explained why they are necessary:

> In theory, ideal behavioural regulation could entirely correct undesirable private incentives, making structural regulation unnecessary. In practice, however, there are circumstances where structural rules solve the problem more effectively, and in the process save on the need for behavioural regulation.[243]

Structural reforms to the banking sector deal broadly with the separation of retail business from investment banking business. Structural separation forces the scale and size of both the retail and parent entities to shrink, thus making either less difficult or perhaps less expensive to resolve. The interconnectedness between the retail and parent entities is reduced and therefore losses occasioned by one entity are less likely to infect the other resulting in a cascade of losses. The Vickers Independent Banking Commission in the UK has affirmed[244] that separation or ring-fencing is the way forward and this approach is now adopted in legislation.[245]

Structural reforms apply to banking institutions in the UK with deposits of £25 billion or more.[246] A similar approach is recommended in an independent expert report commissioned for the European Commission,[247] in the structural separation of 'trading activities' from retail banking for banks with at least 15 per cent of total assets comprising of trading assets. But the resolve to commit to such structural regulation in the EU is relatively lacking. This book will focus discussion on the UK structural reforms.

The Vickers Report proposes to ring-fence banks which accept retail deposits and provide individual and small business loans, in order that they may be structurally separate from the larger parent banking group which may undertake activities exposed to market risk. The Banking Reform Act 2013 adopts this approach by specifying that ring-fenced entities should conduct core retail banking activities such as taking deposits, facilitating customer payments and offering overdrafts on customer

[243] Independent Commission on Banking, *Issues Paper: Call for Evidence* (London: ICB September, 2010) at qed.econ.queensu.ca/faculty/milne/870/Issues-Paper-24-September-2010.pdf, para 4.3.

[244] Independent Commission on Banking, *Final Report* (London: ICB September, 2011) at www.hm-treasury.gov.uk/d/ICB-Final-Report.pdf (the Vickers Report).

[245] Gonzalo Vina and Jennifer Ryan, 'Osborne Will Promise UK Bank Legislation for Vickers Proposals by 2015' *Bloomberg News* (19 December 2011); Treasury White Paper 2012 (n 4); Financial Services (Banking Reform) Act 2013 amending the Financial Services and Markets Act 2000 by inserting s 142Aff.

[246] Financial Services (The Ring-fenced Bodies and Core Activities) Order 2014.

[247] Liikanen, *High-level Expert Group on Reforming the Structure of the EU Banking Sector* (n 4) para 5.5.1.

accounts, but leaves to subsidiary legislation to further specify any other core activities.[248] Ring-fenced banks are prohibited from investing as principals in the Act,[249] and other excluded activities may be provided for in subsidiary legislation:[250] trading activities; sale and purchase of securities; making markets in securities (including structured investment products) or derivatives; secondary market purchases of loans and other financial instruments; conduit financing or securitisation of assets originated outside the ring-fenced bank; the underwriting of securities issues and derivatives trading generally, except legitimate hedging activities;[251] and engaging in wholesale funding arrangements ancillary to the retail deposit taking and lending business. The ring-fenced retail bank may however engage in certain risk management and ancillary activities that expose it to market instruments and market risk.[252]

Besides a prescriptive approach to what a ring-fenced retail bank can or cannot undertake, further economic and legal separation would be mandated. Pursuant to the Banking Reform Act 2013,[253] the specifics of how a ring-fenced entity must be separated in terms of legal structure and corporate governance are to be subject to further detailed rules issued by the PRA.[254] Detailed rules may require minimal overlap of directors, the prohibition of the ring-fenced entity to have an ownership interest in non-ring-fenced entities, and separation in terms of risk management, remuneration, human resource, and internal control policies. Structural separation attempts to 'carve out' the retail bank to a certain extent but does not ban the model of the large financial group as a conglomerate. This is seen to be particularly important in the EU as universal banking has been practised for a long time.[255]

In terms of management separation, the Vickers Report envisaged that the ring-fenced retail bank should have adequate numbers of independent directors from the rest of the group.[256] The Act does not adopt the more

[248] ss 142B, 142C, Financial Services and Markets Act 2000 as amended by the Financial Services (Banking Reform) Act 2013; Financial Services (The Ring-fenced Bodies and Core Activities) Order 2014.

[249] s 142D, Financial Services and Markets Act 2000 as amended by the Financial Services (Banking Reform) Act 2013.

[250] Treasury White Paper 2012 (n 4) para 2.36; Financial Services (The Ring-fenced Bodies and Core Activities) Order 2014.

[251] Treasury White Paper 2012 (n 4) para 2.38ff.

[252] Vickers Report (n 244) para 3.57. Treasury White Paper 2012 (n 4) para 2.46ff; Financial Services (The Ring-fenced Bodies and Core Activities) Order 2014.

[253] s 142H, Financial Services and Markets Act 2000 as amended by the Financial Services (Banking Reform) Act 2013.

[254] PRA, *The Implementation of Ring-Fencing: Consultation on Legal Structure, Governance and the Continuity of Services and Facilities* (Consultation Paper, October 2014).

[255] Liikanen, *High-level Expert Group on Reforming the Structure of the EU Banking Sector* (n 4) para 5.5.1.

[256] Vickers Report (n 244) para 3.64; s 142H, Financial Services and Markets Act 2000 as amended by the Financial Services (Banking Reform) Act 2013.

specific recommendation that only one director on the Board of the ring-fenced retail bank is allowed to have a cross-directorship with another entity in the group.[257] The Government is keen to recommend that at least half the Board be independent, but the final shape of development in this area seems to be that the Chairman must be independent and that at least a third of the Board does not sit on other entities in the group to which the ring-fenced entity belongs.[258] Ring-fenced banks should also have their own independent Board committees on nomination, remuneration, audit and risk.[259]

In terms of legal separation, ideally the ring-fenced retail bank would be a separate legal entity with operational independence. This means that the ring-fenced entity should be independent in terms of its access to resources, staff, operational facilities and infrastructure. This access should not be compromised, irrespective of the health of the group.[260] The Act is however not explicit on this, requiring only that ring-fenced entities structure themselves so as to be able to provide core activities independently of the group, not to be adversely affected in its decision-making by the rest of the group, and is able to undertake continuity of provision of core services in the event of insolvency of the group.

On economic links, the Vickers Report proposes that ring-fenced entities should not transact with the rest of the group in such a manner as to render the fence meaningless. Hence, all dealings with group companies should be on a third-party basis,[261] on arm's length terms that are no more favourable than in third-party relationships. In particular, asset sales or swaps must be on a third-party basis.[262] This proposal is intended to prevent ring-fenced entities from being used to support the rest of the group and thus exposed to the solvency and liquidity risks of the group. This has now been adopted in the Banking Reform Act.[263] In particular, the Vickers Report proposes that the ring-fenced entity's exposure to the rest of the group will be controlled under existing legislation on large exposures; the ring-fenced entity should not provide any form of unlimited guarantee or indemnity to the group; limits should be placed on the total intraday exposures permitted between ring-fenced entities and the rest of the corporate group; and the ring-fenced entity should not be party to agreements which contain cross-default clauses or be subject to similar arrangements

[257] Vickers Report (n 244) para 3.85.

[258] Treasury White Paper 2012 (n 4) para 2.71; PRA, *The Implementation of Ring-Fencing* (n 254) 13.

[259] Treasury White Paper 2012 (n 4) para 2.73; PRA, *The Implementation of Ring-Fencing* (n 254) 14.

[260] Vickers Report (n 244) para 3.74.

[261] ibid, para 3.82ff.

[262] ibid, para 3.89.

[263] Treasury White Paper 2012 (n 4) para 2.69; s 142H, Financial Services and Markets Act 2000 as amended by the Financial Services (Banking Reform) Act 2013.

triggered by the default of entities in the rest of the group.[264] These limitations, as well as whether the ring-fenced entity should be subject to higher individual stand alone capital adequacy requirements are still the subject of debate.[265] Chow and Surti however warn that ring-fenced banks may contract more on an intra-group basis due to the restrictions placed on permitted activities and hence the concentration of intra-group exposure may itself pose a risk to the ring-fenced bank.[266] It may also be important to consider the possibility that ring-fenced subsidiaries have some funding reliance on the parent company,[267] but limits may be imposed on such arrangements.[268]

The structural reforms are to be implemented by banks themselves, and hence it may be argued that structural reforms also have a meta-regulatory character. However, regulators have the power to order restructuring of financial groups and possibly play a significant role in directing such restructuring if doubt as to the resolvability of such groups exists. [269]

The author has elsewhere argued that it remains debatable as to what extent structural reforms can achieve the mitigation of systemic risk and ensure easier resolvability of banks and financial institutions[270] and this book will not belabour these issues further. This chapter will turn to the issue of whether structural reforms may produce an impact upon banking culture. Zingales[271] argues that structural separation allows smaller focused financial outfits to develop in each sector, providing more competition. This development may then unravel the consolidations in the financial sector, which followed earlier liberalisation and deregulation. Such could have a positive impact in terms of de-complexifying and downsizing systemically large and important financial institutions. Such de-complexification may allow banks and financial institutions to focus on particular lines of business, and retail-focused institutions may develop a better customer service culture. The Parliamentary Commission on Banking Standards also seems to accept the view that systemically large and

[264] Vickers Report (n 244) para 3.87.

[265] PRA, *The Implementation of Ring-Fencing* (n 254).

[266] Julian TS Chow and Jay Surti, 'Making Banks Safer: Can Volcker and Vickers do it?' (2011) IMF Working Paper WP/11/236 at www.imf.org/external/pubs/ft/wp/2011/wp11236.pdf.

[267] As provided in EU legislation: see Recovery and Resolution Directive 2014, Art 19.

[268] Treasury White Paper 2012 (n 4) para 2.68.

[269] Recovery and Resolution Directive 2014, Arts 15–18; s 142K, Financial Services and Markets Act 2000 as amended by the Financial Services (Banking Reform) Act 2013.

[270] Iris H-Y Chiu, 'The Vickers Independent Banking Commission Report—Does the Ring-fencing of Retail Banks Mitigate Systemic Risk Concerns in the Banking Sector?' (2012) 9 *International Corporate Rescue* 79; Mads Andenas and Iris H-Y Chiu, *The Foundations and Future of Financial Regulation: Governance for Responsibility* (Oxford: Routledge, 2014) ch 11 generally.

[271] Luigi Zingales, *Capitalism for the People: Recapturing the Lost Genius of American Capitalism* (New York: Basic Books 2012).

important financial institutions that are financial supermarkets combining retail and investment banking tend to allow the trading culture of investment banking to permeate the culture of the organisation in terms of business and compensation practices, resulting in a 'damaging' culture of entitlement.[272] Hence, structural reforms may introduce diversity in business emphases and mitigate the hitherto predominance of predatory and toxic cultures that are attributed to trading environments.

Further, Zingales also argues that smaller focused outfits, divided by sector, are less likely to agree on objectives and consolidate power to form a monolithic and powerful lobbying force.[273] In fact, their objectives may play off against each other, mitigating undue political influence. The mitigation of the political influence of the financial sector may allow the voice of public interest, whether coming from politicians, regulators or stakeholders, to gain ground and create pressure for cultural change in the banking sector.

In sum, structural reforms, although not aimed primarily to force cultural change in the financial sector, could result in dramatic changes to the way banks and financial institutions conduct business and restructure their key relationships. These changes could produce moments of metamorphoses that could, in due course, entail major cultural changes.

F. CONCLUSION

This chapter, together with chapter five, has identified the governance and culture issues at banks and financial institutions that surfaced in the global financial crisis and the subsequent conduct scandals such as LIBOR manipulation. Governance and culture form the broader contexts for internal control at firms and post-crisis reforms have thus addressed various aspects in order to support more robust internal control at firms.

Corporate governance reforms that directly address support for instituting stronger risk and control cultures at banks and financial institutions have been introduced. However, some aspects of corporate governance reforms at the EU level are punctuated by wider agendas in corporate governance generally and do not bear a strong relation to the needs of financial regulation. Further, the policy impetus to encourage more shareholder engagement with risk issues seems contrary to insights offered by corporate governance commentators on the unsuitability of certain conventional perspectives on corporate governance to the financial sector.

272 House of Lords and House of Commons, Parliamentary Commission on Banking Standards, *First Report* (2012–13, HL 98, HC 848) paras 38–39.

273 Zingales, *Capitalism for the People* (n 271).

This chapter has also discussed a number of reforms that are aimed at changing banking culture. The UK reforms in enhancing individual responsibility and personal liability, especially for senior persons, may have an impact upon individual incentives and behaviour. Structural reforms to large banking groups, also introduced only in the UK could, in due course, also produce changes in banking culture. At the EU level, remuneration reforms are targeted at making reward more risk-aligned, hopefully changing the incentives for financial sector employees. However, this chapter has pointed out the limitations and unintended consequences of the prescriptive regulation for bonuses and critically queries if remuneration reforms may indeed achieve incentive changes. This chapter however argues that *malus* and clawback powers may produce powerful incentive-changing effects and encourages that these regimes be better developed in regulation.

As one commentator suggests that banking culture will take a generation to be changed,[274] the effectiveness of the reforms discussed here remain to be seen. On the whole, the tenor of regulation is unequivocally relentless about the importance of robust internal control in firms supported by sound governance and culture contexts. Next, we turn to examine the personal responsibility and liability regimes for internal control personnel in order to flesh out how regulatory expectations of internal control functions are enforced. In doing so, the next chapter will point out that the enforcement regimes reveal an expectations gap between regulatory expectations and internal control personnel perceptions of responsibility. Hence, although post-crisis reforms have engaged with organisational, governance and cultural matters in order to strengthen internal control for securing firms' meeting of regulatory objectives, the reforms have missed a trick in neglecting to ensure that the professional perceptions of internal control responsibilities are aligned with regulatory expectations. Or perhaps the misalignments may highlight where regulatory expectations may be undue. The next chapter highlights the regulatory–professional disjunction and suggests that this disjunction needs to be addressed in order to establish a fair, efficient and effective regime for regulating internal control functions for the broader purpose of securing firm compliance with greatly enhanced regulatory obligations in the post-crisis landscape.

[274] See 'Banks need a generation to change culture, report says' *Financial Times* (26 November 2014).

7

Incentive-Based Approaches to Improve Internal Control Efficacy: Enforcement and Whistle-Blowing

THIS BOOK HAS thus far examined the role of internal control functions in banks and financial institutions and the post-crisis reforms made to boost their capacity, powers and functions in order to assist in securing firms' compliance with new and greatly augmented regulatory obligations. Enhanced regulatory expectations are being placed on internal control personnel in light of the greater demands for firm compliance with the phenomenally increased regulatory burdens. These reforms are largely introduced in the organisational dimension, and the foregoing chapters have looked at prescriptive requirements specific to internal control, as well as in the broader framework of corporate governance and organisational culture. This chapter now examines two incentive-based approaches that are directed at internal control personnel in order to motivate their effectiveness in meeting regulatory expectations. First, regulators could undertake direct enforcement actions against internal control individuals, and such could result in monetary fines and bans from working in the financial services industry. This is the 'stick' aspect of the incentive-based approach. Internal control personnel would not be able to seek shelter behind either the corporate veil or higher levels of responsibility in corporate governance. Direct regulatory enforcement against internal control personnel has been observed to be on the rise in the aftermath of the global financial crisis of 2008–09 and this chapter will discuss several key cases in enforcement by the UK regulator. Second, regulators could incentivise internal control individuals to oversee or carry out whistle-blowing so as to prevent failures in securing compliance with regulatory objectives.

This chapter first discusses the regulatory duties imposed on internal control personnel via the general regime applicable to persons exercising certain functions.[1] This chapter will then discuss key cases in direct

[1] This regime used to be known as 'controlled functions' under s 59, Financial Services and Markets Act and controlled functions are subject to the principles of conduct contained in the regulator's Statements of Principle and Code of Practice for Approved Persons (APER).

enforcement actions taken by the UK regulator against internal control personnel, largely compliance officers. The chapter critically reviews the aspects of the enforcement actions that may reveal a misalignment between regulatory expectations of the professional responsibilities and standards on the part of internal control personnel, and the professional understandings and perspectives on the part of the individuals concerned. Internal control personnel may have been alleged to have breached rules of conduct with the benefit of hindsight and subject to unpredictable forms of liability. The regulatory–professional disjunction is highly unsatisfactory and could undermine the efficacy of internal control. The regulatory–professional disjunction is arguably a result of a mixture of two factors. First, the nascent professional understandings in relation to the scope of responsibilities on the part of internal control functions as discussed in chapters two to four. Internal control personnel may not be entirely clear as to the professional expectations of their work as such expectations are still being developed in the wider emerging context of their professions. Second, regulatory rules are also unclear as to the scope of responsibilities, the standards of execution expected and the nature of liability to be imposed. In particular, the nature of liability to be imposed frames regulatory expectations in terms of the scope of responsibilities and the standard of execution expected.

This chapter will critically query whether individual liability imposed on internal control personnel is a form of primary personal liability or secondary liability. The incurrence of liability on the part of internal control personnel is in connection with a failure by the firm to comply with another substantive obligation. Hence, it is the firm as a legal person that has primarily failed to comply with regulatory obligations or objectives. This chapter will discuss where the internal control individual stands in relation to the primary failure of the firm. Is the individual personally responsible too for the breach of regulatory obligations committed by the firm and on what basis? Or is the liability imposed on the individual a form of secondary liability, in which case the personal responsibility of the individual is more nuanced and the imposition of liability is largely for the purposes of deterrence? This chapter argues that it is not clear whether the current regime of liability for internal control individuals is based on personal or secondary liability, or both, and to what extent. Either characterisation would give rise to certain implications regarding the scope of responsibilities and standard of execution expected of internal control individuals by regulators.

This regime will be known as 'certified' functions in the future, to be distinguished from the senior persons regime discussed in chapter 6, but the code of conduct applicable to certified functions will be largely similar to APER.

This chapter argues that the regulators' enforcement actions against internal control personnel for primary breaches by their firms exposes an expectations gap between what regulators expect internal control functions to achieve and what internal control personnel may perceive to be sufficient discharge of their functions. This regulatory–professional disjunction has the potential to undermine the professional standing and efficacy of internal control functions and be counterproductive to achieving regulatory expectations.

A. REGULATORY REGIME FOR INTERNAL CONTROL PERSONNEL: CODE OF CONDUCT RULES

The UK regulator imposes a system of approvals for certain individuals performing certain functions in financial services firms,[2] going beyond the harmonised system of firm authorisation implemented throughout the European Union. This is to allow the regulator to maintain continuous scrutiny over persons in financial services firms who have a significant influence over the firm, or have customer-facing responsibilities and/or deal with customer assets and monies. Pursuant to the reforms in the Financial Services (Banking Reform) Act 2013 implementing a number of the Parliamentary Commission on Banking Standards suggestions referred to in chapter six, certain internal control personnel would be subject to the new Senior Managers Regime such as the Chief Risk function and the Head of Internal Audit.[3] Other internal control personnel may be subject to the 'Certification' regime. Although the latter regime does not require regulatory pre-vetting, persons subject to the latter regime are subject to a set of Conduct Rules similar to APER but slightly less extensive than the Rules applicable to senior managers.[4] The regulator is empowered to maintain a set of Conduct Rules for senior managers and other certified persons.[5] The Conduct Rules for internal control personnel are evolved from the previously generally applicable Statements of Principle and Code of Practice for Approved Persons (APER) under Handbooks issued by the Prudential Regulation Authority (PRA) for banks and insurers and the Financial Conduct Authority (FCA).

As discussed in the foregoing chapters, the organisational reforms to boost internal control functions need to be supported by professional understanding on the part of internal control personnel in terms of regulatory

[2] s 59, Financial Services and Markets Act 2000.
[3] PRA and FCA, *Strengthening Accountability in Banking: A New Regulatory Framework* (July 2014).
[4] ibid.
[5] s 64, Financial Services and Markets Act 2000.

expectations of those functions and roles. Although organisational reforms go some way in overcoming internal control weaknesses so as to better place internal control functions to meet regulatory expectations, do internal control personnel have a clear professional understanding of their responsibilities and of regulatory expectations? It may be argued that APER is the template upon which regulatory expectations are based and thus internal control personnel and regulators should be on the same page as to the responsibilities imposed on them to meet regulatory expectations. Even if internal control professions have not clearly articulated the scope of their roles and responsibilities, it can be argued that regulatory duties under the Conduct Rules could fill in that gap, so that there should not be any regulatory–professional disjunctions.

However, as will be discussed below, the Conduct Rules contain general principles that apply not only to internal control personnel but to other certified functions, and so they are not profession-specific. Further, the Conduct Rules are widely worded and do not arguably fill in for the professional content for internal control functions. This chapter will argue that the imposition of liability under the Conduct Rules often exposes the disjunctions between regulatory expectations and professional understanding, especially where personal liability seems to be imposed. The cases studied in this chapter will be based on the imposition of APER liability, but as much of the new Conduct Rules is drawn from APER, these cases still provide useful insights into how the new Rules would be applied. Further, this chapter will consider if APER liability is in fact imposed as secondary and not personal liability, in which case the chapter argues that the imposition of secondary liability may threaten to undermine the professional stature of internal control.

The Conduct Rules contain general principles applicable to a wide range of certified persons, not just internal control personnel. The range of persons defined by the PRA and FCA as falling within the definition of certified functions includes: persons in a position to take material risks in the firm; persons performing oversight functions; compliance; oversight functions for client asset and money segregation; money laundering reporting; benchmark administration and submission; systems and control functions; client-facing functions; and significant management functions.[6] Further, the PRA defines actuarial functions and systems and controls functions as falling within the ambit of certified functions.[7] For both the PRA and FCA, staff in compliance, risk management and internal audit would be

[6] PRA and FCA, *Strengthening Accountability in Banking* (n 3).
[7] PRA Handbook, SUP 10B.4.3.

regarded as certified functions as they are functions dealing with systems and controls.[8]

The Conduct Rules have evolved from the seven principles in APER set out in chapter six. However, as the Conduct Rules now provide different sets of Rules for senior managers and other certified persons, the Rules applicable to certified persons are now renamed as 'Individual Conduct Rules' and contain five principles:

Rule 1: You must act with integrity.
Rule 2: You must act with due skill, care and diligence.
Rule 3: You must be open and cooperative with the FCA, the PRA and other regulators.
Rule 4: You must pay due regard to the interests of customers and treat them fairly.
Rule 5: You must observe proper standards of market conduct.

Rules 1, 2, 3 and 5 have been drawn directly from the previous APER, and the interpretation and application of these rules would likely adhere to former APER guidance and enforcement cases. For example, Rule 1 is the same as Statement 1 under APER which is supplemented by non-exhaustive examples in APER 4. Statement 1 is explained by reference to examples in relation to dishonesty and impropriety, such as misleading disclosures. Rule 4 is a new introduction, but this Rule is based on the general Principles of Business Conduct applicable to all authorised firms, the PRIN module under the PRA and FCA Handbooks. One of the principles of business conduct is to treat customers fairly.[9] By incorporating the principle to treat customers fairly into Conduct Rules, regulators are not just making firms, but individuals in responsible positions, liable for customer-facing conduct. This approach reflects the regulators' concerns over conduct scandals at UK financial institutions, especially in mis-selling financial products to customers. Hence, the personal responsibility regime for certified persons is enhanced in order to incentivise individuals to refrain from sharp dealing with customers and to allow regulators to take enforcement actions against identified individuals.

The chapter will now proceed to discuss how APER principles have been used in enforcement action against internal control personnel. These cases are likely to remain very relevant to the Conduct Rules regime which is largely drawn from APER. The cases discussed below will highlight

[8] Commission Directive 2006/73/EC of 10 August 2006 implementing Directive 2004/39/EC of the European Parliament and of the Council as regards organisational requirements and operating conditions for investment firms and defined terms for the purposes of that Directive [2006] OJ L241/26 (MiFID Commission Directive 2006) Arts 6–8.

[9] Principle 6, PRIN 2.1, FCA Handbook.

regulatory expectations placed on internal control personnel and reveal the regulatory–professional disjunctions especially in relation to compliance officers.

B. KEY ENFORCEMENT ACTIONS AGAINST INTERNAL CONTROL INDIVIDUALS IN THE UK

This chapter critically discusses several key enforcement actions taken against compliance officers in the aftermath of the global financial crisis of 2008–09. To date, the internal control individuals who have been subjected to direct enforcement by the UK regulator have all been compliance officers. This is not to say that only compliance officers may be at the forefront of direct enforcement actions, as the general principles supporting liability could also in an appropriate case be applied to risk management or internal audit personnel. This section will first discuss the cases that are based on the failure of compliance officers to 'act with due care, skill and diligence' as required under Principle 6 of APER[10] now in Rule 2 of the Conduct Rules. Next, the case against Robert Addison which is based on breaches of Principles 1 and 7 of APER, now Rule 1 and senior management Rule 3 of the Conduct Rules, will be examined. Finally, this section will discuss the UK regulator's censure of Stephen Morse in relation to the enforcement against Barclays Plc for mis-submissions of the London Interbank Offered Rate to the British Bankers' Association, which seems to be based on collective responsibility of the compliance function.

Compliance Officer Liability in Breach of the Principle to Exercise Due Skill, Care and Diligence

This section deals with three key cases establishing the liability of compliance officers in failure to exercise due care, skill and diligence. Principle 6 APER and now Rule 2 of the Conduct Rules requires an approved person to exercise due skill, care and diligence in managing the business of the firm. This is further fleshed out in APER 4.6 which provides non-exhaustive examples of when due care, skill and diligence has not been achieved. APER 4.6 refers to examples where transactions are carried out without a full appreciation of risks and information, general failure to obtain an adequate understanding of the business and its risks and delegation without due monitoring and supervision. This section will critically consider if breaches of this conduct rule entail a form of personal liability for a form

[10] Principle 6, FCA and PRA Handbooks, APER 2.1A.3. The equivalent under the Conduct Rules would be Rule 2.

of professional failure on the part of the compliance officer concerned, or whether it imposes a form of secondary liability.

Final Notice Against Dr Sandradee Joseph (18 November 2011)

Dr Joseph was an approved person holding the controlled function of compliance oversight in Dynamic Decisions Capital Management Limited (DDCM), a hedge fund management company based in London (and Milan). In late 2008, the fund suffered losses of up to 85 per cent of its total assets under management. In order to conceal the losses, an employee of the fund, known as 'Employee A' in the final notice issued by the then Financial Services Authority (FSA), entered into a number of contracts, on behalf of investment funds managed by DDCM, for the purchase and resale of a bond. The bond was premised on the purported assignment of $10 billion of diesel oil by one company to another. The bond was collateralised by a commodity (diesel oil) and notice could be given to convert the bond into either cash (a cash conversion) or to diesel oil (a commodity conversion) at any time. Once notice is given, cash payments or physical delivery of the commodity would begin after 120 days and continue for 12 months. In the alternative, the bond could be sold to a third party without the need for a cash or physical conversion.

Employee A booked purported profits of approximately $418 million to the fund by purchasing several units of the bond from the company assigned the diesel oil. The fund's acquisitions of the bond were made at deep discounts to the face value of the bond, therefore allowing Employee A to book purported profits to the fund which were slightly in excess of the losses suffered, such that, in each month, a relatively modest profit was reported by the fund. The bond was a fraudulent instrument and this alerted the suspicions of the prime broker which refused to carry out the transactions any further and resigned from the prime brokerage arrangement. Subsequently, two key institutional investors also observed that the bond was in contravention of the investment restrictions placed on the fund and asked to redeem their investments. Dr Joseph was aware of the correspondence with the prime broker and the institutional investors.

Dr Joseph was of the view that the bond transactions would have been vetted by external lawyers and hence she was not in a position to question the propriety of the transactions. She was however never made aware of any correspondence with such external lawyers. In view of the institutional investors' concerns of which Dr Joseph was also made aware, Dr Joseph thought that risk profile reports that were prepared by an independent global professional services firm and sent to the institutional investors would address their concerns.

The FSA was of the view that Dr Joseph had failed to give adequate consideration to the matters raised in the prime broker's and institutional investors' correspondence that ought to have alerted her to possible regulatory breaches in relation to the fraudulent nature of the investment made in the bond transactions. She had failed to undertake any investigations into ascertaining whether the concerns raised were legitimate, and hence failed to detect fraud and escalate matters. The FSA opined that Dr Joseph was seriously lacking in competence in carrying out the compliance function. Dr Joseph was banned from working in the financial services industry and imposed with a fine of £14,000 (discounted from £20,000 for early settlement).

The basis for liability in this case was Principle 6 of APER, relating to the failure of a person appointed to a controlled function to act with due care, skill and diligence in that function. At face value, this was an imposition of personal liability on Dr Joseph, as Dr Joseph was held personally to account for failure to detect irregularities which the FSA felt were sufficiently brought to her notice. The primary irregularity in this case was of course the fraudulent bond transactions that were entered into to conceal losses of the fund from investors in order to stem the possibility of mass redemptions.[11]

The personal liability imposed on Dr Joseph can only be justified if Dr Joseph should have been able to detect the aforementioned irregularities and suspect fraud. The FSA's decision seemed to be based on her awareness of correspondence in which matters of 'red flags' had been mentioned, and her lack of follow-up with the unusual resignation of the prime broker and two clearly worded statements of concern regarding breaches of investment restrictions by institutional investors. The FSA had regulatory expectations of Dr Joseph to be alert to 'red flags' and to follow up with early signs. However, is it clear either in APER or in the professional understanding of the role of compliance what should constitute 'red flags' to a compliance officer and under what circumstances should proactive investigations or follow-up be carried out? Dr Joseph's view that other front line mechanisms had been put in place to take care of concerns shows that there is perhaps uncertainty in the parameters of the oversight and monitoring aspects of the compliance function.

This case arguably highlights a disjunction between regulatory expectations and professional understanding as to the scope of a compliance officer's responsibility where interaction with other internal departments and with external counsel is concerned. If the liability imposed on Dr Joseph is to be understood as personal liability, what is the standard of 'due care, skill and diligence' expected of her in proactive follow-up with unfavourable signs of information, or in working with external counsel in bond transactions, or with professional services firms in direct correspondence

[11] See FSA Decision Notice against DDCM, 20 March 2012 at www.fsa.gov.uk/static/pubs/decisions/ddcm.pdf.

with investors? This chapter is sceptical that the scope of responsibility for compliance officers—particularly in interaction with other internal departments, internal control and external counsel—is a clearly articulated one, either in regulatory duties or objectively understood by the profession. This case should be compared with the final notice against Alison Moran whose failings much more clearly attract liability for failure to exercise due care, skill and diligence.[12] Moran, a compliance officer at Catalyst, distributor of investment products in the UK, had become aware that one of the structured bonds distributed by Catalyst, which was issued by a Luxembourg entity, ARM, was withheld authorisation by the Luxembourg regulator. She turned a blind eye to the fact that the structured bond was ultimately unauthorised and allowed financial promotion to be sent out to investors. In Moran's case, she was given a piece of clearly unfavourable information that she chose to ignore and such conduct quite unequivocally is not that reasonably expected of compliance officers. However, in Dr Joseph's case, the information she came across was arguably much more nuanced and actionable by other persons in the firm. Hence, it may only be with the benefit of hindsight that the then FSA's regulatory expectations are revealed, ie, that compliance officers should proactively follow up early signs of unfavourable information, whether or not such information is more pertinently actionable by other persons.

One may query whether regulatory expectations of the duties of compliance officers have been fairly framed given that the contours of regulatory expectations are broad and ambulatory, and there is a relative lack of professional articulation on the parameters of compliance responsibilities. Further, as chapter two has cautioned, the lack of clearly scoped professional understandings of the parameters of compliance responsibilities could result in the relatively greater influence of organisational factors and culture in shaping the duties of compliance officers. The decision has not been referred to the Upper Tribunal. However, it could also be argued that Dr Joseph did not satisfy herself that external counsel for the transaction of the bonds had been engaged, and in that respect, she did not undertake a thorough appraisal of her information matrix (required under APER 4.6) to determine whether or not proactive follow-up should have been carried out.

In the alternative, we could also view the FSA's enforcement against Dr Joseph as an imposition of secondary liability, the main purpose of which was to incentivise compliance officers to *do more* in order to deter primary regulatory breaches. Secondary liability, often used in imposing directorial liability or external gatekeeper liability (such as upon external auditors and lawyers), is often justified by the insufficiency of

[12] FSA Final Notice against Alison Moran, 30 September 2013, at www.fca.org.uk/static/documents/final-notices/alison-moran.pdf.

primary liability in achieving adequate deterrence.[13] If the nature of liability imposed via the failure to exercise care, skill and diligence is actually one of secondary liability, then the FSA's regulatory expectations of Dr Joseph would relate to her monitoring role in compliance: that insufficient monitoring and control had been carried out to prevent the primary fraud that had taken place within the firm. Are such regulatory expectations clearly articulated in the conduct rule? To what extent would the professional understanding of compliance responsibilities support a fraud prevention or detection role?

This chapter argues that if Dr Joseph was indeed expected to monitor whether conclusions arrived at by other departments, service providers and external counsel are correct, then such a duty is not clearly articulated in the conduct rule relating to 'care, skill and diligence' and is also not explicitly stated as a clear circumstance of breach in APER 4.6. These regulatory expectations are much less clear than the 'duty to supervise' imposed by the US Securities and Exchange Commission (SEC) on compliance officers in broker-dealers.[14] The scope and application of the 'duty to supervise' has been developed in case law jurisprudence and is clearly a form of secondary liability. The nature of 'care, skill and diligence' is less clear as a form of secondary liability by comparison. In Dr Joseph's case, the Final Notice referred to Dr Joseph's failure to monitor for the purposes of securing compliance, a wider formulation than the examples provided in APER 4.6. Is this tantamount to expecting that the monitoring role of compliance would result in successful fraud prevention or detection? It would be rather surprising to compliance officers if zero failures are expected of them whether by regulators or in their professional understanding. This chapter is of the view that if secondary liability is intended to be imposed via the failure to exercise care, skill and diligence, then 'care, skill and diligence' must be further articulated in terms of a positive duty to monitor, and the expectations associated with such monitoring must be fairly and clearly framed. Further, such a duty must also be proportionate to the organisational frameworks within which the compliance function is working. The application of discretionary enforcement by the regulator of unarticulated regulatory expectations within broadly worded conduct rules would only result in the perception of unexpected and unfair 'punishment' for internal control personnel, a demotivating phenomenon which could be counterproductive for the development of their efficacy. Further, the lack of articulation in conduct rules of the specific regulatory

[13] Ke Steven Wan, 'Gatekeeper Liability Versus Regulation of Wrongdoers' (2008) 34 *Ohio Northern University Law Review* 483; Assaf Hamdani, 'Gatekeeper Liability' (2003) 77 *Southern California Law Review* 53.

[14] Discussed in Elizabeth M Knoblock, 'Investment Advisers: The Failure of the Duty to Supervise' (2004) *Journal of Investment Compliance* 35.

responsibilities of compliance officers is not made up for by clear and unambiguous professional understandings—such as where a disjunction may lie between regulatory expectations and the compliance profession. Thus, on the one hand, regulatory expectations need to be clearly articulated in terms of the scope of responsibilities and nature of liability; on the other hand, such expectations should be more clearly framed in dialogue with professional perspectives in order to forge a clearly articulated set of professional responsibilities for internal control functions which may then be fairly enforced, whether pursuant to primary or secondary liability.

We now turn to the enforcement action taken by the FSA against Ten-Holter of Greenlight Investments Inc, a UK-based hedge fund manager.

Final Notice Against Alexander Edward Ten-Holter (26 January 2012)

Ten-Holter was approved by the FSA to perform the controlled functions of partner, trader, money laundering reporting officer and compliance officer at Greenlight Capital UK (LLP), a hedge fund management firm. Greenlight bought two tranches of shares in a UK listed company, Punch Taverns, in June and July 2008 and then bought again in December 2008 and January 2009, building up a stake of about 33 million shares in Punch Taverns in total. On 8 June 2009, the President of Greenlight, David Einhorn, was contacted by Merrill Lynch in relation to a possible issue of equity by Punch Taverns and was asked if he would be prepared to enter into discussions on a wall-crossed basis, ie, to be made an insider and therefore becoming restricted from trading in the shares. Einhorn declined but nevertheless entered into a conversation with the management of Punch Taverns the following day in which he hinted at 'secret bad things' that could be revealed if the wall was crossed. Einhorn declined to be wall-crossed and to sign a non-disclosure agreement, but gave orders to Ten-Holter on the same day to dispose of all Greenlight's shares in Punch Taverns. Between 9 and 12 June 2009, Ten-Holter effected sales of up to a third of Greenlight's holdings in Punch Taverns.

The FSA took enforcement action against Greenlight, Einhorn, Ten-Holter and Greenlight's broker Agnew at JP Morgan. In relation to Ten-Holter, the FSA was of the view that Ten-Holter, in breach of Principle 6 APER, failed to exercise due care and skill in his compliance function to secure compliance with anti-market abuse regulation. Ten-Holter was aware of the conversation between Punch Taverns and Einhorn, and although Einhorn ultimately declined to cross the wall, he had received confidential signals regarding the possibly adverse financial position that Punch Taverns was in. The FSA was of the view that Ten-Holter should have been alert to the dangers of trading such massive volumes of Punch Taverns shares immediately following the telephone conversation between Einhorn and Punch Taverns. The execution of trades by Ten-Holter in the few days before Punch Taverns unscheduled announcement regarding equity raising amounted to insider dealing.

None of the parties in this series of enforcement actions by the FSA challenged the decisions in the Upper Tribunal, although it would have been beneficial for a court to have had the opportunity to develop the jurisprudence on the meaning of 'inside information'. The telephone conversation between Einhorn and Punch Taverns was not wall-crossed and so specific information regarding Punch Taverns financial situation did not pass to Einhorn. Hence, it remains debatable whether a court would hold that hints and signals of 'bad news' are specific enough to constitute information of a 'precise nature'[15] that could be price sensitive amounting to 'inside information'. The somewhat shade of grey in the nature of information received by Einhorn could have been crucial to Ten-Holter's unquestioning disposition taken in relation to the disposal of the shares in Punch Taverns.

Ten-Holter was banned from performing any compliance or money laundering reporting functions in the financial services industry and was also fined in the amount of £130,000. It may be argued that Ten-Holter was imposed with a form of personal liability. This is again a case where the FSA expected a compliance officer to have responded to certain red flags by querying and following up. However, if Ten-Holter genuinely thought that the refusal of Einhorn to be wall-crossed meant that Greenlight was 'safe' to trade, and such an impression could be a legitimate one in industry practice, the imposition of liability upon Ten-Holter may seem surprising. What is exposed in this enforcement action is the regulatory–professional disjunction between a compliance officer's perception of what meets the standard of care and diligence and the corresponding regulatory expectations.

APER 4.6 does not deal with the issue of whether a belief in acting consistently with perceived industry practice would suffice for the purposes of acting with due care, skill and diligence. The question is open as to whether a form of accepted understanding of market practice could shape what compliance officers should perceive to be reasonable professional conduct. This position would be consistent with how professional liability in negligence is established under general law, viz, professional negligence liability is usually based on falling below the standard of care expected of a reasonable body of members of the same profession.[16] The question of how Ten-Holter's conduct should be judged as a matter of professional

[15] s 118C(5), Financial Services and Markets Act 2000. Case law seems to indicate that precise circumstances need to be known, and so it could be contestable whether Einhorn had received precise information. However, it could also be argued that 'bad' financial news is sufficiently precise even if the particulars of adversity are not exactly conveyed.

[16] *Bolam v Friern Hospital Management Committee* [1957] 1 WLR 582.

understanding remains unresolved. Hence, regulatory expectations of how Ten-Holter should have behaved only expose the disjunction between such expectations and professional perspectives, and has not gone any further in clearly articulating the conduct expected of a compliance officer.

In the alternative, the then FSA enforcement could be regarded as having imposed a form of secondary liability on Ten-Holter for the purposes of incentivising compliance officers to do more to deter potential adverse conduct by the firm. Einhorn's dubious conversation with the management of Punch Taverns, albeit under an express understanding of not 'crossing the wall', has somewhat compromised the 'wall' and so there is at least an arguable case that Einhorn engaged in insider dealing according to market abuse regulation in the UK. The imposition of liability on Ten-Holter who executed Einhorn's instructions may be perceived to be on the basis of failure to prevent, ie, a form of secondary liability.

However, one needs to understand the pressures that a compliance officer may face in raising a query that 'blocks' a transaction which has significant financial implications for the firm. On the one hand, internal gatekeepers cannot avoid being unpopular in certain circumstances and post-crisis organisational reforms have gone some way to protect the position and powers of internal control in order that unpopular but objective decisions may be taken when required. On the other hand, imposing secondary liability on internal control overlooks the intra-firm struggles that internal control faces in its perhaps unpopular gatekeeping role. This chapter reiterates that care should be taken so that secondary liability is not imposed to the extent of undermining the professional stature of internal control. It may be argued that the Market Abuse Regulation 2014 now provides for a 'legitimate behaviour' defence that allows defendants to adduce evidence of sound internal control that amounts to Chinese walls within the firm,[17] and so compliance officers who ensure that these defences are well erected should not have much to fear. However, the regulator has ultimate discretion in deciding if the firm's internal control framework is 'sound', and hence regulatory enforcement could still reveal regulatory–professional disjunctions in this regard.

Final Notice Against John Douglas Leslie (26 July 2013)

Leslie ran a firm which was an independent financial adviser based in London. He was approved by the then FSA to perform the controlled

[17] Regulation (EU) No 596/2014 of the European Parliament and of the Council of 16 April 2014 on market abuse (market abuse regulation) and repealing Directive 2003/6/EC of the European Parliament and of the Council and Commission Directives 2003/124/EC, 2003/125/EC and 2004/72/EC, Art 9.

functions of partner, investment adviser, compliance officer and money laundering reporting.

In April 2005, an investment management firm, Burlington, approached Leslie's firm for advice as well as to engage the firm's services to promote a number of retail sector collective investment schemes. The objective of the three schemes was to raise money to invest in land and property developments in Croatia, Bulgaria and Montenegro. Leslie's firm advised Burlington that the schemes could be promoted to investors who had signed eligibility certificates as sophisticated or high net worth investors, and that prospectuses in the three schemes could be sent to them. Burlington engaged Leslie's firm to carry out the relevant financial promotion. Leslie's firm therefore had the responsibility of reviewing and checking the certificates signed by the relevant investors, and of delivering the prospectuses to them. Leslie's firm then outsourced certain administrative aspects of its responsibilities to another firm, AdminCo linked to Burlington.

Leslie gave Burlington and AdminCo access to his firm's records management system and requested that they upload eligibility certificates and other documents so that he could control the investor certification process from his office. Burlington and AdminCo failed to provide the correct records but Leslie did not discover that as he only periodically visited Burlington/AdminCo's offices to spot check a sample of eligibility certificates. Leslie did not in fact check every eligibility certificate and therefore did not ensure that prospectuses were sent only to the correctly identified eligible investors. Sending a prospectus to a person who has not signed an eligibility certificate to receive such promotional material would be in breach of the anti-financial promotion regulations.[18] The FCA took enforcement action against Leslie for failure to exercise due care, skill and diligence, resulting in the firm's non-compliance with the anti-financial promotion regulations.

Leslie was banned from performing any controlled functions in the financial services industry and fined a sum of £28,000. The matter was not further referred to the Upper Tribunal. This case raises fewer concerns than the previous two with regard to what may reasonably have been expected of Leslie. The scope of work Leslie had to carry out was defined in contractual agreement with Burlington and the need to check every eligible investor certificate would have been consistent with precise anti-financial promotion regulations. Leslie did fall short of ensuring that every prospectus was correctly sent to an identified eligible investor, therefore failing to secure compliance with the anti-financial promotion regulations. In this case, the responsibilities of Leslie were clearly set out in contract and precise regulatory requirements and hence there was no

[18] s 21(2), Financial Services and Markets Act 2000.

ambiguity as to the scope of responsibilities. This may be interpreted to be a case of personal liability, as Leslie was liable for failing to carry out clearly articulated responsibilities.

Increased clarity in the scope of responsibilities imposed on internal control personnel is of importance to setting realistic regulatory expectations for fair enforcement and hence reinforcing internal control efficacy. There may however be a limit to how prescriptive regulatory duties can be, and increased prescription could also give rise to gaming behaviour to avoid responsibility. Nevertheless, increased clarity cannot be achieved by merely ramping up regulatory prescription; it can only be achieved by developments in refining the professionalism of internal control personnel in tandem with the realistic setting of regulatory expectations of them. Chapter eight will take this point up to suggest how increased professionalism can interact with the setting of more realistic regulatory expectations of internal control functions in order to achieve an optimal form of internal control efficacy for meeting regulatory objectives.

The other lesson to draw from Leslie's case is that personal liability is more easily justified for internal control functions in smaller firms where such functions are concurrently responsible for business and other functions. In larger organisations where teams of persons may be responsible for one transaction, it is more difficult to identify clearly individual personal liability. The censure of Stephen Morse at Barclays Plc is an example in point. The case also highlights the need for regulatory expectations to be more clearly articulated in terms of the nature of liability, whether it is personal or secondary liability that is imposed on the individual.

Censure of Stephen Morse, Barclays Plc (27 June 2012)

The censure of Stephen Morse, head of compliance at Barclays, took place in the wake of the then FSA enforcement action against Barclays for inaccurate submissions of the London Interbank Offered Rate (LIBOR) and the European Interbank Offered Rate (EURIBOR) in order to manipulate the setting of these benchmark rates. The censure is an example of the imposition of secondary liability on internal control for the primary failing of the firm. It may remain curious in this case why no particular individual compliance officer has been singled out for personal responsibility. Gadinis, in relation to the US SEC's enforcement history, points out that personal responsibility is less often alleged against personnel in large firms and in large scandals, as it is difficult to pinpoint personal responsibility in a complex organisational environment. However, such enforcement preferences may give rise to moral hazard in larger firms.[19]

[19] Stavros Gadinis, 'The SEC and the Financial Industry: Evidence from Enforcement against Broker-Dealers' (2012) 67 *Business Lawyer* 679.

Barclays Plc was fined £59.5 million by the FSA for breaches of principles in conducting business with integrity, due care, skill and diligence and in accordance with proper standards of market conduct.[20] Investigations revealed that between the years 2005 and 2008 where inaccurate LIBOR submissions were made in consequence of conversations between rate submitters and derivative traders, the compliance function had been alerted on three separate occasions regarding the propriety of submissions reflecting the interests of derivatives traders in the bank. However, the compliance function failed to regard the conflict of interest between rate submitters and derivatives traders as posing sufficient risk, and did not undertake investigations such as speaking to the rate submitters. The compliance function also did not draft any policies to manage such conflicts of interest and failed to relay any relevant concern to the regulator even when in conversation with the regulator. However, the FSA took enforcement action principally against the corporation, and censured the head of compliance Stephen Morse.

The censure of Morse could be regarded principally as imposing a form of secondary liability for failing to institute adequate systems and controls even after red flags had been raised by others in senior positions in the corporation. It is queried as to why secondary liability was not made more pronounced in this case as compliance has been put in a position to comment or even mitigate the breaches but has not done so. Further, the facts of the case could have entailed considerations in relation to personal liability, as the failure to follow up and take proactive steps seemed to be treated as personal failures in the case of Dr Joseph mentioned above. This case brings to fore the concern that regulatory expectations embodied in the 'care, skill and diligence' requirement are ambivalent in terms of the content of responsibilities and the nature of liability. Further, concern may also be raised as to whether liability may more easily attach to internal control personnel at smaller firms without a clearly articulated basis and perhaps to an unfair extent. The Upper Tribunal decision in *Arch Cru*[21] seems to confirm that liability may attach to individuals more easily in smaller firms where responsibilities are clearly defined. However, one needs to consider on what basis that should be the case.

This chapter is of the view that it is important to address the unsatisfactory and ambiguous nature of liability attached to the 'care, skill and diligence' requirement. If this requirement relates to primary liability, the regulatory–professional disjunctions have to be addressed, as discussed

[20] Principles 2, 3 and 5, FSA Handbook (up to 1 April 2013), PRIN module. These Principles have succeeded to the PRA and FCA Handbooks, PRIN modules. See Final Notice against Barclays Bank Plc (27 June 2012).

[21] *Arch Financial Products LLP & Ors v The Financial Conduct Authority* [2015] UKUT 13 (TCC) (19 January 2015).

above, to ensure that liability regimes are fairly based on realistic regulatory expectations and clear professional understanding. Primary liability also carries a causal connotation that such individual personal failures have contributed to the primary failure of the firm, and could in some cases attract firm action against the individual. If the 'care, skill and diligence' requirement relates to secondary liability, then the individuals subject to enforcement are more narrowly regarded as responsible for a form of oversight failure; in which case the oversight responsibilities need to be more clearly articulated. Secondary liability would however entail less personal probity as the organisational context and limitations would have to be considered, and would also unlikely be regarded as having causal connotations with the firm's primary breach. The lack of clarity in the nature of liability serves to obfuscate regulatory expectations of internal control functions and would ultimately undermine internal control efficacy.

Compliance Officer Liability Based on Other Grounds in APER

Enforcement Against Robert Stephan Addison (14 September 2012)

The decision against Addison, which was referred to the Upper Tribunal, is interesting as unlike enforcement under the 'care, skill and diligence' requirement, Addison was impeached for breaches of Principles 1 and 7 of APER, the former relating to personal integrity and the latter relating to oversight and monitoring responsibility, in the vein of secondary liability. The discussion here will argue that these two conduct rules are much clearer in their orientation and the clarity also helps to frame regulatory expectations in a more realistic manner. This chapter will argue that such clarity is needed in respect of all conduct rules, in particular with respect to the 'care, skill and diligence' requirement above. This chapter also thinks it is possible to frame 'care, skill and diligence' in respect of both primary and secondary liability, but that each should be clearly articulated and the expectations pertaining to each more clearly defined.

Principle 1, the equivalent which in the Conduct Rules is Rule 1, refers to personal integrity. Principle 7 refers to the responsibility to ensure that the business the individual is overseeing is compliant with regulatory requirements. This is now re-enacted as a senior management rule and more clearly relates to oversight, a form of secondary liability.

Addison was partner, compliance officer and held a controlled function for customer-facing duties in Arch Financial LLP, an investment management firm that manages two UK funds and 22 Guernsey-based companies in which the two UK funds invest. The FSA found that during Addison's tenure as compliance officer, he had specific senior management responsibility (along with the Chief Executive Officer, Farrell) for management of conflicts of interests. Four transactions took place which gave rise to obvious conflicts of interest allowing Arch Financial LLP and its related entities to make gains at the expense of the Guernsey cells, which would have been detrimental to the interests of investors in the Guernsey cells.

Arch Financial LLP caused the Guernsey cells to purchase shares from Farrell in Arch's parent company, Arch Group (UK) Limited at a price determined by Farrell with no independent verification of the price and inadequate contemporaneous recording of the conflict of interest. In another transaction, Arch caused the Guernsey cells to invest £20.2 million into a company which paid Arch and a business associate a fee of £3 million each for undefined services. Arch also caused the Guernsey cells to invest in Cru Investment Management Ltd, the distributor of the UK funds managed by Arch, which was a major business partner of Arch. Finally, Arch caused the Guernsey cells to invest in a company associated with Farrell, which investment disproportionately benefited the company, and consequently Farrell, as compared with the Guernsey cells. Addison failed to subject the above transactions to scrutiny for management of conflicts of interest, and failed to adequately record and report on them to investors in the Guernsey cells. Addison did not put in place systems and procedures for robust monitoring of conflicts of interest and adequate reporting and escalation. The FSA therefore proceeded to ban Addison from performing any controlled function in the financial services industry and to impose a fine of £200,000. Addison referred the matter to the Upper Tribunal.

First, Addison was impeached for acting without integrity. This Principle is likely to be interpreted as one giving rise to personal and not secondary liability as APER 4.1 which fleshes out Principle 1 characterises the Principle by referring to examples of impropriety or dishonesty. Such conduct requires deliberate, knowing or reckless states of mind in perpetuating the conduct,[22] and hence is more appropriate to be attributed to individual personal responsibility. The FSA alleged that Addison had acted recklessly in failing to manage the conflicts of interest issues in the four transactions above. 'Recklessness'[23] is defined as the taking of an unacceptable risk, being aware of the risk or circumstances that entail awareness of certain risks. The awareness of risk is a subjective test, while the acceptability of the risk is based on an objective test of what a reasonable person would regard as an unacceptable risk. The Upper Tribunal held that Addison had been reckless as the transactions posed real and severe conflicts of interest and he did not put in place adequate systems to

[22] The definition of integrity would encompass a few states of conduct and is not limited to dishonesty. See *First Financial Advisors Limited v FSA* [2012] 5 UKUT B16 (TCC).

[23] *Vukelic v FSA* (2009) [2009] UKFSM FSM067; *Amir Khan v The Financial Conduct Authority* FS 2013/002 (January 2014); *Arch Financial Products LLP & Ors v The Financial Conduct Authority* (n 21).

manage them as the business grew and took on novel risks. This Principle is clearly one that imports personal liability where a judgement is made to subject investors to unreasonable levels of risk.

Next, Principle 7 as elaborated upon in APER 4.7 refers to the obligation to put in place adequate systems, policies and control procedures to monitor and prevent non-compliance, and to regularly review and evaluate the efficacy of such systems, policies and procedures. Principle 7 also obliges the relevant approved person to carry out investigations where necessary if significant breaches are suspected. On the one hand, Principle 7 could be viewed as a form of personal responsibility, obliging Addison to put in place adequate systems and controls, and so the lack of such systems and controls is therefore attributed to Addison's personal failure to discharge this responsibility. However, it is rarely the case that firm-wide systems and control could be the individual responsibility of a particular officer, as the institution of firm-wide systems is generally the premise of senior management. Hence, where there is a lack of adequate systems and controls, it would seem that internal control personnel such as Addison in the compliance position should have played a part in influencing the due institution of such systems and controls. The failure to influence and play one's part should be regarded as a form of secondary liability to the firm's primary liability for failure to establish such systems and controls. Even though Addison was also part of senior management, he was only part of a team of which the Chief Executive Officer (CEO) was Farrell. Principle 7 is now exclusively applied to senior managers, and lower level internal control staff would not be affected.

The Upper Tribunal[24] seemed to take the approach of imposing secondary liability upon Addison. The Tribunal first asked the question whether the firm failed to put in adequate systems and procedures to manage conflicts of interest appropriately and concluded that the firm had not. On that basis, responsible persons such as the CEO Farrell and Addision, who was in charge of the compliance function, were held to be also liable. This approach does not look into the personal culpability of the individual as much as was carried out for determining Addison's breach of the integrity principle.

However, it is queried whether secondary liability only attaches to senior manager conduct rules now that these rules deal explicitly with oversight and monitoring responsibilities. If so, is it appropriate that lower level conduct rules are framed only in terms of personal liability? The cases in relation to 'care, skill and diligence' have shown that there may be difficulties in delineating personal responsibility where teams of personnel are involved or where responsibilities may be assumed by an array of

[24] *Arch Financial Products LLP & Ors v The Financial Conduct Authority* (n 21).

intra-firm arrangements. It is submitted that the regulator needs to carefully consider the nature of liability intended to be imposed on internal control personnel and articulate regulatory expectations accordingly and consistently with the nature of such liability.

In light of the Upper Tribunal's clarifications, it is submitted that it is imperative to establish clear regulatory expectations by defining the nature of liability attached to each conduct rule. Personal liability and secondary liability regimes give rise to different implications for internal control behaviour and it is important to articulate clearly the nature of liability in order to frame the relevant regulatory expectations for clearer understanding on the part of internal control personnel. The next section will discuss the nature of personal liability imposed on internal control personnel and the implications for internal control efficacy. Section D will discuss the nature of secondary liability and the relevant implications.

C. IMPOSING PERSONAL LIABILITY ON INTERNAL CONTROL PERSONNEL

It could be argued that the imposition of personal liability on internal control personnel could create incentives for internal control personnel to take personal ownership of the firm's need to secure compliance with regulatory requirements and objectives. However, the counter-argument would be that it is disproportionate to impose a sense of ownership for firm responsibility on internal control personnel at a personal level. Firm compliance should be the responsibility of all relevant chains of command from senior management to front line office personnel. Any responsibility on the part of internal control personnel for securing firm compliance should be secondary and not primary in nature. It is also arguable that personal liability should be based only on personal probity, and personal probity should be measured to some extent against professional standards. Hence, this chapter supports the framing of personal liability regimes only with respect to personal probity and where clear failures of professional standards are observed. Hence, personal liability regimes in regulation should be designed carefully with the input of professional perspectives. As professional standards are still emerging for internal control professions, professional input into the regulatory design process may be relatively weak. This book supports enhanced professionalism in internal control professions and submits that the emerging nature of these professions should not be neglected in the framing of appropriate regulatory expectations.

In the Individual Conduct Rules, Rule 1 which deals with the integrity of approved persons is arguably the only clear principle that deals with personal responsibility. This is an arguably proportionate approach to personal responsibility as individual impropriety and probity could be subject to personal liability.[25] The Upper Tribunal's articulation of what is expected for 'integrity' seems to confirm the approach that this Rule refers to an individual's 'reckless' conduct and decision.[26]

It is arguable whether the rest of the Conduct Rules are in the vein of primary or secondary liability. The ambiguities need to be addressed. As far as Rule 2 on care, skill and diligence is concerned, the above discussions on FSA enforcement cases have fleshed out different implications where liability is framed as personal and where liability is treated as secondary. These implications directly affect the nature and scope of regulatory expectations in relation to the conduct rule. The chapter envisages that it is possible for Rule 2 to attract both personal and secondary liability under different conditions, but such should be clearly articulated. In terms of framing Rule 2 as attracting personal liability, much more work needs to be done to bridge the regulatory–professional disjunctions in terms of what may fairly be expected of due care, skill and diligence in internal control functions. Where Rule 2 attracts secondary liability, the regulator should consider adopting a similar regime such as administered by the US SEC in relation to the explicit duty to monitor imposed on internal control functions.

Further, the PRA and FCA could consider developing a more specific and proportionate Code of Conduct for internal control personnel that maintains consistency between personal liability regimes and professional standards. These will be further discussed in chapter eight in relation to enhanced professionalism for internal control professions. It is argued that the Conduct Rules as they now stand only reveal unsatisfactory regulatory–professional disjunctions and their application risk imposing disproportionate and unfair ex post liability on internal control personnel.

If personal liability is imposed with regard to matters which are more proportionately characterised as secondary responsibility, such personal liability may be regarded as unfair and illegitimate. Where there is insufficient development in professional standards of care, personal liability may only be justified if such liability is imposed for the purposes of punishing individual wrongdoing. Vast extensions of personal liability into the sphere of what is really secondary liability may be perceived as unfair impositions of strict regulatory liability on individuals for breaches that could be attributable to a collectivity of more persons in the firm. Internal control personnel subject to such liability may be scape-goated and this raises the potential of moral hazard for front line functions. Unfair or

[25] E Norman Veasey and Christine T Di Guglielmo, 'General Counsel Buffeted by Compliance Demands and Client Pressures May Face Personal Peril' (2012) 68 *Business Lawyer* 57 discussing the primary and secondary responsibilities of in-house counsel.

[26] *Arch Financial Products LLP & Ors v The Financial Conduct Authority* (n 21).

disproportionate reputation loss for internal control personnel may ensue. Further, the imposition of personal liability may result in challenges for future recruitment of choice and competent personnel into positions subject to such risk of personal liability.[27] On the other hand, secondary liability is more clearly related to duties to monitor, or supervise, or audit and can be more legitimately perceived to incentivise behaviour consistent with deterrence. Individuals in such positions may be more willing to accept and manage the risks in relation to such functions, and correspondingly be more willing to accept strict liability type enforcements for failings,[28] recognising themselves as part of the matrix of responsibility, including the firm and usually senior management. However, it is still imperative to design secondary liability regimes that are clear, fair, proportionate and efficacious, bearing in mind the organisational environment in which internal control is operating, so as not to undermine the efficacy of internal control functions.

Conduct in relation to Rules 3, 4 and 5 on being cooperative with regulators, treating customers fairly, and observing proper standards of market conduct is to a certain extent shaped by the firm's internal systems and procedures in relation to customer relations, market interactions and communications with regulatory authorities. There could be personal elements in individual conduct and decision-making in a retail client-facing situation, or a communication made to the market or to regulators, but it is likely that individual conduct and behaviour is enmeshed within organisational systems and processes. This chapter argues that these rules should be framed within the understanding of secondary liability, so that each internal control officer is incentivised to take part in robust monitoring and oversight of due processes to achieve the expectations in those rules. The failure to achieve those expectations should not be framed as related to individual personal responsibility as it is almost impossible to delineate the extent of individual responsibility within intra-firm arrangements. The treatment as secondary liability is important in disassociating causal connotations with the firm's primary breach. This is important as personal liability has an unnecessarily demotivating impact and should be proportionately used. Only where the failure to treat a client fairly, act in accordance with proper standards of market conduct or cooperate with regulators is due to personal probity such as dishonesty, deliberate concealment or recklessness should personal liability then be attracted under

[27] Analogical reference can be made to Michelle M Mello and Carly N Kelly, 'Effects of a Professional Liability Crisis on Residents' Practice Decisions' (2005) 105 *Obstetrics & Gynecology* 1287.

[28] Tsachi Keren-Paz, 'Liability Regimes, Reputation Loss and Defensive Medicine' (2010) at papers.ssrn.com/sol3/papers.cfm?abstract_id=1639429 on the effect of strict liability as being more acceptable in a context of pooled liability applying to all the relevant professionals across the board.

Rule 1. The clarification of Rules 3, 4 and 5 as rules attracting secondary liability may more clearly serve their deterrence purposes in incentivising robust and proactive internal control functions.

In sum, this chapter supports the overt re-characterisation of the responsibilities under Conduct Rules for internal control personnel as secondary responsibilities, leaving the imposition of personal liability only in the clear cases of individual probity, misconduct and failings in professionalism that are clearly developed as part of the dialogue between the internal control professions and regulatory expectations. In the alternative, more specific codes of conduct could be drawn up for internal control personnel clearly identifying personal and secondary liability regimes and having an informed consistency with professional standards. The next section will discuss the implications of characterising liability for internal control personnel as secondary liability, and suggest reforms to clarify and enhance the deterrence role of internal control functions.

D. SECONDARY LIABILITY REGIMES FOR INTERNAL CONTROL FUNCTIONS

Internal control personnel are well placed to monitor, detect and prevent irregularities and hence imposing secondary liability on them for failing to adequately monitor or mitigate risk and compliance issues is not arguably disproportionate. Such secondary liability regimes should not be framed in terms of the complicity of internal control in the primary wrongdoing by the firm. There may be many shades of complicity involved in conduct, such as assisting, abetting or shutting one's eyes in the face of suspected failure or wrongdoing. Franco argues that indicting on the basis of such shades of complicity is not ideal as it is difficult to interpret behavioural complexities.[29] Thus, this chapter is of the view that secondary liability should be framed in relation to positive duties to monitor, supervise or establish systems of control,[30] so that there is greater clarity as to the expectations placed on the gatekeeper role of internal control personnel to secure firm compliance with regulatory objectives. Such positive framing encourages internal control functions to embrace their deterrence purposes.

The objective of imposing secondary liability on internal control personnel is to secure greater deterrence against the primary violations that the firm may commit.[31] There is much literature discussing the deterrence role

[29] Joseph A Franco, 'Of Complicity and Compliance: A Rules-Based Anti-Complicity Strategy under Federal Securities Law' (2011) 14 *University of Pennsylvania Journal of Business Law* 1.

[30] ibid.

[31] Hamdani, 'Gatekeeper Liability' (n 13).

of external gatekeepers such as auditors and lawyers which supports the imposition of secondary liability in the form of gatekeeper liability. Such gatekeeper liability could serve the purpose of making up for any shortfall in compensation in civil enforcement actions taken against the primary wrongdoer, the firm, or against managers attributed with responsibility for the primary wrongdoing committed by the firm.[32] Or such gatekeeper liability could be imposed as a form of regulatory enforcement in order to impress upon gatekeepers the public interest nature of their role[33] and to induce behavioural change on the part of gatekeepers to more robustly monitor and influence the conduct of the firm.[34] The analogy can be drawn between external gatekeeper liability enforced by regulators and regulatory enforcement against internal control personnel for failures to monitor or prevent wrongdoing. However, it remains imperative to design such secondary/gatekeeper liability for internal control personnel in such a way that is (a) fair, taking into account their capacity and power to monitor; and (b) sufficiently clear, in terms of the parameters of responsibility in monitoring or supervising so that optimal deterrence can be achieved.

Secondary liability imposed on internal control personnel would only be fair if internal control personnel are in a position to influence the conduct of the firm. The capacity for influence depends in large part on the organisational power and positioning of internal control functions. Chapters two to four have provided detailed analyses of regulatory reforms to enhance the power, organisational positioning and capacity of internal control personnel, such as the institution of sufficient seniority in internal control functions, such as in the case of the Chief Risk Officer or risk committee of the Board, and the mandatory requirements to make internal control functions independent, well resourced and sufficiently powerful. These are intended to rectify the excessively open-ended meta-regulatory framework for internal control personnel that existed before the post-crisis reforms, and which have only been weakly implemented in many firms. However, earlier chapters have also pointed out the continuing challenges for internal control functions in terms of the wider framework in corporate governance and organisational culture which are only beginning to change in response to regulatory reforms. Hence, it may be imperative that regulators continue to study the impact of organisational factors upon the efficacy of internal control functions in order to design

[32] Reinier H Kraakman, 'Corporate Liability Strategies and the Costs of Legal Controls' (1984) 93 *Yale Law Journal* 857; Wan, 'Gatekeeper Liability' (n 13).

[33] Noel Wise, 'Personal Liability Promotes Responsible Conduct: Extending the Responsible Corporate Officer Doctrine to Federal Civil Environmental Enforcement Cases' (2002) 21 *Stanford Environmental Law Journal* 283.

[34] Priya Cherian Huskins, 'FCPA Prosecutions: Liability Trend to Watch' (2008) 60 *Stanford Law Review* 1447.

optimal and proportionate secondary liability regimes for deterrence purposes.

Further, this chapter suggests that the conduct expected of internal control functions that would attract secondary liability be expressly and positively framed as duties to monitor or oversee. These should also be developed with input from professional perspectives such as, for example, the professional body for internal auditors which has established generally well-accepted standards of monitoring behaviour for internal audit; and such should feed into regulatory articulations and expectations in order to secure a consistent professional consciousness of expected conduct and behaviour.

However, it may be argued that clarifying the duties of internal control functions may become under-inclusive. Further, clarifications may be used for defensive interpretations of the responsibilities of internal control functions in order to evade liability.[35] One way of achieving this is by excessive proceduralisation to achieve disclaiming effects,[36] but Parker et al's empirical research shows that the institution of procedures could nevertheless be useful in actual mitigation of control failures.[37] Further, internal control functions may also engage in excessive training so that their monitoring responsibility may be largely discharged through educating within the firm. It has nevertheless been commented that ex ante measures such as training could be practically efficacious in securing compliance with regulatory objectives.[38]

Finally, it may be suggested that imposing secondary liability on internal control personnel to secure greater deterrence would create fear and anxiety, and may cause internal control personnel to behave in an adversarial, defensive and opaque manner within the organisation,[39] leading to greater distance between internal control functions and the rest of the organisation. Cunningham suggests, in relation to enhancing external gatekeepers' deterrence capacity (which is discussed here by analogical reasoning), that the gatekeeper deterrence role should be enhanced not by a stick or liability approach, but by a carrot or reward approach.[40]

[35] Veasey and Di Guglielmo, 'General Counsel Buffeted by Compliance Demands' (n 25); Lee Roach, 'Auditor Liability; The Case for Limitation Part I' (2010) 31 *Company Lawyer* 136 discussing external auditor liability, extending to the situation of internal control as gatekeepers by analogical reasoning.

[36] Kimberly D Krawiec, 'Cosmetic Compliance and the Failure of Negotiated Governance' (2003) 81 *Washington University Law Quarterly* 487.

[37] Christine Parker and Vibeke Lehmann Nielsen, 'Corporate Compliance Systems: Could They Make Any Difference?' (2009) 41 *Administration & Society* 3.

[38] Anthony Pirraglia, 'Tangled Web: Compliance Director Liability under the Securities Laws' (2003) 8 *Fordham Journal of Corporate & Financial Law* 245.

[39] Miriam Hechler Baer, 'Governing Corporate Compliance' (2009) 50 *Boston College Law Review* 949.

[40] Lawrence A Cunningham, 'Beyond Liability; Rewarding Effective Gatekeepers' (2007) 92 *Minnesota Law Review* 323.

Cunningham points out that liability-based regimes create incentives to engage in negative behaviour such as undertaking excessive precaution and monitoring, and often such liability regimes are over-inclusive.[41] Liability regimes may also have little effect upon the behaviour of internal control functions if behavioural biases such as backward recursion or the time delay trap occur. Internal control personnel could succumb to the immediate gratification of being aligned with management influence or the pressure of organisational culture.[42] Cunningham therefore suggests that instead of imposing secondary liability, effective gatekeepers should be rewarded with carrots such as awards and public recognition in order to induce greater sensitivity to professional reputation and pride. In terms of application to internal control functions, positive incentives could include recognised organisational status, sponsored professional training and enhancement, and carrots in relation to the enhancement of an individual's career profile.

This chapter supports the carrot-based suggestions earlier outlined and agrees that negative behavioural responses to the deterrence regime need to be mitigated. This chapter does not however think an overhaul of secondary liability regimes is necessary as there is a point in instituting deterrence regimes that support the efficacy of gatekeeper functions, as discussed above. The only issues are that such regimes should be based on clearer articulations of responsibilities and duties and should be proportionately enforced paying careful consideration to the organisational contexts in which internal control functions are working.

Next, the chapter discusses whether the proximity of internal control functions to sensitive information in the firm could be used to promote internal control responsibilities for overseeing whistle-blowing or indeed engage in constructive whistle-blowing. This chapter will compare the whistle-blowing framework in the UK with the framework applicable to the US in respect of the use of financial incentives to encourage whistle-blowing in the financial sector under the Dodd–Frank Act 2012.

E. INTERNAL CONTROL FUNCTIONS AND THE WHISTLE-BLOWING REGIME

Regulatory supervision of financial sector firms could be enhanced by a flow of information and knowledge from inside the firm. However, for reasons of confidentiality, although internal control personnel are situated

[41] ibid.

[42] Donald C Langevoort, 'Chasing the Greased Pig Down Wall Street: A Gatekeeper's Guide to the Psychology, Culture and Ethics of Financial Risk-taking' (2011) 96 *Cornell Law Review* 1209.

in positions which allow them to become aware of information that could put firms in a precarious position vis a vis regulators, regulatory prescriptions have rightly not gone so far as to demand direct accountability from internal control functions. Such direct accountability would put internal control personnel in a difficult position as they would neither be overtly appointed in public interest nor be regarded as part of the organisational fabric. Regulators have therefore sought to encourage internal detection and gatekeeping by instituting whistle-blower regimes that apply generally to employees not confined to internal control functions. Hence, internal control functions could be protected by robust whistle-blowing policies and structures in firms, and they could also be part of the whistle-blowing systems and structures in firms. The involvement of internal control functions in whistle-blowing systems and structures may contribute to their monitoring and oversight efficacy.

Whistle-blowing does not necessarily mean disclosure to regulators or to external persons such as legal advisers. Much whistle-blowing is internal in nature, escalated to higher levels of senior management so that the organisation has a first opportunity to put things right. The UK has instituted a whistle-blower protection regime since 1998 in order to encourage legitimate whistle-blowing in the public and corporate sectors.[43] In the wake of the global financial crisis, the US has however enhanced its whistle-blower regime to encourage more whistle-blowing directly to regulators,[44] a controversial regime that the UK has hesitated to follow.[45] This section will outline the comparison in discussing how whistle-blowing regimes may support internal control efficacy.

The UK whistle-blowing regime is not based on incentivising such behaviour, but rather on ex post protection of a person if a legitimate disclosure has been made. The person seeking protection has to be a 'worker' defined in legislation, and the protected disclosure is confined to information that:

a. a criminal offence has been committed, is being committed or is likely to be committed;
b. a person has failed, is failing or is likely to fail to comply with any legal obligation to which he is subject;
c. a miscarriage of justice has occurred, is occurring or is likely to occur;
d. the health or safety of any individual has been, is being or is likely to be endangered;

43 Public Interest Disclosure Act 1998.

44 s 922, Wall Street Reform and Consumer Protection Act 2010 (Dodd–Frank Act) (Pub.L. 111–203, HR 4173) at www.sec.gov/about/offices/owb/dodd-frank-sec-922.pdf.

45 BIS, *The Whistleblowing Framework: Call for Evidence* (July 2013).

e. the environment has been, is being or is likely to be damaged;
f. information tending to show any matter falling within any one of the preceding paragraphs has been, is being or is likely to be deliberately concealed.[46]

The whistle-blower may report internally to higher levels of the employer or externally to certain prescribed persons, and the Act intends to confer protection on such a person against suffering detriment for having made such a report.[47] A protected person who has suffered detriment may bring a complaint to the Employment Tribunal.[48] This regime has not prevented a high-profile whistle-blower from being treated detrimentally at the Halifax Bank of Scotland (HBOS) in 2004,[49] and who has since been vindicated in his views when HBOS almost collapsed in the global financial crisis in 2008. The UK whistle-blowing regime has however not undergone much reform since. In 2013, the Enterprise and Regulatory Reform Act extended the definition of 'worker'[50] for the purposes of protected disclosures but the scope of protected disclosures remained the same. Further, whistle-blowers have to reasonably believe in the public interest[51] in carrying out whistle-blowing. This measure seems intended at ensuring that any protection offered to whistle-blowers is based on socially acceptable justifications rather than more liberally incentivising such behaviour. The Department for Business, Innovation & Skills is continuing to consult upon the design of a regime with a wider scope of protection.[52] This chapter is of the view that protection regimes do not actively incentivise whistle-blowing. Whistle-blowing is left to take place as a self-disciplining or correction phenomenon against corporate entities that arises out of voluntary initiatives.[53] Inadequate protection of whistle-blowers is arguably a form of market failure and thus, the nature of a protection regime is a response to correct the market failure.

[46] s 43B, Public Interest Disclosure Act 1998 amending the Employment Rights Act 1996.

[47] ibid, s 47B.

[48] ibid, s 48(1A).

[49] 'Whistle-blowing almost Killed Me' *Financial Times* (5 June 2013).

[50] s 20, Enterprise and Regulatory Reform Act 2013 amending s 43K of the Employment Rights Act 1996.

[51] ibid, s 17, amending section 43B of the Employment Rights Act 1996.

[52] BIS, *The Whistleblowing Framework* (n 45).

[53] Much research point out that whistle-blowers are largely encouraged by the firm's culture and policies that encourage whistle-blowing to report upwards. A supportive environment in the firm itself is key. See Pailin Trongmateerut and John T Sweeney, 'The Influence of Subjective Norms on Whistle-Blowing: A Cross-Cultural Investigation' (2013) 112 *Journal of Business Ethics* 437; Jessica R Mesmer-Magnus and Chockalingam Viswesvaran, 'Whistleblowing in Organizations: An Examination of Correlates of Whistleblowing Intentions, Actions, and Retaliation' (2005) 62 *Journal of Business Ethics* 277; Joan E Sieber, 'The Psychology of Whistleblowing' (1998) 4 *Science and Engineering Ethics* 7; Julia Zhang, Randy Chiu and Li-Qun Wei, 'On Whistleblowing Judgment and Intention: The Roles of Positive Mood and Organizational Ethical Culture' (2009) 24 *Journal of Managerial Psychology* 627. However, individual characteristics do also matter such as tenure and seniority that affect

There is however recognition that whistle-blowing regimes can form an important part of the risk and control cultures at firms, and hence, European initiatives suggest that whistle-blowing should form part of the internal control framework.[54] No further details are provided, but this suggests that internal control functions should be involved in administering whistle-blowing systems and structures in order to ensure greater protection for whistle-blowers (perhaps due to their independence) and to gain access to information revealed by whistle-blowers. The protection regimes for whistle-blowers would remain the same as under general law as discussed above.

There are proposals however to treat whistle-blowers in the financial sector differently. The Parliamentary Commission on Banking Standards proposes that internal whistle-blowers and informers should be encouraged and offered a greater degree of protection[55] in order to overcome the unhealthy 'fear' culture that persists in the financial sector as discussed in chapter five. The Parliamentary Commission on Banking Standards recommends that internal whistle-blowing systems should be improved so that employees may not be put in fear of making known their concerns regarding disconcerting practices. Systems and mechanisms must be put in place to ensure that employees feel confident that they would be heard.[56] Proper records should be kept of whistle-blowing incidents, and such records may be made available to regulators for purposes of intelligence to aid in their supervisory processes.[57] The Parliamentary Commission also suggests that regulators should scrutinise firms' internal whistle-blowing systems as part of their evaluation of firm culture.[58]

an individual's perception of job security: see Gregory A Liyanarachchi and Ralph Adler, 'Accountants' Whistle-Blowing Intentions: The Impact of Retaliation, Age, and Gender' (2011) 57 *Australian Accounting Review* 167; for individual ethical orientations and perceptions of severity of issue at hand, see Randy K Chiu, 'Ethical Judgment and Whistleblowing Intention: Examining the Moderating Role of Locus of Control' (2003) 43 *Journal of Business Ethics* 65; Randi L Sims and John P Keenan, 'Predictors of External Whistleblowing: Organizational and Intrapersonal Variables' (1998) 17 *Journal of Business Ethics* 411; for individual personality traits such as extraversion, proactivity and low agreeableness, see Brita Bjørkelo, Ståle Einarsen and Stig Berge Matthiesen, 'Predicting Proactive Behaviour At Work: Exploring the Role of Personality as an Antecedent of Whistleblowing Behaviour" (2010) 83 *Journal of Occupational and Organizational Psychology* 371.

[54] European Banking Authority, *EBA Guidelines on Internal Governance* (November 2011) at www.eba.europa.eu/News--Communications/Year/2011/The-EBA-has-published-today-its-Guidelines-on-Inte.aspx, para 17.2.

[55] To this end the government is generally consulting on legal protection for whistle-blowers in general and not limiting it to the financial sector: see Department of Business, Innovation and Skills (BIS), *Whistleblowing Framework: Call for Evidence* (12 July 2013) at www.gov.uk/government/consultations/whistleblowing-framework-call-for-evidence.

[56] House of Lords and House of Commons, Parliamentary Commission on Banking Standards, *Changing Banking for Good* Vol II (HL 27-II, HC 175-II) chapter 6 generally, para 786.

[57] ibid, paras 792–96.

[58] ibid, para 797.

Further, in order to ensure that firms take seriously the obligation to put in place appropriate systems for internal whistle-blowing, the Parliamentary Commission recommends that a senior person be made responsible for overseeing such systems, preferably the Chairman. The relevant senior person or Chairman should also have personal responsibility for ensuring that the whistle-blower is protected so that the whistle-blower does not experience retaliation.[59] It remains uncertain whether the regulator will enact rules to institutionalise whistle-blowing in banks and financial institutions and offer a heightened degree of protection to whistle-blowers than under general law. Law reform in this area continues to proceed as a general matter of employment law led by the Department for of Business, Innovation & Skills.[60] Policymakers are looking into better protection for whistle-blowers, but whistle-blowers are at the same time to be subject to higher standards to justify such protection. The thresholds of public interest and good faith are to apply to whistle-blower protection.

In this light, the US whistle-blowing regime for the financial sector may provide an interesting comparison with the UK regime. The US regime for the protection of corporate whistle-blowers features an anti-retaliation regime, but it has been commented that the administration of the regime is sub-optimal as the procedural hurdles for claimants who wish to challenge retaliation after whistle-blowing are tremendous.[61] The US Dodd–Frank Act 2010 now provides for positive incentives for whistle-blowers to report directly to regulators such as the US SEC with original information about a violation of the securities laws. Such whistle-blowers are then entitled to share in part of the penalties recovered by the regulator in the proportion of 10 to 30 per cent in a successful enforcement action against the firm concerned, if monetary sanctions exceeding $1 million are recovered. Commentators acknowledge that bounties could incentivise intelligence provision to regulators.[62] Further, bounties could also act as a form of protection for financial sector whistle-blowers who may find themselves at a disadvantage in seeking future employment in the sector. However, in this process new dimensions of direct regulatory relationships with firm 'insiders' are forged for the purposes of supporting regulatory governance. Concerns can be raised with regard to the dual nature of loyalties on the part of potential whistle-blowers. Further, it can be questioned if selfish motivations on the part of whistle-blowers would adversely affect the quantity and quality of intelligence received.

[59] ibid, paras 787, 791.

[60] BIS, *The Whistleblowing Framework* (n 45).

[61] Richard Moberly, 'Sarbanes–Oxley's Whistleblower Provisions: Ten Years Later' (2012) 64 *Southern California Law Review* 1.

[62] ibid; and Geoffrey Christopher Rapp, 'Mutiny by the Bounties? The Attempt to Reform Wall Street by the New Whistleblower Provisions of the Dodd–Frank Act' (2012) *Brigham Young University Law Review* 73.

New dimensions of direct regulatory relationships with insiders could also have uncertain consequences for the organisational fabric of firms.

Some commentators have argued that financial motivations would incentivise a flood of non-consequential and low quality tips from whistle-blowers that are not particularly important from a public interest point of view for enforcement.[63] For example, large-scale issues such as the JP Morgan whale loss[64] was not uncovered by whistle-blowing. Individuals with an axe to grind, or who could be persuaded to behave in an individualistic manner, are more likely to be persuaded to take advantage of financial bounties. Nevertheless, when one considers the empirical research on what motivates individuals to whistle-blow, it would seem that selfish or self-concerned financial motivations are particularly irrelevant. Empirical research seems to support findings regarding the communitarian or ethical motivations for whistle-blowers. These motivations are largely flanked by perceptions of organisational or cultural support, and individual personality traits that tend towards being vocal. It may be argued that since whistle-blowing is motivated by communitarian and ethical concerns in the majority of empirical studies, encouraging whistle-blowing using financial incentives could corrupt the natural incentives to whistle-blow and should be discouraged. But the contrary may also be argued: that if whistle-blowing motivations are not affected by selfish desires anyway, then financial bounties only act as ex post protections for whistleblowers. Nevertheless, it remains to be seen if financial incentives provide new motivations for persons who otherwise would not whistle-blow. Further, if financial incentives result in increased incidents of whistle-blowing, then it needs to be considered if an adverse impact may be caused to the organisational fabric of firms. Increased internal adversarialism and defensiveness in firms would not be desirable as such would impede the institution of a robust firm-wide risk and control culture and may pose challenges for internal control functions. If fear of whistleblowers results in impediments to internal information flows and the fostering of an open and auditable environment for internal control, then incentivising direct whistle-blowing to regulators for reward may be counterproductive to the regulatory objective of making internal control effective. Focusing excessively on individual whistleblowers may encourage maverick behaviour rather than organisational

[63] See Dave Ebersole, 'Blowing the Whistle on the Dodd–Frank Whistleblower Provisions' (2010–11) 6 *Ohio State Entrepreneurial Business Law Journal* 123; John Ashcroft, Catherine Hanaway and Claudia L Oñate Greim, 'Whistleblowers Cash in, Unwary Corporations Pay' (2011) 40 *Hofstra Law Review* 367.

[64] United States Senate Permanent Subcommittee on Investigations, *JP Morgan Chase Whale Trades: A Case History of Derivatives Risks and Abuses: Majority and Minority Staff Report* (2012) at www.hsgac.senate.gov/subcommittees/investigations/hearings/chase-whale-trades-a-case-history-of-derivatives-risks-and-abuses.

reform and impetus towards instituting a changed culture and environment for internal control.[65]

This chapter is sceptical of regulatory efforts to deliberately stoke whistle-blowing, and of direct relations between whistle-blowers and regulators. Nevertheless, a case may be made for direct recourse to regulators as a last resort if whistle-blowers find themselves in abjectly unsupportive organisational cultures. This chapter sees the potential of a healthy whistle-blowing framework as being part of internal control systems and structures. Internal control functions can be made more efficacious by having access to such critical information, as such access is essential to the monitoring and oversight roles of internal control functions. Whistle-blowing systems and structures within firms can contribute to the overall institution of a sound risk and control culture in firms. Whistle-blowing systems and structures should also be underpinned by organisational reforms and it may perhaps be beneficial to spell these out in the organisational reforms already applicable to internal control functions. Further, it would be apt to consider the extent of specific senior manager responsibility for establishing an adequate and credible system for whistle-blowing in order to support the role of internal control functions in this regard. Internal control personnel would also need to be assured of adequate protection if they become whistle-blowers themselves. This is an area that seems ripe for further development and reform in the overall scheme of enhancing internal control efficacy at banks and financial institutions.

F. CONCLUSION

This chapter highlights two incentive-based approaches to enhancing the efficacy of internal control: via liability regimes and whistle-blowing systems. The chapter has presented a critical view of the current personal and secondary liability regimes for approved persons, applied to compliance officers in a number of cases. The chapter argues that personal liability cases have revealed disjunctions between regulatory expectations and professional perceptions of the scope of responsibilities which remain unresolved. Further secondary liability regimes are also not based on clearly articulated duties for internal control functions. This chapter suggests that reforms should be made to clearly articulate the conditions for personal liability, which this chapter has argued ought to be confined to personal probity and clearly developed professional standards with professional input. Secondary liability regimes should also be developed to clarify the scope of oversight and monitoring responsibilities for internal control functions and should be proportionately enforced such that

[65] Ashcroft, Hanaway and Oñate Greim, 'Whistleblowers Cash in' (n 63).

optimal deterrence is achieved without instilling counterproductive responses that impede internal control efficacy.

This chapter then provides an overview of the UK whistle-blowing framework that applies generally to all workers within the protection of employment law. This chapter is sceptical that the current regime is sufficient (a) to support whistle-blowers in the financial sector, or (b) to support the development of robust internal whistle-blowing systems to contribute to enhanced internal control efficacy. However, the chapter does not regard as a solution the position taken in the US that uses financial incentives to encourage more whistle-blowing directly to regulators. This chapter supports the reform proposals suggested by the Parliamentary Commission on Banking Standards and it remains to be seen if more reform will be undertaken in this area.

8

The Need for Enhanced Professionalism for Internal Control Functions

A. INTERNAL CONTROL FUNCTIONS AS 'GATEKEEPERS'

ENHANCED REGULATORY OBLIGATIONS for banks and financial institutions have been introduced since the global financial crisis of 2008–09. It has been opined that at least 50,000 new regulations have been introduced since 2008,

> [and these] represent a barely-scalable barrier to entry for new participants and a huge disincentive for all but the largest firms. Even the [too-big-to-fail] behemoths, ensconced in their fortress of paper, run an increasing risk of falling foul of regulations whose sheer volume impedes comprehension and implementation.[1]

Internal control functions at firms are at the forefront of securing firms' meeting of these new regulatory burdens. Regulators see internal control functions as well placed to gate-keep misconduct and excesses from the inside the firm, and have thus introduced regulatory reforms to empower internal control functions to act as internal 'gatekeepers' in order to secure firms' meeting of new regulatory requirements. Enhanced regulatory expectations are now placed on the roles and capacity of internal control functions.

This book has thus far discussed the regulatory emphasis on organisational reforms to boost internal control efficacy. Arguably, the pre-crisis weaknesses of internal control functions have to a certain extent been mitigated by regulatory reforms that seek to improve their organisational positioning, power, resources and profile. However, the earlier chapters, in critically evaluating the reforms in the organisational dimension, suggest that such reforms may not be sufficient to place internal control functions in a position to meet new and enhanced regulatory expectations of their 'gatekeeping' roles. Chapter seven in particular has exposed the crucial disjunction between regulatory expectations and the professional understanding on the part of internal control personnel as to their roles and responsibilities. This regulatory–professional disjunction has hitherto

[1] Nick Railton-Edwards of Derivatives Risk Solutions, commenting on a blog on 19 December 2014: see drsllp.com/blog.

not been addressed in post-crisis reforms. Such a disjunction is arguably exposed in a number of enforcement actions taken by the UK regulator against compliance officers for failing to exercise due care, skill and diligence as discussed in chapter seven. Chapter seven has argued as to how such a disjunction may undermine the efficacy of internal control and is counterproductive to achieving regulatory expectations. Such a disjunction may also be exploited by firms who could turn internal control functions into scapegoats for firm failures. This would result in internal control functions becoming less practically efficacious than envisaged and yet having to bear significant liabilities for the primary non-compliance of firms.

This chapter argues that the regulatory–professional disjunction needs to be mitigated or overcome in order to frame internal control responsibilities in a clearer and more achievable manner, and to put regulatory expectations on a firmer footing. This chapter argues that enhanced professionalism is needed in order to secure a better articulated framing of internal control functions' 'gatekeeping' roles and responsibilities and regulators have a part to play in securing such enhanced professionalism.

Coffee defines gatekeepers as 'some form of outside or independent watchdog or monitor—someone who screens out flaws or defects or verifies compliance with standards or procedures'.[2] Gatekeepers are often thought of as third parties external to the firm who are engaged for specific purposes, and hence the idea of extending the notion of gatekeeping to internal control functions that are hired by and occupy a position in the organisational structure of the firm may sound implausible. Laby[3] argues that even with external third-party gatekeepers, there are gatekeepers who are 'independent' and those who are 'dependent', and the quality of gatekeeping to be expected from the two groups would differ significantly with the 'dependent' ones being relatively ineffective. 'Independent' gatekeepers are defined as agents hired in order to check whether the principal/firm has violated a law or otherwise, and hence the role is performed overtly as a watchdog against the firm. Laby cites auditors and securities analysts as being poised to be 'independent' gatekeepers even if in reality some are compromised. 'Dependent' gatekeepers are agents hired to provide advice and recommendations to assist the client in meeting a goal, and hence they often owe fiduciary duties to the client and are put in a mindset of loyalty and cooperation with the client. Dependent gatekeepers are also often motivated by a continuing business relationship with the client. Examples of dependent gatekeepers would be external lawyers and securities underwriters. Laby doubts that dependent gatekeepers would make effective gatekeepers as their role, and the heuristics and biases that infuse their

[2] JohnC Coffee, *Gatekeepers* (Oxford: Oxford University Press, 2006) 2.

[3] Arthur B Laby, 'Differentiating Gatekeepers' (2006) 1 *Brooklyn Journal of Corporate, Financial & Commercial Law* 119.

facilitative roles, would make them unlikely to be able to act as effective watchdogs against their clients.[4] The watchdog stance could even arguably be contrary to fiduciary and contractual duties that are owed. Hence, a reduction in reliance on dependent gatekeepers is urged, although fashioning them as intelligence providers subject to overt regulatory duties could help in supplementing regulatory governance over firms.

Going on Laby's argument, characterising internal control functions in financial institutions as gatekeepers would be contrary to their 'dependent' nature being part of the firm and owing duties of loyalty in employment. Thus, even if regulatory reforms in the organisational context and structures of firms were to enhance the profile, responsibilities and resources of internal control functions, they may not be best placed to act as gatekeepers from the inside. Their 'inside' positions could inherently be counterintuitive to the notion of 'gate-keeping'.

However, as firms regard internal control functions as lines of defence, and such a perspective is increasingly emphasised and imposed by regulators,[5] internal control functions do have the potential to overcome the binary 'independent–dependent' classification in Laby's paradigm and assume a form of quasi-independent gatekeeping albeit in a dependent context. The regulatory reforms in the organisational dimension do contribute towards reducing the 'dependency' aspect of internal control functions, but this book suggests that the gatekeeping role of internal control functions needs to be sustained by an enhanced professionalism that maintains objectivity and independence in professional perspectives, flanked by clear regulatory expectations that both guide and protect internal control functions.

Enhanced professionalism may be related to an increased sense of autonomy due to a stronger professional identity[6] which reinforces respect for the competence of professionals. Commentators have observed that although employment by organisations has changed the nature of occupational professionalism in many professions into an organisational form of professionalism, there are various dynamics that shape the relative independence, objectivity, power, position and profile of professions hired within an organisational framework.[7] Bovens argues that professional

[4] See discussion of Linklater's role in providing clean advice for Lehman Brothers' now infamous Repo 105 transactions that were designed to manipulate the presentation of financial information, in David Kershaw and Richard Moorhead, 'Consequential Responsibility for Client Wrongs: Lehman Brothers and the Regulation of the Legal Profession' (2013) 76 *Modern Law Review* 26.

[5] Simon Ashby, Tommaso Palermo and Michael Power, *Risk Culture in Financial Organisations* (Interim Report, Nov 2012; Research Report, 2014).

[6] Eliot Friedson, *Professionalism: The Third Logic* (Cambridge: Polity Press, 2001, 2004 rep).

[7] See Julia Evetts, 'Professionalism in Turbulent Times: Changes, Challenges and Opportunities' (Propel international conference, Stirling, May 2012); Paul R Tremblay and Judith A McMorrow, 'Lawyers and the New Institutionalism' (2011) 9 *University of Saint Thomas Law Journal* 568.

values may contribute towards autonomy of values and power for individuals or groups even if hired to work within an organisation.[8] A number of commentators are also of the view that professionals hired within an organisation may be able to exercise 'expert power' to influence the organisation and continue to be able to exercise discretion and maintain a certain extent of autonomy and respect.[9] Enhanced professionalism is often also related to a strong and distinct articulation of professional ethics[10] which helps to ameliorate the 'dependency' position of internal control personnel who are employed in-house. It therefore cannot be concluded that dependent gatekeepers hired within an organisation are as such ineffectual. Hence, it is important that internal control functions are framed and supported in such a way that distinguishes them from being merely constituents within their organisations, and they should have a sense of professional pride in their work and a more precise understanding of the standards, conduct, competence and behaviour expected on their part. This chapter however notes that there is scepticism in academic commentary regarding the superiority of professionalism and that we should not have rose-tinted expectations of superior integrity, competence, standards and ethics on the part of those who call themselves 'professionals'.[11] It is acknowledged that professionalism is not a magic bullet or a panacea for the weaknesses on the part of internal control functions. However, the book has argued that some weaknesses relating to internal control efficacy may be attributed to the emerging nature of the current state of professionalism. Thus, enhanced professionalism may provide part of the answer. The book also argues that enhanced professionalism for internal control functions needs to be supported by regulatory involvement as much of internal control responsibilities are aimed at meeting regulatory expectations anyway, and such expectations need to be shaped in dialogue with the professions in order to be fairly, clearly and realistically framed. Hence, the enhanced

[8] Mark Bovens, *The Quest for Responsibility: Accountability and Citizenship in Complex Organisations* (Cambridge: Cambridge University Press, 1998).

[9] See Eugene McKenna, *Business Psychology and Organizational Behaviour*, 4th edn (New York: Taylor & Francis Psychology Press, 2006) 423; Friedson, *Professionalism* (n 6) chs 6, 7 and 9.

[10] Magali Sarfatti Larson, *The Rise of Professionalism* (London: Transaction Publishers, 2013). However, other researchers have argued that professional identities are not always supported by a strong commitment to ethics. Kouchaki argues that some in the profession use strong professional identities instrumentally and perversely to legitimate unethical behaviour, while Moorhead and Hinchly's empirical research shows that commitment to professional ethics may be over sounding for a minimalist commitment to a professional code which would be interpreted liberally to further commercial interests if grey areas are present. See Maryam Kouchaki, 'Professional Identities and Moral Behavior: Does a Professional Identity Make Individuals More Unethical?' (2013) at www.ssrn.org; Richard Moorhead and Victoria Hinchly, 'Professional Minimalism? The Ethical Consciousness of Commercial Lawyers' (2015) *Journal of Law and Society* (forthcoming).

[11] Richard Moorhead, 'Precarious Professionalism: Some Empirical and Behavioural Perspectives on Lawyers' (2014) *Current Legal Problems* 1.

professionalism called for in this book would be unlikely to result in an insular, self-regarding and self-congratulatory form of professionalism that becomes endogenously justified. The development of enhanced professionalism for internal control functions also serves as a countervailing force against undue imposition of regulatory expectations.

The next section will discuss what enhanced professionalism for internal control functions means broadly and make some suggestions as to how this can be achieved. The advantages of the book's proposal and its potential drawbacks will also be discussed. Section C will then discuss how liability regimes may be appropriately structured for internal control failings and section D concludes.

B. ENHANCING PROFESSIONALISM

The term 'professionalism' has evolved over time and could refer to being part of a recognised profession or more broadly as a general manner of conduct in work.[12] This chapter suggests that a trawl of the relevant literature defining professionalism yields the following common characteristics:

a. Specialised knowledge and skills, generally acquired through formalised training or education,[13] such specialised expertise acquired through dedicated study in higher education rather than in workplace experience,[14] and such expertise not thought of as commodified in the labour marketplace but as a more ideological calling that serves the social good.[15]
b. Specialised expertise defining an exclusive zone of work which allows control of the work processes, systems and priorities in the zone of work,[16] and the exercise of discretionary judgement that entails trust.[17]
c. The support of self-regulatory bodies that determine admission to the profession, qualifications required, codes of conduct, continuing development and disciplinary issues.[18]

[12] Evetts, 'Professionalism in Turbulent Times' (n 7); Lila Despotidou and Gregory P Prastacos, 'Professionalism in Business: Insights from Ancient Philosophy' (2013) at ssrn.com/abstract=2030614.

[13] Hudson Birden, Nel Glass, Ian Wilson, Michelle Harrison, Tim Usherwood and Duncan Nass, 'Defining Professionalism in Medical Education: A Systematic Review' (2014) 36 *Medical Teacher* 47; Institute for Learning, 'Professionalism and the Role of Professional Bodies' (2009) at www.ifl.ac.uk; Jerry R Lynn, 'Professionalism is a State of Mind' (1974) 3 *Journal of Advertising* 13; Baris Parkan, 'Professionalism: A Virtue or Estrangement from Self-Activity?' (2008) 78 *Journal of Business Ethics* 77.

[14] Friedson, *Professionalism* (n 6) ch 1.

[15] ibid, chs 6, 7 and 9; Larson, *The Rise of Professionalism* (n 10) ch 5.

[16] Evetts, 'Professionalism in Turbulent Times' (n 7); Friedson, *Professionalism* (n 6) ch 1.

[17] Evetts, 'Professionalism in Turbulent Times' (n 7) and Parkan, 'Professionalism' (n 13).

[18] Evetts, 'Professionalism in Turbulent Times' (n 7); Birden et al, 'Defining Professionalism in Medical Education' (n 13).

d. The perpetuation and maintenance of power by such self-regulatory bodies in maintaining the autonomy and preserve of the profession.[19]
e. The characterisation of professional service as going beyond self-interest and encompassing wider social interest,[20] as part of an ideologising process[21] that sustains the aura of and respect for the profession.
f. Commitment to ethical conduct and a code of standards and values[22] as part of the ideology[23] of the profession.

These characteristics combine expertise with social esteem and trust, although the self-regulation of professions is not necessarily a distinguishing characteristic any more due to increased regulatory intervention and monitoring of professional responsibilities in the public interest.[24] Most commentators converge on the esteem surrounding the acquisition of expertise as that which distinguishes a profession from merely commodified labour. The esteem surrounding a profession is supported by institutions of professionalism such as dedicated educational pathways and professional organisations. Professional institutions are traditionally developed as bottom-up forces[25] that consolidate the economic market and social position of professions. Further, professional stature or esteem can be derived from the framing of a profession as a calling, and the relation of the profession to performing a social good to the highest standards of expertise and ethics. Barnett acknowledges that state regulation could 'hollow out' a profession, but the ideology surrounding the epistemological authority of a profession could continue to sustain and hold a profession together as a distinct boundary of expertise and calling.[26]

[19] Willem Schinkel and Mirko Noordegraaf, 'Professionalism as Symbolic Capital: Materials for a Bourdieusian Theory of Professionalism' (2011) 10 *Comparative Sociology* 67; Dick W Olufs, 'The Limits of Professionalism' (1985) 9 *Public Administration Quarterly* 96.

[20] Despotidou and Prastacos, 'Professionalism in Business' (n 12); Parkan, 'Professionalism' (n 13).

[21] Larson, *The Rise of Professionalism* (n 10) chs 9 and 12; Friedson, *Professionalism* (n 6) chs 7 and 9. See also Ronald Barnett, 'Critical Professionalism in an Age of Super-complexity' in Bryan Cunninghm (ed), *Exploring Professionalism* (London: Institute of Education Press, 2008) 190.

[22] Larson, ibid; Friedson, ibid; Donald C Langevoort, 'Someplace between Philosophy and Economics: Legitimacy and Good Corporate Lawyering' (2006) 75 *Fordham Law Review* 1615; Institute for Learning, 'Professionalism and the Role of Professional Bodies' (n 13); Benjamin P Hayek, 'Morality, Professionalism and Happiness' (2007) 8 *Engage* 135.

[23] Ingrid Lunt, 'Ethical Issues in Professional Life' in Bryan Cunninghm (ed), *Exploring Professionalism* (London: Institute of Education Press, 2008) 73; Larson, *The Rise of Professionalism* (n 10) ch 12.

[24] Such as the Financial Reporting Council's Accounting Standards Board which is an independent agency setting accounting standards and having disciplinary jurisdiction over accountants and auditors in the UK; the PCAOB in the US; the Solicitors' Regulation Authority, an independent agency that sets standards and has disciplinary jurisdiction over solicitors in England and Wales:see Christopher J Whelan, 'The Paradox of Professionalism'—Global Law Practice Means Business' (2009) 27(2) *Penn State International Law Review* 465.

[25] Larson, *The Rise of Professionalism* (n 10).

[26] Barnett, 'Critical Professionalism' (n 21) 190.

Hence, professionalism is undergoing evolution in the face of regulatory intervention. However, the development of professionalism need not be seen as necessarily undermined by interaction with regulatory requirements. This book is of the view that professionalism can still be sustained by partnering with regulatory discourses and expectations in developing the parameters of responsibility, the objectives of service, ie, acting with the wider public interest in mind, and the standards of ethical conduct, in order to continue sustaining social trust reposed in professional discretion and judgement.[27] This development is viewed by this book as a positive one in relation to developing quasi-independent/dependent gatekeepers such as internal control functions towards enhanced professionalism.

As bottom-up forces in relation to internal control professions are relatively modest in sculpting distinct professional identities and standards for these professions, except perhaps in the case of the internal auditor profession, this chapter argues that regulators who are keen to ensure that internal control functions act as effective gatekeepers from the inside could play an active role in encouraging enhanced professionalism on the part of internal control professions, and be engaged in clarifying responsibilities and standards. Regulators should not impose expectations in a top-down fashion without dialogue as this is counterproductive to raising the profile of the internal control professions. The enhancement of internal control professionalism could usefully be preceded by greater consolidation of voice on the part of these professions and regulators can play a part in forging such forums and catalysing bottom-up forces so that a meaningful dialogue can be achieved. Further, regulatory involvement in enhancing internal control professionalism can also mitigate development of the dark sides of professionalism, pointed out by commentators, such as in relation to disguising unethical conduct under cosmetic and minimalist ethical adherence[28] or indeed engaging in unethical conduct by legitimating such conduct through a veneer of professionalism.[29]

Chapters two to four have looked at the developments in professionalism with respect to the functions of compliance, internal audit and risk management. Internal audit is arguably more professionalised as it is supported by a professional body than is the case with the compliance and risk management functions. In terms of evaluating whether each of the three internal control functions may be regarded as having attained the characteristics of professionalism set out above, this chapter makes the following observations in the Table below. It further suggests where improvements may be needed in relation to each of the following professional characteristics outlined above.

[27] ibid; and Lunt, 'Ethical Issues in Professional Life' (n 23) 73.

[28] See Moorhead and Hinchly, 'Professional Minimalism?' (n 10).

[29] See Kouchaki, 'Professional Identities and Moral Behavior' (n 10).

Table 1: Extent of Professionalism in Internal Control Professions

Characteristics of Professionalism	Compliance	Internal Audit	Risk Management
Specialised knowledge and skills, generally acquired through formalised training or education, specialised expertise acquired through dedicated study in higher education rather than in workplace experience, and such expertise not thought of as commodified and being offered in the labour marketplace but as a more ideological calling that serves the social good.	If the compliance officer is legally trained, the specialised expertise is drawn from law and the professional aura of the legal profession. But legal qualifications do not define the role exclusively. Hence it remains questionable what specialised knowledge or skills distinguish the compliance profession. Legally trained compliance officers would likely view themselves as legal professionals and not as 'compliance' professionals as such.	If the internal auditor is trained in accounting, the specialised expertise is drawn from accounting and the professional aura of the accounting profession. But accounting qualifications do not define the role exclusively. However, an internal auditor may more confidently assert herself as an internal audit professional by virtue of other institutional aspects such as the role of the Institute of Internal Auditors worldwide.	Used to be part of a wider business management or financial engineering course in higher education, but this is changing as more higher education institutions are offering MSc degrees dedicated to risk management or financial risk management. It is however doubted that risk management has attained an ideological status in relation to the expertise as compared with other traditional professions such as law, medicine and accounting.
Such knowledge and skills defining an exclusive zone of work which allows control of the work processes, systems and priorities in the zone of work.	An exclusive zone of work is more or less the case, especially now protected by mandatory requirements as to organisational independence, but the content of such an exclusive zone may not be well clarified, as chapters two and seven have discussed.	An exclusive zone of work, especially now protected by mandatory requirements as to organisational independence. The content of such an exclusive zone is in an ever-expanding state in practice. Hence, the growth of the	A zone of work that depends largely on organisational structure and leadership, may permeate the organisation as in enterprise-wide risk management. Now supported by mandatory requirements as to enhancing

(Continued)

Table 1: (*Continued*)

Characteristics of Professionalism	**Compliance**	**Internal Audit**	**Risk Management**
		remit of internal audit may undermine the notion of an 'exclusive zone', such as in the advisory aspects of work undertaken.	the organisational profile of risk management, via the appointment of the Chief Risk Officer and Board risk committees. The zone of work is becoming more defined due largely to regulatory requirements.
Exercise of discretionary judgement that entails trust	Yes largely, it is questioned if compliance officers acting in advisory roles may defer to business concerns.	Yes largely, it is questioned if internal audit officers acting in advisory roles may defer to business concerns.	May work closely with front lines of business but the enhanced profile of Chief Risk Officer may boost the power of risk managers to influence the organisation.
The support of self-regulatory bodies that determine admission to the profession, qualifications required, codes of conduct, continuing development and disciplinary issues.	No.	Only in relation to standards and code of conduct.	No.

(*continued*)

Table 1: (*Continued*)

Characteristics of Professionalism	Compliance	Internal Audit	Risk Management
The perpetuation and maintenance of power by such self-regulatory bodies in maintaining the autonomy and preserve of the profession.	No.	No.	No.
The characterisation of professional service as **going beyond self-interest and encompassing wider social interest as part of an ideologising process** that sustains the aura of and respect for the profession.	Hitherto no, although this aspect may be subject to changing regulatory expectations.	Hitherto no, although this aspect may be subject to changing regulatory expectations.	Hitherto no, although this aspect may be subject to changing regulatory expectations. That said, the ideologising process for risk management as a profession is emerging at best.
Commitment to ethical conduct and a code of standards and values as part of the ideology of the profession.	Depending on whether the compliance officer is legally trained and hence drawing from ethics in legal practice. Compliance officers could also act as ethics officers in corporations and as such be responsible for upholding the organisation's code of conduct and values.	Yes largely, drawing from the Institute for Internal Auditors' Codes.	No, but could be drawing from the organisation's code of conduct and values.

This chapter proposes that enhanced professionalism can and needs to be achieved in respect of the internal control functions in the following manner set out in the Table below. The text following the Table explains further.

Table 2: Enhanced Professionalism in the Internal Control Professions

	Enhanced Professionalism needed in the following:
Compliance	(i) Specialised knowledge and skills, largely in professional development. (ii) Exclusive zone of work and more clarity in the content of such responsibilities. (iii) Overt characterisation of professional service as going beyond self-interest and encompassing wider social interest. (iv) Commitment to ethical conduct and a code of standards and values. (v) Perhaps supported by a dedicated professional body that represents the voice of the profession.
Internal Audit	(i) Specialised knowledge and skills, acquired through formalised training or education or professional development. (ii) Exclusive zone of work and more clarity in the content of such responsibilities. (iii) Overt characterisation of professional service as going beyond self-interest and encompassing wider social interest.
Risk Management	(i) Specialised knowledge and skills, generally acquired through formalised training or education. (ii) An exclusive zone of work and more clarity in the content of such responsibilities. (iii) Exercise of discretionary judgement that entails trust. (iv) Overt characterisation of professional service as going beyond self-interest and encompassing wider social interest. (v) Commitment to ethical conduct and a code of standards and values. (vi) Perhaps support of a professional body representing the voice of the profession.

Where the compliance profession is concerned, this chapter argues that enhanced professionalism may be achieved by more precisely specifying the competencies and skill sets relating to compliance as well as by ideologising the profession towards service of the wider public interest. On competencies, although these may be drawn from legal expertise, they could go beyond legal expertise to other regulatory-related expertise. Increased precision in specifying compliance skill sets and competencies could improve the 'expert' profile of compliance in the organisation, and encourage the perception that 'compliance' is a specialised position and not a graveyard post in occupational rotation in the organisation.

The more precise specification of competencies and skill sets could support the clearer articulation of the responsibilities of compliance, such as how compliance should relate to external service providers and external counsel. This chapter suggests that a major component of the competencies and skill sets of the compliance function should based on legal and regulatory training, as compliance officers need to interpret and understand regulatory texts[30] and perhaps deal with regulatory authorities. It is observed that specific qualifications in higher education are being developed dedicated to accrediting compliance expertise.[31]

The emerging International Compliance Association in the UK is a young professional body that is starting to undertake accreditation of compliance qualifications in partnership with higher education. Hence, a nascent voice seems to be positioned to articulate the specific competencies and skill sets of compliance officers. As such accreditation programmes are new developments, it takes time for such programmes to gain credibility, and incumbents in the compliance profession may resist the increasing prescriptions for competencies and skill sets required of compliance officers. However, this book views positively the role of bottom-up forces in the compliance profession in shaping the professional profile of the compliance function and urges that UK and EU-level financial regulation authorities work with such representative bodies in order to achieve meaningful dialogue in clarifying the expectations of roles, functions, responsibilities and liabilities for compliance officers, which can then feed into the processes for developing training and accreditation. Such clarification could reinforce the burgeoning professionalism of compliance officers and ensure that the compliance function is well placed to take advantage of the new empowering organisational reforms introduced in regulation, therefore keeping to a minimum any professional–organisational disjunctions that affect internal control efficacy. Such clarification is also especially useful for overcoming the regulatory–professional disjunctions already discussed at length.

[30] Marc Lenglet, 'Ambivalence and Ambiguity: The Interpretive Role of Compliance Officers' in Isabelle Huault and Chrystelle Richard (eds), *Finance: The Discreet Regulator* (Abingdon: Palgrave Macmillan, 2012) 59.

[31] eg, compliance certificates and diplomas are being awarded by the International Compliance Association in partnership with the Manchester Business School (MBS). The MBS also has an undergraduate programme awarding a BSc in management with compliance and a postgraduate programme, the MSc in management and compliance: see www.mbs.ac.uk/undergraduate/courses/management-with-compliance.

As the book supports the articulation of clearer regulatory expectations with regard to the responsibilities and standards of compliance officers, this chapter also suggests that regulators develop specific Conduct Rules for internal control personnel instead of relying on the widely worded Conduct Rules that apply to all persons in the 'Certification' regime. This chapter suggests that the national regulator or the European authorities in the form of the European Banking Authority (EBA) or European Securities and Markets Authority (ESMA) should take the lead in drafting a Code of Competencies and Responsibilities for compliance officers in financial institutions, in partnership with relevant professional associations such as the International Compliance Association, and subject to the safeguard of extensively consulting compliance officers across the UK and EU. The involvement of regulators is essential as the responsibilities for compliance officers are to a large extent determined by regulatory objectives, and regulators are therefore well placed to articulate their expectations of what such a role should entail for the compliance function. The achievement of clarity in professional responsibilities allows specificity in the competencies and skill sets of compliance officers to develop and contributes towards enhancing professionalism. Compelling regulators to articulate their expectations of competencies and responsibilities also helps prevent the imposition of silent and undue expectations on compliance officers subsequently subject to liability surprises. However, this should not become a platform for regulators to impose excessive expectations on internal control functions and the book advocates partnership with the profession so that regulatory expectations can be fairly shaped with the input of a bottom-up voice.

It is not unusual for regulators to specify the professional roles and responsibilities of specific persons in relation to securing certain regulatory objectives. One example is the regulatory requirement that financial institutions obtain an auditor's assurance that client money is properly handled in accordance with regulation. Under EU legislation,[32] auditors are required to verify the compliance by an investment firm with rules requiring the handling of client assets and money in such a way as to protect client rights in the event of firm failure or insolvency.[33] The UK

[32] European Parliament and Council Directive 2004/39/EC of 21 April 2004 on markets in financial instruments amending Council Directives 85/611/EEC and 93/6/EEC and Directive 2000/12/EC of the European Parliament and of the Council and repealing Council Directive 93/22/EEC [2004] OJ L145/1 (Markets in Financial Instruments Directive) (MiFID) Art 13(7) and (8); Commission Directive 2006/73/EC of 10 August 2006 implementing Directive 2004/39/EC of the European Parliament and of the Council as regards organisational requirement and operating conditions for investment firms and defined terms for the purposes of that Directive [2006] OJ L241/26 (MiFID Commission Directive 2006) Art 20 and MiFID II Directive, Arts 16(8)–(10).

[33] MiFID Art 13(7) and (8).

Financial Services Authority (FSA) specified in subsidiary legislation what may be expected of auditors.[34] It is specified[35] that auditors have to report on the firms' state of compliance with client money and assets handling rules and should also assess the adequacy of internal control (including the internal control of outsourcees) that enable compliance with the client asset and money handling rules. Auditors must also be 'independent' and free from conflicts of interests.[36] The Financial Conduct Authority (FCA) Handbook sets out the few express duties[37] imposed on auditors: auditors have a duty to submit a report on client compliance and to gain access to information in the firm in order to discharge their verification function. The main enforcement measure that may be taken against auditors who fall short of their duties is the power of disqualification under section 345 of the Act.[38] However, auditor failings in verifying client compliance with money and asset handling rules may also be subject to disciplinary action taken by the Financial Reporting Council (FRC). The Council monitors the development of accounting standards and the quality of audits. It carries out inspections and audits of major auditors.[39] The Professional Discipline Board under the Council may discipline auditors generally and this includes auditors' work in relation to verifying client compliance with money and asset handling rules in financial regulation. In light of the UK regulator's revelation of severe weaknesses in auditors' work relating to verifying financial sector compliance with money and asset handling rules, the Board took action against Pricewaterhouse Coopers in relation to their client JP Morgan's breaches of money and asset handling rules.[40] JP Morgan was fined by the UK regulator in 2012. In view of the FRC's purview over the auditing profession, the FSA deferred to the FRC to undertake professional discipline of the auditors concerned. In relation to the specific responsibility of vetting financial institutions' client money and asset handling, the duties and responsibilities imposed on auditors can be shaped by regulatory duties working in tandem with professional bodies.

The marked trend towards more articulation of regulatory duties for those working in the financial services industry is set to continue. For example, chapter six has discussed how senior persons may be subject to more defined statements of responsibilities and codes of conduct.

[34] FCA Handbook, SUP 3.

[35] ibid, SUP 3.10.

[36] ibid, SUP 3.5.

[37] ibid, SUP 3.8 and SUP 3.10

[38] FCA Handbook, EG 15 further provides circumstances where such power may be exercised.

[39] Professional Oversight Board, part of the Financial Reporting Council.

[40] Jonathan Guthrie, 'PwC fine underplays auditors' responsibilities' *Financial Times* (6 January 2012).

This may be viewed as a form of increased prescription by powerful regulators in the conduct of business and professional activity, but may also be regarded as an opportunity for professions and regulators to work together to shape duties and obligations that are consistent with organisational environments, proportionate to professional competencies and constructive to the securing of regulatory objectives by the firm. This is an opportunity to overcome regulatory–professional and professional–organisational disjunctions so that the expectations gap between regulators and internal control professions may be mitigated.

Further, professionalism can be enhanced by the framing of professional services within a paradigm of wider social good beyond self-interest. This chapter argues that such enhanced professionalism plays a part in improving the general stature of internal control functions and resisting organisational manipulation of such functions. This chapter suggests that the development of an appropriate Code of Ethics for internal control functions would be desirable and it is proposed that regulatory engagement can also play a role in shaping the Code.

It is suggested that national or EU regulators should, in extensive consultation with compliance officers, draw up a Code of Ethics and Values in relation to their conduct. Such a Code could reinforce the gatekeeping role of the compliance function towards meeting regulatory expectations by improving professional consciousness in compliance individuals. Although it is 'non-traditional' for professional codes of ethics to be drawn up between a profession and regulators, this chapter argues that: (a) the bottom-up forces motivating the profession are still emerging and regulatory endeavours could supply the relevant impetus to shape and bring such a Code into existence; (b) regulatory involvement is likely a win-win for regulators and the profession alike, as consciousness of the wider good in the discharge of internal control responsibilities is consistent with the gatekeeping expectations regulators place on such functions; and (c) the profession itself could be viewed as invested with increased credibility, which can be helpful in the context of generally increased social scepticism of professions.[41] Further, such a Code may inculcate professional pride in compliance officers and further support the organisational structures of independence and capacity intended to enhance the objectivity and efficacy of the compliance function. In other words, regulatory intervention could be used (albeit non-traditionally and perhaps surprisingly) to assist in the ideologising process that sustains the compliance function as a distinct and respectable profession, and this may be constructive for making the compliance function more effective in meeting regulatory expectations.

[41] Lunt, 'Ethical Issues in Professional Life' (n 23) 73.

The chapter suggests that the Code of Ethics for the compliance function should be separate from the general Code of Conduct the FCA has established for all financial sector employees in the 'Certification' regime. The latter Code has a wide coverage and is likely to be broadly worded without specific reference to the special role of internal control functions. As internal control functions such as the compliance function has special gatekeeping responsibilities and needs to meet regulatory expectations revolving around those responsibilities, clearer articulations of expected scope of responsibilities and standards of conduct are important to frame fairer regulatory expectations and liability regimes. The Code of Ethics will be able to feed into the particular standards of conduct expected of the compliance function. Such a Code should also involve more extensive input from the compliance industry, and the engagement with professional associations such as the emerging International Compliance Association would also help improve the professional body's profile and boost the general professional stature of the compliance function. It may be suggested on the contrary that a separate Code is not needed and that the compliance function would adhere to the organisation's Code of Conduct anyway, which is likely based on business ethics or corporate values. However, Bucklin[42] argues that the tendency is for corporate Codes of Ethics or values to be rather minimalist and cosmetic as corporate Codes are often disengaged from individual moral compasses and centre upon lowest common denominator behaviour such as legal and literal compliance. Hence, corporate Codes are unlikely to be adequate to secure the much needed enhanced professionalism on the part of the compliance function and would instead subsume the profession within the organisational context.

The discussion above applies in many respects to the internal audit and risk management professions. For internal audit, the Institute for Internal Auditors (IIA) has to some extent achieved a measure of professionalism for the internal audit profession. However, chapter four has pointed out that the IIA has made only very general references to competencies and skills in the IIA's Code.[43] That said, the generality of reference may be due to the fact that internal auditors work in many sectors and hence greater precision would be difficult in light of sectoral differences. This chapter suggests that greater clarity and precision of internal auditors' competencies, roles and responsibilities in financial institutions may be needed in view of regulatory expectations of their roles in gatekeeping. The IIA and regulators should work together towards drawing up a more precise Code

[42] Leonard Bucklin, 'More Preaching, Fewer Rules: A Process for the Corporate Lawyer's Maintenance of Corporate Ethics' (2009) 35 *Ohio Northern University Law Review* 887.

[43] Section B, chapter 4.

of Competencies, functions and responsibilities for internal auditors at banks and financial institutions, in order to secure realistic and fair regulatory expectations and liability regimes, and better support the organisational reforms that have already taken place to enhance the powers of internal audit functions. Further, a more specific Code of Ethics and values drawn from the IIA's general provisions[44] may be considered for internal audit functions in the financial sector. In particular, it may be necessary to clarify to what extent internal auditors at banks and financial institutions may be able to act in management consulting capacities as is the trend in many other sectors. This chapter urges that in view of enhanced regulatory expectations of internal control functions, more partnership and dialogue should take place between the IIA and financial regulators such as the Prudential Regulation Authority (PRA) and FCA. Such dialogic platforms provide opportunities for regulatory expectations to be more clearly articulated and shaped by the professional understandings and capacities of internal auditors. Such dialogic engagements would likely provide a boost to the professional stature of internal auditors, as being distinct players in the financial regulatory space apart from the organisations for which they work.

As for the risk management function, this chapter suggests that enhanced professionalism for risk management also involves greater clarity in specifying the competencies and skill sets, roles and responsibilities of the risk management function. Risk management was not a dedicated discipline of study in many higher education programmes in the pre-crisis era, being subsumed under general business management or financial engineering programmes. Hence, the risk management profession may face more challenges in distinguishing itself as a distinct professional function. Post-crisis, leading institutions in the UK have now started developing undergraduate[45] and Masters degree programmes for risk management especially in the financial sector.[46] Hence, there are bottom-up market forces shaping the conception of risk management expertise and training as an independent discipline. It is arguable whether higher education accreditation should become a core criterion for risk management competencies, as the requirement for distinct qualifications may create barriers to entry although the development of such qualifications could achieve the effect of more

[44] IIA, *Code of Ethics* at na.theiia.org/standards-guidance/mandatory-guidance/pages/code-of-ethics.aspx.

[45] eg, the BSc (Hons) programme in Investment and Financial Risk Management offered by City University, London, see www.cass.city.ac.uk/courses/undergraduate/courses/investment-and-financial-risk-management/2015; the BA (Hons) programme offered by Glasgow Caledonian University, see www.gcu.ac.uk/study/undergraduate/courses/risk-management-3rd-year-entry-8946.php?loc=uk.

[46] eg, The London Business School, Imperial College London and the University of Southampton all run specialist MSc programmes in risk management.

precisely defining skill sets, competencies and training to support distinct and enhanced professionalism. Further, endeavours made to distinguish the competencies and skills relating to risk management are important in supporting the distinction of the function in the organisational context as organisational manipulation of the risk management function would be less difficult if the boundaries of the function were more clearly established. Chapter three has discussed the organisational context for risk management and how management and organisational structures have in the pre-crisis era played a large part in making the risk management function relatively weak in a number of banks. Hence, there may be a strong case for developing professionalism in risk management competencies and skill sets that help in making the profession more distinct, less susceptible to organisational manipulation and consequently maintaining the distinctness of the profession. However, would such an approach run counter to the 'enterprise-wide' risk management system and culture that risk management experts suggest is beneficial for financial institutions?[47] In firms that adopt enterprise-wide risk management, establishing such a system and culture does not run counter to empowering a centralised, professionalised and respected risk management function in the firm. In fact the centralised function would coordinate the enterprise-wide system in the firm. Adopting an enterprise-wide risk management system and culture does not conflict with making the risk management function a more professionalised one with clearer articulations of responsibilities, roles and competencies.

The bottom-up forces in developing more specific training and education in risk management can feed into the process of clearer articulations of risk management responsibilities and regulatory expectations. This chapter suggests, consistent with the other internal control functions discussed above, that the risk management function should also be subject to a distinct Code of Responsibilities drawn up in dialogue between the profession and the regulators. Such a dialogic process should be carried out in order to shape fairer and more realistic regulatory expectations in light of professional understandings of the scope of responsibilities and skill sets for such responsibilities. The regulatory involvement in shaping a distinct Code for the risk management function may arguably have the same positive and reinforcing effect upon enhanced professionalism as

[47] Brian W Nocco and René M Stultz, 'Enterprise Risk Management: Theory and Practice' (2006) 18 *Journal of Applied Corporate Finance* 8; Lisa K Meulbroek, 'A Senior Manager's Guide to Integrated Risk Management' in Donald H Chew (ed), *Corporate Risk Management* (New York: Columbia Business School Publishing, 2008); René M Stultz, 'Rethinking Risk Management' in Donald H Chew (ed), *Corporate Risk Management* (New York: Columbia Business School Publishing, 2008); Annetta Cortez, *Winning at Risk* (Chichester; John Wiley & Sons, 2011) 142ff.

discussed for the compliance function above. In terms of representative voices in the risk management profession, the Institute of Risk Management (IRM) mentioned in chapter three is an emerging body for certification and networking that is well placed to grow in profile and stature. The chapter suggests that constructive dialogic processes should be established between the financial regulators and the IRM so that a distinct Code of Responsibilities that protects risk managers from organisational manipulation and from undue and unarticulated regulatory expectations can be drawn up. Such a distinct Code helps to secure enhanced professionalism that is more consistent with meeting fair and realistic regulatory expectations.

Further, this chapter supports the drawing up of a Code of Ethics and Values for risk managers that can be distinguished from the Code of Conduct for persons in the 'Certification' regime, as discussed above in relation to the compliance and internal audit functions. As risk management is a relatively emerging profession compared with internal audit or compliance, the application of a separate Code of Ethics and Values to them would likely reinforce professional distinction. This could be important for enhanced professional consciousness of the gatekeeping roles and capacities of the risk management function. The role of such a Code can set more precisely articulated standards of conduct expected of risk managers in order to mitigate organisational manipulation and secure fairer and more realistic regulatory expectations and liability regimes.

This book has so far argued that there is a marked rise in regulatory expectations for internal control functions to act as internal gatekeepers in securing the firm's meeting of regulatory objectives whether in prudential or conduct regulation. Such regulatory expectations have exposed an regulatory-organisational disjunction in terms of the powers and capacities of internal control functions, and post-crisis reforms have to a significant extent addressed this issue. However, organisational reforms to boost the positioning, powers and profile of internal control have to be complemented by enhanced professionalism on the part of internal control functions, and regulatory expectations can only be met if they are shaped fairly and realistically with professional input. As post-crisis reforms have neglected to address the professional dimension of internal control functions while subjecting such individuals to extensive liability regimes, this book calls for greater awareness of the limitations of post-crisis organisational reforms and potential adversities resulting from the imposition of liability regimes on internal control individuals, and reforms to enhance the professionalism of internal control functions.

Enhanced professionalism entails greater specification of competencies and responsibilities for internal control, therefore making recruitment a more distinguished exercise, and improves the organisational positioning of such 'expert' profiles. This may mean that candidates with just general skill sets may face barriers to entry, but this book does not conclude on the matter and suggests that qualifying competencies should be subject to dialogue between the professions, industry and regulators. A trade-off may be necessary in terms of limiting access to the labour market for internal control, in order to distinguish a profession by enhancing its professional power and gatekeeping capacity. There is indeed a dilemma between allowing elitism to evolve in order to address specific needs and maintaining egalitarianism in the labour market.[48] This book is mindful of Larson's arguments that the rise of professionalism although surrounded by an ideological aura, is in fact a creation of a market monopoly.[49] Is the ideological special-ness of certain expertise and skill sets overstated in order to maintain a market monopoly?[50] However, increased elitism in the distinguishing of professions can also be accompanied by greater social responsibility, and in the case of internal control functions in the financial sector, greater regulatory accountability. It is arguably not disproportionate to distinguish the internal control professions in tandem with enhanced regulatory expectations of their roles and responsibilities and the rather demanding liability regimes discussed in chapter seven.

However, one could argue that there are unintended consequences in enhancing the professionalism of internal control professions. Perhaps organisations could take advantage of enhanced professionalism on the part of internal control functions so that their responsibilities may be increased and internal control may be more exposed to blame when things go wrong. Internal control functions could become overtly responsible for an augmented scope of matters and be required to perform an impossible extent of internal checking and gatekeeping, which makes zero failure unlikely, but in the event of which would position such internal control functions for blame. Perverse forms of organisational manipulation need to be subject to supervisory monitoring and scrutiny. Another adverse development could be that internal control professionals may maintain a precise but minimised set of responsibilities, and seek to dodge blame when things go wrong. Clearer delineation of internal control competencies and responsibilities may narrow down responsibilities and serve as a means to protect internal control functions from liability. The opportunity to clarify responsibilities and competencies towards enhanced professionalism can be used opportunistically to meet these self-interested ends. However, in light of the unsatisfactory aspects of regulatory enforcement discussed in chapter seven, this chapter is of the view that securing greater clarity and fairness in regulatory expectations for internal control

[48] See, however, Friedson, *Professionalism* (n 6) ch 9.

[49] Larson, *The Rise of Professionalism* (n 10).

[50] David Crook, 'Some historical Perspectives on Professionalism' in Bryan Cunninghm (ed), *Exploring Professionalism* (London: Institute of Education Press, 2008) 10.

functions is desirable at this time. The relevant Codes suggested in this chapter should also be subject to regular dialogic review between regulators and professional bodies.

As a longer-term development, it is observed that higher education and professional accreditation is developing for the emerging professions such as compliance and risk management, in tandem with the emergence of representative bodies such as the International Compliance Association and IRM. The book considers these to be positive developments in the interests of enhanced professionalism. Although self-regulatory organisations have teetered at the brink of social trust, with auditors and lawyers suffering from low social perceptions,[51] it is important for the internal control industry to be given a voice as the relative autonomy of an industry reflects its professional achievements, and it is arguably contrary to the spirit of enhancing professionalism if professional competencies and responsibilities are dictated solely by regulators. The professional distinction, autonomy and power of groups based on knowledge and expertise provide an ideological basis[52] for such groups to have a distinct public profile, to mediate social trust and have an outward-facing pride beyond an organisational-specific role that is inward looking.[53] A knowledge-based professional distinction and outward-facing profile also provide the basis for the consolidation of governance power by the professional body with such epistemic authority and autonomy.

In the de-centred, complex and pluralistic landscape of the financial sector, the growth of actors with governance capacity is important to regulators, as regulators' governance is often supplemented by them. The author has commented extensively elsewhere that the de-centred landscape in financial regulation is dominated by financial sector firms which bring extensive expertise in designing bottom-up systems and self-regulatory initiatives to condition the imposition of regulatory governance.[54] Although the financial sector has contributed much to its own governance, their governance deficits have been exposed during the global financial crisis. However, although regulators have rushed to regulate extensively, regulatory expertise is still developing in the face of

[51] Langevoort, 'Someplace between Philosophy and Economics' (n 22); William H Simon, 'After Confidentiality: Rethinking the Professional Responsibilities of the Business Lawyer' (2006) 75 *Fordham Law Review* 1453; John C Coffee, 'Understanding Enron: "It's About the Gatekeepers, Stupid"' (2002) 57 *Business Lawyer* 1403; Coffee, *Gatekeepers* (n 2); Juan Jose Ganuza and Fernando Gomez, 'Should we Trust the Gatekeepers? Auditors' and Lawyers' Liability for Clients' Misconduct' (2007) 27 *International Review of Law and Economics* 96.

[52] Friedson, *Professionalism* (n 6) ch 9; Larson, *The Rise of Professionalism* (n 10) chs 5 and 12.

[53] Despotidou and Prastacos, 'Professionalism in Business' (n 12); Parkan, 'Professionalism' (n 13).

[54] Mads Andenas and Iris H-Y Chiu, *The Foundations and Future of Financial Regulation: Governance for Responsibility* (Oxford: Routledge, 2014) ch 3.

the increased demands to supervise sophisticated financial sector firms. Regulatory expectations placed on internal control functions is one way of co-opting supporting governance capacity from other actors, but such other actors need to be developed in power and capacity in the de-centred landscape to act as effective countervailing forces to the dominance of financial sector firms. Hence, enhanced professionalism on the part of internal control functions is necessary if they are envisaged to play this part in the governance landscape. Wilke also supports diversity in actorhood in contemporary governance, given the limitations of state control and the diffusion of expertise among many knowledge-based groups.[55]

The next section will discuss the appropriate design of liability regimes for internal control personnel based on the suggestions in this section.

C. LIABILITY REGIMES

Chapter seven has discussed the trend of regulatory enforcement in the UK against internal control personnel such as compliance officers in the form of personal and secondary liability based on general principles of conduct in regulatory rules such as the Code of Practice for Approved Persons (APER). However, enforcement decisions have revealed an expectations gap between regulatory expectations and the profession's perceived understanding of the scope of responsibilities and standard of professional conduct. This gap is a regulatory–professional disjunction that needs to be addressed or else the imposition of liability on internal control personnel would result in cognitive dissonance and demoralisation from becoming effective internal gatekeepers. This chapter has argued thus far that enhanced professionalism will play a major part in addressing such a disjunction by clarifying internal control responsibilities and framing regulatory expectations in a fair and realistic manner with professional input.

The development of enhanced professionalism on the part of internal control also entails reconsiderations of appropriate liability regimes for internal control individuals. This section will make some suggestions in this respect.

As the policy trend going forward is the enhancement of responsibility and liability for banking professionals,[56] internal control personnel are not spared from the trend. This section suggests that an appropriate liability regime for internal control personnel consistent with enhanced

[55] Helmut Wilke, *Governance in a Disenchanted World* (Cheltenham: Edward Elgar, 2009).

[56] House of Lords and House of Commons, Parliamentary Commission on Banking Standards, *Changing Banking for Good* Vol II (HL 27-II, HC 175-II) (12 June 2013); ss 65A, 66A and 66B, Financial Services and Markets Act 2000 as amended by the Financial Services (Banking Reform) Act 2013.

professionalism should be based on a clear but limited scope for personal liability. Secondary liability upon internal control personnel may be imposed if professional failings contribute to the primary breach by the firm.

This book argues that personal liability for internal control personnel should only be based on a breach of the relevant Code of Ethics and Conduct, akin to individual accountability in a professional disciplinary situation. In order to support the enhanced professionalism of internal control, internal control personnel should be treated in a similar manner as other established professions where individual accountability is called for. Individual liability should be based on individual probity, failure in ethical standards or personal wrongdoing. This chapter also argues that enforcement against individual internal control officers in personal liability cases should be carried out by a professional body and not by the PRA or FCA, akin to the sanctions carried out against PriceWaterhouseCoopers by the FRC, not the FSA (for breaches in relation to auditing client money handling by JP Morgan). As the book supports the development of specific Codes of Ethics and Values for the three internal control professions, such a Code also forms an appropriate basis for any personal liability. This development would mitigate the problems discussed in chapter 7 with regard to the ambiguous nature of liability in the general Code of Conduct (APER) that applies to controlled functions in banks and financial institutions.

This chapter is hesitant to support the imposition of personal liability on internal control personnel for issues relating to care, skill or competence unless in accordance with the Code of Ethics and Values that is proposed or in the clearest of cases. Internal gatekeeping failures may reflect wider issues in firm culture and structure, and may implicate other departments, senior management and the organisational and governance structures in the firm. Hence, one should exercise caution in pinning down responsibility for internal control failures on internal control personnel as such. Further, it is noted in chapter seven that some empirical research in the US points out that enforcement decisions taken against individual compliance officers in a small firm where compliance may be assumed by a single individual are markedly harsher[57] than enforcement decisions taken against the internal control functions of large financial institutions where responsibility is more diffuse[58] among a group of internal control personnel. In other words, internal control personnel in smaller firms may bear disproportionate liability apart from the severity of the failing. This could result in the perverse consequence that where internal control personnel

[57] See Stavros Gadinis, 'The SEC and the Financial Industry: Evidence from Enforcement against Broker-Dealers' (2012) 67 *Business Lawyer* 679.

[58] Bovens, *The Quest for Responsibility* (n 8).

work in more resource-constrained organisational contexts, they are personally punished and held more severely accountable for the firm's primary breach. The assumption that internal control personnel could be more powerful or in a better position to influence firm behaviour cannot be readily made without an in-depth understanding of the organisational context. This section argues that there is no clear basis for making a distinction between internal control personnel in a small outfit and in a large firm where the imposition of personal liability is concerned. It is suggested here that where a firm commits a primary breach and regulators are of the view that internal control personnel have not done enough within reasonable means to prevent such an occurrence, the indictment of internal control personnel should only be based on secondary liability. This reasoning applies to internal control personnel in both large and small firms and the organisational context should not lend itself to undue assumptions on the part of regulators regarding the level of culpability of internal control officers.

Hence, the threat of personal liability in relation to care, skill and competence should be applied sparingly and it is argued that narrowing down the regime of personal liability for internal control individuals to deal mainly with individual probity and conduct issues would bring about a fairer regime of primary liability for all internal control personnel. Such a development would also avoid the conflation between personal and secondary liability for internal control personnel in smaller firms who would perceive themselves to be targeted just because they are the only individuals bearing the office.

This chapter does not object to regimes of secondary liability as secondary liability regimes can be consistent with enhanced professionalism. Professional failings in care, skill and diligence that result in or contribute to a firm's primary breach should be made accountable, as such accountability and liability could serve a deterrence purpose. Drawing from Kershaw and Moorhead's recommendations regarding the secondary liability of transactional lawyers advising clients in commercial matters,[59] this chapter supports the arguments that expert professionals could be placed in a position of secondary liability if such expert professionals are actively assisting in a matter of some probity.

Such secondary liability is modelled after accessory liability in criminal law which requires the accessory to be aware that real and substantial risk of illegality would entail upon the assistance given. The authors mentioned above have argued that transactional lawyers as professionals should assume a broader public interest duty of fidelity to the law and not be allowed to use excessive zeal for the client as an excuse. They argue

[59] Kershaw and Moorhead, 'Consequential Responsibility for Client Wrongs' (n 4).

that transactional lawyers should assume consequential liability for the illegality of their clients if they could reasonably foresee the likelihood of non-compliance or illegality, and that their assistance creates a real and substantial risk of such non-compliance or illegality materialising. This chapter suggests that internal control personnel could be subject to secondary liability if the neglect or failure of professional responsibilities could foreseeably create a real and substantial risk of firm non-compliance. This position would arguably be consistent with the enhanced professionalism of internal control professions. But it does mean that internal control personnel should endeavour to avoid being pressured by business lines[60] to refrain from being vigilant and critical, and should hold fast to what is required as a matter of professional care and competence.

This chapter therefore advocates reforms in the framing of personal and secondary liability regimes for internal control personnel, consistent with enhancing their professionalism, away from the general regime of Conduct Rules established by the financial regulator which makes no distinction between the different 'certified functions' in the firm. In sum, personal liability should be limited and aligned with similar premises for professional discipline in other professions, and secondary liability should be based on a form of professional assistance rendered towards the firm within the reasonable foreseeability of ultimate firm non-compliance. However, this chapter acknowledges that the behavioural impact of designs of liability regimes upon internal control personnel should be further studied in order to ascertain how they affect the efficacy of internal control.

So far this book has taken stock of enhanced regulatory expectations of internal control functions at banks and financial institutions and argued that the role of internal control functions as internal gatekeepers can be made effective not only through organisational empowerment of such functions, but through enhanced professionalism that would help frame regulatory expectations more fairly and realistically, and provide support for the organisational reforms. However, Laby has argued that gatekeepers with a 'dependent' relationship to the corporation they are connected with may be inherently limited as gatekeepers. Hence, there is the question of whether we can expect internal control functions to act as internal gatekeepers at all. The positive duties of loyalty that sustain such dependent relationships may cause conflict with the demands of a gatekeeping role and/or psyche, and could result in confusion as to whose interests are to be served by internal control functions. Are regulatory expectations imposed on internal control functions inherently misplaced and unsustainable?

[60] E Norman Veasey and Christine T Di Guglielmo, 'The Tensions, Stresses, and Professional Responsibilities of the Lawyer for the Corporation' (2006) 62 *Business Lawyer* 1.

This question should be critically considered and reviewed although the book supports the post-crisis framing of internal control functions as gatekeepers within the firm. However, at a more minimal level, regulators could also consider leveraging upon the roles of internal control functions in terms of intelligence provision and reporting[61] in order to assist in regulatory supervision.

An intelligence-based role for internal control personnel could be appropriately framed based on the model of the UK regulators' relationship with external auditors of financial institutions. One of the duties imposed on auditors is the passing of information to the regulators, particularly in periodic meetings that the regulators schedule with auditors of financial institutions.[62] It has also been established as a rule that auditors should cooperate with the UK regulators in the discharge of their functions.[63] Such cooperation has been defined as regular bilateral or trilateral meetings (at least annually) between auditors of 'high impact' financial institutions and regulators. The bilateral meeting would involve the leader of the supervisory team on the side of the regulators and the lead audit partner; the trilateral meeting would also involve one independent non-executive director of the audit firm, such as the Chairman of the audit committee. Such meetings are to be open and cooperative and are designed to assist the regulators in their supervisory capacity. It is queried if similar interaction could be required between internal control functions and regulators. International developments already indicate such a trajectory.[64] Such would also provide support for whistle-blower protection if reporting to regulators needs to take place due to the lack of supportive systems and cultures in the firm.

D. CONCLUSION

This book has discussed enhanced regulatory expectations of internal control functions at banks and financial institutions and argued that the role of internal control functions as internal gatekeepers can be made effective not only through organisational empowerment of such functions, but through enhanced professionalism that would help frame regulatory expectations more fairly and realistically, and provide support for the organisational

[61] Already championed in Basel Committee on Banking Supervision, *Guidelines: Corporate Governance Principles for Banks* (Consultation Paper, October 2014) Principle 13, para 160, which envisages direct regulator communications with internal control functions in the supervisory process.

[62] PRA and FCA Handbooks (as of 30 April 2013, formerly FSA Handbook) SUP 3.8.2.

[63] ibid, SUP 3.8; FSA, 'Code of Practice for the Relationship between the External Auditor and the Supervisor' (May 2011) FG11/09 at www.fsa.gov.uk/pubs/guidance/fg11_09.pdf.

[64] Basel Committee, *Guidelines* (n 61) Principle 13, para 160.

reforms. This chapter discusses the nature of emerging professionalism in the compliance and risk management functions, and to a lesser extent the internal audit function. This chapter suggests areas of enhancement in the professionalism of the three internal control professions, and in particular calls upon regulators to develop a clearer set of regulatory expectations in the form of duties and liabilities, as well as standards of conduct, in partnership with the professions. Such distinct Codes of Responsibilities and Standards are important for the predictability of responsibilities and liability for internal control personnel.

The chapter sees enhanced professionalism on the part of the internal control professions as not only an emerging bottom-up development, but as influenced and shaped by regulators, in light of the extensive demands of financial regulation generally imposed on firms. The role of internal control functions as gatekeepers suffers from organisational–regulatory, regulatory–professional and professional–organisational disjunctions discussed in chapter one, and this book hopes that the analyses of these disjunctions and the suggestions to enhance professionalism in the internal control professions would go so way to overcome these disjunctions, and to achieve the efficacy of internal control functions in meeting fair and realistic regulatory expectations of their roles and responsibilities.

9

Concluding Remarks

LEGISLATIVE REFORMS HAVE been relentlessly introduced to change the financial sector since the global financial crisis of 2008–09. In light of increased demands on banks and financial institutions to meet regulatory obligations, regulators are increasingly looking to the internal control functions in firms to play a greater part in securing firm compliance.

Enhanced regulatory expectations of the roles and responsibilities of internal control functions have led to regulatory reforms to beef up the organisational positioning, profile and capacity of such functions. These regulatory reforms are couched in a meta-regulatory framework that has to be implemented by the organisation concerned. Internal control functions situated within this meta-regulatory framework are used to performing firm-centric functions. Now they are also subject to 'gatekeeping' expectations. The question is whether they are able to effectively meet such regulatory expectations and provide a form of governance support to securing regulatory objectives through firm compliance.

This book discusses the general rationales for meta-regulation in financial regulation, and explores the potential and weaknesses of meta-regulation. One of these weaknesses was manifested in the relative impotence of internal control functions in banks in the pre-crisis era. The meta-regulation of internal control functions means that firms have to undertake design and implementation of internal control functions to meet regulatory objectives, and in this process, firms enjoy a certain latitude of discretion. Banks and financial institutions in the pre-crisis era have not made internal control functions particularly robust or influential in the organisational context in order not to impede business purposes. The organisational manipulation of internal control functions manifests the general weakness of meta-regulatory frameworks, ie, that they can be subject to organisational manipulation.

Post-crisis reforms have grappled with this key weakness and ushered in many reforms in the organisational dimension for internal control functions. The compliance, internal audit and risk management functions have all become more important in organisational profile, and regulatory reforms protect their independence, power and resources. Further, appropriate accountability channels have been designed to support their independence and objectivity. This book critically reviews these reforms and argues that although these go some way to mitigating the meta-regulatory weaknesses that afflicted internal control functions previously, they may not be sufficient to help internal control functions meet new regulatory expectations. On the one hand, one may argue that such structural reforms to internal control and corporate governance are merely cosmetic as firms are still left with the discretion as to how exactly the prescribed structures are to be implemented and would do the minimum to adjust to regulatory requirements in order to carry on business as usual. In other words, new structural requirements for internal control and corporate governance could produce a box-ticking exercise of ever expanding checklists of procedures, structures and systems that look measurable, credible and acceptable to regulators. These reforms need therefore not be directly related to substantive outcomes such as changing firm behaviour. However, Parker and Nielsen have carried out empirical research on the nature and efficacy of reforming structures and procedures in firms and conclude that these reforms could result in a substantive effect upon firm culture and behaviour.[1] Therefore, organisational reforms are important to a certain extent, but this book argues that these reforms need to be further supported in order to make internal control functions effective in assuming a gatekeeping role.

The book does not assume that new regulatory expectations are excessive, as there is good reason to view internal control functions as being able to supply governance support to secure firms' meeting of regulatory objectives. However, the potential to assume gatekeeping roles by internal control functions is arguably at the moment not matched by their practical capacity. Even if internal control functions have gained more organisational power and stature as a result of legislative reforms, their efficacy in gatekeeping is also shaped by their professional understanding and commitment to such a role. An effective professional understanding is based on clarity in the scope of responsibilities and in the standards for discharging such responsibilities. An effective professional commitment needs to be based on the profession's generally accepted consciousness of the social value of its role and its contribution to the wider good.

The book is of the view that the compliance and risk management professions are only experiencing an emerging form of professionalism, and to a lesser extent the internal audit function. Relatively nascent levels of professionalism could affect internal control functions meeting regulatory expectations as the lack of clarity in scope of responsibilities or standards of conduct could result in (a) organisational manipulation of the roles and powers of internal control functions and (b) an expectations gap between

[1] Christine Parker and Vibeke Lehmann Nielsen, 'Corporate Compliance Systems: Could They Make Any Difference?' (2009) 41 *Administration & Society* 3.

regulators and internal control professions which may result in unfair and unpredictable forms and extents of liability imposed on internal control personnel for the primary breaches by firms. The book refers to the former as giving rise to regulatory–organisational and professional–organisational disjunctions, and the latter as giving rise to regulatory professional disjunctions, all of which may undermine internal control functions in meeting regulatory expectations.

This book suggests that more is needed in terms of enhancing the professionalism of internal control functions, and such can be achieved by a partnership between bottom-up initiatives—led by the professions' emerging trade bodies—and regulators who need to articulate their expectations more clearly and frame them fairly and realistically taking on board professional input.

In general, this book also suggests that its arguments may have more general application in addressing the weaknesses of meta-regulation. Meta-regulation is an important and essential regulatory strategy and it is arguable that its chief weakness, ie, firm implementation, can be mitigated by internal gatekeeping that checks on such firm implementation. Effective internal gatekeeping could be based on the enhanced professionalism of such gatekeepers. The book's suggestions could provide wider insights towards informing the theory of knowledge-based contemporary governance dominated by experts.[2] Wilkes has posited this theory to argue that the trajectory in contemporary governance and regulation in general will be expert dominated, as specialist knowledge will become the main criterion for securing a voice in governance. Governance by experts in international financial regulation is already observed.[3] Increasing the expert capacity of internal gatekeepers in a firm may shape these gatekeepers into a governance role that can resist organisational manipulation. Such internal gatekeepers may thus be better placed to secure firm compliance with ever increasing regulatory burdens.

[2] Helmut Wilke, *Governance in a Disenchanted World* (Cheltenham: Edward Elgar, 2009).

[3] Geoffrey Underhill, 'Theorizing Governance in a Global Financial System' in P Mooschlechner, H Schuberth and B Weber (eds), *The Political Economy of Financial Market Regulation* (Cheltenham: Edward Elgar, 2006); Geoffrey Underhill and Xiaoke Zhang, 'Norms, Legitimacy, and Global Financial Governance' (2006) WEF Working Paper 13 at papers.ssrn.com/sol3/papers.cfm?abstract_id=941389.

Bibliography

Acharya, Viral and Richardson, Matthew (eds), *Restoring Financial Stability: How to Repair a Failed Financial System* (Chichester: Wiley Finance, 2009).

Adams, Renee, 'Governance and the Financial Crisis' (2009) ECGI Finance Working Paper 248/2009).

AIRMIC, ALARM and IRM, 'A Structured Approach to Enterprise Risk Management (ERM) and the Requirements of ISO 31000' (2010).

Akinbami, Folarin, 'Is Meta-Regulation All it is Cracked Up to Be? The Case of UK Financial Regulation' (2013) 14 *Journal of Banking Regulation* 16.

Aldamen, Husam, Duncan, Keith, Kelly, Simone, McNamara, Ray and Nagel, Stephan, 'Audit Committee Characteristics and Firm Performance during the Global Financial Crisis' (2012) 52 *Accounting & Finance* 971.

Alexander, Kern, 'Principles v Rules in Financial Regulation: Re-assessing the Balance in the Credit Crisis' (2009) 10 *European Business Organization Law Review* 169.

—— 'UK Corporate Governance and Banking Regulation: The Regulator's Role as Stakeholder' (2004) 33 *Stetson Law Review* 991.

Alfieri, Anthony V, 'Big Law and Risk Management: Case Studies of Litigation, Deals, and Diversity' (2011) 24 *Georgetown Journal of Legal Ethics* 991.

Allen, Linda and Saunders, Anthony, 'Incorporating Systemic Risk Influences into Risk Measurements: A Survey of the Literature' (2004) 26 *Journal of Financial Services Research* 161.

Al-Shetwi, Mohammed, Ramadili, Shamsher Mohamed, Hassan, Taufiq, Chowdury, Shah and Sori, Zulkarnain Muhamad, 'Impact of Internal Audit Function (IAF) on Financial Reporting Quality (FRQ): Evidence from Saudi Arabia' (2011) 5 *African Journal of Business Management* 11189.

Altamuro, J and Beatty, A, 'How does Internal Control Regulation Affect Financial Reporting?' (2010) 49 *Journal of Accounting and Economics* 584.

Alvesson, Mats, *Understanding Organizational Culture* (London: Sage, 2012).

Andenas, Mads and Andersen, Camilla (eds), *Theory and Practice of Harmonisation* (Cheltenham: Edward Elgar, 2012).

Andenas, Mads and Chiu, Iris H-Y, *The Foundations and Future of Financial Regulation: Governance for Responsibility* (Oxford: Routledge, 2014).

Andenas, Mads and Wooldridge, Frank, *European Comparative Company Law* (Cambridge: Cambridge University Press, 2009).

Andruszkiewicz, Grzegorz, Davis, Mark HA and Lleo, Sébastien, 'Taming Animal Spirits: Risk Management with Behavioural Factors' (2013) 9(2) *Annals of Finance* 145.

Arena, Marika and Jeppesen, Kim J, 'The Jurisdiction of Internal Auditing and the Quest for Professionalization: The Danish' (2011) 14 *International Journal of Auditing* 111.

Armour, John, Deakin, Simon and Konzelmann, Suzanne J, 'Shareholder Primacy and the Trajectory of UK Corporate Governance' (2003) 41 *British Journal of Industrial Relations* 531.
Armour, John and McCahery, Joseph A (eds), *After Enron: Improving Corporate Law and Modernising Securities Regulation in Europe and in the US* (Oxford: Hart Publishing, 2006).
Arsalidou, Demetra, 'The Regulation of Executive Pay and Economic Theory' (2011) 5 *Journal of Business Law* 431.
Ashbaugh-Skaife, H, Collins, D and Kinney, W, 'The Discovery and Consequences of Internal Control Deficiencies Prior to SOX-Mandated Audits' (2006) Working Paper, University of Wisconsin-Madison.
Ashby, Simon, Palermo, Tommaso and Power, Michael, *Risk Culture in Financial Organisations* (Interim Report, November 2012; Research Report, 2014).
Ashcroft, John, Hanaway, Catherine and Oñate Greim, Claudia L, 'Whistleblowers Cash in, Unwary Corporations Pay' (2011) 40 *Hofstra Law Review* 367.
Awrey, Dan, Blair, William and Kershaw, David, 'Between Law and Markets: Is there a Role for Culture and Ethics in Financial Regulation?' (2013) 38 *Delaware Journal of Corporate Law* 191.
Baer, Miriam Hechler, 'Governing Corporate Compliance' (2009) 50 *Boston College Law Review* 949.
Bainbridge, Stephen, 'Caremark and Enterprise Risk Management' (2009) 34 *Journal of Corporation Law* 967.
Bamberger, Kenneth A, 'Regulation as Delegation: Private Firms, Decisionmaking, and Accountability in the Administrative State' (2006) 56 *Duke Law Journal* 377.
—— 'Technologies of Compliance: Risk and Regulation in a Digital Age' (2009/10) 88 *Texas Law Review* 669.
Banerjee, SB, *Corporate Social Responsibility: The Good, the Bad and the Ugly* (Cheltenham: Edward Elgar, 2007).
Banks, Erik, *Risk Culture* (Basingstoke: Palgrave Macmillan, 2012).
Barker, Roger M, *Corporate Governance, Competition, and Political Parties: Explaining Corporate Governance Change in Europe* (Oxford: Oxford University Press, 2010).
Barnett, Ronald, 'Critical Professionalism in an Age of Super-complexity' in Bryan Cunninghm (ed), *Exploring Professionalism* (London: Institute of Education Press, 2008).
Bartram, Söhnke M, 'Corporate Risk Management as a Lever for Shareholder Value Creation' (2000) 9 *Financial Markets, Institutions & Instruments* 279.
Barua, Abhijit, Rama, Dasaratha V, Sharma, Vineeta, 'Audit Committee Characteristics and Investment in Internal Auditing' (2010) 29 *Journal of Accounting and Public Policy* 503.
Basel Committee on Banking Supervision, *Compliance and the Compliance Function in Banks* (April 2005).
—— *Implementation of the Compliance Principles: A Survey* (August 2008).
—— *Principles for Enhancing Corporate Governance* (October 2010).
—— *The Internal Audit Function in Banks* (Consultation Paper, December 2011).
—— *The Internal Audit Function in Banks* (Final Report) (Basel: BIS, June 2012).
—— *Consultative Document Operational Risk–Revisions to the Simpler Approaches* (October 2014).
—— *Guidelines: Corporate Governance Principles for Banks* (Consultation Paper, October 2014).

Bazley, Stuart and Haynes, Andrew, *Financial Services Authority Regulation and Risk-based Compliance* (London: Tottel Publishing, 2006).

Beasley, MS, 'An Empirical Analysis of the Relation between the Board of Director Composition and Financial Statement Fraud' (1996) 71 *Accounting Review* 443.

Bebchuk, Lucian, Cohen, Alma and Spamann, Holgar,'The Wages of Failure: Executive Compensation at Bear Stearns and Lehman 2000–2008' (2010) 27 *Yale Journal on Regulation* 257.

Bebchuk, Lucian and Fried, Jesse M, *Pay without Performance: The Unfulfilled Promise of Executive Compensation* (Boston, MA: Harvard University Press, 2006).

—— 'Paying for Long Term Performance' (2009) 158 *University of Pennsylvania Law Review* 1915.

Bebchuk, Lucian and Spamann, Holger, 'Regulating Bankers' Pay' (2010) 98 *Georgetown Law Journal* 247.

Beecher-Monas, Erica, 'The Risks of Reward: The Role of Executive Compensation in Financial Crisis' (2011) 6 *Virginia Law & Business Review* 101.

Belinfanti, Tamara C, 'Beyond Economics in Pay for Performance' (2012) 41 *Hofstra Law Review* 91.

Belmont, David P, *Value Added Risk Management in Financial Institutions* (Chichester: John Wiley & Sons, 2004).

Bender, Ruth and Moir, Lance, 'Does "Best Practice" in Setting Executive Pay in the UK Encourage "Good" Behaviour?' (2006) 67 *Journal of Business Ethics* 75.

Bénéplanc, Gilles and Rochet, Jean-Charles, *Risk Management in Turbulent Times* (New York: Oxford University Press, 2011).

Bennett, Tim, *Money Laundering Compliance*, 2nd edn (W Sussex: Tottel Publishing, 2007).

Berson, Yair, Oreg, Shaul and Dvir, Taly, 'CEO Values, Organizational Culture and Firm Outcomes' (2008) 28 *Journal of Organizational Behavior* 615.

Bessis, Joël, *Risk Management in Banking* (Chichester: John Wiley & Sons, 2011).

Birden, Hudson, Glass, Nel, Wilson, Ian, Harrison, Michelle, Usherwood, Tim and Nass, Duncan, 'Defining Professionalism in Medical Education: A Systematic Review' (2014) 36 *Medical Teacher* 47.

Birindelli, Giuliana and Ferretti, Paola, 'Compliance Risk in Italian Banks: The Results of a Survey' (2008) *Journal of Financial Regulation and Compliance* 335.

BIS, *The Kay Review of UK Equity Markets and Long-Term Decision Making* (Final Report, 23 July 2012).

—— *The Whistleblowing Framework: Call for Evidence* (July 2013).

—— *Transparency & Trust: Enhancing the Transparency of UK Company Ownership and Increasing Trust in UK Business* (April 2014).

Bjørkelo, Brita, Einarsen, Ståle and Matthiesen, Stig Berge, 'Predicting Proactive Behaviour At Work: Exploring The Role Of Personality As An Antecedent Of Whistleblowing Behaviour' (2010) 83 *Journal of Occupational and Organizational Psychology* 371.

Black, Julia, *Rules and Regulators* (Oxford: Clarendon, 1998).

—— 'Mapping the Contours of Contemporary Financial Services Regulation' (2002) 2 *Journal of Corporate Law Studies* 253.

—— 'Enrolling Actors in Regulatory Systems: Examples from UK Financial Services Regulation' [2003] *Public Law* 63.

—— 'The Emergence of Risk-Based Regulation and the New Public Risk Management in the United Kingdom' [2005] *Public Law* 512.

—— 'Paradoxes and Failures: "New Governance" Techniques and the Financial Crisis' (2012) 75 *Modern Law Review* 1037.

Black, Julia and Baldwin, Robert, 'When Risk-based Regulation Aims Low: A Strategic Framework' (2012) 6 *Regulation & Governance* 131.

Black, Julia, Hopper, Martyn and Band, Christa, 'Making a Success of Principles-based Regulation' (2007) 6 *Law and Financial Markets Review* 191.

Blowfield, M and Murray, A, *Corporate Responsibility* (Oxford: OUP, 2009).

Boatright, John R, 'Risk Management and the Responsible Corporation: How Sweeping the Invisible Hand?' (2011) 116 *Business and Society Review* 145.

Bolt, Wilko and Tieman, Alexander F, 'Banking Competition, Risk and Regulation' (2004) 106 *The Scandinavian Journal of Economics* 783.

Boubakri, Narjess, 'Corporate Governance and Issues from the Insurance Industry' (2011) 78 *Journal of Risk and Insurance* 501.

Bovens, Mark, *The Quest for Responsibility: Accountability and Citizenship in Complex Organisations* (Cambridge: Cambridge University Press, 1998).

Bower, James B and Schlosser, Robert E, 'Internal Control—Its True Nature' (1965) 40 *The Accounting Review* 338.

Braithwaite, John, *Regulatory Capitalism* (Cheltenham: Edward Elgar, 2008).

Brown, Ian, Steen, Adam and Foreman, Julie, 'Risk Management in Corporate Governance: A Review and Proposal' (2009) 17 *Corporate Governance* 546.

Bruner, Christopher M, 'Corporate Governance Reform in a Time of Crisis' (2011) 36 *Journal of Corporation Law* 309.

—— 'Conceptions of Corporate Purpose in Post-Crisis Financial Firms' (2012) 36 *Seattle University Law Review* 527.

—— *Corporate Governance in the Common Law World: The Political Foundations of Shareholder Power* (Cambridge: Cambridge University Press, 2013).

Brunnermeier, M, Crockett, A, Goodhart, C, Persaud, AD and Shin, Hyun, *The Fundamental Principles of Financial Regulation* (London: Centre for Economic Policy Research, Geneva Reports on the World Economy, 2009).

Brytting, Tomas, Minogue, Richard and Morino, Veronica, *The Anatomy of Fraud and Corruption* (Farnham: Gower Publishing, 2011).

Bucklin, Leonard, 'More Preaching, Fewer Rules: A Process for the Corporate Lawyer's Maintenance of Corporate Ethics' (2009) 35 *Ohio Northern University Law Review* 887.

Bundred, Stephen, 'The Future of Regulation in the Public Sector' (2006) 26 *Public Money and Management* 181.

Burnaby, Priscilla and Hass, Susan, 'Ten Steps to Enterprise-Wide Risk Management' (2009) 9 *Corporate Governance* 539.

Büschgens, Thorsten, Bausch, Andreas and Balkin, David B, 'Organizational Culture and Innovation: A Meta-Analytic Review' (2013) 30 *Journal of Product Innovation Management* 1.

Cadbury, Sir Adrian, *Report of the Committee on the Financial Aspects of Corporate Governance* (London, Gee, 1992).

Cahill, Edward, 'Audit Committee and Internal Audit Effectiveness in a Multinational Bank Subsidiary: A Case Study' (2006) 7 *Journal of Banking Regulation* 160.

Carey, Mark and Stulz, René M, 'Introduction' in Mark Carey and René M Stulz (eds), *The Risks of Financial Institutions* (Chicago, IL: University of Chicago Press, 2006).

Carmichael, DR, 'Hypotheses of Internal Control' (1970) 45 *The Accounting Review* 235.

Carrel, Philippe, *The Handbook of Risk Management: Implementing a Post-Crisis Corporate Culture* (Chichester: John Wiley & Sons, 2010).

Cheffins, Brian R, 'Did Corporate Governance "Fail" During the 2008 Stock Market Meltdown? The Case of the S&P 500' (2009) ECGI Law Working Paper 124/2009.

—— 'The Stewardship Code's Achilles' Heel' (2010) 73 *Modern Law Review* 1004.

Chew, Donald H (ed), *Corporate Risk Management* (New York: Columbia Business School Publishing, 2008).

Chiu, Iris H-Y, *Regulatory Convergence in EU Securities Regulation* (The Hague: Kluwer Law International, 2008).

—— 'Institutional Shareholders as Stewards: Toward a New Conception of Corporate Governance' (2012) 6 *Brooklyn Journal of Corporate, Financial & Commercial Law* 387.

—— 'The Vickers Independent Banking Commission Report—Does the Ring-fencing of Retail Banks Mitigate Systemic Risk Concerns in the Banking Sector?' (2012) 9 *International Corporate Rescue* 79.

—— 'Turning Institutional Investors into "Stewards"—Exploring the Meaning and Objectives in "Stewardship"' (2013) *Current Legal Problems* 443.

Chiu, Randy K, 'Ethical Judgment and Whistleblowing Intention: Examining the Moderating Role of Locus of Control' (2003) 43 *Journal of Business Ethics* 65.

Choi, Stephen J, Fisch, Jill E and Kahan, Marcel, 'The Power of Proxy Advisors: Myth or Reality?' (2010) 59 *Emory Law Journal* 869.

Cioffi, John W, *Public Law and Private Power. Corporate Governance Reform in the Age of Finance Capitalism* (Ithaca, NY: Cornell University Press, 2010).

Coates, John, *The Hour Between Dog and Wolf. Risk Taking, Gut Feelings, and the Biology of Boom and Bust* (New York: Penguin Press, 2012).

Coates, John, Gurnell, Mark and Sarnyai, Zoltan, 'From Molecule to Market: Steroid Hormones and Financial Risk-Taking' (2010) 365 *Philosophical Transactions of the Royal Society B: Biological Sciences* 331.

Coates, John and Herbert, Joe, 'Endogenous Steroids and Financial Risk Taking on a London Trading Floor' (2008) 105 *Proceedings of the National Academy of Science* 6167.

Coffee, John C, *Gatekeepers* (Oxford: Oxford University Press, 2006).

—— 'Understanding Enron: "It's About the Gatekeepers, Stupid"' (2002) 57 *Business Lawyer* 1403.

Coglianese, Cary and Lazer, David, 'Management-Based Regulation: Prescribing Private Management to Achieve Public Goals' (2003) 37 *Law & Society Review* 691.

Coglianese, Cary and Mendelson, Evan, 'Meta-Regulation and Self-Regulation' in R Baldwin, M Cave and M Lodge (eds), *The Oxford Handbook of Regulation* (Oxford: Oxford University Press, 2010).

Committee of Sponsoring Organizations of the Treadway Commission, *Enterprise Risk Management: Integrated Framework* (September 2004).

Conley, John M, Broome, Lissa L and Krawiec, Kimberley D, 'Dangerous Categories: Narratives of Corporate Board Diversity' (2010) 89 *North Carolina Law Review* 759.

Cortez, Annetta, *Winning at Risk* (Chichester: John Wiley & Sons, 2011).

Couppey-Soubeyran, Jézabel, 'Financial Regulation in the Crisis: Regulation, Market Discipline, Internal Control: The Big Three in Turmoil' (2010) 123 *International Economics* 13.

Cox, Paul, Brammer, Stephen and Millington, Andrew, 'Pension Fund Manager Tournaments and Attitudes towards Corporate Characteristics' (2007) 34 *Journal of Business Finance & Accounting* 1307.

CRM Policy Group, 'Containing Systemic Risk: The Road to Reform—The Report of the CRMPG III' in Melvin R Turley (ed), *Reforming Risk in Financial Markets* (New York: NovaScience Publishers, 2009).

Crook, David, 'Some historical Perspectives on Professionalism' in Bryan Cunninghm (ed), *Exploring Professionalism* (London: Institute of Education Press, 2008).

Crouhy, Michel, 'Risk Management Failures During the Financial Crisis' in Robert W Kolb (ed), *Lessons from the Financial Crisis* (New Jersey: John Wiley & Sons, 2010).

Cummings, Thomas G and Worley, Christopher G, *Organization Development and Change*, 8th edn (Boston, MA: South-Western College Publishing, 2004).

—— 'Beyond Liability; Rewarding Effective Gatekeepers' (2007) 92 *Minnesota Law Review* 323.

—— 'Rediscovering Board Expertise: Legal Implications of the Empirical Literature' (2008) 77 *University of Cincinnati Law Review* 465.

Cunninghm, Bryan (ed), *Exploring Professionalism* (London: Institute of Education Press, 2008).

Dallas, Lynne, 'Short-Termism, the Financial Crisis, and Corporate Governance' (2012) 37 *Journal of Corporation Law* 265.

Damodaran, Aswath, *Strategic Risk Taking: A Framework for Risk Management* (New Jersey: Pearson Education Inc, 2008).

Davidson, R, Goodwin-Stewart, J and Kent, P, 'Internal Governance Structures and Earnings Management' (2005) 45 *Accounting & Finance* 241.

Davies, Howard, *The Financial Crisis: Who is to Blame?* (Cambridge: Polity Press, 2010).

Davies, MBT, 'The Objectives of Internal Auditing' (1956) 31 *The Accounting Review* 227.

De Haan, Jakob, Oosterloo, Sander and Schoenmaker, Dirk, *European Financial Markets and Institutions* (Cambridge: Cambridge University Press, 2009).

Deakin, Simon, 'What Directors Do (and Fail to Do): Some Comparative Notes on Board Structure and Corporate Governance' (2010/11) 55 *New York Law School Law Review* 525.

—— 'Corporate Governance and Financial Crisis in the Long Run' in Peer Zumbansen and Cynthia A Williams (eds), *The Embedded Firm: Corporate Governance, Labor, and Finance Capitalism* (New York: Cambridge University Press, 2011).

DeMott, Deborah A, 'The Discrete Roles of General Counsel' (2005) 74 *Fordham Law Review* 955.

—— 'The Stages of Scandal and the Roles of General Counsel' (2012) *Wisconsin Law Review* 463.

Diebold, FX, Doherty, N and Herring, RJ (eds), The Known, *The Unknown and The Unknowable in Financial Risk Management* (Princeton, NJ: Princeton University Press, 2010).

Dignam, A, 'Capturing Corporate Governance: The End of the UK Self-regulating System' (2007) 4 *International Journal of Disclosure and Governance* 24.

Dignam, Alan and Galanis, Michael, *The Globalization of Corporate Governance* (Aldershot: Ashgate, 2009).

Di Renzo, B, Hillairet, M, Picard, M, Rifaut, A, Bernard, C, Hagen, D, Maa, P and Reinard, D, 'Operational Risk Management in Financial Institutions: Process Assessment in Concordance with Basel II' (2007) 12 *Software Process Improvement and Practice* 321.

Dombalagian, Onnig H, 'Requiem for the Bulge Bracket? Revisiting Investment Bank Regulation' (2010) 85 *Indiana Law Journal* 777.

Draghi, Mario, 'Observations on Risk Management Practices During the Recent Market Turbulence' in Melvin R Turley (ed), *Reforming Risk in Financial Markets* (New York: NovaScience Publishers, 2009).

Dragomir, Larisa, *European Prudential Banking Regulation and Supervision* (Oxford: Routledge, 2010).

Drori, Gili S, 'Governed by Governance' in Gili S Drori, John W Meyer and Hokyu Hwang (eds), *Globalization and Organization* (Oxford: Oxford University Press, 2009).

Drori, Gili S and Meyer, John W, 'Global Scientization: An Expanded Environment for Organization' in Gili S Drori, John W Meyer and Hokyu Hwang (eds), *Globalization and Organization* (Oxford: Oxford University Press, 2009).

Drori, Gili S, Meyer, John W and Hwang, Hokyu (eds), *Globalization and Organization* (Oxford: Oxford University Press, 2009).

Easterbrook, Frank H and Fischel, Daniel R, *The Economic Structure of Corporate Law* (CambridgeMA: Harvard University Press, 1996).

EBA, *Guidelines on the Assessment of the Suitability of Members of the Management Body and Key Function Holders* (22 November 2012).

—— *Consultation Paper: Draft Regulatory Technical Standards On the specification of the assessment methodology for competent authorities regarding compliance of an institution with the requirements to use the IRB Approach in accordance with Articles 144(2), 173(3) and 180(3)(b) of Regulation (EU) No 575/2013* (12 November 2014).

—— *Draft Guidelines on Product Oversight and Governance Arrangements for Retail Banking Products* (November 2014).

Ebersole, Dave, 'Blowing the Whistle on the Dodd–Frank Whistleblower Provisions' (2010–11) 6 *Ohio State Entrepreneurial Business Law Journal* 123.

Edelman, Lauren B, Krieger, Linda H, Eliason, Scott R, Albiston, Catherine R and Mellema, Virginia, 'When Organizations Rule: Judicial Deference to Institutionalized Employment Structures' (2011) 117 *American Journal of Sociology* 888.

Edelman, Lauren B, Uggen, Christopher and Erlanger, Howard S, 'The Endogeneity of Legal Regulation: Grievance Procedures as Rational Myth' (1999) 105 *American Journal of Sociology* 406.

Eden, Dov and Moriah, Leah, 'Impact of Internal Auditing on Branch Bank Performance: A Field Experiment' (1996) 68 *Organizational Behavior and Human Decision Processes* 262.

Edmunds, Rod and Lowry, John, 'The Failure of RBS and HBOS: Holding Banking Directors to Account via the Disqualification Regime' in Iris H-Y Chiu and Michael McKee (eds), *The Law of Corporate Governance in Banks and Financial Institutions* (Cheltenham: Edward Elgar, 2015 at ch 3.

Edwards, Douglas O, 'An Unfortunate "Tail": Reconsidering Risk Management Incentives after the Financial Crisis of 2007–2009' (2010) 81 *University of Colorado Law Review* 247.

Ellinson, Robert Elliot, 'Circles within a Circle: The Condition for the Possibility of Ethical Business Institutions within a Market System' (2004) 53 *Journal of Business Ethics* 17.

Ellul, Andrew and Yerramilli, Vijay, 'Stronger Risk Controls, Lower Risk: Evidence from US Bank Holding Companies' (2013) 68 *Journal of Finance* 1757.

Enriques, Luca, 'Conflicts of Interest in Investment Services' in Guido Ferrarini and Eddy Wymeersch (eds), *Investor Protection in Europe: Corporate Law Making, the MiFID and Beyond* (Oxford: Oxford University Press, 2006).

Enriques, Luca and Zetzsche, Dirk, 'The Risky Business of Regulating Risk Management in Listed Companies' (2013) 103 *European Company and Financial Law Review* 271.

Erkens, David H, Hung Mingyi and Matos, Pedro, 'Corporate Governance in the 2007–2008 Financial Crisis: Evidence from Financial Institutions Worldwide' (2012) 18 *Journal of Corporate Finance* 389.

Ernst & Young and the Institute of International Finance, *Progress in Financial Services Risk Management: A Survey of the Major Financial Institutions* (2012).

ESMA, *Consultation Paper: Guidelines on Certain Aspects of the MiFID Compliance Function Requirements* (December 2011).

—— *Guidelines on Certain Aspects of the MiFID Compliance Function Requirements* (6 July 2012).

—— *Consultation Paper on MiFID II and MiFIR* (22 May 2014).

—— *Final Report: ESMA's Technical Advice to the Commission on MiFID II and MiFIR* (December 2014).

Facciolo, Francis J, 'A Broker's Duty of Best Execution in the Nineteenth and Early Twentieth Centuries' (2005) 26 *Pace Law Review* 155.

Fahlenbrach, Rüdiger, Prilmeier, Robert and Stulz, René M, 'This Time is the Same: Using Bank Performance in 1998 to Explain Bank Performance during the Recent Financial Crisis' (2012) 67 *Journal of Finance* 2139.

Fanto, James A, 'Anticipating the Unthinkable: The Adequacy of Risk Management in Finance and Environmental Studies' (2009) 44 *Wake Forest Law Review* 731.

—— 'The Role of Financial Regulation in Private Financial Firms: Risk Management and the Limitations of the Market Model' (2009) 3 *Brooklyn Journal of Corporate Financial & Commercial Law* 29.

Fanto, James A, Solan, Lawrence M and Darley, John M, 'Justifying Board Diversity' (2011) 89 *North Carolina Law Review* 901.

Fehle, Frank and Psyplakov, Sergey, 'Dynamic Risk Management: Theory and Evidence' (2005) 78 *Journal of Financial Economics* 3.

Fernandez-Laviada, Ana, 'Internal Audit Function Role in Operational Risk Management' (2007) *Journal of Financial Regulation and Compliance* 143.

Ferola, Peter, 'Internal Controls in the Aftermath of Sarbanes-Oxley: One Size Doesn't Fit All' (2006) 48 *South Texas Law Review* 87.

Ferran, Eilis, 'Regulatory Lessons from the Payment Protection Insurance Mis-Selling Scandal in the UK' (2012) *European Business Organisation Law Review* 248.

Ferrarini, Guido, Moloney, Niamh and Ungureanu, Maria-Cristina, 'Executive Remuneration in Crisis: A Critical Assessment of Reforms in Europe' (2010) 10 *Journal of Corporate Law Studies* 73.

Ferrarini, Guido and Ungureanu, Maria Cristina, 'Economics, Politics, and the International Principles for Sound Compensation Practices: An Analysis of Executive Pay at European Banks' (2011) 64 *Vanderbilt Law Review* 432.

Financial Reporting Council, *Developments in Corporate Governance 2012: The Impact and Implementation of the UK Corporate Governance and Stewardship Codes* (December 2012).

Financial Stability Board, *Principles for an Effective Risk Appetite Framework: Consultative Document* (17 July 2013).

—— *Assessment Methodology for the Key Attributes of Effective Resolution Regimes for Financial Institutions* (28 August 2013).

—— *Guidance on Supervisory Interaction with Financial Institutions on Risk Culture: Consultation Document* (18 November 2013).

—— *Principles for an Effective Risk Appetite Framework* (18 November 2013).

—— *Adequacy of Loss-Absorbing Capacity of Global Systemically Important Banks in Resolution* (10 November 2014).

—— *Global Shadow Banking Monitoring Report 2014* (November 2014).

Fisch, Jill and Rosen, Kenneth M, 'Is there a Role for Lawyers in Preventing Future Enrons?' (2003) 48 *Villanova Law Review* 1097.

Folkman, Peter et al, 'Working for Themselves: Financial Intermediaries and Present Day Capitalism' (2007) 49 *Business History* 552.

Ford, Cristie, 'New Governance, Compliance, and Principles-Based Securities Regulation' (2008) 45 *American Business Law Journal* 1.

—— 'New Governance in the Teeth of Human Frailty: Lessons from Financial Regulation' (2010) *Wisconsin Law Review* 441.

—— 'Macro- and Micro-Level Effects on Responsive Financial Regulation' (2011) 44 *University of British Columbia Law Review* 589.

Ford, Cristie and Hess, David, 'Can Corporate Monitorships Improve Corporate Compliance?' (2009) 34 *Journal of Corporation Law* 679.

Foreman, Samuel R, 'Bored Boards: The Directorial Disengagement Dilemma' (2010) 50 *Washburn Law Journal* 174.

Fort, Timothy L, Ethics and Governance: Business as Mediating Institution (Oxford: Oxford University Press 2001)

Franco, Joseph A, 'Of Complicity and Compliance: A Rules-Based Anti-Complicity Strategy under Federal Securities Law' (2011) 14 *University of Pennsylvania Journal of Business Law* 1.

Fried, Jesse M and Shilon, Nitzan, 'Excess Pay Claw-backs' (2011) 36 *Journal of Corporation Law* 722.

Friedson, Eliot, *Professionalism: The Third Logic* (Cambridge: Polity Press, 2001, 2004 rep).

FSA, *Consumer Redress Scheme in Respect of Unsuitable Advice to Invest in Arch Cru Funds* (December 2012).

—— *Final Guidance: Risks to Customers from Financial Incentives* (January 2013).

—— *Commercial Insurance Intermediaries—Conflicts of Interest and Intermediary Remuneration: Report on the Thematic Project* (May 2014)

—— *Thematic Review: Best Execution and Payment for Order Flow* (31 July 2014).

FSA, *Conflicts of Interests between Asset Managers and their Customers: Identifying and Mitigating the Risks* (November, 2012).

Funk, Russell J and Hirschman, Daniel G, 'Endogenous Legal Change: How Organizations Re-Shaped Glass-Steagall' (2012) University of Michigan Working Paper.

Ganuza, Juan Jose and Gomez, Fernando, 'Should we Trust the Gatekeepers? Auditors' and Lawyers' Liability for Clients' Misconduct' (2007) 27 *International Review of Law and Economics* 96.

G30 Working Group on Macroprudential Policy, *Enhancing Financial Stability and Resilience: Macroprudential Policy, Tools and Systems for the Future* (Washington DC: Group of Thirty, 2010).

Gabbi, Giampaolo, Tanzi, Paola Musile and Nadotti, Loris, 'Firm Size and Compliance Costs Asymmetries in the Investment Services' (2011) *Journal of Financial Regulation and Compliance* 58.

Gadinis, Stavros, 'The SEC and the Financial Industry: Evidence from Enforcement against Broker-Dealers' (2012) 67 *Business Lawyer* 679.

Galavielle, Jean-Pierre, 'Business Ethics is a Matter of Good Conduct and of Good Conscience?' (2004) 53 *Journal of Business Ethics* 9.

García, Laura Sierra, Barbadillo, Emiliano Ruiz and Pérez, Manuel Orta, 'Audit Committee and Internal Audit and the Quality of Earnings: Empirical Evidence From Spanish Companies' (2012) 16 *Journal of Management & Governance* 305.

Georgosuli, Andromachi, 'Regulatory Interpretation: Conversational or Constructive?' (2010) 30 *Oxford Journal of Legal Studies* 361.

—— 'The FSA's Treating Customers Fairly (TCF) Initiative: What is so Good About it and Why it May not Work' (2011) 38 *Journal of Law and Society* 405.

Gerding, Erik F, 'Code, Crash and Open Source' (2009) 84 *Washington Law Review* 127.

Gersbach, Hans and Wenzelburger, Jan, 'Sophistication in Risk Management, Bank Equity, and Stability' (2010) 10 *International Review of Finance* 63.

Gevurtz, Franklin A, 'The Role of Corporate Law in Preventing a Financial Crisis: Some Reflections on *In Re Citigroup Inc Shareholder Derivative Litigation*' in PM Vasudev and Susan Watson (eds), *Corporate Governance after the Financial Crisis* (Cheltenham: Edward Elgar, 2011).

Ghafran, Chaudhry and O'Sullivan, Noel, 'The Governance Role of Audit Committees: Reviewing a Decade of Evidence' (2012) *International Journal of Management Review* 1.

Ghosh, DN, 'Quirks of the Market Regulator' (2004) 39 *Economic and Political Weekly* 1550.

Gilad, Sharon, 'It Runs in the Family: Meta-regulation and its Siblings' (2010) 4 *Regulation & Governance* 485.

—— 'Process-Oriented Regulation: Conceptualisation and Assessment' in David Levi-Faur (ed), *Handbook on the Politics of Regulation* (Cheltenham: Edward Elgar, 2011).

—— 'Institutionalizing Fairness in Financial Markets: Mission Impossible?' (2011) 5 *Regulation & Governance* 309.

Gilligan, George, 'Jerome Kerviel the "Rogue Trader" of Société Générale: Bad Luck, Bad Apple, Bad Tree or Bad Orchard?' (2011) 32 *Company Lawyer* 355.

Gleeson, Simon, *International Banking Regulation* (Oxford: Oxford University Press, 2009).

Goyal, Amit and Wahal, Sunil, 'The Selection and Termination of Investment Management Firms by Plan Sponsors' (2008) 63 *Journal of Finance* 1805.

Gray, Joanna and Hamilton, Jenny, *Implementing Financial Regulation: Theory and Practice* (Chichester: John Wiley & Sons, 2006).

Greenbury, Richard, *Report: Directors' Remuneration* (17 July 1995).
Grove, Hugh, Patelli, Lorenzo, Victoravich, Lisa M and Xu, Pisun (Tracy), 'Corporate Governance and Performance in the Wake of the Financial Crisis: Evidence from US Commercial Banks' (2011) 19 *Corporate Governance* 418.
Hallett ,Tim, 'Symbolic Power and Organizational Culture' (2003) 21 *Sociological Theory* 128.
Hamdani, Assaf, 'Gatekeeper Liability' (2003) 77 *Southern California Law Review* 53.
Hansmann, Henry and Kraakman, Reinier, 'The End of History for Corporate Law' (2000-2001) 89 *Georgetown Law Journal* 439.
Harner, Michelle, 'Barriers to Effective Risk Management' (2010) 40 *Seton Hall Law Review* 1323.
—— 'Ignoring the Writing on the Wall: The Role of Enterprise Risk Management in the Economic Crisis' (2010) 5 *Journal of Business & Technology Law* 45.
Harris, Stephen L, 'Regulating Finance: Who Rules, Whose Rules?' (2004) 21 *Review of Policy Research* 743.
Hau, Harold and Thum, Marcel, 'Subprime Crisis and Board (In-)Competence: Private vs Public Banks in Germany' (2009) 24 *Economic Policy* 701.
Hayek, Benjamin P, 'Morality, Professionalism and Happiness' (2007) 8 *Engage* 135.
Hellmann, Thomas F, Murdock, Kevin C and Stiglitz, Joseph E, 'Liberalization, Moral Hazard in Banking, and Prudential Regulation: Are Capital Requirements Enough?' (2000) 90 *The American Economic Review* 197.
Hendry, John, *Between Enterprise and Ethics* (Oxford: Oxford University Press, 2003).
Heremans, Dirk and Bosquet, Katrien, 'The Future of Law and Finance after the Financial Crisis: New Perspectives on Regulation and Corporate Governance for Banks' (2011) 5 *University of Illinois Law Review* 1551.
Herring, Richard J, 'The Known, the Unknown, and the Unknowable in Financial Policy: An Application to the Subprime Crisis' (2009) 26 *Yale Journal on Regulation* 391.
HM Treasury, *Banking Reform: Delivering Stability and Supporting a Sustainable Economy* (White Paper, Cm 8356, June 2012).
Ho, Karen, 'Disciplining Investment Bankers, Disciplining the Economy: Wall Street's Institutional Culture of Crisis and the Downsizing of "Corporate America"' (2009) 111 *American Anthropologist* 177.
Hoffman, W Michael et al, 'An Investigation of Ethics Officer Independence' (2008) 78 *Journal of Business Ethics* 87.
Hoffman, Michael W, Neill, John D and Stovall, O Scott, 'Mutual Fund Compliance Officer Independence and Corporate Governance' (2008) 16 *Corporate Governance: An International Review* 52.
Hoffman, W Michael and Rowe, Mark, 'The Ethics Officer as Agent of the Board: Leveraging Ethical Governance Capability in the Post-Enron Corporation' (2007) 112 *Business & Society Review* 553.
Holland, John, 'Banks, Knowledge and Crisis: A Case of Knowledge and Learning Failure' (2010) *Journal of Financial Regulation and Compliance* 87.
Hopt, K, 'Labor Representation on Corporate Boards: Impacts and Problems for Corporate Governance and Economic Integration in Europe' (1994) 14 *International Review of Law and Economics* 203.

—— 'Corporate Governance of Banks after the Financial Crisis' in E Wymeersch, KJ Hopt and G Ferrarini (eds), *Financial Regulation and Supervision: A Post-Crisis Analysis* (Oxford: Oxford University Press, 2012).

Horn, Laura, 'Corporate Governance in Crisis? The Politics of EU Corporate Governance Regulation' (2012) 18 *European Law Journal* 83.

House of Commons and House of Lords, Parliamentary Commission on Banking Standards, *An Accident Waiting to Happen: The Failure of HBOS* (2012–13, HL 144, HC 705).

—— *First Report* (2012–13, HL 98, HC 848).

—— *Proprietary Trading* (2012–13, HL 138, HC 1034).

—— *Changing Banking for Good* Vols 1 and 2 (12 June 2013).

Howson, Nicolas Calcina, 'When "Good" Corporate Governance Makes "Bad" (Financial) Firms: The Global Crisis and the Limits of Private Law' (2009) 108 *Michigan Law Review* 44.

Hoyt, Robert E and Liebenberg, Andre P, 'The Value of Enterprise Risk Management' (2011) 78 *Journal of Risk and Insurance* 795.

Hu, Henry TC, 'Too Complex to Depict? Innovation, "Pure Information" and the SEC Disclosure Paradigm' (2012) 90 *Texas Law Review* 1601.

Huault, Isabelle and Richard, Chrystelle (eds), *Finance: The Discreet Regulator* (Abingdon: Palgrave Macmillan, 2012).

Hubbard, Douglas, *The Failure of Risk Management: Why It's Broken and How Do we Fix It?* (Chichester: John Wiley & Sons, 2009).

Hughes, Peter, 'Bank Internal Audit—Third Line of Defence or First Line of Attack?' in *Interim Management* (ICAEW, August 2011).

Husisian, Gregory, 'US Regulation of International Financial Institutions: It's Time for an Integrated Approach to Compliance' (2010) 127 *Banking Law Journal* 195.

Huskins, Priya Cherian, 'FCPA Prosecutions: Liability Trend to Watch' (2008) 60 *Stanford Law Review* 1447.

ICAEW, *Internal Control: Guidance for Directors on the Combined Code* (Turnbull Report) (1999, 2005 rev).

Inderst, Roman, 'Retail Finance: Thoughts on Reshaping Regulation and Consumer Protection after the Financial Crisis' (2009) 10 *European Business Organization Law Review* 455.

Inderst, Roman and Ottaviani, Marco, 'Misselling Through Agents' (2009) 99 *American Economic Review* 993.

IIA, *Characteristics of an Internal Audit Survey* Executive Summary (2010).

—— *Core Competencies for Today's Internal Auditor* (2010).

Ireland, Paddy, 'Shareholder Primacy and the Distribution of Wealth' (2004) 68 *Modern Law Review* 49.

Jensen, M and Meckling, W, 'Theory of the Firm: Managerial Behavior, Agency Costs and Ownership Structure' (1976) 3 *Journal of Financial Economics* 305.

Jobst, Andreas A, 'The Credit Crisis and Operational Risk—Implications for Practitioners and Regulators' (2010) 5 *Journal of Operational Risk* 43.

John, Kose, Saunders, Anthony and Senbet, Lemma W, 'A Theory of Bank Regulation and Management Compensation' (2000) 13 *Review of Financial Studies* 95.

Johnston, R Barry and Abbott, John, 'Placing Bankers in the Front Line' (2005) 8 *Journal of Money Laundering Control* 215.

Joosen, Bart PM, 'The Limitations of Regulating Macro-Prudential Supervision in Europe' (2010) 25 *Journal of International Banking Law and Regulation* 493.

Jorion, Phillippe, 'Risk Management Lessons from the Credit Crisis' (2009) 15 *European Financial Management* 923.

Kanter, Rosabeth Moss, *Men and Women of the Corporation* (New York: Basic Books, 1977, rep 1983).

Keay, Andrew, *The Corporate Objective* (Cheltenham: Edward Elgar, 2011).

Kershaw, David and Moorhead, Richard, 'Consequential Responsibility for Client Wrongs: Lehman Brothers and the Regulation of the Legal Profession' (2013) 76 *Modern Law Review* 26.

Kim, Sung Hui, 'Gatekeepers Inside Out' (2008) 21 *Georgetown Journal of Legal Ethics* 411.

Kinsella, Ray (ed), *Internal Controls in Banking* (Chichester: John Wiley 1995).

Grant Kirkpatrick, 'The Corporate Governance Lessons from the Financial Crisis' (2009) 96 *OECD Financial Market Trends* 1.

Kling, Arnold, 'The Financial Crisis: Moral Failure or Cognitive Failure?' (2010) 33 *Harvard Journal of Law & Public Policy* 507.

Knights, David and O'Leary, Majella, 'Reflecting on Corporate Scandals: The Failure of Ethical Leadership' (2005) 14 *Business Ethics: A European Review* 359.

Knoblock, Elizabeth M, 'Investment Advisers: The Failure of the Duty to Supervise' (2004) *Journal of Investment Compliance* 35.

Kolb, Robert W (ed), *Lessons from the Financial Crisis* (New Jersey: John Wiley & Sons, 2010).

Kraakman, Reinier H, 'Corporate Liability Strategies and the Costs of Legal Controls' (1984) 93 *Yale Law Journal* 857.

Krawiec, Kimberly D, 'Cosmetic Compliance and the Failure of Negotiated Governance' (2003) 81 *Washington University Law Quarterly* 487.

—— 'The Return of the Rogue' (2009) 51 *Arizona Law Review* 127.

Kross, Wilhelm, *Organised Opportunities: Risk Management in Financial Services Operations* (Chichester: John Wiley & Sons, 2007).

Kumpan, Christoph and Leyens, Patrick C, 'Conflicts of Interest of Financial Intermediaries' (2008) 5 *European Company and Financial Law Review* 72.

Kuritzkes, Andrew and Schuermann, Til, 'What We Know, Don't Know and Can't Know about Bank Risk: A View from the Trenches' in FX Diebold, N Doherty and RJ Herring (eds.), *The Known, The Unknown and The Unknowable in Financial Risk Management* (Princeton, NJ: Princeton University Press, 2010).

Laby, Arthur B, 'Differentiating Gatekeepers' (2006) 1 *Brooklyn Journal of Corporate, Financial & Commercial Law* 119.

Lam, James, *Enterprise Risk Management: From Incentives to Controls* (Chichester: John Wiley & Sons, 2003).

Lang, William W and Jagtiani, Julapa A, 'The Mortgage and Financial Crises: The Role of Credit Risk Management and Corporate Governance' (2010) 38 *Atlantic Economic Journal* 123.

Langevoort, Donald C, 'Internal Controls after Sarbanes–Oxley: Revisiting Corporate Law's "Duty of Care as Responsibility for Systems"' (2006) 31 *Journal of Corporation Law* 949.

—— 'Chasing the Greased Pig Down Wall Street: A Gatekeeper's Guide to the Psychology, Culture and Ethics of Financial Risk-taking' (2011) 96 *Cornell Law Review* 1209.

Langevoort, Donald C, 'Someplace between Philosophy and Economics: Legitimacy and Good Corporate Lawyering' (2006) 75 *Fordham Law Review* 1615.

Langevoort, Donald C and Thompson, Robert B, '"Publicness" in Contemporary Securities Regulation after the Jobs Act' (2013) 101 *Georgetown Law Journal* 337.

Larcker, David and Tayan, Brian, *Corporate Governance Matters: Closer Look at Organisational Choices and their Consequences* (New Jersey: Pearson, 2011).

Larson, Magali Sarfatti, *The Rise of Professionalism* (London: Transaction Publishers, 2013).

Lastra, Rosa, 'Systemic Risk, SIFIs and Financial Stability' (2011) 6 *Capital Markets Law Journal* 197.

Lee, Gun Ho, 'Rule-based and Case-based Reasoning Approach for Internal Audit of Bank' (2008) 21 *Knowledge-Based Systems* 140.

Lenglet, Marc, 'Ambivalence and Ambiguity: The Interpretive Role of Compliance Officers' in Isabelle Huault and Chrystelle Richard (eds), *Finance: The Discreet Regulator* (Abingdon: Palgrave Macmillan, 2012).

Levi-Faur, David, 'The Global Diffusion of Regulatory Capitalism' (2005) 598 *The Annals of the American Academy of Political and Social Science* 12.

Liikanen, Erkki, *High-level Expert Group on Reforming the Structure of the EU Banking Sector* (Final Report, October 2012).

Lipson, Jonathan C, Engel, Beth and Crespo, Jami, 'Foreword: Who's in the House? The Changing Nature and Role of In-house and General Counsel' (2012) *Wisconsin Law Review* 237.

Liyanarachchi, Gregory A and Adler, Ralph, 'Accountants' Whistle-Blowing Intentions: The Impact of Retaliation, Age, and Gender' (2011) 57 *Australian Accounting Review* 167.

Lloyd-Bostock, Sally and Hutter, Bridget M, 'Reforming Regulation of the Medical Profession: The Risks of Risk-Based Approaches' (2008) 10 *Health, Risk and Society* 69.

Lunt, Ingrid, 'Ethical Issues in Professional Life' in Bryan Cunninghm (ed), *Exploring Professionalism* (London: Institute of Education Press, 2008).

Lynn, Jerry R, 'Professionalism is a State of Mind' (1974) 3 *Journal of Advertising* 13.

Lyons, Sean, 'In Defense of the Corporation' (2009) 66 *Internal Auditor* 1.

Macey, Jonathan R and O'Hara, Maureen, 'The Law and Economics of Best Execution' (1997) 6 *Journal of Financial Intermediation* 188.

Maijoor, Steven, 'The Internal Control Explosion' (2000) 4 *International Journal of Auditing* 101.

Majewski, Thomas M, 'Conflicts of Interest Chief Compliance Officers Face in Implementing Compliance Programs for Investment Funds and Investment Advisers' (2006) 7 *Journal of Investment Compliance* 23.

Malloy, Timothy F, 'Regulation, Compliance and the Firm' (2003) 76 *Temple Law Review* 451.

Markham, Jeremy W, 'Super-Regulator: A Comparative Analysis of Securities and Derivatives Regulation in the US, UK and Japan' (2003) 28 *Brooklyn Journal of International Law* 319.

Martin, Joanne, *Organisational Cultures: Mapping the Terrain* (London: Sage, 2001).

Matthews, Kent and Matthews, Owen, 'Controlling Bankers' Bonuses: Efficient Regulation or Politics of Envy?' (2010) *Institute of Economic Affairs* 72.

Matthieu, Emilie, 'Beyond Wall Street: Germany, the United States, and Executive Compensation' (2013) 38 *Brooklyn Journal of International Law* 579.

Maxwell, Andrew, Eichhorn, Michael, Seddighi, Hamid and Smith, Peter, 'Measuring Operational Risk in the Context of Basel II: Are Internal Audit Functions on the "Right" Hymn Sheet?' (2010) *Journal of International Banking Law and Regulation* 543.

—— 'Measuring Operational Risk in the Context of Basel II: How Can the Internal Audit Function Strengthen Its Role?' (2012) *Journal of International Banking Law and Regulation* 161.

McAleer, Michael, Jiménez-Martin, Juan-Angel and Pérez-Amaral, Teodosio, 'What Happened to Risk Management During the 2008–2009 Financial Crisis?' in Robert W Kolb (ed), *Lessons from the Financial Crisis* (New Jersey: John Wiley & Sons, 2010).

McCormick, Roger, *Legal Risk in Financial Markets*, 2nd edn (Oxford: Oxford University Press, 2010).

McDermott, Kathryn, Spence Laschinger, Heather K and Shamian, Judith, 'Work Empowerment and Organizational Commitment' (1996) 27 *Nursing Management* 44.

McGee, Suzanne, *Chasing Goldman Sachs: How the Masters of the Universe Melted Wall Street Down … And Why They'll Take Us to the Brink Again* (New York: Crown Business, 2010).

McKenna, Eugene, *Business Psychology and Organisational Behaviour*, 4th edn (New York: Taylor & Francis Psychology Press. 2006).

McNeese, John B IV, 'The Ethical Conflicts of the Hybrid General Counsel and Chief Compliance Officer' (2012) 25 *Georgetown Journal of Legal Ethics* 677.

McNulty, Terry, Florackis, Chris and Ormrod, Phillip, 'Boards of Directors and Financial Risk during the Credit Crisis' (2013) 21 *Corporate Governance* 58.

Mello, Michelle M and Kelly, Carly N, 'Effects of a Professional Liability Crisis on Residents' Practice Decisions' (2005) 105 *Obstetrics & Gynecology* 1287.

Mendales, Richard E, 'Collateralized Explosive Devices: Why Securities Regulation Failed to Prevent the CDO Meltdown, and How to Fix it' [2009] *University of Illinois Law Review* 1359.

Mesmer-Magnus, Jessica R and Viswesvaran, Chockalingam, 'Whistleblowing in Organizations: An Examination of Correlates of Whistleblowing Intentions, Actions, and Retaliation' (2005) 62 *Journal of Business Ethics* 277.

Meulbroek, Lisa K, 'A Senior Manager's Guide to Integrated Risk Management' (2002) 14 *Journal of Applied Corporate Finance* 56.

Meulbroek, Lisa K, 'A Senior Manager's Guide to Integrated Risk Management' in Donald H Chew (ed), *Corporate Risk Management* (New York: Columbia Business School Publishing, 2008).

Mikes, Anette, 'Risk Management and Calculative Cultures' (2007) at papers.ssrn.com/abstract=1138636.

Miller, Geoffrey P, 'Intellectual Hazard: How Conceptual Biases in Complex Organizations Contributed to the Crisis Of 2008' (2010) 33 *Harvard Journal of Law & Public Policy* 807.

Miller, Robert T, 'Oversight Liability for Risk-Management Failures at Financial Firms' (2010) 84 *Southern California Law Review* 47.

Mills, Annie, *Essential Strategies for Financial Services Compliance* (Chichester: John Wiley & Sons, 2008).

Mitchell, Lawrence E, 'The Legitimate Rights of Public Shareholders' (2009) 66 *Washington and Lee Law Review* 1635.

Mitts, Joshua, 'Recoupment under Dodd–Frank: Punishing Financial Executives and Perpetuating "Too Big To Fail"' (2012) 122 *Yale Law Journal* 507.

Moberly, Richard, 'Sarbanes–Oxley's Whistleblower Provisions: Ten Years Later' (2012) 64 *Southern California Law Review* 1.

Mohamed, Zulkifflee, Zain, Mazlina Mat, Subramaniam, Nava and Fadzilah, Wan, Yusoff, Wan, 'Internal Audit Attributes and External Audit's Reliance on Internal Audit: Implications for Audit Fees' (2012) 16 *International Journal of Auditing* 268.

Moore, Marc T, 'The Evolving Contours of the Board's Risk Management Function in UK Corporate Governance' (2010) 10 *Journal of Corporate Law Studies* 279.

Moorhead, Richard, 'Precarious Professionalism: Some Empirical and Behavioural Perspectives on Lawyers' (2014) *Current Legal Problems* 1.

Morgan, Gareth, *Images of Organization* (London: Sage Publications, 2006).

Mulig, Elizabeth E and Smith, L Murphy, 'Understanding and Preventing Money Laundering' (2004) 19 *Internal Auditing* 22.

Murphy, Michael E, 'Assuring Responsible Risk Management in Banking: The Corporate Governance Dimension' (2011) 36 *Delaware Journal of Corporate Law* 121.

Musile Tanzi, Paola, Gambi, Giampaolo and Previati, Daniele, 'Managing Compliance Risk after MiFID' (2013) *Journal of Financial Regulation and Compliance* 51.

Nestor, S, 'The Impact of Changing Corporate Governance Norms on Economic Crime' (2004) 11 *Journal of Financial Crime* 347.

Newton, Andrew, *The Handbook of Compliance: Making Ethics Work in Financial Services* (London: Financial Times Management, 1998; rep Mind Into Matter, 2002).

Nocco, Brian W and Stultz, René M, 'Enterprise Risk Management: Theory and Practice' (2006) 18 *Journal of Applied Corporate Finance* 8.

Norman, Wayne, 'Business Ethics as Self-Regulation: Why Principles that Ground Regulations should be Used to Ground Beyond-Compliance Norms as Well' (2012) 102 *Journal of Business Ethics* 43.

O'Sullivan, Kenneth Patrick Vincent and Kinsella, Stephen, 'Financial and Regulatory Failure: The Case of Ireland' (2013) 14 *Journal of Banking Regulation* 1.

OECD, *Corporate Governance and the Financial Crisis: Key Findings and Main Messages* (June 2009).

Okamoto, Karl S, 'After the Bailout: Regulating Systemic Moral Hazard' (2009) 57 *UCLA Law Review* 183.

Okamoto, Karl S and Edwards, Douglas O, 'Risk-Taking' (2010) 32 *Cardozo Law Review* 159.

Olufs, Dick W, 'The Limits of Professionalism' (1985) 9 *Public Administration Quarterly* 96.

Orenstein, Alec E, 'A Modified Caremark Standard to Protect Shareholders of Financial Firms from Poor Risk Management' (2011) 86 *New York University Law Review* 766.

Osborne, Stephen P (ed), *The New Public Governance?: Emerging Perspectives on the Theory and Practice of Public Governance* (Oxford: Routledge, 2009).

Pacces, Alessio M, 'Consequences of Uncertainty for Regulation: Law and Economics of the Financial Crisis' (2010) 7 *European Company and Financial Law Review* 479.

Pagano, Michael S, 'How Theories of Financial Intermediation and Corporate Risk-Management Influence Bank Risk-Taking Behavior' (2001) 10 *Financial Markets, Institutions & Instruments* 277.

Parkan, Baris, 'Professionalism: A Virtue or Estrangement from Self-Activity?' (2008) 78 *Journal of Business Ethics* 77.

Parker, Christine, *The Open Corporation* (Cambridge: Cambridge University Press, 2002).

Parker, Christine, and Gilad, Sharon, 'Internal Corporate Compliance Management Systems: Structure, Culture and Agency' in Christine Parker and Vibeke Lehmann Nielsen (eds), *Explaining Compliance: Business Responses to Regulation* (Cheltenham: Edward Elgar, 2011).

Parker, Christine and Nielsen, Vibeke Lehmann, 'Corporate Compliance Systems: Could They Make Any Difference?' (2009) 41 *Administration & Society* 3.

—— (eds), *Explaining Compliance: Business Responses to Regulation* (Cheltenham: Edward Elgar, 2011).

Parker, Christine E, Rosen, Robert Eli and Nielsen, Vibeke Lehmann, 'The Two Faces of Lawyers: Professional Ethics and Business Compliance With Regulation' (2009) 22 *Georgetown Journal of Legal Ethics* 201.

Peni, Emilia and Vähämaa, Sami, 'Did Good Corporate Governance Improve Bank Performance during the Financial Crisis?' (2011) *Journal of Financial Services Research* 19.

Petra, ST, 'Do Outside Independent Directors Strengthen Corporate Boards?' (2005) 5 *Corporate Governance* 55.

Pfeffer, Jeffrey, *Managing with Power: Politics and Influence in Organizations* (Boston, MA: Harvard Business School Press, 1992).

Pfister, Jan, *Managing Organizational Culture for Effective Internal Control* (Berlin: Physica-Verlag, 2009).

Piccioto, Sol and Haines, Jason, 'Regulating Global Financial Markets' (1999) 26 *Journal of Law and Society* 351.

Pichadze, Aviv, 'Institutional Investors as Blockholders' in PM Vasudev and Susan Watson (eds), *Corporate Governance after the Financial Crisis* (Cheltenham: Edward Elgar, 2011).

Pichet, Eric, 'What Governance Lessons Should Be Learnt from the Societe Générale's Kerviel Affair?' (2008) 3 *La Revue Française de Gouvernance d'Entreprise* 117.

Pirraglia, Anthony, 'Tangled Web: Compliance Director Liability under the Securities Laws' (2003) 8 *Fordham Journal of Corporate & Financial Law* 245.

Pirson, Michael and Turnbull, Shann, 'Corporate Governance, Risk Management, and the Financial Crisis: An Information Processing View' (2011) 19 *Corporate Governance: An International Review* 459.

Pooran, Priya Nandita, 'Macro-prudential Supervision—A Panacea for the Global Financial Crisis?' (2009) 3 *Law and Financial Markets Review* 534.

Power, Michael, *The Audit Society* (Oxford: Oxford University Press, 1997).

—— *Organized Uncertainty: Designing a World of Risk Management* (Oxford: Oxford University Press, 2008).

PRA, *The Implementation of Ring-Fencing: Consultation on Legal Structure, Governance and the Continuity of Services and Facilities* (Consultation Paper, October 2014).

PRA and FCA, *Strengthening Accountability in Banking: A New Regulatory Framework* (July 2014).

—— *Strengthening the Alignment of Risk and Reward: New Remuneration Rules* (July 2014).

Prawitt, DF, Smith, JL and Wood, DA, 'Internal Audit Quality and Earnings Management' (2009) 84(4) *Accounting Review* 1255.

Quagliariello, Mario (ed), *Stress Testing the Banking System: Methodologies and Applications* (Cambridge: Cambridge University Press, 2011).

Ramirez, Steven A, 'Lessons from the Subprime Debacle: Stress Testing CEO Autonomy' (2009) 54 *Saint Louis University Law Journal* 1.

Rapp, Geoffrey Christopher, 'Mutiny by the Bounties? The Attempt to Reform Wall Street by the New Whistleblower Provisions of the Dodd–Frank Act' (2012) *Brigham Young University Law Review* 73.

Rappaport, Alfred, *Creating Shareholder Value: The New Standard for Business Performance* (New York: Free Press, 1986).

Rathz, James, 'Compliance as the Competitive Differentiator' (2009) 12 *Duquesne Business Law Journal* 13.

Ravasi, D and Schultz, M, 'Responding to Organizational Identity Threats: Exploring the Role of Organizational Culture' (2006) 49 *Academy of Management Journal* 433.

Ray, Christina, *Extreme Risk Management: Revolutionary Approaches to Evaluating and Measuring Risk* (New York: McGraw-Hill, 2010).

Rebonato, Riccardo, *Plight of the Fortune Tellers: Why We Need to Manage Financial Risk Differently* (Princeton NJ: Princeton University Press, 2007).

Rodrigues Usha, 'Corporate Governance in an Age of Separation of Ownership from Ownership' (2011) 95 *Minnesota Law Review* 1822.

Roach, Lee, 'Auditor Liability; The Case for Limitation Part I' (2010) 31 *Company Lawyer* 136.

Rose, Anna M, Rose, Jacob M and Norman, Carolyn S, 'Is the Objectivity of Internal Audit Compromised when the Internal Audit Function is a Management Training Ground?' (2013) 53 *Accounting & Finance* 1001.

Rose, Paul, 'Regulating Risk by "Strengthening Corporate Governance"' (2010) 17 *Connecticut Insurance Law Journal* 1.

Rosella, Michael R. and Pugliese, Domenick, 'The Investment Company Chief Compliance Officer: Three Years Later: An Assessment of the Evolution of the Role of the CCO' (2006) 7 *Journal of Investment Compliance* 16.

Rosen, Dan and Zenios, Stavros A, 'Enterprise-Wide Asset and Liability Management: Issues, Institutions, and Models' in SA Zenios and WT Ziemba (eds), *Handbook of Asset and Liability Management*, Vol 1 (North Holland: Elseiver, 2006).

Rosen, Robert Eli, '"We're All Consultants Now": How Change in Client Organizational Strategies Influences Change in the Organization of Corporate Legal Services' (2002) 44 *Arizona Law Review* 637.

Rosenau, James N and Czempiel, Ernst-Otto, *Governance without Government: Order and Change in World Politics* (Cambridge: Cambridge University Press, 1992).

Rosenberg, Joshua V and Schuermann, Til, 'A General Approach to Integrated Risk Management with Skewed, Fat-Tailed Risks' (Federal Reserve Bank of New York Staff Reports, 2004).

Rostain, Tanina, 'General Counsel in the Age of Compliance: Preliminary Findings and New Research Questions' (2008) 21 *Georgetown Journal of Legal Ethics* 465.

Rupp, Deborah E and Williams, Cynthia A, 'The Efficacy of Regulation as a Function of Psychological Fit: Reexamining the Hard Law/Soft Law Continuum' (2011) 12 *Theoretical Inquiries in the Law* 581.

Salz, Anthony, *The Salz Review: An Independent Review of Barclays' Business Practices* (April 2013).

Santoro, Michael A and Strauss, Ronald J, *Wall Street Values: Business Ethics and the Global Financial Crisis* (Cambridge: Cambridge University Press, 2012).

Sarens, Gerrit, Allegrini, Marco, D'Onza, Giuseppe and Melville, Robert, 'Are Internal Auditing Practices Related to the Age of the Internal Audit Function? Exploratory Evidence and Directions for Future Research' (2011) 26 *Managerial Auditing Journal* 51.

Sarens, Gerrit, 'Internal Auditing Research: Where are we Going? Editorial' (2009) 13 *International Journal of Auditing* 1.

Sarens, Gerrit and Abdolmohammadi, Mohammad J, 'Monitoring Effects of the Internal Audit Function: Agency Theory versus other Explanatory Variables' (2011) 15 *International Journal of Auditing* 1.

Sarens, Gerrit, De Beelde, Ignace and Everaert, Patricia, 'Internal Audit: A Comfort Provider to the Audit Committee' (2009) 41 *The British Accounting Review* 90.

Schein, Edgar H, *Organizational Culture and Leadership* (NY: Jossey-Bass, 2010).

Schiller, Frank and Prpich, George, 'Learning to Organise Risk Management in Organisations: What Future for Enterprise Risk Management?' (2013) 17 *Journal of Risk Research* 999.

Schinkel, Willem and Noordegraaf, Mirko, 'Professionalism as Symbolic Capital: Materials for a Bourdieusian Theory of Professionalism' (2011) 10 *Comparative Sociology* 67.

Schroeck, Gerhard, *Risk Management and Value Creation in Financial Institutions* (Chichester: John Wiley & Sons, 2002).

Schroeder, Jeanne L, 'Mad Money: Wall Street's Bonus Obsession' (2012) 33 *Cardozo Law Review* 2307.

Schwartz, Mark S, 'A Code of Ethics for Corporate Code of Ethics' (2002) 41 *Journal of Business Ethics* 27.

Schwarcz, Steven L, 'The "Principles" Paradox' (2009) *European Business Organization Law Review* 175.

—— 'Systemic Risk' (2008) 97 *Georgetown Law Journal* 193.

Schwarcz, Steven L and Chang, Lucy, 'The Custom to Failure Cycle' (2012) 62 *Duke Law Journal* 767.

Schwizer, P, Casiraghi, R and Stefanelli, V, 'Boards at Work: Why and How Induction and Training Could Enhance Directors' Effectiveness in the Boardroom' (2011) 11 *International Journal of Regulation and Governance* 1.

Sharfman, Bernard S, 'How the Strong Negotiating Position of Wall Street Employees Impacts the Corporate Governance of Financial Firms' (2011) 5 *Virginia Law & Business Review* 350.

Scott, Colin, 'Reflexive Governance, Meta-regulation and CSR' in Nina Boeger, Rachel Murray and Charlotte Villiers (eds), *Perspectives on Corporate Social Responsibility* (Cheltenham: Edward Elgar, 2008).

—— 'Regulating Everything: From Mega- To Meta-Regulation' (2012) 60 *Administration* 61.

Scott Simmons, Omari, 'The Corporate Immune System: Governance from the Inside Out' (2013) *University of Illinois Law Review* 1131.

Scott Simmons, Omari and Dinnage, John D, 'Innkeepers: A Unifying Theory of the In-House Counsel Role' (2011) 41 *Seton Hall Law Review* 77.

Segon, Michael and Booth, Christopher, 'Business Ethics and CSR as part of MBA Curricula: An Analysis of Student Preference' (2009) 5 *International Review of Business Research Papers* 72.

Selim, Georges, Woodward, Sally and Allegrini, Marco, 'Internal Auditing and Consulting Practice: A Comparison between UK/Ireland and Italy' (2009) 13 *International Journal of Auditing* 9.

Sensarma, Rudra and Jayadev, M, 'Are Bank Stocks Sensitive to Risk Management?' (2009) 10 *Journal of Risk Finance* 7.

Sepe, Simone M, 'Making Sense of Executive Compensation' (2011) 36 *Delaware Journal of Corporate Law* 189.

Servaes, Henri, Tamayo, Ane and Tufano, Peter, 'The Theory and Practice of Corporate Risk Management' (2009) 21 *Journal of Applied Corporate Finance* 60.

Shapiro, Sidney A and Glicksman, Robert L, *Risk Regulation at Risk* (Stanford, CA: Stanford University Press, 2003).

Sheedy, Elizabeth, 'The Future of Risk Modelling' in Robert W Kolb (ed), *Lessons from the Financial Crisis* (New Jersey: John Wiley & Sons, 2010).

Shont, Esther M, *Internal Bank Auditing* (New York: John Wiley & Sons, 1982).

Short, Jodi L and Toffel, Michael W, 'Making Self-Regulation More than Merely Symbolic: The Critical Role of the Legal Environment' (2010) 55 *Administrative Science Quarterly* 361.

Sieber, Joan E, 'The Psychology of Whistleblowing' (1998) 4 *Science and Engineering Ethics* 7.

Siems, Mathias, 'Convergence in Corporate Governance: A Leximetric Approach' (2010) 35 *Journal of Corporation Law* 729.

Simkins, Betty and Ramirez, Steven A, 'Enterprise Wide Risk Management and Corporate Governance' (2007–08) 39 *Loyola University of Chicago Law Journal* 571.

Simon, William H, 'After Confidentiality: Rethinking the Professional Responsibilities of the Business Lawyer' (2006) 75 *Fordham Law Review* 1453.

Sims, Randi L and Keenan, John P, 'Predictors of External Whistleblowing: Organizational and Intrapersonal Variables' (1998) 17 *Journal of Business Ethics* 411.

Sloan, Frank A et al, 'Liability, Risk Perceptions, and Precautions at Bars' (2000) 43 *Journal of Law and Economics* 473.

Smith, Roy C and Walter, Ingo, *Governing the Modern Corporation* (Oxford: Oxford University Press, 2006).

Smithson, Charles and Simkins, Betty J, 'Does Risk Management Add Value? A Survey of the Evidence' (2005) 17 *Journal of Applied Corporate Finance* 8.

Snider, Laureen, 'The Conundrum of Financial Regulation: Origins, Controversies, and Prospects' (2011) 7 *Annual Review of Law and Social Science* 121.

Sobol, Rob, 'Conversations at the Top: The Tone of the Independent Chief Compliance Officer' (2009) 10 *Journal of Investment Compliance* 10.

Soh, Dominic SB and Martinov-Bennie, Nonna, 'The Internal Audit Function: Perceptions of Internal Audit Roles, Effectiveness, and Evaluation' (2011) 26 *Managerial Auditing Journal* 605.

Spencer Pickett, KH, *The Essential Guide to Internal Auditing*, 2nd edn (Chichester, John Wiley & Sons, 2011).

Spira, Laura and Page, Michael, 'Risk Management: The Reinvention of Internal Control and the Changing Role of Internal Audit' (2003) 16 *Accounting, Auditing and Accountability Journal* 640.

Stansfield, George, 'Some Thoughts on Reputation and Challenges for Global Financial Institutions' (2006) 31 *The Geneva Papers* 470.

Stultz, René M, 'Risk Management Failures: What Are They and When Do They Happen?' (2008) 20 *Journal of Applied Corporate Finance* 58.

Suarez, Sandra and Kolodny, Robin, 'Paving the Road to "Too Big to Fail": Business Interests and the Politics of Financial Deregulation in the United States' (2011) 39 *Politics & Society* 74.

Sweeting, Paul, *Financial Enterprise Risk Management* (Cambridge: Cambridge University Press, 2011).

Talukdar, Ashoke S, 'The Voice of Reason: The Corporate Compliance Officer and the Regulated Corporate Environment' (2005) 6 *UC Davis Business Law Journal* 2.

Tarraf, Hussein, 'The Role of Corporate Governance in the Events Leading up to the Global Financial Crisis: Analysis of Aggressive Risk-Taking' (2011) 5 *Global Journal of Business Research* 93.

Tett, Gillian, *Fool's Gold: How Unrestrained Greed Corrupted a Dream, Shattered Global Markets and Unleashed a Catastrophe* (London: Abacus Books, 2010).

Thannasoulis, John, 'The Case for Intervening in Bankers' Pay' (2012) 67 *The Journal of Finance* 849.

Tomasic, Roman, 'Corporate Governance Failure: The Role of Internal and External Gatekeepers in UK Banks and Financial Institutions' (2010) 10 *Corporate Governance: International Journal for Enhanced Board Performance* 8.

Tomasic, Roman and Akinbami, Folarin, 'Towards a New Corporate Governance after the Global Financial Crisis' (2011) *International Company and Commercial Law Review* 237.

Tremblay, Paul R and McMorrow, Judith A, 'Lawyers and the New Institutionalism' (2011) 9 *University of Saint Thomas Law Journal* 568.

Trevino, Linda Klebe, Weaver, Gary R, Gibson, David G and Toffler, Barbara Ley, 'Managing Ethics and Legal Compliance: What Works and What Hurts' (1999) 41 *California Management Review* 131.

Trongmateerut, Pailin and Sweeney, John T, 'The Influence of Subjective Norms on Whistle-Blowing: A Cross-Cultural Investigation' (2013) 112 *Journal of Business Ethics* 437.

Underhill, Geoffrey, 'Theorizing Governance in a Global Financial System' in P Mooschlechner, H Schuberth and B Weber (eds), *The Political Economy of Financial Market Regulation* (Cheltenham: Edward Elgar, 2006).

Underhill, Geoffrey RD, 'Markets beyond Politics? The State and the Internationalisation of Financial Markets' (1991) 19 *European Journal of Political Research* 197.

Uzun, H, Szewczyk, SH and Varma, R, 'Board Composition and Corporate Fraud' (2004) 60 *Financial Analysts Journal* 33.

Vallascas, Francesco and Hagendorff, Jens, 'CEO Remuneration and Bank Default Risk: Evidence from the US and Europe' (2013) *Financial Markets, Institutions & Instruments* 47.

Van den Berg, Peter T and Wilderom, Celeste PM, 'Defining, Measuring, and Comparing Organisational Cultures' (2004) 53 *Applied Psychology: An International Review* 570.

van Essen, Marc, Engelen, Peter-Jan and Carney, Michael, 'Does "Good" Corporate Governance Help in a Crisis? The Impact of Country- and Firm-Level Governance Mechanisms in the European Financial Crisis' (2013) 21 *Corporate Governance* 201.

van Nunen, Anton, *Fiduciary Management: Blueprint for Pension Fund Excellence* (Hoboken, NJ: Wiley Finance, 2008).

Vasudev, PM, 'Credit Derivatives and Risk Management: Corporate Governance in the Sarbanes–Oxley World' [2009] *Journal of Business Law* 331.

Veasey, E Norman and Di Guglielmo, Christine T, 'The Tensions, Stresses, and Professional Responsibilities of the Lawyer for the Corporation' (2006) 62 *Business Lawyer* 1.

—— 'General Counsel Buffeted by Compliance Demands and Client Pressures May Face Personal Peril' (2012) 68 *Business Lawyer* 57.

Walker, David, 'A Review of Corporate Governance in UK Banks and other Financial industry Entities: Final Recommendations' (26 November 2009).

Wallace, W and Kreutzfeldt, R, 'Distinctive Characteristics of Entities with an Internal Audit Department and the Association of the Quality of Such Departments with Errors' (1991) 7 *Contemporary Accounting Research* 485.

Walter, Ingo, 'Reputational Risk and Conflicts of Interest in Banking and Finance: The Evidence So Far' in J Richard Aronson, Harriet L Parmet and Robert J Thornton (eds), *Variations in Economic Analysis* (New York: Springer, 2010).

Wan, Ke Steven, 'Gatekeeper Liability Versus Regulation of Wrongdoers' (2008) 34 *Ohio Northern University Law Review* 483.

Want, Jerome, *Corporate Cultures* (New York: St Martin's Press, 2006).

Weber, Robert F, 'New Governance, Financial Regulation, and Challenges to Legitimacy: The Example of the Internal Models Approach to Capital Adequacy Regulation' (2010) 62 *Administrative Law Review* 783.

Weinstein, Martin J, 'The World of International Compliance: What Transactional Lawyers Need to Know to Perform Ethically and Responsibly' (2007) 29 *Houston Journal of International Law* 311.

Wernz, Johannes, *Bank Management and Control: Strategy, Capital and Risk Management* (Heidelberg: Springer, 2014).

Wexler, Mark, 'Financial Edgework and the Persistence of Rogue Traders' (2010) 115 *Business & Society Review* 1.

Wheatley, Martin, *The Wheatley Review of LIBOR* (September 2012).

Whelan, Christopher J, 'The Paradox of Professionalism'—Global Law Practice Means Business' (2009) 27(2) *Penn State International Law Review* 465.

White, Lawrence J, 'Corporate Governance and Prudential Regulation of Banks: Is there any Connection?' in James R Barth, Chen Lin and Clas Wihlborg (eds), *Research Handbook on International Banking and* Governance (Cheltenham: Edward Elgar, 2012).

Wilke, Helmut, *Governance in a Disenchanted World* (Cheltenham: Edward Elgar, 2009).

Williams, JW, 'Envisioning Financial Disorder: Financial Surveillance and the Securities Industry' (2009) 38 *Economy and Society* 460.

Wilmarth, Arthur E, 'The Transformation of the Financial Services Industry: 1975–2000, Competition, Consolidation and Increased Risks'' (2002) 2 *University of Illinois Law Review* 2 15.

Windram, Richard, 'Risk-Taking Incentives: A Review of the Literature' (2005) 19 *Journal of Economic Surveys* 65.

Winter, Soren & May, Peter J, 'Information, Interests, and Environmental Regulation' (2002) 4 *Journal of Comparative Policy Analyses: Research and Practice* 115.

Wise, Noel, 'Personal Liability Promotes Responsible Conduct: Extending the Responsible Corporate Officer Doctrine to Federal Civil Environmental Enforcement Cases' (2002) 21 *Stanford Environmental Law Journal* 283.

Wong, Simon CY, 'Why Stewardship is Proving Elusive for Institutional Investors' [2010] *Butterworths Journal of International Banking and Financial Law* 406.

Wright, John SF, Dempster, Paul G, Keen, Justin, Allen, Pauline and Hutchings, Andrew, 'The New Governance Arrangements for NHS Foundation Trust Hospitals: Reframing Governors as Meta-Regulators' (2012) 90 *Public Administration* 351.

Yeh, Yin-Hua, Chung, Huimin and Liu, Chih-Liang, 'Committee Independence and Financial Institution Performance during the 2007–08 Credit Crunch: Evidence from a Multi-country Study' (2011) 19 *Corporate Governance* 437.

Zhang, Julia, Chiu, Randy and Wei, Li-Qun, 'On Whistleblowing Judgment and Intention: The Roles of Positive Mood and Organizational Ethical Culture' (2009) 24 *Journal of Managerial Psychology* 627.

Zingales, Luigi, *Capitalism for the People: Recapturing the Lost Genius of American Capitalism* (New York: Basic Books 2012).

Conference Papers

Danielle Blanchard and Georges Dionne, 'Risk Management and Corporate Governance' (The Crisis of Corporate Governance: What's Next? conference, Montreal, May 2003).

Mary Condon, 'Canadian Securities Regulation and the Global Financial Crisis' (The Walter S Owen Lecture, University of British Columbia, 26 March 2009).

Evetts, Julia, 'Professionalism in Turbulent Times: Changes, Challenges and Opportunities' (Propel international conference, Stirling, May 2012).

Dignam, Alan, 'Understanding the Financial Crisis: Pay, Risk and Responsibility in the 21st Century' ('Current Legal Problems' lecture at Bentham House, University College, London, 4 November 2010).

Newspaper Articles

'Archbishop of Canterbury criticises bankers for 'culture of entitlement' *Guardian* (27 April 2013).

Samuel Brittan, 'Use the UK's state bank holdings to speed a recovery' *Financial Times* (22 September 2011).

Kate Burgess, 'Myners Lashes out at Landlord Institutional shareholders' *Financial Times* (21 April 2009).

'Bank of England Signal Possible HSBC Tax Probe' *Financial Times* (13 February 2015).

'Banks need a generation to change culture, report says' *Financial Times* (26 November 2014).

'Barclays hit with £290m Fine over LIBOR Fixing' *Daily Telegraph* (27 June 2012).

'Barclays suspends six foreign exchange traders' *Financial Times* (1 November 2013).

'Britain Abandons Banker Bonus Fight after EU Court Blow' *Bloomberg* (21 November 2014).

'Citigroup forex trader fired amid global probe' *Financial Times* (10 January 2014).

'Commerzbank must pay €50m of bonuses after losing legal battle' *Financial Times* (16 April 2013).

'Corzine Blasted in MF Global Autopsy' *The Wall Street Journal* (4 April 2013).

Crisis-torn Co-op Bank suffers cash breakdown' *Daily Telegraph* (2 June 2013).

'Deutsche Bank braced for fines in forex probes: sources' *Reuters* (28 May 2014).

Helia Ebrahimi, 'Institutional Institutional Shareholders Admit Oversight Failure on Banks' *Daily Telegraph* (27 January 2009).

'Ex-Co-op Bank chairman Paul Flowers charged with drug offences' *Financial Times* (16 April 2014).

'Foreign Exchange: The Big Fix' *Financial Times* (12 November 2013).

'Foreign exchange trading faces SFO criminal investigation' *Guardian* (21 July 2014).

John Gapper, 'There is no such thing as the banking profession' *Financial Times* (12 February 2014).

—— 'Trading Floor Culture no longer Acceptable' *Financial Times* (5 July 2012).

Francesco Guerrera, 'Welch condemns share price focus' *Financial Times* (12 March 2009).

Jonathan Guthrie, 'PwC fine underplays auditors' responsibilities' *Financial Times* (6 January 2012).

Jennifer Hughes, 'FSA Chief Lambasts Uncritical Investors' *Financial Times* (11 March 2009).

'HBOS executives "threatened" colleagues who questioned risk-taking' *Guardian* (30 October 2012).

'Higher Bank Salaries Poised to Offset Brussels Bonus Cap' *Financial Times* (17 July 2013).

'HSBC to Pay £1.2bn over Mexico Scandal' *Guardian* (11 December 2012).

Richard Lambert, 'Sir Ralph's lessons on short-termism' *Financial Times* (22 May 2011).

Andrea Leadsom, 'How an Old Hand would Change Barclays' *Financial Times* (5 July 2012).

'LIBOR Manipulation: Done for you, Big Boy' *Financial Times* (27 June 2012).

'London banks and brokers face research business shake-up' *Financial Times* (24 July 2014).

David Oakley, 'Biggest UK Investors Plan Joint Move on Excess' *Financial Times* (16 June 2013).

—— 'Financial System Waiting for Next Crisis' *Financial Times* (6 June 2013).

—— 'Spotlight on Shareholder Advice Groups' *Financial Times* (9 June 2012).

Frank Partnoy, 'On Rogues, Risk-taking and Restoring Trust in Banks' *Financial Times* (23 September 2011).

John Reed, 'Culture clash means banks must split, says former Citi chief' *Financial Times* (9 September 2013).

'RBS Fined £390m for Rigging LIBOR Interest Rate' *Guardian* (6 February 2013).

Martin Sandbu, 'Flexibility Decided by States is a Wrong Move for Europe's Banks' *Financial Times* (26 June 2013).

'Sants' Resignation from Barclays Shows Pitfalls of Poaching' *Financial Times* (18 November 2013).
'Shop Talk: Dodd-Frank and Data Overload' *Compliance Week* (17 April 2012).
'Société Générale uncovers £3.7bn fraud by rogue trader' *Guardian* (24 January 2008).
Gillian Tett, 'The Banks that are too Complex to Exist' *Financial Times* (8 June 2012).
'UBS First to Report FX Rigging Shows EU Immunity Flaws' *Bloomberg News* (2 April 2014).
'UBS Latest Bank to be Hit with Multimillion LIBOR Fine' *Guardian* (13 December 2012).
'UK Watchdog to Tackle HSBC on Standards' *Financial Times* (16 February 2015).
Gonzalo Vina and Jennifer Ryan, 'Osborne Will Promise UK Bank Legislation for Vickers Proposals by 2015' *Bloomberg News* (19 December 2011).
'Welch condemns share price focus' *Financial Times* (12 March 2009).
Whistle-blowing almost Killed Me' *Financial Times* (5 June 2013).

Index

Introductory Note

References such as '178–79' indicate (not necessarily continuous) discussion of a topic across a range of pages. Wherever possible in the case of topics with many references, these have either been divided into sub-topics or only the most significant discussions of the topic are listed. Because the entire work is about the 'internal control', the use of this term (and certain others which occur constantly throughout the book) as an entry point has been minimised. Information will be found under the corresponding detailed topics.

www.ingramcontent.com/pod-product-compliance
Lightning Source LLC
LaVergne TN
LVHW050301210926
848481LV00014BA/247
* 9 7 8 1 5 0 9 9 2 0 0 9 9 *